D0906679

FEVER

THE DARK MYSTERY OF
THE BRE-X GOLD RUSH

JENNIFER WELLS

VIKING

VIKING
Published by the Penguin Group
Penguin Books Canada Ltd, 10 Alcorn Avenue, Toronto, Ontario, Canada M4V 3B2
Penguin Books Ltd, 27 Wrights Lane, London W8 5TZ, England
Penguin Putnam Inc., 375 Hudson Street, New York, New York 10014, U.S.A.
Penguin Books Australia Ltd, Ringwood, Victoria, Australia
Penguin Books (NZ) Ltd, cnr Rosedale and Airborne Roads, Albany Aukland 1310,
New Zealand

Penguin Books Ltd Registered Offices: Harmondsworth, Middlesex, England

First published 1998
10 9 8 7 6 5 4 3 2 1

Printed and bound in Canada on acid free paper ∞

CANADIAN CATALOGUING IN PUBLICATION DATA

Wells, Jennifer, 1955–
    Fever: the dark mystery of the Bre-X gold rush

ISBN 0-670-87815-4

1. Bre-X (Firm). 2. Gold mines and mining – Indonesia. 3. Fraud. I. Title.

HD3536.I544W44 1998   338.2'741'09598   C98-930353-5

Visit Penguin Canada's website at www.penguin.ca

For my three sons: Chris, Jake and Will
Love you big as the sky

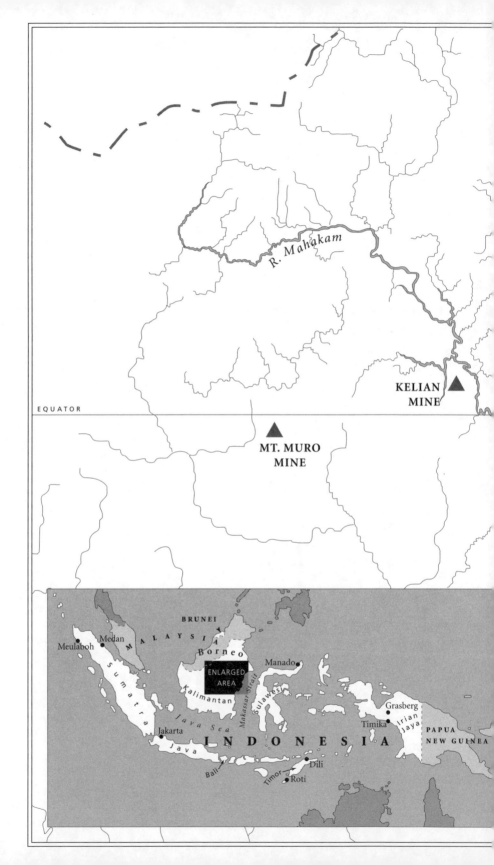

R. Mahakam

KELIAN
MINE

EQUATOR

MT. MURO
MINE

BRUNEI

Meulaboh Medan

MALAYSIA

Borneo

Manado

ENLARGED
AREA

Kalimantan

Sumatra

Makassar Strait

Sulawesi

Grasberg

Timika Irian
Jaya

PAPUA
NEW GUINEA

Java Sea

Jakarta

I N D O N E S I A

Java

Bali

Timor Dili

Roti

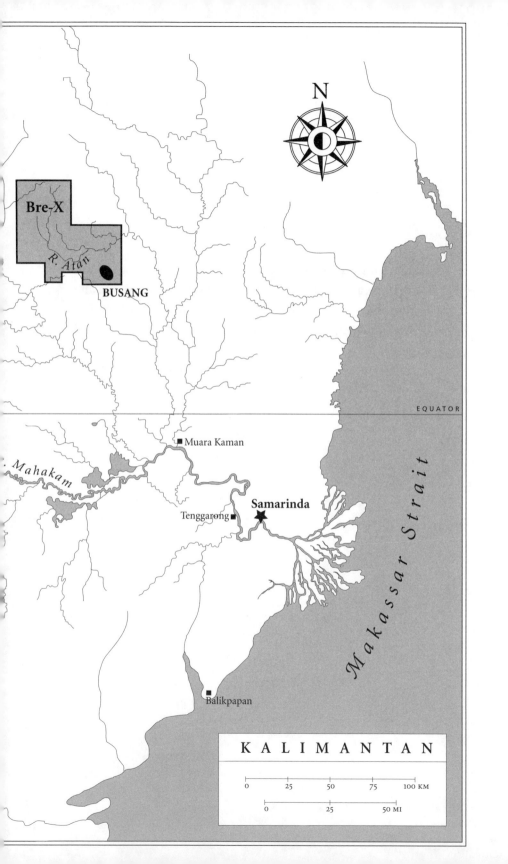

Bre-X

R. Atan

BUSANG

N

EQUATOR

Muara Kaman

Mahakam

Samarinda

Tenggarong

Makassar Strait

Balikpapan

KALIMANTAN

0   25   50   75   100 KM

0   25   50 MI

Hunters for gold or pursuers of fame, they had all gone out on that stream ... What greatness had not floated on the ebb of that river into the mystery of an unknown earth! ... The dreams of men, the seed of commonwealths, the germs of empires.

—Joseph Conrad, *Heart of Darkness*

CONTENTS

Post Mortem   1

Beginnings   35

Up River   59

Putz   97

The Dreams of Men   126

All that Glisters   155

The Black Hand   176

Sinews of War   203

Grasping at the Shadow   227

The Fix   254

Bob, Jim Bob   292

The Crackup   320

Conspiracy Theories   345

All to Dust   371

Acknowledgments   383

Bibliography   386

Index   389

FEVER

POST MORTEM

Waynefred Villarba, his head tilted back, passes the strips of negatives high above his face, trying to catch the fluorescent light. This place is so damn dim. How to see? There. Frame: head. Frame: torso. Frame: legs. Mr. Villarba's eyes scan, side to side, searching. Titch. Titch, titch. Are there no shots of this man in one piece? A dozen negatives. Two dozen. Three. Not a single full-body image.

Mr. Villarba is chief of the photography and publishing division at the National Bureau of Investigation in Manila. On his desk in his cramped, dreary quarters sits open an instruction booklet on tie-knotting: four-in-hand; half-Windsor; Windsor. "What's difficult," he says, peering skyward at the negatives of body parts, his tie hanging limp and unattended about his neck, "is getting the ends the same length." Just so. For the moment he has put aside a small mirror, his instructional aid, to attend to what may be the only official business of the day. "Well," he says at last, "three frames will have to suffice.

I

Please, wait a minute."

Dr. Eduardo Antonio Kalalo studies Villarba as the division chief steps from his office. It is hot, oppressive. The air does not stir. NBI workers hang in doorways, seemingly with nothing to do. Best to stay still. The heat presents a sensation of having one's skin shrink-wrapped, a thin film of oil spreading beneath the Saran.

Dr. Kalalo is a solid, blocky man. He frets about his weight. His glasses hang stringed about his neck. His face is broad; his eyes are small, but comforting, friendly. His mouth, in repose, turns up at the edges, giving him a look of the persistently bemused. Unlike Mr. Villarba, Dr. Kalalo is a busy man. He is head of the forensic dental investigation unit at the NBI, and he also keeps up his private dental practice. The dead and the undead. He is keenly interested in the unsolved. He keeps an adult human skull in a plastic shopping bag and carries it about as one would a melon, home from the shops. He has taken forensics courses at Interpol in Paris and so has become the Inspector Maigret of the NBI. "My first case was the naval ship *Datu Kalantiao*, sideswiped by a strong typhoon in Manila Bay," he says. "The crew went down with the ship. But the lieutenant's brother said, 'I don't think that's my brother. He's too short.' We identified him finally, using dental records from Annapolis."

Dr. Kalalo would like to see all his files similarly closed. "We must be rigid in gathering evidence," he says. "In the interests of justice." This is offered in the manner of an oath.

Mr. Villarba seems to have been gone forever—or is it the steam heat that slows time? At last he flaps back toward his desk and lays down three still-wet black-and-white prints. The smell of fixative rises from the flaccid photos, heightening the slightly surreal atmosphere. Dr. Kalalo pulls his chair closer and peers intently at cadaver No. N-97-591: Michael Antonio Tuason de Guzman.

Dr. Alberto Reyes, chief of the NBI's medico-legal division, has given clearance for this viewing. Reyes holds court across the way, in a mint-green office with pea-green venetian blinds. He motioned for his secretary to pull the de Guzman file with all the casualness of a bar patron ordering a gin fizz. With jet-black hair iced into an aspiring pompadour, his name engraved grandly on a marble scroll in front of him, holding his cigarette high in the air, twisting and flourishing it to accentuate his very important words, he exudes the aroma of an engaging tinpot dictator. Bung Sukarno comes to mind—the most engaging tinpot dictator of all. But that was Indonesia, circa 1950, and this is the Philippines, and these are the 1990s.

Reyes's computer sits snug in its bubble wrap. Instead, typewriters of a certain vintage are still much in use, their carriages clacking across the autopsy forms documenting all manner of horrors. Throughout the morning, scrums of people move in and out of his curious lair. He interrupted a sombre-sounding conversation with a man wearing fat black suspenders under his sheer, shirt-like barong and smiled broadly. "Are you getting everything you need? Hmmm?"

In musty, miasmal corridors through the NBI, fetuses sit pickled in jars, eyes filmed, mouths agape—specimens from criminal abortions. An adult's pasty hand floats under a screw-top lid. "It appears old man lost his left hand in parrying the blow to a heavy, sharp bolo, while trying to rescue his niece from her abductors," says the accompanying sign.

Down the hall is the anti-graft division, a cluster of ancient wooden desks around which workers appear to be doing little of anything. The firing range nearby features pin-ups of criminals about as menacing as the bad guys in a Tintin adventure, which is to say, not very. In the courtyard below, an address by Santiago Toledo, head of the NBI, is being broadcast on closed-circuit television, the sets sunk in concrete boxes. There swarms of people commingle, waiting, hoping to clear the NBI paperwork to get the hell out of the Philippines.

It was Dr. Kalalo who led me through this throng, to Mr. Villarba, and then to the final photographic record of Michael de Guzman. Kalalo is intensely curious about this case. He worked on the de Guzman autopsy two months earlier, with a full team from the NBI. He had requested dental records from the family of the deceased, which they had failed to provide. Kalalo's file is still very much open. Together we eyeball the disjointed, cadaverous images. Who was this man, now displayed in pieces? What was the trajectory of his life? What did his mother expect of him? Was he a good boy? What were his politics? Was he punctilious? A creative lover? A man of wit? Someone... eye-catching?

Was he indeed Michael de Guzman?

Two months earlier. La Funeraria Paz, Garaneta Avenue, Manila. April 3, 1997.

Dr. Noel Minay is not used to working at this hour, 12:45 a.m. But this is a rush job. There is only one consolation: he did not have to face the wretched Manila traffic.

Minay is the chief anatomic pathologist at the NBI, and as such is leading the team in the autopsy of cadaver No. N-97-591. He has been joined by Dr. Kalalo, whom everyone calls Ed, as well as a representative of the dactyloscopy crew who will study the fingerprints, a photographer and two people from the morgue. In an adjacent room Laurence de Guzman, brother of the deceased, known in the de Guzman family as Owie, waits with his father, Simplicio, whom everyone calls Mike.

Owie is the appointed one, the overseer of the autopsy of the man he no longer knew, a man who had many wives, and innumerable girl-friends—in Sulawesi, in Samarinda, in Java. Michael had been gone from the Philippines for a decade, hunting for gold in Indonesia, making his riches there. He swore that he had found the biggest, richest gold mine ever, at the behest of a punky Canadian mining company called Bre-X Minerals Ltd. The discovery was called Busang, and Owie knew, for Michael had told him, that it was the most remarkable gold discovery in history.

Owie and Mike say very little. They make no pre-emptive mention of identifying characteristics, of birthmarks, to Minay and his autopsy team.

The plastic body bag has been unzipped and the familiar stench is now crawling up Minay's nostrils, the scent of a steak left forgotten in the sun for days, a week. Minay lights a cigarette. He always smokes in the morgue. It helps chase the stink away. That and taking a "big inspiration," as he calls it. Breathe in, deeply. Get it over with. He wears no face-mask. The NBI is in dire financial straits, and face-masks are regarded as extras.

Owie and Mike step forward to view what is left of their golden boy. There has been heartbreak before in the family, but nothing as gruesome as this. Owie stands, heavy-set, the brother the family says looks most like Michael. "These," says Owie, "appear to be Michael's feet." They cannot recognize the body that has them, momentarily, transfixed. There have been many rumours. That the masterful Michael de Guzman faked his own demise. That a body-double had been planted in his place. A fresh corpse, purchased in Indonesia. What would that cost? Ten thousand rupiahs? Not a problem.

What is taking the X-ray team so long? Two hours for this? Yes, yes, yes, of course we must be thorough. Traces of metal? No. No obvious signs of foul play. No bullet wounds. No stab wounds.

Well, this will be an easy assignment. Look at this body. Already autopsied, cut and sutured by a pathologist in Indonesia. First, the measurement: 164 cm.

Minay is in his street clothes, as he is for all his NBI autopsies. No scrubs, no shoe covers. He cuts as many as ten a day. The volume of work is overwhelming. The bureau is badly understaffed, so work is done in haste and perhaps without the utmost professionalism. Here in Manila, autopsy time means bring your own instruments and wear whatever you were wearing at the dinner table a couple of hours before. At the Royal Darwin Hospital in Sydney, Australia, where Minay worked in forensics for three years, he would dress for an autopsy as if for surgery. Those were the days. Minay was happy in his work, just as he had been in his studies, as the lone student of clinical and anatomic pathology at Manila's Far Eastern University in the early 1980s. He liked the fact that this specialty was not crowded, and he enjoyed laboratory work. Minay sounds bitter that his time in Sydney was cut short. He was removed from his post, he says, on account of his accent. Is he being wry?

The body that awaits him is grossly smooth, swollen, pale. In Minay's assessment it has the look of pork that has been on the boil for a few hours. He puts a fresh blade in his scalpel and sets to work, cutting first 32 centimetres, ear to ear, across the coronal plane, which seems very polished, the hair sloughed away by water. The continuous sutures pop neatly open. The bone has already been cleaved, not horizontally across the cranium, but arcing over the top. What was used? An old handsaw possibly. Or perhaps a Stryker's saw. The skull is empty: the brain perhaps has been removed and retained in Indonesia. So hard to do any quick work on a brain, so soft, gelatinous. Better to keep it in formalin until it is nice and firm and can be cut like headcheese and examined. Minay assumes that that is just what his Indonesian counterpart had in mind, though there are no notes to that effect. Would they be planning any diagnostic work? An examination for malarial parasites perhaps? Who knows? Possibly portions of the brain spilled out of the fractured skull upon crash landing in a jungle so far away.

Minay glances at the autopsy report delivered from Indonesia. This is certainly not up to international standards. One lousy page. It is not an autopsy report at all. Why has one not been sent? Typical Indos.

Look at the face. The left ear, almost totally gone. Eaten. Right eye closed. Left eye partially open, a sunken white ball in there. An indentation where the nose used to be: "superficially eaten," in Minay's description. Lacerations on the left side of the face. Minay draws hastily on a sheet of paper offering up a body outline. Avulsion type, he notes, as if the skin has been plucked. He thinks of rats. Sutures starting at the bottom of where the nose used to be, at the philtrum. The identifying mole on the upper left lip is not visible. The once sparse and unattractive moustache is gone. Sutures run down the chin, down the neck. At its base, a series of black drippings where the sutures have pulled away, then tightened, running 78 centimetres along the anterior median line down to the level of the symphysis pubis. Not a Y incision, coming down either side of the clavicle, but a relatively linear rivulet. The Y incision gives the pathologist better exposure but it eventually requires more stitching, more time.

Minay pops the stitches, as fat as binder twine, and inhales the sharp pungent aroma of formalin. Perhaps some dye has been added, for this cadaver is slightly peachy in skin tone, not brown as it would naturally be by now. Minay pulls back the loose flaps of skin and peers inward. There is not much to see. Cadaver No. N-97-591 has been wholly excavated and has collapsed in the middle. No heart, no liver, no intestines. Minay thinks of wild boars, which he has heard run in the jungles of Kalimantan. The wild boars are very neat in their work, tidily snorfling the offal without tearing the surrounding flesh.

Minay shifts his gaze lower. There is no genitalia. The sutures have trussed the skin from the thigh right across, a Sunday roast effect that is not pretty.

Long vertical incisions run along the forearms. Minay follows them, centimetre by centimetre. He notes abrasions on the small, ring and middle fingers of the left hand. Bits of skin have been plucked off. Contusions: mid-line, anterior chest. Lower third, anterior aspect, right arm. Ditto left. Minay neatly trims a three-centimetre piece from the area of the chest contusion, thinking to himself that these trimmings can be tested later, for hepatitis, for DNA. But of course the NBI's testing equipment is not fully operational, and anyway this is not the bureau's case to investigate. Any pursuit of such testing would have to be carried out at the behest of the de Guzman family. In the meantime, the tissue samples will be preserved in paraffin blocks.

Fractures: ulna, right. Fibula, left and right. Scapula, both sides. First, second, third and fourth vertebrae. Pelvis at multiple points. Femur, both sides. The right leg badly broken just above the ankle. The feet splayed. Laceration, left instep. The toenails are intact.

Minay enjoys the intrigue of such cases. It is a game to him. He thinks this man landed on his feet, making the pelvis the weakest point. A descent of nearly 250 metres, they say. The fellow is actually in pretty good shape for all that. Minay recalls that this man was once a skydiver, and that reminds him of the Alice Springs case. A ballooning accident. The bodies were autopsied by Dr. Kevin Lee, Minay's supervisor in the mortuary of the Royal Darwin Hospital. Lee presented the slides of the accident victims to a medical staff conference of the pathology department, offering the hypothesis, based on breaks and fractures, that the passengers had landed vertically. Minay sees similarities here.

Now it is Ed Kalalo's turn, and he makes a neat incision under the cadaver's chin. The mandible has already become semidetached from the muscle, so Kalalo's work is as easy as passing a hot knife through butter. The mandible has been fractured in two. The maxilla also. He makes a notation: two wisdom teeth, the third molar on either side, are all that remain on the upper jaw. The smooth sockets that run the U between the two are overgrown and smooth, so this man wore an upper bridge of fourteen teeth. He checks the record. No dental plate was recovered with the body. On the bottom, the deceased had three teeth, though only two remain in the jaw. Kalalo can see clearly from a fresh indentation that a third tooth was knocked out, perhaps upon landing. He makes a request to the family for the dental records of the deceased.

Perhaps the dactyloscopy crew will have better luck. Prints are taken, forefinger and thumb. By 3:00 a.m., the autopsy team has completed its work. All is done. Nothing is finished.

JAKARTA, INDONESIA

On the morning of March 18, 1997, Mike de Guzman stepped through the mahogany French doors of his home in a quiet, gated community in the Jakarta suburb of Bogor. A child's two-wheeler was leaning against the doorjamb. Two lustrous membeo birds, their glossy plumage black as tar, their beaks a bright tangerine, fussed in their wire cages, offering wolf whistles and the Indonesian national anthem to passersby. The Javanese call them beo birds and their skill at mimicry makes them popular pets. From the red clay rooftop of the de Guzmans' home rises a whomping satellite dish. It is a very fine house by Indonesian standards, but far from palatial. The much grander house that Mike was building for life here with his wife, Genie, was not yet finished. Genie was eager to make the move.

Nineteen-ninety-seven promised to be Michael's great year. He began it by celebrating the New Year in Manila with his Filipino family—with his number-one wife, Teresa, whom he called Tess, his mother, Leila, and his siblings. There had been so many difficult times for Michael during his ten years in Indonesia: threatened expulsion from the country years before, financial hardship, illness. But that was all behind him now. He had discovered there the greatest gold mine ever, Busang, buried in the wilds of Kalimantan—a fabulous find that had grown suddenly, exponentially. A million ounces. Then ten. Then ten times that. Then double again. It was time for the family to share in the glory.

On his flight to Manila, Michael had lost a gold ring on the plane. "Whoever finds that ring will have a good year," he said to Diane, an older sister who works as a nurse in California. Superstition. The serendipity of good fortune. So typical of Chel, which is what the family called him, pronouncing it with a hard "k" sound. He laughed. One gold ring. What did that matter? What could that be worth? There was a time when such an object would have held tremendous significance. Years before, Genie had sold a piece of her own gold jewellery, pawned to make ends meet in the life she had taken up with Michael. Before he had become a rich man.

Michael had paid for Diane to make the trip to Manila to share the celebration of his good fortune. It would be her birthday on January 7, and the trip was Michael's present to her. The family called

Diane, who was christened Diana, Inday. Michael often called her Ate, a more generic name for an older sister, a sign of respect.

Early in the New Year, he took Diane and another sister, Marissa, who lives in Germany, along with his mother and Tess, to Jakarta. They checked into the Shangri-La Hotel. With busboys in gold *pitji* caps, cocktail waitresses in sleek sarongs, it was a glittering palace, a favourite hotel for many western visitors to Jakarta. It was a hang-out for locals with money, who showed off their luxury cars that sell for obscene sums, their rag-top, cherry-red BMWs buffed to a mirrored sheen. Tess had made the trip several times before, at least twice with the children, but never in such style as this.

Michael showed his family through the Bre-X office, where they met his good friend Mike Bird, who worked just down the hall, and Greg MacDonald, the office manager. Michael and Tess hosted a dinner at the Empire Grill in the Menara Imperium Building. John Robertson, manager of engineering for PT Kilborn Pakar Rekayasa, came with his wife. Kilborn had been contracted by Bre-X to draft the feasibility studies for the Busang project. Kilborn was anticipating the contract to build what would likely be a US$1.5-billion mine.

One day Michael took the family for a long drive, to Bogor. They certainly did not stop at Mike's house there, where Genie was ensconced. He was careful to keep his various wives and families separate from each other, and Tess knew nothing of Genie. Instead they drove through picturesque fields of tea plants. Michael explained how the women labourers would snip the tea leaves with their fingers. He enjoyed squiring his family, showing off his knowledge of this exotic place

He showed them where he used to sky-dive, a hobby he had taken up after his move to Indonesia a decade earlier. They watched a diver take the plunge, dropping through a cerulean sky. Michael stared, enraptured, studying the skydiver closely behind his ever-present sunglasses.

"Ate, look at that man's positioning," he said to Diane. "See how he has bent his knees?"

"Why did you choose that sport?" asked Diane.

"Because it relaxes me," said her little brother. But, he added, he had given it up.

"Why, Chel?"

"Because I don't want to die with my body scattered all over the place."

Two of Michael's sisters had already died: Leilani, in 1978, of complications during childbirth, and Mary Ann, in 1986, of leukemia. Both were twenty-eight when they died. The de Guzman family would be all right now, they knew. Mike would take care of them. He shot many rolls of film and promised to send prints to the family later. He seemed relaxed, content, and he was certainly jovial. He was just as eager to talk about new mineral prospects as he was about Busang. He said there would be an intensely busy time ahead at work.

There was some relief for the family in this; they had been worried that something strange was happening. Tess had received mysterious phone calls the previous summer, and Michael had said he had to watch his back. Paranoia? Perhaps. But then Michael had told the family that Bre-X had hired an investigator. There was some kind of sabotage, the family had come to understand. Directed, they believed, not just at Michael, but at Bre-X itself.

Now it was March. Mike and Genie had just returned from Singapore, having spent two days in the Marriott Hotel on Orchard Road. Genie had followed her husband's directions before making the trip, travelling first to the Bre-X office, claiming his $7,000 pay packet in cash and taking it to Singapore with her. De Guzman's office-mates knew Genie well, would comment on her sleek black Mercedes, and knew too the children she had had with Michael, Paula and Michael, Jr.

There was nothing out of the ordinary in Michael making such a trip. The previous month he had scrawled an itinerary in his large, loopy handwriting, leaving it for his office assistant to attend to. "7/2 JKT-SNG MTG, Genie. 9/2 SNG-MNL MTG. 11/2 MNL-SNG MTG. 12/2

SNG-JKT MTG, Genie." Jakarta, Singapore, Manila, Singapore. Typical busyness for the latest leg of Michael de Guzman's largely airborne life.

Before leaving Singapore on February 12, de Guzman had undergone a complete health checkup at the Mount Elizabeth Medical Centre; he made it a habit to have one annually. He had handed the cashier $1,000 to pay for the $673.62 health screen. On March 7 a memo was sent to Mount Elizabeth requesting an appointment to discuss the test results.

The hospital returned its confirmation by fax for an appointment March 17. "If you are still in Singapore your results will be ready for review with the doctor at 2 p.m. on 19/3/97.... Please fast from midnight before the check-up.... If you open your bowels before coming to the hospital, please collect a sample of your stool in a clean container."

As Bre-X had grown, so had de Guzman. In 1993, when he had started working for the company, he was leaner and far more desperate. Now he was verging on fat, plumping over his belt.

Within Bre-X, everyone was aware of de Guzman's health troubles: the recurring malaria that left him weak. He would lean into an office door frame when talking to his office staff, struggling, it seemed, to concentrate. This distorted mental state was debilitating and fed bouts of depression. He could not think straight. The Ancient Chinese blamed such illness on the demons. The native Dayak, whose land it was that de Guzman had come to Indonesia to explore, saw supernatural forces everywhere. Evil spirits who reside in the jungle deep had brought this illness, they would say, and the black magic of sorcerers could have it befall whom they chose.

At 8:30 in the a.m. of March 17, de Guzman arrived for his appointment at Mount Elizabeth carrying with him a small white booklet containing the test results of the examinations he had undergone the previous month. "The cardiac shadow is normal in size and configuration," said the concluding report. "No active lung lesions are seen. Pulmonary vascularity appears normal." He had undergone an ultrasound of the abdomen. "The liver is normal in size and shape. There is no focal hepatic lesion demonstrated.... The gallbladder is normal in size and shape... kidneys and spleen are normal in size and show normal features and normal echogenicity. The tail of the pancreas is obscured by bowel gas.... There is no focal lesion seen in the kidneys and the spleen."

There was little to alarm in the February tests. Raised cholesterol; he was advised to cut back on dairy and beef. A risk of hyperuricaemia, with a predisposition to gout and urinary stones. Dr. Achamma Cheriyan went over all the results with this patient, whom she did not know. Most critically, de Guzman's tests recorded an indication of hepatitis B antigenaemia, or raised liver enzymes. "My company wants to know about the hepatitis B," he said to Cheriyan. He did not seem alarmed, or overly anxious. Cheriyan repeated what had already been stated in the report: if the condition persisted for more than six months de Guzman would be a hepatitis B carrier. His blood was infectious, and he faced an increased risk of chronic liver disease. "There is at present no safe effective way of curing hepatitis B," said the report. Cheriyan turned to her patient. "Many many people are hepatitis B carriers," she said. It was not the end of the world.

Dr. Cheriyan also sent de Guzman to Dr. Leslie Lam for a stress test. In eight minutes on a treadmill, de Guzman achieved a maximum heart rate of 186 bpm, 103 percent of the predicted maximum heart rate for a man of forty-one. The test was terminated and declared negative, or normal. "I have reassured and discharged patient back to your capable hands," wrote Dr. Lam in his reference letter to Cheriyan.

After the hospital visit, Genie and Mike together attended to some business at the United Overseas Bank. De Guzman had made a known profit of more than $4 million in exercising Bre-X share options granted to him in four agreements, beginning in the spring of 1994.

At 10:30 that night Mike and Genie headed home to Bogor. They had been together for almost a decade, and even though there would be many other women, even other wives, Mike was closer to Genie than any of them, save Tess. He held her close. He said he was sorry he had failed her. "If I should die, do not remarry."

The following day, de Guzman made his way from Bogor to the downtown Jakarta offices of Bre-X Minerals, in the Aspac Center on Rasuna Said. The Aspac Center, topped with a clock tower, was a more than respectable office address. De Guzman passed the familiar Chinese statue of four horses and their driver sitting atop a reflecting pool, passed the polished building directory pointing visitors to PT Westralian Atan Minerals. No mention was made of Bre-X Minerals, now a company with a market capitalization (the number of shares outstanding multiplied by the stock price) of $6 billion. Bre-X operated here as PT Westralian, or PT WAM for short.

It had taken fewer than four years to vault the penny-ante Bre-X to the status, at least in stock market terms, of a major corporate player. At $6 billion, Bre-X was trading on exchanges in Toronto and New York and had the market cap of long-lived, profit-making blue-chip companies. It had even taken its place on the Toronto Stock Exchange 300, an index of "high cap" companies that bestows a measure of respectability.

On the ninth floor, Mike de Guzman walked the few short steps to the Westralian, aka Bre-X, offices wearing his standard casual office attire: a cheap polyester shirt and slacks. He had been spending more time than usual in his office here. The month before had been a nightmare of deal-making, which had not helped his health. He became even less communicative than usual. Still, these were heady days for the company, which was now touting Busang as a 200-million-ounce gold discovery. Months of ownership wrangling had finally been resolved, and corporate representatives, at least publicly, were proclaiming themselves pleased. Bre-X now had a fearsome partner in Freeport-McMoRan Copper and Gold Inc. of New Orleans. The Indonesian government was in for a piece. And a guy named Bob Hasan, a relative unknown beyond the world of Asian tycoons, had managed to spread his own tentacular empire right into Busang for

20 percent. Still, 200 million ounces was a big prize. Bre-X had come through the deal-making with a 45 percent share of the greatest single gold resource the world has ever known.

De Guzman spoke briefly that morning with Bernhard Leode, the company's accountant and a long-time associate. Leode has short black hair that he likes to spike with gel, which, given his five-foot-flat height, makes him look rather like a hedgehog. Nice guy, Leode. The beer crowd on mining night at Jakarta's Cilandak Commercial Estates called him Lumpy. "Up off your knees, Lumpy," they would say in jest. Leode had left his job at ICI Chemicals in North Sulawesi, switching to Bre-X's Jakarta operations because he knew, just knew, that Bre-X would be "the fucking largest gold mine in the world." He had shares: 25,000 in Bre-X at $20.50, and 50,000 in Bresea, its sister company, at $14.

De Guzman gave Leode a copy of a memo detailing the pay owed to him by a previous employer, PT Hunamas Putra Interbuana. Hunamas had acquired interests in fertilizer, in broadcasting and, latterly, mining. The company had employed de Guzman four years earlier. De Guzman claimed he was owed something on the order of $22,000 from that time. Leode knew John Nainggolen, an Indonesian who was number two at Hunamas. The real power at Hunamas was a young entrepreneur named Takala Hutasoit, but Nainggolen was the make-things-happen guy. Not yet forty, Nainggolen was a high-flier with a number of residences, a Mercedes fleet and a penchant for gold jewellery. It was to Nainggolen that the memo was addressed. "When the money arrives, transfer it to Genie's account," said de Guzman to Leode. "And Puspos is owed too," he added, referring to his very good friend and right-hand man, with whom he had worked for years at a number of jobs, Cesar Puspos. De Guzman gave a copy of the memo to Mike Bird.

It was astonishing, really. De Guzman was a millionaire many times over. But those who worked with him saw his futzy nature, his persnickety attention to detail. It cost Bre-X US$1.5 million, maybe $1.6 million, a month to keep Busang running. The monthly drill bill alone was $600,000. Yet de Guzman insisted on authorizing every little expenditure. His insistence on pursuing past debts, this tidying up of affairs, certainly did not seem out of character. And given his bitch of a temper, it was not worth anyone's while to complain about having to attend to his non-Bre-X-related housekeeping. It was in his Hunamas days, when he was on his uppers, that he had hocked some of Genie's gold jewellery to make ends meet, to buy "a mouthful of rice," he had said. So there was a bit of romance about his insistence on repayment, about doing right by Genie.

In the early hours of the evening of March 18, Michael de Guzman was driven to Jakarta's Sukarno Hatta International Airport by Dulla, a Bre-X driver. De Guzman had the look of the frequent traveller—carry-on baggage only. He checked onto the last Sempati Airlines flight of the day headed to Balikpapan, an oil town on the east coast of Kalimantan. He had taken this eighty-minute flight, same airline, hundreds of times before, across the Java Sea and the southern tip of Kalimantan.

Waiting for him in Balikpapan was Iwan, a Bre-X employee who had driven the two hours from Samarinda to retrieve the boss man. With Iwan was Rudy Vega, a Filipino metallurgist who worked for Bre-X. De Guzman had phoned Vega in advance, saying he wanted to discuss sampling procedures. But when the boss man arrived, he had other ideas. He would overnight in Balikpapan, he announced.

Iwan was instructed to drive the two men to their hotel, stopping first at a general store where de Guzman purchased stationery and a 2,000-rupiah *meterai*, a stamp. In Indonesia, no document can be officially sealed without a *meterai*. De Guzman had a hacking cough. For this he picked up a large bottle of cough medicine.

At 8:03 p.m., de Guzman and Vega checked into the Benakutai Hotel. The men took Club Rooms 910 and 914, the high-end offerings of the somewhat worn-at-the-edges Benakutai, where the beds are king-sized and the welcome fruit and flowers probably go unnoticed.

The newer Dusit, which sits just behind the shoreline of the Macassar Strait, was much more popular with discerning business clientele. But the Benakutai had been the swish hotel in de Guzman's impoverished years, and it had an edge, a personality, and the rocking Luwai Music Lounge off the lobby that kept hotel patrons awake long after the rest of Balikpapan had tucked in for the night.

At 9:00 p.m. de Guzman left his room and headed down to the hotel's reception desk, where he handed the deskman a fax to be sent to Bre-X's top man in Indonesia, John Felderhof, care of the company's Jakarta office. De Guzman asked his secretary, Linda, to type up the following:

To: Mr. John B. Felderhof
From: Mike de Guzman
Copy: Messrs G.C. MacDonald, B. Leode
Re: Urgent Info

Dear John:

I spent half day 18/3 at office to catch up with desk notes, then traveled to Balikpapan. I will proceed to Busang morning of 19/3. I am not feeling well with my flu but will manage. URGENT info for your attention are listed below:

A. PT WAM F.S. presentation of mines department on 26/3.
   I think it is necessary for Mr. Harsono (PT AKM) and Dave
   Potter (Freeport) to be made aware of this meeting. More
   so, we may need Mr. Harsono's presence in case the
   "Merukh gang" shows up.

   Bernhard to prepare details of financial data and Greg to
   prepare "corporate" history. I suggest Mike Bird's presence
   be required also.

B. I met Adam Tobing at our office re: Limestone Quarry. Two letters copies [*sic*] issued from office of the government to be delivered to Bupati and Camat pertaining to "site evaluation" mainly for formality reason, after which a report needed to be submitted. I will write out the draft, then Greg to co-ordinate with Adam Tobing to finalize.

C. Health situation. I passed the treadmill test 17/3 at Mt. Elizabeth. However, I was adviced [*sic*] to seriously consult a specialist internist pertaining to my liver. I will do this as soon as I am back in Jakarta.

Details of my health exam I will leave at your desk.

I intend to be back in Jakarta 23 or 24/3 will advice [*sic*] you on more details from site.

Best regards
Mike de Guzman

There was nothing to alarm in any of this office talk. The meetings and discussions with the country's Department of Mines and Energy had been ongoing for months, and so to refer to yet another, this one scheduled for March 26, involving Freeport and Bre-X's minority partner, PT AKM, would not have caught anyone's notice. Bre-X had been attempting to fend off Jusuf Merukh, an erstwhile politician with a fistful of mining concessions, since early 1996, when he started hounding the Department of Mines, complaining that he had been shut out of Busang when, in his view, his rights were clear.

Adam Tobing, a close friend of Felderhof's, was well known about the Bre-X offices. Tobing had opened a bar-cum-discotheque in Jakarta some months before, and invitations had gone out to many Bre-X staffers. Tobing and Felderhof were in the process of setting up a limestone business in Samarinda, on the east coast of Kalimantan. The quarry would provide the Busang mine operation with limestone, but getting their hands on the quarry meant squiring government officials in Samarinda, and that job fell to Tobing. (*Bupati* is an Indonesian term for the regent who heads a territorial administration; *Camat* is the head of a region that lies within the Bupati's territory.)

In pursuit of the quarry, Tobing would call in at Bre-X's office for the money he would need to cover expenses, travel and hotel. No invoices were submitted, for while de Guzman kept a close eye on most of his underlings, relationships with some, such as Tobing, were very loose.

With his administrative tasks attended to, de Guzman picked up Vega and sought out a local restaurant for dinner, then wound back to a karaoke bar near the Benakutai. De Guzman had a weakness for karaoke. It was his favourite pastime, now that he had given up sky-diving. When he took the microphone he started to croon—not "Little Red Corvette" or "MacArthur Park," but "My Way," Frank Sinatra's signature song: "And now, the end is near and so I face the final curtain."

At approximately 1:00 a.m., the two men, who had never spent much social time in one another's company, retired for the evening. De Guzman paused before opening his hotel room door. "Stay awake for an hour," he told Vega. "I have something to give you." Half an hour later, de Guzman gave Iwan a note to take to a woman at a disco, offering her a job at Bre-X. He did not call Vega.

Iwan later told Rudy Vega that de Guzman had been soaking wet in the middle of the night. He said the boss man had consumed the bottle of cough syrup and had tried to drown himself in the bathtub.

On the morning of March 19, de Guzman phoned Grace Kapal, his administrative secretary in the Bre-X office in Manado, at the northernmost tip of the island of Sulawesi. He instructed Grace to have ready 20 million rupiahs in cash, which his Manado wife, Susani Mawengkang, would pick up that day. Susani had married Michael two years earlier and had borne him a son, Anthony. Michael had added the two to his growing list of support payments. But this was a large sum of money to hand over without Bernhard Leode's say-so. Though de Guzman often borrowed such large sums, Kapal gave Susani just 10 million rupiahs.

De Guzman phoned Lilis, his wife in Samarinda, spouting declarations of love and affection and filling her in on the basic details of his plan to head directly to Busang, thereby pre-empting their possible reunion. And he phoned Genie. He related the bathtub escapade and told her that he would be back in Jakarta from Busang on March 21. He told her to pick him up at the airport, and said she should come alone.

At 8:19 on the morning of March 19, de Guzman and Vega checked out of the Benakutai. "Shit, I shouldn't have done that," said de Guzman. He said it more than once. Vega wanted to know what had happened. De Guzman said he had fallen asleep, in the tub, after drinking the medicine.

At the Sepinggan Airport in Balikpapan, de Guzman had a coffee with one of the managers at PT Indonesia Air Transport (IAT). De Guzman seemed his normal self, though he had checked in an hour late. No one asked why; Bre-X was a good customer. Vega phoned the Bre-X office in Samarinda to get them to purchase a pair of jeans for de Guzman and take them to him at the airport there. De Guzman and Vega boarded the chopper. The charter company had been ferrying the Bre-X guys for three years now, and this particular chopper, an Alouette III coded PK-TRY, was a regular on the Busang route.

At 9:12 Central Indonesia Time, PK-TRY left Sepinggan Airport with pilot Edy Tursono at the controls, accompanied by engineer Andrian Meilan, Vega and de Guzman. Tursono, a retired lieutenant-colonel in the Indonesian Army, had flown de Guzman before, and had flown with IAT for five years.

At 9:50 the Alouette landed at Temindung Airport in Samarinda, where children lazily walked the runway, flying kites that would sharply cut the air and fray the nerves of the chopper pilots. Vega and de Guzman went into the airport lounge, a sparse holding tank for passengers waiting for the pink-and-blue Bali Air prop planes. De Guzman changed out of his shorts and into the newly purchased jeans. He joked with the girls from the Samarinda office.

After twenty minutes in Samarinda, de Guzman reboarded the helicopter. Tursono assisted him with his seatbelt. The Alouette had two seats across the front. De Guzman climbed onto the rear bench, with his gear, placing the yellow denim jacket he was carrying over the back of the seat in front of him. Yellow, the colour of infidelity and corruption.

The front passenger door was duly snapped shut. Check. The rear door was then pushed forward and closed firmly. Lock. Check.

Edy Tursono ran his hand over the controls. The helicopter sat on a small, square metal pad amid the Kodachromatic Kalimantan scene. Nearer to the control tower, red-and-white Pertamina trucks had come in for refuelling. Orange hibiscus sprang from plaster pots. Splashy green palm fronds danced above trim lawns. Beyond the airstrip, modest houses ran in neat rows, and beyond that one could just see the beginnings of the hilly jungle terrain.

Tursono powered up. The high crackle of Bahasa Indonesia came in from the control tower. "*Selamat Pagi*, good morning. Tursono to tower." Tursono requested clearance. The slight vibration of the windows, the thwupping of the blades. Tursono sat with one hand on the cyclic control, the other on the collective and both feet on the rudders. Vega watched the chopper lift off, then drove to the Bre-X offices on the outskirts of the city.

Two minutes out of Samarinda, the chopper drifts across the blanketed green of Borneo, an aerial Constable. The height is so deceiving. To step out and float, to catch a branch, then nestle into the leafy canopy below. So blissful. But then, quickly, great swaths of clear-cut come into view, ugly and violent, places where the timber companies have done their business. Strips of trees have been left standing, but they are thin sentinels. Reforestation efforts have introduced baby acacia and eucalyptus where ramin, jongkong and mangrove once stood tall. The shifting cultivation habits of the local farmers, too, have created a cycle of burnoff that the island can no longer withstand. In the early 1980s the great fires took out more than three million hectares of forest in East Kalimantan. The slide-show scenery changes swiftly, beckoning, then hateful.

The helicopter flies over a transmigration camp, neat rows of boxed futures. The authorities have heaved inhabitants off the island of Java, out of its population of 115 million, and into Kalimantan, sparsely populated with fewer than 11 million.

The chopper bobbles lower, tipping toward the peat swamp, marsh and fen. Timing one's departure from a chopper would be a tricky business. A helicopter pilot knows when 100 kilos are on the move in his machine.

Sir Malcolm Watson marched this mire. "Among the roots of these trees move the salt and brackish waters which at low tide keep the mud clammy and stinky. Poisonous snakes abound. Wild pigs hunt under the mangroves for nuts and roots, and in turn are hunted by tigers who often develop a taste for woodchoppers. Crocodiles are by no means scarce. In the stomach of one I found a dog license and a monkey's skull intact."

The route to Busang is so familiar to de Guzman. Co-ordinates 0 degrees 44.208' 116 22.803'. A trip he has made repeatedly, uneventfully. Time normally for a brief nap.

Edy Tursono keeps the chopper at 250 metres, or 800 feet, travelling at 95 knots. The scenery slides beneath, moving as a child's Kinetoscope. With headsets on, each passenger is isolated in this bubble environment. Easy to let one's mind wander to another place. The chopper blades tap time. Seconds pass to minutes. Five. Ten. Fifteen. Sixteen. Stop. Something is wrong. A blast of air. Tursono pitches down to reduce the speed, turns, sees nothing. The left-hand door is fully opened to its latched stop. Tursono freezes his GPS receiver. The Global Positioning System records co-ordinates S 00 06 29 and E 116 57 62.

Look at your watch. Tap this time. The rate of initial acceleration is 32 feet a second. It would take seven to ten seconds to fall 800 feet. Tap. Second. Tap. Second. It seems to take forever. Can you breathe? Can you focus?

Tursono swings back to search and as he does, he radios the tower at Temindung. "My passenger is jump from the helicopter." Another chopper is dispatched. The control tower instructs Tursono to return to Temindung, where he arrives at 10:50.

It was approaching the lunch hour when Greg MacDonald took the call in Bre-X's Jakarta office from Indonesia Air Transport. De Guzman was gone. MacDonald let out a cry. He told Mike Bird, who was in his office down the hall. "What the hell is going on?" Bernhard Leode wondered aloud. "Were there technical problems at Busang? Was de Guzman trying to hide something?" Bird and MacDonald turned on their associate. What the hell was he on about? What was he suggesting? Mike? Never. The trio tried to keep the news quiet. There was no hope.

The personal belongings of Michael de Guzman were duly confiscated by the Indonesian police in Tenggarong, the capital of East Kalimantan. Included in his belongings was an authorization letter. "Full authority given to Mr. Bernhard Leode to represent, act on my behalf and for my behalf in case of disability or my death. Voluntarily issued 18 March 1997." On this was affixed the 2,000-rupiah stamp. The letter was signed by Michael de Guzman.

A second letter was addressed to Rudy Vega. "My final request," it said. "To Rudy. Rm 914. Pls. Bring my black bag w/ all my very important notes. Hand carry to office and Bogor. Key here. Thanks. Mike."

A third was to John Felderhof "+ All my friends." De Guzman's script ballooned across the page, so familiar to those who had worked with him and had received his vituperative faxes. "Sorry I have to leave. I can not think of myself a carrier of Hepatitis 'B.' I can not jeopardise your lifes. Same w/ my loved ones. God bless you all. No more stomach pains!!! No more back pains!!"

His request to his wife Teresa, addressed to Leode, was simple enough. "Do not bury me. Burn—cremate me in Manila."

Leode was called up in Jakarta. His presence was requested in Tenggarong, at the police office, a journey he made with Greg MacDonald. De Guzman had left a number of instructions for Leode: to accompany de Guzman's body to Manila; to hand-carry documents and passport and deliver to Teresa. "Do not bring my body to Bogor. Stay at funeral parlour while waiting for travel to Manila. Settle accounts personal. Thank you very much my dear friend."

There were, too, notes to Felderhof. "Dear John, I need money to finish these unit, part of boarding house adjacent to school. Pls. Spare me." "Dear John, I need money to finish the school. Pls. Spare me." The notes accompanied floor plans for a school at Busang that was to be named for de Guzman.

Spare me, spare me. Was Michael de Guzman begging forgiveness of his friend? Had he deceived him? Or was he merely exhibiting the psychology of the suicidal? He had been so careful, it seemed, to put his life in order before ending it. Money to Genie. Money to Susani. This tidy business about the school. The suicidal often attend to the banal. An example from *Pathways to Suicide: A Survey of Self-Destructive Behaviors*: "Dear Rob. Forgive me darling... There is no other way out... Laundry due Friday... Please cancel all charge accounts . . . Find out if you can continue Blue Cross yourself . . . Love Janet."

Business matters. Vanity projects. Was de Guzman in a state of emotional upheaval? Or had he plateaued on that icy calm psychiatrists talk of before the final exit? Perhaps one, then the other, in quick succession. Powerlessness: a basic conceptual state for the suicidal. The understanding that one has no control over the personal loss, or the voices, or the illness, or the feelings, or the occupational failure, or life's course, or whatever. Sexual eagerness. Taking risks. Were these habits part of the aggressive make-up of someone who had already given up? Anomie. Moral decay. De Guzman was a good Catholic boy in his day. Now to kill himself and assume God's prerogative. If there is a religion more damning of suicide than Catholicism it is the Muslim faith. De Guzman had turned to Islam in recent years. Double damn.

The notes to the family were heartbreaking. "Sweetheart. Tess Mahal," Tess my love, "I must leave you now I am very sorry my sadness is killing me. I tried my best for you and our children. Please forgive me for any misgiving Mahal, you must be strong and continue. I will die without regrets—Lord God have bless us more than I ever love you. I love all our children. Watch you health. Love forever Mike."

He wrote his children. "Please love your Mama, respect her . . . please protect your mama—All of you, All the time . . . ."

Mike addressed his boys, Paul (known as Birl) and Mike, Jr. "Take my responsibilities now. . . . Stay together all the time. Never blame each other. I will die even 10x for your Mommy because I love, respect her. All of my children—Remember me. Papa. Lots of love."

He suggested that Tess sell an apartment, that she save the boats at Balawan, or sell them one by one. The business neatness again. Michael signed these small notes "Love Chel."

Michael de Guzman lay in the swamp of Kalimantan for four days. There is no dry season in Borneo, or at least there wasn't that March. The rains came. The humidity climbs to 80, the temperature to the high 90s. A few minutes north of the Equator, at noon the sun is virtually overhead. His body hosted pigs, leeches, maggots and crocodiles, the panoply of jungle life that becomes monotonous to those who live and work here. De Guzman had seen it all before, the misery in these swampy, malarial lowlands. Martinus, a Bre-X employee, and Thahir, a local villager, found de Guzman's putrid body, soft and swollen as a marshmallow, not 200 metres from Tursono's co-ordinates. Martinus marked the spot with a red gasoline container.

In the stale police office in Samarinda, a uniformed officer typed out his report on an aged typewriter.

Report on the progress of the handling of the case of the fall of a foreign citizen named Michael de Guzman from a helicopter in Kutai, East Kalimantan. Police report No.: LP/05/lll/1119/Sek Makaman.

In accordance with Letter of Confiscation No. Sprin/18/lll/ 1997/Serse, dated March 20, 1997, victim's belongings were confiscated and placed under the care of the Head of Temindung Airport, Samarinda. They are as follows:

a. A white Vanguard suitcase containing:
  – 20 rolls of Fuji film
  – 16 ordinary letters and one telegram.

b. A black Assima leather bag containing:
  – a Motorola handphone and its charge
  – a Seiko and Rolex wristwatch
  – two diamond studded gold rings
  – a gold bracelet
  – a Casio calculator
  – a small wallet containing:
    • Rp 252,850 in cash
    • US$35 in cash
    • CAN$20 in cash
    • Two certificates Nos. 003409 and 003424 respectively
    • Alfred Dunhill card No. JF-80285488
    • SM Card No. 608-1386-8 in the name of Mike de Guzman
    • American Express Card No. 3769609554 11005 in the name of Mike de Guzman
    • Two Universal cards Nos. 0730 0101 6106 8801 and 5899 2801 6016 8650 respectively in the name of Mike De Guzman

- Citi Bank Card Nos. 4541 7890 1117 3187 in the name
    of Mike de Guzman
  – a Versus belt
  – important business letters
  – a green vest
  – a small case containing a ruler
  – Letters of Last Will written before falling out of helicopter

c. A black plastic bag containing:
  – A brown cloth jacket
  – A brown shirt
  – Three T-shirts and several briefs and singlets

d. Three cases of Bintang beer (72 cans)

2. After having letters written in English left by victim translated into Indonesian, it was found, among others:
   a. Problem at workplace
   b. Disease suffered (Hepatitis B)
   c. Request for sending victim's remains to Manila, The
      Philippines
   d. Apologies to friends
   e. Request for sending document to victim's mother and
      wife (Teresa)
   f. Request for sending the black bag and important papers
      to victim's office in Bogor; and a letter for victim's wife in
      Manila, the Philippines, and the result of a medical per-
      formed in Singapore was found in the suitcase.
   g. Letter for victim's wife arranging the division victim's
      wealth: 40% for his wife and 10% respectively for each
      of his six children.

On March 25, 1997, at 10:45 a.m., Doctor Daniel Umar, a physician at the A. Wahab Syachrani Hospital in Samarinda, found himself staring at the remains of Michael de Guzman in the hospital morgue. "Dokter Daniel" lived 25 metres down a mud road that rejected most vehicles in Sempaja, a small village just outside Samarinda. Across the way an old man lived in a wooden shack, which had, as its lone decoration, a collection of running shoes hanging from nails on its front. Dokter Daniel's home was very neat by contrast. Middle class.

Each day Dr. Umar would make his way to town, past the fruit vendors, along streets where chickens and scooters seemed to dart along in equal numbers. On that morning, a Tuesday, he found himself alongside police Captain Dr. T.B. Rijanto and Lieutenant Dr. Sugeng, doctors of the East Kalimantan Police Medical and Health Service, staring at the cadaver of a man declared to have died at the timber estate of PT Sumalindo Lestari Jaya, Block 85-86, Kutai District.

He commenced his external examination. The corpse was placed on an examination table in room No. 2. It was covered in white plastic bearing the name of the Kasimo Foundation, a local group representing the Filipino community in Kalimantan. The pink label of the Kutai Police was affixed to the plastic, describing the corpse as one Michael de Guzman. Sex: male. Nationality: Filipino. Religion: Catholic.

Dr. Umar removed the corpse's white plastic wrapping. The body was face down, slanting slightly to the right. Dark-blue jeans. A bright violet T-shirt, batiked in the Indonesian manner. White underwear.

Hair: straight, black, four and a half centimetres long, mostly removed from the head. Eyebrows, eyelashes, moustache: missing. Eleven by six centimetres of scalp peeled from the left side of the head, at the back, above the left ear. Right eyeball: missing. Left eyeball: shrunken and hollow. Open, jagged wounds around the nose and mouth. Tongue: pale. Teeth: mostly missing.

Dr. Umar recorded an open, jagged wound in the abdomen extending to about five fingers below the navel. The skin and muscles on one-third of the upper part of the left thigh were severely damaged and decomposed. The joint between the second and third groin bones had broken off. No genitals were found. No chest bones. No innards. Dr. Umar wrote: "The contents of the chest and abdomen were not found." The surface of the back was uneven. Dr. Umar pressed down, feeling a broken backbone.

No broken bone was found in the skull. Umar cleaved the cranium, removed the brain, and by 12:30, nearly two hours after he had commenced this task, Dr. Umar concluded that the cause of death was unknown.

From the facts and analysis above, said the police, it may be concluded as follows:

1. There are no indications and evidence of act/acts of violence against victim Michael Antonio de Guzman, as such no crimes of violence can be proven to have been committed against victim.
2. Testimonies of witnesses and existing evidence indicate that victim Michael Antonius [sic] de Guzman did not fall by accident but that he deliberately ended his life by dropping himself from the helicopter.

By dropping himself from the helicopter. Safe to say the police had never written words to that effect before.

Dr. Umar injected the body with 4 percent formalin. The corpse was placed in a zinc-laminated wooden box, soldered "until no air can going in and out." Two officers of the counter-smuggling unit, office of the director general of customs and excise taxes in Samarinda, affixed two seals of paper on the coffin. At 2:15 p.m. on the afternoon of Tuesday, March 25, the corpse of Michael de Guzman was loaded aboard a Garuda Airlines flight to Jakarta.

John Felderhof was at his palatial Cayman Islands home when he heard the news of his good friend's demise. He made plans to return to Jakarta posthaste. On the afternoon of March 28, he arrived at a hastily organized memorial service with his wife, Ingrid. The Bre-X crowd was there. Bernhard Leode. A trio of Canadian geologists who had been working at Busang. Bre-X support staff from the Jakarta office. Many journalists. Felderhof was looking heavy and wet in an ill-fitting, oversized suit. All eyes were on him—if anyone had the answers to their questions it would be Felderhof. Father Van der Schurren celebrated a mass for the soul of the departed.

Tess de Guzman, a woman in her forties, wore sunglasses and the inexpensive gold jewellery that she favours. She chose a simple navy blue jumper over a daisy T-shirt. At a later memorial service in Manila, she stayed close to the six children she had had by Michael. Their eldest, Birl, looked as slim as Michael himself had in his early mining days, working for Benguet Corp. at their Acupan gold mine, fathering babies, leading a pretty fine life. Photographs taken during that happy time were on display. Teresa and the six children she had borne had constructed a heroic image of their conquering husband and father, the valiant explorer.

Tess approached Tom Malihan, who still worked at Acupan. "Could you get Michael's dental records, Tom?"

"Are you sure he underwent dental treatment at our dispensary?" asked Malihan. Of course he had. There was that high night of revelry when Michael, blasted and ginned up, barfed his plate down the toilet. It was the Benguet dental policy that paid for the replacement. Malihan promised to look into it.

Many of de Guzman's former Benguet pals were there. Paul Damasco. Pedro Oyam. John Salamat, who had worked at Busang, had to be smuggled in to avoid a media inquisition. Cesar Puspos was notable by his absence. The long-time de Guzman acolyte had not been seen in days.

It is June, and on the road to Holy Cross Memorial Park, in Quezon City, the Philippines, the children are enthusiastic participants in St.-Jean Baptiste Day, trying to water-soak travellers in wildly coloured jeepney buses. There is a roadside sign that says: "Ask not what your country can do for you. Ask what you can do for your country." It is, interestingly, attributed not to John Fitzgerald Kennedy, pace Oliver Wendell Holmes, but rather to someone named Jeffrey San Jose.

Entering the verdant glade of Holy Cross, searching for Michael de Guzman, the driver passes the Lawn of Tranquillity One and the Lawn of Serenity Two. Michael is entombed in the Estate of Peace Three. It is still under construction, and Armado, Sivarena and Mario the Blind are hard at work. Mario's left eye is just a white ball barely visible in its socket. His chest is bare under pale-blue overalls. Bags of Continental cement are piled high in Mario's digs, a roughly assembled wooden barrack with a corrugated tin roof and a bare light bulb hanging from the ceiling. Mario lives with the final display of Michael de Guzman's remains. Cook pots are on the boil. In front of the tomb is a very small offering of flowers, gone brittle. Soon the raw look of cement will be clad in granite and it will look very fine.

The de Guzmans do not particularly want any outsiders visiting here. They have retained a Filipino lawyer, William Chua, who has a mop of dark hair, very Beatle-ish, and craterous inky folds under his eyes. His manner is unassuming, almost embarrassed. The family is prepared to accept the worst news, he says, to accept that Michael, such a religious little boy, has taken his own life. But of course they want proof, and the family will conduct its own investigation. Tess is terribly anguished. By the loss of her spouse, the father of her children, and by these allegations of so many wives. How can it be true? She asks many people if they have heard news of this, but she does not want the truth. She phones Michael's secretary, Linda, in Jakarta. "Is it true, Linda? Did Michael have this wife in Bogor?" Yes, she is told, it is true. Investigators say her husband masterminded the most brilliant gold scam of the century. Oh pray that it is not true.

Over a late dinner one evening, attorney Chua touches on a number of curiosities in this case. Why did the Indonesian government let the Filipino workers at Busang leave the country? That does not sound like the Indonesian way, if these men are guilty of something, if there has been a fraud in the gold fields. Chua seems to have little affection for Indonesia, which, in truth, is a distaste directed at its leader, Pak Suharto. "Dictators die," he says dryly. "Ours did." Does he believe this man Michael de Guzman devised one of the greatest scams of all time? He laughs. He does not know if this is true, and out of courtesy to his clients will not speculate that it is. But if it is true? Attorney Chua finds a small amusing note in this. "It took the Filipinos to screw the Suhartos."

The de Guzman family also retained the services of Dr. Jerome Bailen, associate professor in anthropology at the University of the Philippines. He was provided with the official identification of Bayani Palad, chief of the dactyloscopy division at the National Bureau of Investigation in Manila. The dactyloscopy crew confirmed the identification of Michael de Guzman, matching the right thumbmark with the right thumbmark on de Guzman's identification card. "In the view thereof, the unknown male cadaver and de Guzman, Michael Antonio are one and the same person," wrote Palad. The de Guzman family was suspicious of this Indonesian identification. An identification from Michael's days working for Benguet was retrieved. On the basis of this the NBI changed its opinion. "After thorough examination, thumbmarks in the above document do not match.... In view thereof, de Guzman Michael Antonio and Michael T. de Guzman are TWO DIFFERENT PERSONS."

Bailen studied the case. As to the first conclusion, the positive identification: "The so-called right thumbprint taken by the NBI from the cadaver (through, I presume, the usual printer's ink roller technique) is so practically washed out, that not enough details could be found to enable a reputable dactyloscopy expert from a credible forensic laboratory to come out with such a cocksure conclusion." Further, the NBI had matched the right cadaver thumbprint to a left thumbprint from the Indonesian ID card.

"Naturally," wrote Bailen, "the right thumbmark of the former ID should not match the left thumbmark.... However, from this finding the NBI could not jump to the opinion/conclusion that de Guzman Michael Antonio and Michael T. de Guzman are TWO DIFFERENT PERSONS. Not necessarily.... Moreover, according to his family de Guzman's birth certificate and therefore passport as well as foreign documents (in Indonesia) carries the name Michael Antonio de Guzman. While still in the Philippines, Mike used the shorter name— Michael T. de Guzman."

Bailen obtained another thumbprint, from de Guzman's Social Security Form, which he superimposed on the Indonesian identification card. They appeared to match. He advised that the NBI should try again.

I have a piece of Busang core, given to me by one of the Bre-X geologists, and I have taken it to a fine geologist at the University of Toronto. It is 6 centimetres in diameter, 2.5 centimetres thick. The rock's background is a soft grey colour, speckled with cloudy, flesh-tone spots. Close to one side runs a greenish black vein, and this is intersected by another of the same colour that runs across the middle of the piece. Bleeding off of these veins is a rusty stain, echoing the shape of the veins to perhaps twice their thickness.

Ed Spooner studies what to me looks like nothing more than a round of roquefort. "In the host rock, you can see little grains, some kind of felsic." (Felsic: from feldspar and lenad and silica, a term applied to an igneous rock having abundant light-coloured minerals in its mode.) Spooner wets the tips of his fingers and rubs his saliva across the sheer surface of this volcanic host rock, giving it, briefly, a glossy sheen. "In some of the cavities here you can see tiny little specks of something reflective. They're reflecting light quite strongly. From their colour, I'm pretty sure they're just pyrite. You can see in the core of this little vein here the same brassy-yellow reflective material. It's not gold. When you see gold like that it's a really intense yellow. When you see it you never forget it. Again, this is pyrite. Pyrite is fine-grained. Normally in this kind of sample the gold is even more fine-grained and is intergrown with the pyrite.

"The dark colour, I don't know what that is. When lead and zinc sulphides are very fine-grained they make a dark colour like that. The brownish echo is an iron staining. In the subsurface, iron sulphides are stable underground. But when those sulphides come in contact with atmospheric oxygen, the sulphides become totally unstable. If you have erosion of the surface layers going on, a rock that was formed fairly deep in the subsurface comes closer to the surface and comes in contact with high-level groundwater carrying oxygen."

It's a grey, spitting day outside Spooner's window. Very unpleasant. This piece of rock seems just as drab. And Spooner? If here were at a drill site in the godforsaken middle of nowhere and he sliced a piece of core like this? "Oh. I'd send it out for assay right away. Actually, it's quite good-looking stuff."

It holds the small promise of clues, this tiny taste of Busang. To a geologist, it holds the distant promise of a discovery. "Sometimes it runs gold," says Spooner. "Sometimes it doesn't." The truth can be got, should be got, pretty darned quickly. "If you put a couple holes into this stuff and didn't get anything, not a whisper, you're in trouble."

BEGINNINGS

"THE AUTHORITIES SAY MICHAEL de Guzman jump, suffering some personal problems, or whatever. There is a foul play." The taxi turns and drives past the Ma-Anne Student Canteen in Manila. The cabby's identification card hangs in the taxi window, an impression of his right thumbprint permanently plasticized. Of course, the cabby knows about Michael de Guzman and his baroque demise. The newspapers in the Philippines have been full of it.

The taxi takes a corner at San Marcelino. A three-storey concrete bunker behind a high wire gated fence is the administration building of Adamson University. Students in their Adamson uniforms—white shirts, straight ties, dark-blue slacks or skirts for the women, grey flannels for the men—flash their identification badges to clear security standing watch at the San Marcelino entrance. This is a country of proved identities. Up a metal staircase and across a foul canal visitors arrive at a honeycomb of doorless classrooms opening onto open-air corridors that overlook the quad. The chief feature of the cement-columned courtyard is a fountain that has been left dry. Grimy ochre walls, old wooden school desks, a crucifix at the front of each class above each and every chalkboard. There is nothing to evoke *Brideshead Revisited* here, no Oxbridge hues.

Scrums of young people hang out at the pastoral office, waiting to air their admission grievances. A security guard with a smart and very shiny brass belt buckle keeps a revolver in a snappy oxblood leather holster. "You are duly informed," says a posted sign, "that the administration has not authorized any one, student or otherwise, to accept money from any enrollees allegedly to expedite enrollment."

Of course there would be the aroma of graft, even here in these unassuming academic environs. Ferdinand Marcos was elected to the presidency in 1965. Seven years later he declared martial law. His wife, Imelda, was awash in shoes, her squat personage topped by a prow of very hard hair. Together they fronted a grotesque play of human rights violations. Financial ones, too. Offshore transfers, Swiss bank accounts, officials on the take, a corrupt police force. Marcos and his wife stole an estimated $10 billion, according to Philippine government claims. Their regime was the backdrop to Michael de Guzman's life in the Philippines.

Adamson was the college for the poor and lower-income students, then as now. The top students and the well-to-do would enrol in the University of the Philippines, much grander in style and repute. Adamson is housed in the former home of the Vincentian Fathers on San Marcelino. The three Greek cousins who founded the college in the 1930s formally turned it over to the Fathers in 1964. There is a heavy overlay of Christianity and dedication to the spirit of St. Vincent de Paul, patron saint of charity. The students here are expected to know their school prayer: "Give me the heart of the poor so that I may strive to develop with loving patience and perseverance the intellect and talents you have given me; give me prudence—fill me with the Holy Spirit—be my Friend, my Light and Strength as I pursue a life of honesty, truthfulness, humility and loving service each day as a student." The university's hymn is a touch more Ivy League:

Adamson Alma Mater dear
All Hail thy name
In our wand'ring far or near
We'll spread thy fame

Adamson's stated mission is to mould its students into mature Catholics, competent professionals, responsible citizens, integrated persons, "capable of making sound moral judgement by discerning the values which dignify them from those that degrade them." In the foyer of the college's administration building, a statue of St. Vincent de Paul, the Gascony peasant, looms over all visitors. His raiment is filthy, seemingly untouched by any cleaning staff, and he's missing the tips of two fingers. But his eyes are as warm as polished chestnuts. What appears to be a note has been tucked behind his crucifix: "I am the vine and you are the branches."

Liquor is not allowed on campus. The pastoral officer says campus rules are very strict. Why are there so many armed personnel? "You never know," he says. "There might be students harbouring some grudges against us." And the campus must be protected from the outside world, apparently. Just the other day, someone was being chased out there on the street by "a notorious criminal," who, when he saw the armed guards, ran the other way.

This is a dour place, this community rooted in Jesus, evangelizer of the poor. Yet in the streets of Manila beyond, it is clear that Jesus is coming. He must be, for the messages are everywhere, flashing on street signs, printed on bumper stickers. They convey a confidence and urgency. *Jesus Alone Saves.*

Michael Antonio Tuason de Guzman was born at the University of Santa Thomas Hospital in Manila, Valentine's Day, 1956. The fifth child born to Simplicio and Leila de Guzman, Michael had pride of place in the family, for he was the firstborn son.

The family was not well-to-do. Simplicio, universally called Mike, was a surveyor and geodesic engineer. Young Chel spent his first two years as a student attending the Nazareth School, registered there initially, Leila recollects, because it was the only school that would take him at the age of six. Two years later, he was switched to Holy Trinity Academy, where he joined his sisters. He was a good student, bringing home ribbons of excellence on a quarterly basis. He did well in maths and sciences and religion. He would, with his sisters, receive the Blessed Sacrament every day before class.

The family roamed a fair bit, living in the Bicol region, in southeast Luzon, before moving to Manila when Chel was two. As a young boy, Chel would sell newspapers and comics—there was an industriousness about him. And he was close to his mother, who was enterprising too. Leila was a licensed cosmetologist, though she never practised that trade. Instead, she would buy PX goods from American army bases and deliver them to stores in Manila. With twelve children to support, Leila had to be resourceful. Chel adored her. He was not close to his father.

In 1972, Michael graduated from the Quezon City Science High School and entered Adamson, where he pursued studies in geology. He had been offered a place at the Baguio campus of the University of the Philippines, but the family wanted their son nearer to the home base in Manila, so Michael chose Adamson. Diane, the eldest of the de Guzman children, who moved to the United States in 1974 to practise nursing, helped him out financially from time to time.

In 1977, Benguet Consolidated Inc., which would later change its name to Benguet Corp., perused the list of potential hirees from the Adamson graduating class. UP was by far the university grad pool of choice, but Adamson had a good reputation for producing technically proficient graduates, and Benguet then was a powerful mining company that hired legions of green geologists. Benguet rated de Guzman as Adamson's best. It would have been a coup to be hired by Benguet then. In the Philippines it had corporate presence, even prestige.

Benguet also had a reputation for paying minuscule salaries. Criticisms of this practice were dismissed with standard corporate arguments—hirees should be grateful to be taken into the Benguet fold, should appreciate the corporate benefits: dental, medical, housing. De Guzman, fresh out of college, would have been paid fewer than 19 pesos a day ($2.77 in 1977 dollars).

Immediately he was thrown into the company's training program, which had a good reputation. Mapping, sampling, core-logging. De Guzman would have taken on the standard duties of a field geologist. After training, de Guzman was assigned to the company's Acupan mine, just outside of Baguio.

The bus pulls out of the Victory Liner station in Cubao, a Manila subdivision where the de Guzman family still runs what they call their "buy-sell" operation. The traffic is, of course, nose to bum. The second-worst traffic in the world; Jakarta's is worse. The bus passes the popular Goldilocks bakery franchise, then goats, garbage and quail eggs for sale. The energetic flow of commerce-on-foot is never-ending: newspapers, car accessories, foodstuffs. Signs advertise *Gilbey's London Dry Gin, Gilbey's By Choice*; there is still the sense of foreign occupation, a colonial air. A building boasts a proud corporate moniker: Integrity Lending Investor Corp. Belying the energetic commercial bustle, the homeless fill the streets. The city is so overrun the government has aggressively pursued a policy of transferring out the slum-dwellers, the squatters.

On the trip to Baguio, the Sony television that hangs from the front of the bus can blare through two Hollywood action pictures, when the tube is not tuned to local teen talent shows of morphed, Osmond-like families. Pavarotti is due in Manila soon, and for 20,000 pesos ($1,064) the people of Manila can attend his concert. Gas is 10 pesos a litre. The bus passes a toll gate, with a young woman inside stamping and filing small squares of paper. When the television is not blaring, the tape system replaces the cacophony. "Stairway to Heaven" is hugely popular still. Quiet seems to be a concept that holds little interest for the passengers.

A skyway, to be called the Metro Manila, is being built to ease traffic congestion. It will cost 30 billion pesos and will be constructed by the Citra Metro Manila Tollway Corp., a partnership between a state-run Philippine construction company and PT Citra Lamtoro Gung Persada, an Indonesian company owned by Siti Hardyanti Rukmana, daughter of Indonesia's eternal leader, Suharto. Siti is better known by her nickname, Tutut.

The trip to Baguio winds through agriculturally lush countryside, which, as the roads push farther north, is occasionally dusted by *lahar*, the volcanic mud flow that erupted from Mount Pinatubo in the summer of 1991. When Pinatubo spread its deadly grey ash, they say there was no daylight in Zambales that season. Benguet sent food and supplies during the relief effort. Seven years later, the lahar still blankets sections of what was once rich farming soil.

The bus makes pit stops. Salesmen hop up the high steps laden with plastic buckets from which wafts the heavy, buttery smell of peanuts. They jostle down the narrow bus corridors, holding aloft paper cones for the peanuts, stepping over passenger parcels. Fresh *buko* juice is offered at roadside stands. The bus climbs higher. The journey to Baguio, through emerald rice paddies, could be a trip through any Asian countryside, until, round a bend just outside the city, a giant likeness of Marcos rises through the mist, an incongruous mountain of concrete, the visage of an evil wizard. Acid has discoloured the stone under his nose, but any other efforts undertaken by the Filipino people to destroy this likeness have failed.

Prominent Filipinos built their summer homes in this mountain air, and Baguio is still called the summer capital of the Philippines, the nation's cleanest city. The countryside is lush; the air is fresh. The town itself is built around Burnham Park, named after Daniel Hudson Burnham, a Chicago architect. Children rent small wooden boats to paddle in the park. Willows bend near the water. A strip of open-air food stalls adjoins the park: the Four Kids Eatery and Joce-lyn Bulakena Fastfood. Whole fresh fish are grilled on barbeques at breakfast time. Hotly coloured jeepney buses, in turquoise, sienna and cinnamon, await passengers, who are perhaps meant to be drawn by their kitschy look. Some are personalized. One bears the brave and bracing name Anus Young Guy. The jeepneys come in two sizes: family-sized, called Honour Jeepneys, sell for 180,000 pesos. The passenger version, which can carry up to twenty-two people, sells for almost twice that.

American prospectors arrived here in the Cordillera Highlands with pack horses at the turn of the century. Tex Revis, an American soldier turned prospector, panned for gold as far back as 1905. Hun-dreds of years before the Americans, the native Igorots were success-ful miners, and after them the Spanish in the sixteenth century. Gold was as captivating a siren for the conquistadors as God was for the missionaries who sought to convert the native peoples, furthering the co-conspiratorial pursuits of economic gain and religious conversion. "I and my men suffer from a disease of the heart," said Hernán Cortés, "that can only be cured by gold." The gold mines of Luzon would cause Fernando Riquel to proclaim that "there is more gold in this island than there is iron in Biscay."

In a Benguet history, the exuberant optimism of Riquel "dissipated about as quickly as the easily collectible gold disappeared. While the Filipinos did mine gold, they did so only in small quantities, both because of their limited need for the metal as well as the primitive state of their mining techniques. They used some gold in the form of nuggets for trade but more often for personal adornment in the form of earrings and bracelets. The basic techniques consisted of pounding the gold-bearing ore with a stone hammer and then repeatedly wash-ing the particles in a wooden bowl or coconut shell. Adding the sap of a green vine in the washing operation helped prevent the fine gold particles from floating away."

Still, gold was gold was gold, in any quantity "a magnet to men's hearts," someone once said. Through the early 1620s the Spanish conducted a number of *entradas*, incursions that established garrisons in the highlands, attempting to expel the Igorots from the mines in the region. Numerous Igorot mines were discovered, as well as placer operations where they would mine gold from the streams. And the Igorots would conduct the occasional head-hunting raid against the Christian interlopers, leading the missionaries to argue that conquest of the Igorot gold reserves would assist in the pacification of the natives and thence their conversion. But the cost to Spain in manpower and equipment proved too great for so small a reward, and the conquest of the Igorot, and thereby the Baguio mines, was ultimately abandoned in 1623. Though Spain's colonial rule continued for very nearly another three hundred years, its mining law, a licensing system that provided tenuous title comfort to the licensee, did little to spur the development of Luzon's mineral wealth. The conquistadors' dream of El Dorado was never realized in the Philippines.

After the annexation of the Philippines by the United States in 1898, those mining concessions held by the Spanish were unilaterally cancelled, and a new freehold system granted property rights to prospectors who maintained a minimum level of expenditures on exploration work. Ultimately, the land claim was patented, giving the title-holder effective ownership of surface and subsurface mineral rights. Confident in the right to exercise legal control over their discoveries, buccaneers of the Spanish-American war, scanning the frontier for their fortunes, made the same run up the Baguio hills that their Spanish predecessors had made hundreds of years earlier.

Nelson Peterson was one of these, and in 1903 he and two partners formed the Benguet Consolidated Mining Co. Its initial authorized capital was a million shares at one dollar a share. The three founders drew 100,000 shares each in exchange for the twelve mining claims they together held in the region. To raise cash they sold 100,000 shares to the public at twenty cents a share. By 1905 the partners were in production, using cyanide to process the gold ore. Five years later, all three were wiped out, their gold-spinning dreams devastated by typhoons.

Benguet was revived in 1915, after issuing fresh shares to the public and refurbishing the mine. As its mineral resources later dwindled, Benguet risked capital on new drilling on claims that had been prospected, drilled and abandoned by less successful companies. The Balatoc Mining Co. was one. Balatoc, the Igorot word for gold, had attempted to develop the so-called Acupan mines, one of a string of original Igorot mine camps to which foreign venture capitalists had returned. Benguet acquired Balatoc in 1927, and by 1930 Acupan was in full operation, treating 140 tonnes of rock a day at its mill. Benguet would go on to invest in other young mining companies, what would later be called "junior" mining companies. "The smaller organizations cannot always develop their properties to the best advantage," said John Haussermann, a long-serving Benguet president. "The lack of resources, and often the lack of experience in a specific field makes it difficult for them to take their place in the producing category." Benguet grew by seeking joint ventures with these young corporate prospectors, a practice still popular with senior mining companies to this day.

The 1930s were boom times in Baguio, and throughout the Philippine gold-mining industry. It was, too, a period of low interest rates and big winnings in other industries, such as sugar and coconut. The country was awash in capital seeking a home, and the mining industry was an immediate and direct beneficiary. In 1933, President Franklin Roosevelt took the United States off the gold standard. This divine confluence of circumstances created a claims-staking rush not seen since the Klondike in 1898. The Philippine Bureau of Science remarked that prospectors were laying claims over all manner of geology known to be non-gold-bearing.

Such is the history of penny mine booms. Born of an uptick in commodity prices, served by buoyant stock markets, such exploration rushes create baby companies that issue shares at a penny, a nickel, ten pennies a share. The insiders—the promoters and their pals—get the cheapest stock. The general investing public buys in at higher prices, gambling, punting, wishing, hoping that the bet placed on the latest play will pay off. The game has not changed substantially in a hundred years.

It takes only one gold discovery to excite the minds of wishful investors. Acre upon acre of moose pasture has been and will forever be claimed amidst such fever, infecting investors with dreams of limitless stock winnings. A corporate history of Benguet has an unattributed contribution from an astute observer of the day: "The penny-share trick had been popularized, taking in clerks and day labourers who got to preferring mining shares to *jueteng* [an illegal numbers game] or the sweepstakes as a device for gambling. When a new company was organized, whole schools of these little customers overwhelmed the offices with eagerness to get in on the ground floor. Board averages were rising; no one asked much about what property was to be exploited or about prospector's assays and reports, or who was behind the project." The number of mining stocks on the Manila Stock Exchange went from six to seventy in just three years. The trajectory followed its historically proven course. A great run-up of stocks, many companies promoting bogus properties getting in on the bull run, and the ultimate stock crash, in this case in 1937, in which investors lost their shirts.

Benguet was not substantially shaken by the crash, though it was made nervous by a change in Philippine mining law that decreed that all mining rights belonged to the state. Prospectors were now granted fifty-year leases, maximum, instead of freehold property rights. The new law was not backdated to cover previous claims, and so the company's Acupan operations remained unaffected. After the Second World War, which saw the destruction by the Japanese of much of the company's operations, Herbert Allen, Sr., head of Wall Street's Allen and Co., took a 40 percent interest in the company and underwrote a listing on the New York Stock Exchange.

The company suffered, as did all gold mining companies, in the 1950s and '60s. Rising labour costs, ore that was deeper and more dispersed and thus more difficult to get at, and a poor gold price forced it to turn to the government for support and subsidies. Many mining companies diversified: financial services, oil and gas, anything to try to keep their financial statements in the black. Herbert Allen recommended expansion into the Grand Bahama Port Authority, partly owned by Herbert Allen. This Benguet did, and the gold mining company became a player in a waterway and various amusements in Grand Bahama Island.

In the late 1960s, a copper mining boom propelled the shares of small mining companies upward on various stock exchanges. The junior companies had promising, albeit non-producing, properties. Their fortunes fizzled once the market was informed that the deposits had been overstated. Many did well as a result of market manipulation. The Manila Stock Exchange struck a commission to investigate.

Moves to nationalize the Philippine economy in the 1960s pushed the full conversion of Benguet from an American-ruled fiefdom to one with a Filipino president, Jaime (Jimmy) Ongpin. Natural resources became an obvious target for nationalization: for the development of a national labour force, for the retention of resource ownership by the Philippines itself, for the forestalling of plundering foreign hordes.

Under Ongpin, the company expanded its mineral base, taking control of the Dizon copper mine in southeastern Zambales in 1975. There was expansion in nickel and chromite. And by 1977 the price of gold had risen to $168,* making the company's Acupan mine almost profitable. Benguet by then had produced 10 million ounces of gold. The company was on the upswing. Canada's Export Development Corp. and the Bank of Montreal had stepped in to finance start-up of the Dizon property. They were good times for the company's mining prospects. Ongpin would later enter politics as finance minister. In September 1987 he was forced from the cabinet for his pro-business views. On December 6, 1987, Ongpin had a three-party phone conversation

---

*Gold prices are quoted in U.S. dollars throughout.

with Herb Allen and Benguet executive Birl Worley. Ongpin was happy, laughing. He had decided to accept a post with Allen and Co. in New York, but he wanted to spend Christmas with his family first. The next day he was found dead of a gunshot wound. The authorities ruled it a suicide. The gun was in his right hand, tucked in his barong. Jimmy Ongpin was left-handed. Many at Benguet would never believe that Ongpin had taken his own life.

In 1977, Michael de Guzman moved into very modest quarters at the Acupan mine site, in a second-storey flat above Arzadon's Kitchenette and Grocery. A basketball court was a few feet away, and de Guzman helped organize a bush league. There was a dispensary, a cinema—all the requisite offerings of a mining community, built for the short term, its lifeline determined not only by the minerals that lay beneath her but by the company's ability to retrieve those minerals at a profit.

The verdant scenery lent a more pleasant atmosphere to Acupan than is found at most mine sites. Housing was built into the hillsides, mostly two-storey apartments with verandahs. At its peak, three thousand miners were employed at the mine. One man a year, on average, would lose his life underground.

De Guzman started in Benguet's training program, a rigorous introduction to field work: a month in the field, followed by four days at home, then back again. Mapping, sampling, core-logging. The work was detailed, fussy, but de Guzman liked it, just as he liked the liberating feeling of not having to answer to anyone, and even the pent-up desire for a raucous good time when those leave days arrived. All geologists at Benguet spent their first six months with the company on probation. Any "geo" rated average or below could be dismissed. De Guzman was rated very good, outstanding, exceptional. Top class.

The Benguet Gold Operations, Southern Division, were locked to outsiders, the entranceway marked by a nine-metre statue of a hard-rock miner, helmeted with mining lamp, swinging a pickaxe. The men of Acupan were mining at a depth of 457 metres, mucking ore onto rail cars, the rail lines running past the sub-warehouse and on to the mill.

The mine portal was a conventionally grim entranceway to the bowels of this operation, to a peculiar underground life that first opened to men in 1927: shitting underground without latrines, dangerously smoking where they should not, experiencing the peculiar existence of lightlessness. Safety advances in the industrial workplace always came decades later to the depths. George Orwell described a miner as a "grimy caryatid," standing as solid as stone, "upon whose shoulders nearly everything that is *not* grimy is supported. . . . Most of the things one imagines in hell are there—heat, noise, confusion, darkness, foul air, and, above all, unbearably cramped space."

At shift's end the miners would rise to the surface, to a dour stretch of locker space above ground where workers could attempt to shed the day's grime. Such circumstances have bred revolutionaries in many times, in many lands.

Outside the portal, nailed to the wall, a red-lettered sign instructed miners to "DROP YOUR CHAPA HERE. Failure to drop your chapa: written warning." The chapa was the miner's numbered metal identification tag, which was supposed to be pegged to the board so management would know who was underground. Above the portal maw a hand-lettered sign read: "Through this portal passed the best miners in the world." Another said: "Stop the Highgrading."

Acupan was plagued by high-grading. Underground miners would take sledgehammers to rock that was supposed to be shipped above ground. Day after day they would manually smash and grind this rock in secret. When the rock was ground as fine as they could make it, they would add mercury, which they had smuggled underground. They often used old axle caps from the mine cars to contain their chemistry. The mercury would liberate the gold, leaving an amalgam. There were a number of options for spiriting the result out of the mine undetected—miners would hollow out a portion of a rock drill, or an underground saw. The easier method was to shape the amalgam into a small sausage, wrap up the gold sausage and coat it in a little oil, then stick it up the anus.

Half an ounce of gold was equivalent to a month's pay for the miners who toiled underground. It might take a week's labour to work up the illicit amalgam. If the amalgam had a relatively high presence of gold, say, 20 or 30 percent, the high-grader could get as much as five ounces of gold for a week's work, the equivalent of ten months' pay. High-graders who were caught were prosecuted and imprisoned. The practice cost the company the equivalent of a million pesos a month. In 1976 Benguet invested in metal-detectors at the mine entrance, but still in de Guzman's day the financial reward for stealing gold made it irresistible.

De Guzman spent almost ten years of his life at Acupan. He married Teresa Cruz during his time there. The company then transferred him to a modest three-bedroom home, fully furnished. Four of his six children were born there: Birl, John, Michael and Nina. His life at Benguet was laid out before him: a future of modest income and accommodation, eventual retirement. This was not the place for stock options, the penny mine run, the big score.

De Guzman was an energetic partier. On particularly high-spirited nights he would leave Tess and the children and head down the mountain road to Baguio. At its outskirts he would frequent the Chapparel, featuring "playmates," as the club advertised them, laser karaoke and the See Thru Club, Baguio's version of the Mustang Ranch. Anything de Guzman craved girl-wise was there for the taking.

Session Road is the city's main strip, almost San Franciscan in the demands it makes of pedestrians as it rises and falls over the hilly terrain. On Session Road, de Guzman's favourite bars were Rumours, a staid gathering place for more restrained drinking, and the pub in the Patria Building. Fifteen minutes away, toward the city's sprawling market, lay the red-light district and the Peek-a-Boo strip joint, another de Guzman hangout.

When the rains come to Baguio, the terraced concrete steps that are cut into the pavement are slick and treacherous. Hydro wires hang low overhead, running along the streets that run parallel to, and behind, Session Road. These streets have the look of old Asia, not the colonially imported look of Session itself. Tinkers and tailors run two-metre stalls in the back streets, and signs such as Xerox and Typing do nothing to lend a more modern air to the commerce that goes on.

The market lights the city prettily at night. Light bulbs have been strung for what seems like miles. In daytime, one can see more clearly the animal offal beside dog shit beside bowls of rice topped with green chilies. There are hocks on hooks, cleaved cow heads on chopping blocks, a cornucopia of fresh produce. Young boys monotonously tap the bottoms of wooden cigarette boxes, strung about their necks like something from a 1940s-era supper club, offering Marlboro and Salem. Garlands of marigolds are threaded by the hundreds alongside buckets of daisies and roses.

Michael de Guzman had dreams at Acupan. He dreamed over and over again about the gold underneath her, about new, unexplored reserves, which, given half a chance, he could prove. He could find the gold. He, Michael de Guzman, could extend the life of this rickety operation. He had studied the work of Grover Whitney de l'Mari. De l'Mari was a geologist who had worked at Acupan in the 1960s and who expounded a theory of gold mineralization in what is known as a diatreme setting. On this basis, de l'Mari discovered recoverable ore reserves for Benguet at its operations near Baguio, and as a result became something of a heroic figure in Benguet lore.

Geology is not a science of stagnant matter. A geologist who worked at Busang wrote to me, attempting to open up this misunderstood science for an amateur, describing the life cycles that rocks undergo—shrinking, expanding, cracking with pressure and temperature changes, the cracks healing with the addition of new elements. Rock-forming minerals may precipitate from molten magma at great depth or near the surface, at higher and lower pressures. A variety of elements combine to form minerals and the minerals then combine to form rocks, all in a variety of chemically pre-established ways. If you add a component, or take one away, if you raise the temperature or reduce it, the result will be far different.

The rock forming at the edge of a lava flow might ultimately be buried, or it might be pounded by ocean waves or disintegrated by centuries of surface chemical weathering. It might also be picked up by a later lava flow and be fully or partially remelted. Rocks undergo constant chemical and physiochemical abuse. "There are only two real differences between humans and rocks and those are in the domains of consciousness (humans only) and life-spans (rocks usually last longer)."

De l'Mari's analysis focused on breccias, fragmented rocks that serve as a good host for mineralization because they are permeable. The diatreme is simply a vent, the form in which a gaseous explosion has taken place deep below ground and erupted to surface. The surface expression of the diatreme is circular, or ovoid, and appears either like a collapsed crater, or is raised in the shape of a dome.

On these formations, de Guzman became something of a scholar. With the help of his sister, Mary Jane, who would search mineral records in Manila, he started penning studies of the gold mineralization in the Acupan diatreme. His papers were full of historical references; he speculated that the history of the Acupan diatreme spanned the Early Miocene period to the Pleistocene period. He noted that a dacite, or extrusive rock, marked the vent in the shape of a plug dome. The diatreme was the central vent, or column, in this volcanic morphology, and the column had underlain a maar, or lake. In quick sketches such a shape would resemble a tuberous vegetable, rooted deep, like a parsnip.

There were as many as a dozen known breccia orebodies peripheral to the Acupan diatreme. De Guzman theorized that there were more. Even at Benguet, here near Baguio, decades after the mine commenced its life, de Guzman could envision the prospect for discovery, and the recognition that would attend that, as it had for de l'Mari.

The key, knew de Guzman, lay in convincing his superiors to give him permission to make the tunnels to find the gold. Gold is a numbers game. The mineralization is rarely obvious. The run of the gold can be fickle: plentiful in spots, then leaving the host rock barren, unimpregnated by mineralization. Proving an economically recoverable deposit becomes a mathematical puzzle. In oil and gas the winnings can be instantaneous. But hard-rock mining is for the patient. The discovery is but the first piece.

In the Book of Job, miners put an end to darkness and "search out to the farthest bound the ore in gloom and deep darkness. They open shafts in a valley away from human habitation.... They put their hand to the flinty rock, and overturn mountains by the roots. They cut out channels in the rocks, and their eyes see every precious thing. The sources of the rivers they probe; hidden things they bring to light."

Michael de Guzman searched for the hidden thing, and at Acupan he found it. His work at Benguet did expose untapped dimensions of the Acupan mine, and as a result he was heralded as a top-class geologist. De Guzman was still a young pup when he and his supervisor, Paul Damasco, made a presentation on these breccias before a geological seminar at Baguio's Pines Hotel. As his career progressed, de Guzman would turn the writing of studious geological papers and their presentation at international conferences into a mini-industry, extending as far afield as Melbourne.

The geological lexicon would mean little to the lay person. No matter. The investor, neophyte and expert alike, would not come looking for an understanding of how this gold, or this copper, or this nickel came to be. The polysyllabic explanations would wash over them as they waited patiently for the punch line: there was gold, and lots of it. Investors would look elsewhere for reassurances that the discovery was all it was cracked up to be and not a modern-day snake oil play. There were industry analysts, experts trained in the ways of geology and mining, to offer just those assurances or, conversely, issue warnings when the discovery seemed suspect.

De Guzman proposed an open pit to extract this newly defined gold. But little moves quickly in major mining companies, and approvals for this mine extension would not be easily won at Benguet. It was not until 1992, long after de Guzman had left Benguet, that the company pursued the possibility of development. Opposition from non-governmental organizations, expressing environmental concerns, stopped the project prior to development.

There was then no adventure in this job for de Guzman. His days would eventually be spent supervising the Acupan "beats," the teams of miners who had daily quotas of material to be delivered to the mill at Balatoc. The beats—A, B, C and so on—would compete for tonnage, and would be awarded bonuses accordingly. They worked eight-hour shifts, blasting, mucking with shovels to mine cars, then sending the cars over the ore pass. As quitting time neared, they would take the usual dumb-ass risks, cutting blasting fuses shorter and shorter, eight minutes, five minutes, furiously trying to retrieve more tonnage before shift's end.

As gold ran up in price, breaking the $800-an-ounce barrier in January 1980, so did Benguet's share price. From a 9 peso stock, the company's shares moved to 60, then doubled. Investors were doing very well betting on gold and Benguet's prospects. But workers did not share in the good fortune. De Guzman had no hope of profiting from Benguet's rise on the Manila Stock Exchange.

Yet, despite the oppressive, old-world atmosphere of the mining operations, de Guzman remained eager to test his geological insight, to prove how smart he was. Such confidence flourishes in the presence of an acolyte, who in the life of Michael de Guzman appeared in the form of a handsome young man named Cesar Puspos.

Puspos arrived at Benguet in 1983. He was, first, an exploration geo, then a mine geologist, and he worked for Mike de Guzman. Puspos had an unsophisticated résumé. Graduate with honours and recipient of Children's Museum and Library Inc. Model Pupil Award, Dasmariñas Elementary School, 1974. First place East Cavite Secondary Physical Science Quiz, 1977. In 1983 he graduated with a B.Sc. in geology from the Mapua Institute of Technology and headed to Benguet. His older brother, Emmanuel, or Manny, already worked there. There was little for them to look forward to in these almost-spent mine operations, marriages and children, eventually pensions. Their futures would be constrained by moderate income.

Puspos was not known for his honed intellect or an ability to carry on insightful conversation. Yet de Guzman, who liked to boast of a high IQ, became a mentor to Puspos, no doubt impressing the young man with his analysis of the site's breccia deposits. De Guzman was already losing patience with Benguet by the time Cesar Puspos showed up. At a minimum he was due a promotion. Benguet owed him at least that much. He had taken the company's in-house management course in 1985 and, three years before that, had graduated in the non-degree course at the Asian Institute of Management. The company did eventually make him chief geologist at Benguet's Baguio gold operations, but the pay was still too scant. Even with the free housing, plus the medical and dental care for his family, his monthly salary of 15,000 pesos (about US$1,000 at the time) was too scant, he believed, for a man of his talents. He had gone for three years without a pay raise. The promotion, when it came, was too little, too late for de Guzman's liking.

Where was the hunt? Where did the excitement for mineral discovery lie? Where was the next geological hotspot?

An Australian geologist named Mike Bird paid a visit to Baguio. According to Paul Damasco, Bird was looking for geologists to join in the exodus to Indonesia. The Philippines had a reputation for producing top-notch geologists, and Indonesia, overrun with an Australian junior mining boom, was desperate for qualified personnel.

One evening in Baguio, de Guzman and Damasco had dinner with Bird. Bird was very high on the prospects for promoting young mining companies in Indonesia. To de Guzman, who was not enamoured of mine management and was much more enthused by the possibility that the next day might be discovery day, Indonesia seemed a break-through prospect. Jobs were plentiful, the pay was twice that in the Philippines, and there was the potential of stock market winnings.

In 1987 Mike de Guzman quit Benguet and took up a position with an Indonesian company called PT Kasongan Bumi Kencana. Kasongan was one of a mittful of mining prospects managed by an Australian outfit called Pelsart Resources N.L. Kasongan had tenure, what the Indonesian government called a "contract of work," on a hard-rock gold/silver prospect in Central Kalimantan known as Mirah. The project was run as a joint venture with another company, Jason Mining. The two companies were also joint venture partners in PT Amphalit Mas Perdana, which was dredging an alluvial, or riverbed, gold deposit, also in Central Kalimantan. Pelsart and Jason were players. Now de Guzman was too. The Australians were look-ing for numbers. Cesar Puspos seemed an obvious second-round draft pick. Before long, both professor and pupil were packing their bags for the wilds of Indonesia. Awaiting them there was a well-known geologist who carried a storied reputation in those parts. His name was John Felderhof.

I have gone back to Acupan to see what the place smells of, what it feels like. Climb the same narrow flight of stairs de Guzman would have ascended daily to a large airy office space. Surveying maps still sit in their slim drawers, a variety of rock samples are scattered atop filing cabinets, fibreglass bags of samples sit on the floor. There is a sign on a wall: "Whatever power is responsible for the universe made mineral deposits; but mines are made by the genius of men." The quote is attributed to someone named Parson and dated 1933. A lone cartographer sits at a drafting table, but the workers are few. It does not take long to realize that there is no future here, or within Benguet, for that matter.

In an adjacent office, Tom Malihan continually, and somewhat ner-vously, adjusts his wire-framed glasses. At this moment, Malihan is head of exploration for Benguet. A lousy job, really, when one considers the pitiful pay and the fact that the company's exploration efforts have been cut to very nearly nil. Malihan knew de Guzman and certainly knew Cesar Puspos well, for Cesar is Tom's nephew. Years after Cesar took off to follow Mike to Indonesia, Michael de Guzman would woo his brother Manny away, too. This has Malihan, who says he believes in the innocence of his nephews, particularly stumped. "If Cesar knew he was doing something fishy, why would he hire his brother? Manny was top staff here. If you know you're doing something bad..." Malihan's voice trails off, then recovers. "He didn't want to leave Dizon [Benguet's mine in Zambales]. He had a good compensation package." On Benguet's personnel records, Manny Puspos is listed as AWOL after nine years and ten months' employment.

In the hillsides that rise behind this building the burrowing holes made by local miners trying to get at the gold are still in evidence. Paint peels from the two-storey apartments, which have fallen into a bad state of disrepair, though many people still live here. The corrugated tin roofs run with rust. The steel rails for the ore cars are intermittently buried by dirt and gravel.

The Baguio earthquake of 1990 destroyed the power lines at Acupan. The mine was already losing money. With production costs at US$400 an ounce, and with the gold price halved from its 1980 heyday, mining gold here was bleeding Benguet dry. Before the war, the company was retrieving more than one ounce of gold per tonne from these rocks; by 1990 that number had fallen to six grams. In July of that year the mine was flooded, a common practice when mining companies want to seal off an operation. The portal now is for the ghosts of Benguet to guard. The sign claiming that the best miners in the world walked through this entranceway has been removed, though the reference to high-grading remains.

I head back to the Belfranlt Hotel, where Paul Damasco has agreed to meet me for lunch. Damasco has a tic, the effect of which is a continual fast-cracking of the neck over to one side. It takes getting used to. Damasco left Benguet years ago and headed to Indonesia, part of what became a great transmigration of Filipino geologists to that country. He would eventually go to work for Pelsart, after de Guzman left. At Pelsart they called him Weng Weng, Comic Dwarf.

Damasco has named himself an unofficial emissary for the Filipino geologists who worked with de Guzman at Busang and are now back home, hiding out. The Puspos brothers. Bobby Ramirez. Sonny Imperial. John Salamat. Damasco sounds rather ambassadorial as he reports that the boys swear they were not involved in any funny business.

Damasco fancies himself a singer and songwriter in addition to the strengths he claims as a geologist. He has brought along a tape cassette and, as I have a recorder at hand, begins to play it. "Swift were the rivers and jungles were endless, fierce with the sounds of the wild! Walls blocked the way in mountains of badlands where, showed no mercy, the sun!" He sounds, perhaps, like one of the Bee Gees having a difficult day.

A few days later, in Benguet's headquarters in Manila, Malihan has before him the faxed résumés of Bre-X employees Sonny Imperial and John Salamat. They were too late to capitalize on their stock options, he says, and they need work. Salamat has removed the Bre-X name from his résumé.

Benguet is resident in the basement of a once-grand corporate estate the company had built in the 1980s as a monument to its success. Rock was hauled down from the highlands to build its walls. There was once a tennis court, and vast tracts of adjacent land, and a helicopter pad for the quick ferrying of the company's top executives. In de Guzman's early Benguet days this was the profile the company held. Now it is down on its luck and its image is very worn. Banco do Oro, owned by Henry Sy, who built his fortune through the SM shopping mall chain, has bought the building and taken over the grander upper chambers. Tom Malihan's office is utterly depressing. Looking at the dowdy Benguet of today, de Guzman's decision to quit the company seems prescient. As much as Malihan tries to put a positive spin on the company's prospects, the fact that he has to hand-write his title on his business card does not bode well. In just a few weeks' time, Tom Malihan will leave Benguet and head to Indonesia, to Jakarta, to work for Pelsart Resources.

An hour outside Manila, in the town of Dasmariñas, Cesar Pus-pos's mother opens the accordion door of her house to commence another day's business. She runs a Sari Sari store, which, roughly translated, means Mixed Mixed. Packages of pumpkin seeds and small candies are strung overhead. The strawberry hibiscus is fat in bloom. Local ladies come to sit on her wooden bench and chat. Her black hair is cut very short and plain. Her glasses are owlishly large for her face. She wears a simple blue patterned housedress and about her neck hangs a cross on a black string. Her husband Rene tenants the rice fields nearby, but a real estate broker aims to put a subdivision in there and so has come to talk to the Pusposes about this.

She ladles sago, a sugary drink mixed with the juice of the sago palm, into long, thin plastic bags, letting tiny balls of gelatin drift to the bottom. She talks quietly. She says she is afraid. Her son was held for three days in Indonesia, she says, referring to Cesar's older brother, Manny. And his manager was pushed from a helicopter. It was murder, she is sure. "There was a foul play," says the rent-a-car driver who brought me here and is helping to translate Mrs. Puspos's careful words. "There is gold there."

Neither the Pusposes, nor the Filipino community at large, have cornered the market on conspiracy theories. Many observers, investors and delusionists (the categories are not mutually exclusive) have been stoking the conspiracy fires. There were anonymous calls to my office before I left for Manila: "I work independently. Another company. I have a story to tell. There is a lot of gold there. Not at Busang. Nearby. Michael de Guzman. Suicide? Bullshit. Government over there is very corrupt. Bre-X mine known to be a flop. Spoke to Mr. de Guzman on several occasions. There were drugs involved. Another company right now trying to get the daughter of the president to give them exclusivity. The Bre-X mine was a bust. Known long before that. Mr. de Guzman believed everything would work out. Get this other deposit. Somebody in government pulled a wanger on them. They make their own bloody rules. There's a company paying huge amounts of money to ensure the mine is given to certain interests."

He would call again. "There was a man named Allyseou." How do you spell that? "Not sure. He was at the Hilton in September. The 21st to the 23rd. A large gentleman. De Guzman was paying him off, U.S. dollars. He carried huge amounts of cash. Allyseou was at the warehouse at Loa Duri. He supplied the gold. I'm very sure of that. The five people involved, they did not orchestrate what happened. De Guzman had a mole on his left shoulder. There was a fourth person in the helicopter. Only five people in the world know what I know."

Mind-bending. Nothing was making any sense. Was he a wacko? He would only say his name was Jeff. There were so many unanswered questions. Some days what Jeff had to say seemed less fantastic, more plausible. Then there was another anonymous call, this one with no identifier at all. "I have some information regarding the Bre-X guy. I'm going to tell you the way it is. The body was dead in the helicopter. I know for an absolute fact he was dead inside the helicopter. He went out in a fetal position. I had a vision. Through the power of the Holy Spirit. I was gonna tell the RCMP but I changed my mind. I'm kinda on the outs with the RCMP."

In the city streets of Dasmariñas, Michael de Guzman is everywhere, in his ever-present aviator shades, sporting his sparse moustache. A handsome jeepney passes, with a horse hood ornament outfitted with purple and amber wings. Schoolgirls bounce in green gingham tunics and canvas runners. This is a pleasant place. Cesar Puspos has returned here; the roguish Errol Flynn of the Busang saga who ran the site in Kalimantan has come home. Now what kind of plan is that?

UP RIVER

SAMARINDA, CAPITAL OF EAST Kalimantan, Indonesian Borneo. The rains have come again, and when they do, the afternoons seem more languorous. A middle-aged gentleman sits on his verandah, carefully tweezing stray hairs from his chin. The bicycle ladies quietly ferry their goods, a deft move of the foot shifting their sacks, heavy with squash and potatoes, out of the way of the bike gears. Their conical straw hats, the traditional *lawung*, striped in soft pastels, do better service than any umbrella. Lean men jog to market, bamboo rods held across thin shoulders, flexing with their smooth rhythm. A girl pulls a freshly cut piece of bamboo, green sprigs still clinging to the rod. The day's washing is not yet retrieved from the laundry lines.

Nonchalant mothers sit sidesaddle on motorcycles, clutching their babies, behind drivers in peaked black helmets. Six-passenger mini-vans suck and burp passengers. A statue of King Tenggarong stands as a central signpost, signalling that this is a city of import. He is a two-feathered warrior, holding his sword high, staying the foreigners. Naturalist Carl Bock came here, in the spring of 1878, "through the liberality of the late and much-lamented Marquis of Tweeddale." He sought the Dutch East Indies to examine its fauna, and his *Head-Hunters of Borneo*, the narrative of his trip up the Mahakam and down the Barito, proclaimed Samarinda "[t]he most miserable place I have ever seen." He noted its commerce. "Every one is a trader," he said, sounding less than complimentary. Today, Samarinda, a city of 335,000, retains the character of a frontier town, of transience, of goods and people passing through, a flux that swells when the world's commodities markets are on the upswing, fattening the prospects for Borneo's natural resources.

In the town proper, neon and shopping malls have introduced a modern urgency. But just a short distance away, the mighty Mahakam River transports visitors to an earlier time. Passel upon passel of logs, sheared of bark, slumber in the harbour of the Mahakam, symbol of a relatively modern barony. The timber tycoons who strip this island are experts in clear-cutting, cynics of reforestation. The export of logs was banned in 1985, and so plywood became the big industry here. When the workers for the Sumalindo plywood company, in their factory blues, end their day, the mill disgorges them by the hundreds. The traffic snarls, the buses inch.

The Mahakam is a mile wide at its mouth, a near-sea of milky coffee that has bred sultanates and trading empires for hundreds of years. Kalimantan may mean River of Gems. Mahakam certainly means Great River, and as the mightiest on the island, she has a greater right to this title than any other. She has carried camphor and coal and bezoar stones—concretions from monkey gallbladders highly prized for their medicinal and magical powers. Betel nut, pepper, tortoiseshell, gutta-percha, beeswax and the pheromonal musk of civet. The Chinese brought silk, porcelain and beads. The riches of Borneo were shipped in return.

On this island, spreading over 750,000 square kilometres, the native Dayak tribes pluck birds' nests in the caves by firelight. White-bellied swiftlets spin the nests of saliva, and they can fetch $1,000 a kilo. These 1,500-year-old culinary delicacies are shipped to Jakarta or exported to Hong Kong. White gold, they call them. In the late 1700s, four million nests passed through what became Batavia, the capital of Java. Retrieving them is a careful duty, for there are spirits in the caves.

Arab traders came to Borneo in the fourteenth century, and the conversion to Islam of indigenous peoples living in the region as far back as 38,000 B.C. began. Borneo was known as Java the Great, and the southern regions were called Puradvipa, or Diamondland. From this time, Bornean trade became legendary.

The Chinese came in the next century, hunting for gold. In the early sixteenth century, the Portuguese captain, Jorge de Albuquerque, proclaimed Borneo "one of the richest islands that exists in these parts, where there is much gold, camphor and great trade to many places." By the 1700s, the Chinese had established gold operations in the western portion of the island. Gambling houses and opium dens followed.

Kalimantan is carved into four provinces, East, South, Central and West, and within these the land is still ruled by sultans. The sultan of Kutai, one of the island's richest, lords it over the Mahakam from his seat at Tenggarong, 145 kilometres upriver from Samarinda. Hundreds of years ago his trading empire was called Kertanegara, and Tenggarong was (until the twentieth century, when it was upstaged by Samarinda and Balikpapan) its largest urban centre. In 1878 the sultan showed Carl Bock diamonds of the "purest water," and others green, yellow and black. The emperor of Siam, said the sultan, was keen to purchase the gems, having sent "an influential officer for the purpose of negotiating the sale." The sultan had forty-two wives: four "privileged" and thirty-eight concubines. His wives bore him eighty-four children. He levied a 10 percent tax on all goods imported and exported, except in the salt and opium trades, over which he had a monopoly. "The Sultan has no great scruple about breaking an agreement made with one contractor if he can afterwards get a better bid from another," wrote Bock.

Under the Dutch, Indonesia's colonial rulers, the search for minerals commenced in the 1840s, and substantial tin and coal production then got underway. But they never unearthed the much-touted pot of gold.

The gold mines in West Kalimantan, under the Chinese, had gone into production in the mid-1700s. The Dutch pursued a small deposit on the southern extreme of the island, but to the east and into the centre of this Dutch territory, gold workings were left to the locals. Reconnaissance work carried out before the Second World War would prove useful to explorationists later, but the war put a halt to the country's search for the precious metal.

From Tenggarong, the sultan drew "grants" of money from his citizens, and certainly from any foreigners who wanted to exploit the region's riches. But it was oil, not gold, that generated fat royalties. A refinery was built at Balikpapan in 1898, and the names Shell and Royal Dutch became a familiar part of the local lexicon. A community of expatriate workers sprang up. The two companies created a joint venture, Bataatsche Petroleum Maatschappij, or BPM, which soon dominated Kalimantan's oil production.

Similarly, foreigners were determined to dominate the island's forestry. The Malay and Chinese established themselves as important concession-holders prior to the Second World War. While Balikpapan prospered as an oil town, Samarinda's trade was linked more to lumber than to any other commodity. Still, in 1911, a visitor described it as "a dirty town of small squat houses with Atap roofs," thatched with the leaves of palm trees.

In the mid-nineteenth century, James Brooke, the white rajah of Sarawak, extolled the God-given wealth of his province, that gold was its most valuable commodity and that it was procurable in large quantities. The riches of the island of Borneo were not to be questioned, he said, presuming that the wealth of Sarawak extended across the island.

The foreigners' pursuit of wealth soon opened the door to its traditional running mate, missionary conversion. Borneo had long been ignored by the Dutch, at least in religious pursuits. Fewer than twenty missionaries were listed as active in Dutch Borneo at the time of the First World War. In 1915, the Christian conversion of Dutch Borneo commenced in earnest, with Protestants moving up the coast and Catholics moving into the interior. This was the land of the Dayak, nomadic peoples of perhaps as many as two hundred indigenous tribes. Churches were built and the Dayak Christianized.

Carl Bock sketched the Dayak, their intricately tattooed bodies, the longhouses on stilts. He did careful work on the visage of Sibau Mobang, chief of the cannibal Dayaks who, said Bock, had a paralysed right arm and a deft touch for left-handed decapitation. "As he sat conversing with me through my interpreter, and I sketched his portrait, he had fresh upon his head the blood of no less than seventy victims, men, women and children, whom he and his followers had just slaughtered and whose hands and brains he had eaten." Thus was Victorian England taken into the heart of Borneo, and thus were set the day-dreaming adventures of children tracking the presumed wild men through the jungle.

The cliffs that rise from the Mahakam's shores have the look of carved umber, a backdrop to ragged shoreline rows of houses on stilts bleached of all colour. A two-year-old dwelling can seem one hundred. Nothing lasts long, save, perhaps, the satellite dishes that perch hat-like above these homes. Barges and masted *praus* share the laneway with *ketinting* that putt along, low-slung boats with propellers jutting straight back from the stern. Boat-taxis pass, loaded with passengers and drums of gasoline. *Surya Kalimantan* is one taxi's name, displayed in proud red lettering. Its destinations: Melak, Long Iram, Long Bagun, scripted along the boat's side. Those who can afford to, zoom by in speedboats, cutting days into hours.

Into the shore, coconut fronds spray skyward, an evocation of bird feathers, or Dayak headdresses. This is an island of bird exotica. Brahminy kites, hornbills, the rufous piculet, the scarlet-rumped trogon, the white-rumped shama. A beautiful white-throated creature swoops low to the water, his wings seeming to go from buttercup to amber, as they lighten and darken, flapping across the sky—peaceful imagery in a land of king cobras, alligators and pythons.

Villagers come to the Mahakam via her tributaries, selling their wares. She is a giant teat, a waterway to wash in, feed from and defecate in. Her rivers are her highways; her riverines give birth to settlements whose inhabitants sporadically pan for placer gold, nuggets to sell. "We're only after some kitchen money, not like those poor foreigners," a local told a travel writer. "For them, gold and *gaharu* are everything, and when they find none they get desperate." Gold. *Mas*, in Islam. *Kencana*, in Bahasa Indonesia, the country's official language. For foreigners in Kalimantan, there has always been the belief that a motherlode of *kencana* will be found somewhere. "I have been shown samples of gold by the Dayaks, who, however, keep the places where it is found secret, as they have no desire that Europeans should come into their territory," wrote Carl Bock.

The local miners later grew more enterprising, not just panning for gold in the streams, but mining along quartz veins, too. They would break off rock from the vein at the surface, pieces the size of a fist. The rock would be broken into half-inch pieces with a hammer, then smashed all day until the size of small stones. Then it would be thrown into one-metre cast-iron pipes with cyanide and turned to a powdery mix. Mercury would be added to the mix, which would attract the gold from the cyanide solution. Then the mercury would be burned off, oxidizing into the air and into one's lungs. The remaining poisonous rock powder would be dumped into the creek.

The water is low. There has not been enough rain in the hills to raise the river basin and allow the speedboats to pass. For travellers headed farther north, the slow boat is the lone option. This is good news for Heldi, who waits aboard his floating prawn restaurant–cum–refuelling station at Muara Kaman, at the junction of the Kaman and Mahakam rivers. No one calls him Heldi. He prefers Eddy.

Eddy has a girl, a guitar and a sentimental nature. His hair is black as coal, his skin as silken as a baby's bottom. He has a fat purple mole under his right eye, is of dwarfish stature, and has a right leg so withered that sometimes he has to hobble about with the aid of a crutch; at other times, he tosses it aside to swing up and through the glassless window frames of his prawn shack with the dexterity of an orangutan. Eddy's place is popular, for the prawns, the *udang galeh* of the Mahakam, can grow to 40 centimetres, and Eddy always keeps the fryer on a high flame, ready to feed the next lot of travellers headed upriver. If you come, please bring American cigarettes.

Fresh-water dolphins frolic in the Mahakam delta, and they are real. Deeper in her waters the Naga dragons dwell—creatures of the spiritual realm. There are certainly spirits in the hills, "in trees where during storms the souls of children cried," as writer Ernest Hillen described it.

Everyone knows there is witchery in this place. The spirits can turn the trees to stone. There are many *balians*, sorcerers. Bock made it sound like the realization of Arthur Rackham's fantasies. "Here, surrounded by the eternal forest, and hidden from human gaze, the spirits were believed to hold high revel beneath the wooded shade, preparing their enchantments for the confusion of man."

Modern-day seekers of gold come in waves, and they come past Eddy's place: the upriver journey to riches has remained unchanged for centuries. The geology of Borneo has been only partially explored, but even the areas that have been surveyed, sampled and perhaps drilled are worth another look, particularly when the stock markets are riding high. Bull markets are made for sucking investment dollars from gamblers willing to place a bet on the one-in-a-thousand chance that a potential gold discovery in God-knows-where just might prove to be real.

The speedboats sidle up to Eddy's empire. The wooden platform is bleached grey from the sun. Tables are set with blue-and-white checked tablecloths, just as they were when Michael de Guzman came by and dropped a fishing line through the floorboards of the restaurant into the river, as the boys are doing today. De Guzman was usually in the company of Dzia Uddin, an Indonesian who handled administrative jobs for Bre-X in the early days. The site drillers from PT Drillinto Tiko would stop by, the men who would sink hundreds of holes into the Busang site. Once, but only once, a big Canadian came, and his name was David Walsh. John Felderhof knew Eddy's place, and he certainly knew this water from the days when he took a slow boat up the Mahakam, in the mid-1980s, headed for a gold prospect deep in the island.

Felderhof's own journey started long before that, in the tiny fishing village of Spakenburg on the Zuider Zee. Herman Felderhof was the town doctor, though his many offspring were born in a hospital in nearby Amersforrt.

John was the fifth child born to Herman and Hermine, whom everyone called Mien. Henk, Ubbo, Ineke and Els all came before John, who was born in the summer of 1940. The prolific Felderhofs would go on to beget Clarence, Gerald, Marius, Dick, Cathy and finally the twins, Herman and William. Twelve children in all, a family as rich as that of Leila and Simplicio de Guzman.

It was an idyllic country life. Children at play in the fields. A month every summer spent holidaying at the North Sea. John was always the lucky one in his family. He would scour the shoreline and return home trumpeting treasures found.

In Spakenburg, Mien kept a garden, which she loved, where she grew kale and berries. During the war the family owned a goat. Mien and Herman were nature-lovers.

The family belonged to the Dutch Reformed Church, which they attended twice on Sundays. Father and mother always read from the children's Bible before each meal, and there was prayer before and after.

When John was five the family moved to 123 Schiekade in Rotterdam, a grand, four-storey house in which Herman set up his medical practice. The move was made for the children's sake—the pursuit of opportunity, better education. John was a good student, though not stellar. The children fell into two groups: the bookworms, and the more gregarious, outgoing siblings, including John.

After nine years, however, Herman and Mien were restless. Herman's brother Clarence had long before moved to the Ontario farming community of Dutton, and he was happy there. Then Herman's best friend in Rotterdam, Jan Kok, who was in the clothing trade, moved to Canada too. In 1953 Herman Felderhof took a trip to Nova Scotia and was smitten. He moved his entire brood there in 1954.

John, then fourteen, was immediately sent, with his brother Clarence, to stay with his uncle Clarence (there is much name repetition in the Felderhof clan). The two spent a hard year working on the farm before rejoining the family in New Glasgow. After high school John headed into the geology program at Dalhousie University and then spent his summers working as a novice field geologist, earning his tuition. By the time John Felderhof graduated with his B.Sc. in 1962, he was looking for adventure. There was something about the pursuit of geology at fifty below zero in the Canadian bush that did not appeal. He went to Africa.

In the late 1960s, Bob Hutchinson, managing director for Kennecott, the Australian mining giant, headed for Toronto looking for energetic geologists set for adventure. Bill White, an Aussie geologist with Kennecott, had developed an exploration plan for Papua New Guinea (PNG). But there was a mining boom in Australia, and, as Hutchinson says, "geologists could get good employment at home without going into a hell hole like New Guinea."

By mid-1968, Kennecott had filed applications to explore huge areas of PNG, beating out Placer Exploration Pty by mere days. It did not matter that it was hell and gone—it was a mining rush. Mining companies were touting the so-called "Ring of Fire," or "Rim of Fire." Press releases from companies that over the years entered this hot zone would repeat boilerplate introductions: "The Rim of Fire, which stretches through New Zealand, Fiji, the Solomon Islands, Vanuatu,

PNG, Indonesia and the Philippines, is an area where volcanic activity was caused by the collision of the Pacific and Indo-Australian continental plates." Hutchinson interviewed, and immediately hired, John Felderhof.

Papua New Guinea was wild and remote. The only place on site where the helicopter could land naturally was where two streams came together and made a little delta. The geologists would be spotted in by chopper in the morning, each with a field assistant. They would head upstream and take sediment samples for later analysis.

The geologists established their base camp at Goroka. Three weeks in the bush would be followed by one week at base camp, where they would write up field notes and give their heads a shake. The focus of Kennecott's exploration was right at the crest of the Star Mountains. There was rain in the southeast monsoon season. There was rain in the northwest monsoon season. There was always rain, 8000 millimetres a year, 325 days on average. In what the locals called the dry days, it rained at night. In the afternoon, the sky would turn a battleship grey, bringing rain in thundershowers. So the boys would try to get out very soon after first light. It was an isolated life, made bearable, perhaps, only by the eternal optimism a geologist carries in his belly. Tomorrow might be "it." The big find.

Malaria was a given. Felderhof had it bad in PNG. The goose flesh, burning fever, the insatiable thirst as the body bathes itself in sweat. It is the female mosquito, with her sharp mandibles, that sucks the blood. The ancient Greeks would carry a nutshell containing a spider to ward off the disease. (One morning, years later, Felderhof had breakfast and headed for the bus to take him to the Kennecott offices in Sydney. On the trip he felt fine. At work he started to shiver and shake. When they found him he was curled up under a drafting table, unconscious. For many years afterward Felderhof would grouse that Kennecott did not pay his hospital bills during that time.)

The PNG prospect was in an area now known as Fly River Province. The indigenous Min people in the Fly River region were reliant on the river and its fish for their economy: prawns, crayfish, barramundi. The area was rich in bird life, with more than two hundred indigenous species. The Min relied on the birds for food and decoration. Plodding through streams that ran through the swampland off the Fly River, Felderhof and co-geologist Doug Fishburn, each on his own course, came upon a rich "skarn" on the same day, in February 1969. A skarn is a rock formation that surrounds the intrusive. Because it denotes an "alteration envelope" around a potential ore body, the skarn can provide an exploration guide or model. Fishburn and Felderhof had found copper and they had found gold, shed from Mount Fubilan, at an altitude of more than 2,000 metres. The discovery was dubbed Ok Tedi. (One account, however, credits an Australian patrol officer with discovering the first signs of mineralization in 1963.) Eighteen kilometres away, a spit in the wind, was the Indonesian province of Irian Jaya.

Long after the viability of the Ok Tedi discovery had been proven, however, it remained undeveloped. Papua New Guinea was on its way to independence from Australia then. Kennecott was negotiating with PNG's transitional self-government and, fearing nationalization, tried to build strict caveats into its negotiations, including protection from expropriation. The political risk was high. The company spent three years wrangling over such terms as the Additional Profits Tax until, in 1975, the same year PNG won its independence, Kennecott's prospecting rights were terminated. After 1975, standing alone, PNG had not a single home-grown mining engineer, let alone the bureaucratic infrastructure to oversee a project through all its labyrinthine turns—permitting, taxation, production and export—and ultimately to reclamation. What would be the cultural effects on the Min people? And what about the environmental aftershocks? What would happen to the fish, to the wildlife?

It would be twelve years before construction was even begun. Kennecott, unable to come to terms with the PNG government, was replaced by Broken Hill Proprietary Co. The cry of economic nationalism would be heard through the decade. Multinationals pulled out of PNG, complaining of adverse tax and mineral policies. Years later, nationalistic fervour in Indonesia would echo the Ok Tedi experience. In his book on Ok Tedi, William Pintz said, "The general disarray of early administrative policy undoubtedly made Kennecott uncertain as to exactly who was speaking for the government." That would sound familiar, too.

Felderhof stayed with the project through the euphoria of the first drill results, as the first hole intersected 46 metres of ore grading an average 3 percent copper. He was there for the prototypical early stages: the splitting of the core, logging the core into boxes, preparing it for assay. All of this early Kennecott work conformed to international standards. As the drills were sunk and the core retrieved, it was split lengthwise, down the middle. Half would be crushed and "assayed," tested for mineralized content. The other half would be retained by the company, to be cross-checked later, or perhaps offered to another company interested in striking a partnership. A year after the discovery, Bob Hutchinson commenced negotiations on Kennecott's contract of work for Ok Tedi. The process took eighteen months. John Felderhof attended some of those meetings.

The geology of Ok Tedi was complex, and the initial euphoria gave way to trepidation. Perhaps the promise of a massive deposit had been overstated at the start. It would be years, and Felderhof would be long gone, before Ok Tedi would prove its world-class status.

The big-company life seemed not to suit Felderhof, who drifted out of Kennecott and made his way back to Canada, and also to Virginia. In the 1970s he went to work for Peter Howe, whose international geological consulting firm, A.C.A. Howe, would flit to whichever region was deemed hot for prospecting. Felderhof worked for Howe in South Africa and Australia. In 1980, he headed for Indonesia to be Howe's man in Jakarta.

They were not terribly heady days, at least not initially. Howe would take up properties or try to farm out properties. Nothing really big was happening on the development side. Yet gold itself had gained intense investor interest, particularly after the $800 spike in 1980. In 1982, A.C.A. Howe was trying to sell some mining prospects in West Kalimantan. Felderhof would squire potential buyers about the properties, trying to convince them of the ground's untapped potential.

One of these was a property called Mandor, and one day, the Indonesian arm of Rio Tinto, a large and respected mining firm, came calling. Umar Olii, an Indonesian geologist, was part of the site visit team. Felderhof proceeded with his shtick, going on and on about the geochemistry of a promising porphyry copper prospect. "But I can't see the surface expression of the target," said Olii, over and over again. He took some soil samples and headed on his way. Rio Tinto took a pass, but Olii, even though he disagreed with his fellow geologist, decided there was something about the man he quite liked. The country was on the cusp of what geologist Theo van Leeuwen, who wrote a history of mining in Indonesia, termed "a major gold rush" that would result in the drill-testing of more than eighty primary and alluvial gold prospects. With all the alluvial gold on the island, many shared the belief that there had to be a monumental deposit somewhere.

Felderhof's corporate pursuits in Indonesia led him to a couple of high-flying Australian hopefuls. Jason Mining Ltd. was an Australian exploration company based in Sydney. Pelsart International Ltd. was part of the Kevin Parry empire. (Parry, then the Australian department store king, would later wipe out a good chunk of his fortune financing his bid for the America's Cup.) Parry entered the mining game at the suggestion of Mike Novotny, a geologist who would say around the bars in Jakarta that he had set the spark that started the 1980s penny mine boom in Indonesia. Together Pelsart and Jason invested as joint venture partners in a series of Indonesian mining prospects. Pelsart was the cash cow in the relationship.

With 42.5 percent a piece, Jason and Pelsart partnered in PT Amphalit Mas Perdana. An Indonesian mining partner, PT Yunawati, had the remaining 15 percent. The exploration costs were shared equally between the two Australian outfits, while the projects created in their exploration portfolio were managed by A.C.A. Howe Australia Pty. Ltd. Peter Howe was chief executive; John Felderhof was one of four directors.

Amphalit was an alluvial gold prospect in Central Kalimantan. The company pegged "proven and probable" reserves (meaning the reserves that were recoverable) at 21.5 million cubic yards, and further "possible" reserves of more than 8 million m3. The property spread across two so-called "contracts of work," which, at the time of Jason's bullish pronouncements, had merely been initialled by the Indonesian Department of Mines. Final presidential approval, Jason quickly reassured shareholders, was expected momentarily.

The mining method adopted for Amphalit was a dredging operation, a suction cutter that would strip the clay that overlaid the gravel beds on the Amphalit River, and a bucket-wheel dredge that would mine close to three million cubic metres a year. Small dredges were brought in from Australia for the task. Jason expected an 85 percent recovery rate. Based on the assumption that it could fetch US$400 an ounce for its gold, the revenues from Amphalit were projected at US$7.3 million. Which meant what precisely? 21.5 million cubic yards, divided into $7.3 million, gets revenue of 34¢ a yard, which suggests a gold grade of .001 ounces per yard. Ridiculous. This was not a viable dredging operation. Not even close.

The technology, the mineral and the money. Jason spun out its annual and quarterly reports, but it was the press releases that were meant to catch the eye of investors—who would have been wooed by brokers, who would have been brought into the story by underwriters, who, like the principals of the company themselves, would have been flush with the cheap stock that comes from getting in on the story at its earliest stages. And they would have been foreign investors, in the main. Europeans, Canadians, Australians. The Indonesians had not floated any such junior mining companies on the Jakarta Stock

Exchange, and even if they had, they had no penny mine history and did not fit the profile of risk-takers.

To help allay foreign investors' concerns about wading into far-off lands, particularly those with less than democratic tendencies, the Indonesian government had established its Foreign Capital Investment Law in 1967, and soon thereafter its contract of work (COW) legislation. Given the country's rather stark failure to discover and develop its own mineral resources, a contract that enshrined an outsider's right to develop, and take profits from, Indonesian lands was an essential move. And given the country's investment history under the sixteen-year rule of Sukarno, a progressive wooing of foreign interests was imperative if Indonesia under Suharto were ever to break the impoverished Third World mould.

From the government's point of view, however, the encroachment of offshore commercial interests was never meant to be colonial, that is to say, limitless. In Point A of the preamble of the COW regulations it is stated that all mineral resources contained in the territories of the Republic of Indonesia, including the offshore areas, are the national wealth of the Indonesian Nation. The government expected to enjoy the predictable offshoots from prosperous mining endeavours: employment opportunities, skills development, a transfer of technological know-how to Indonesian nationals.

The company was compelled to give labour preference to Indonesian nationals, and to "provide direct Indonesian participation in the Enterprise through the inclusion of Indonesian nationals in the management of the Company and among the members of its Board of Directors." There were numerous standard stipulations. Shareholders in the company, for example, must not transfer shares in the company without the prior written consent of the mines minister. The legislated permitting process would take would-be mine operators through a series of incremental steps—from surveying, to exploration, on to a feasibility study, construction, ultimately to mining, processing and marketing. John Felderhof's descriptions of the contract of work system would be oft-repeated years later when he became a central figure in advancing Bre-X in Indonesia: "For the foreign company, it provides assurances that if economic mineralization is found, the Indonesian government guarantees title to the deposit, fixes taxation rates, permits export..." and so on. Credit for the clarity of the COW legislation should be given to two individuals, he said then: Sutaryo Sigit, director general of mining, and Ridwan Mahmud, director of mining development.

The first mining company to make an investment under the new law was PT Freeport Indonesia, owned by an American company then known as Freeport Kaolin Co. In 1960, Freeport Indonesia had discovered a massive copper deposit in Netherlands New Guinea, which had been retained by the Dutch after the independence of Indonesia in 1949. The Dutch had initially identified the deposit, in 1936, but the war had intervened, and the prospect was ignored until Freeport took notice in 1959. Suharto routed the Dutch from West Irian in 1961, and then routed Sukarno himself five years later, so the folks at Freeport went from dealing with the Dutch to Sukarno to Suharto. The deposit was called Ertsberg, Dutch for "Ore Mountain."

Nils Kindwall, a member of the Freeport negotiating team, later related the Sidney Greenstreet ambience in Indonesia to George Mealey, a Freeport mining engineer who wrote: "'When we first arrived in Jakarta in early 1966, Suharto had just taken over, there was no Foreign Investment Law, we had competition for Ertsberg, the infrastructure was a mess, there was only one hotel in Jakarta, the economy was in tatters, the legal basis for an agreement was vague.... The small problems were numerous. There was one typewriter in the hotel, which we rented by the hour and on which we did our own typing. Our telexes—no faxes then—back to the U.S. could be read by anybody. The "characters" around at the time and the rundown airport made it all seem like an Ian Fleming novel. We rode in a 15-year-old Chevy with no instruments, bad tires, and certainly no air conditioning.'"

Forbes Wilson was PT Freeport's president, and when he later related the experience of Ertsberg to Mealey, the difficulty of developing a mine at 1,097 metres paled beside the trials of negotiations with Jakarta. The capper was an eleventh-hour demand for tax payments that would have quashed the economic viability of Ertsberg. "The sharp and sudden swings in our fortunes," he said, "were beginning to make me feel a little manic-depressive." It was only after the deal was done that Freeport learned that someone within the Department of Mines had tried to woo a Japanese group to develop Ertsberg, undercutting Freeport.

In April 1967, Freeport Indonesia signed the first COW under the Foreign Investment Law. Freeport built its mine camp, set up its core shack and hired a team of Canadian drillers. The core was split lengthwise, as per the accepted practice, and one half was left, according to Mealey, with the government to file. "That way if the company decided not to proceed with developing the deposit, the government would have an independent record of what Ertsberg contained, a system that is still used today."

Ertsberg went into production in 1972. Freeport's plan to ferry North American hard-rock miners to West Irian proved a disaster. Mealey describes the hard-drinking hirees as a group capable of getting themselves into trouble fast. Of the forty hired, just two remained after six months. So Freeport recruited out of the Philippines, hiring fifty men from the copper mines. "Not only were the Filipinos quality miners, but they also had an excellent attitude toward their work and got along well with the Indonesians," said Mealey. In 1983, Freeport applied to Indonesia's Department of Manpower to import additional Filipino labour, an idea that the Indonesian bureaucrats quashed. They further advised Freeport that the work permits for those Filipino miners already working at Ertsberg would be rescinded. So Freeport appealed to the Department of Mines. Still, the Freeport board in New York had concerns about the emotional mood swings of their Indonesian landlords. "One thought that our increasing reserves just made us a target for nationalization, or for unwanted interest from one of the growing group of Indonesian tycoons."

Unofficially, the Freeport team of geologists had no intention of shutting down its efforts in Indonesia, and Jim Bob Moffett, who became chief executive officer of Freeport in 1984, supported them in this view. The following year, Dave Potter, Freeport Indonesia's chief of exploration, sank a drill hole three kilometres from Ertsberg. He called it a "training hole." Not having the proper permits, he was not supposed to be there at all, but Potter was always looking over to the other side of the fence, and in Irian Jaya, that meant what the Dutch had dubbed Grasberg, appropriately "Grass Mountain."

The hole was a bitch. A Caterpillar engine was too heavy to lift by helicopter, and with management resistant to Potter's expansionist dreams, he ended up fashioning a Rube Goldberg contraption featuring Toyota truck engines. The drillers had to haul 40-kilogram sacks of concrete on their backs. But Potter had gold intuition, a gold smell, a sense that the precious metal was there somewhere. His early days working for Freeport, in the late 1970s, were based in Elko, Nevada, working on the company's Jerritt Canyon gold mine. Though Jerritt was only a middling gold producer, Potter had been smitten—and he was prepared to be smitten again.

In 1986, Moffett moved Freeport's offices to New Orleans, and he issued a new directive. He wanted the company's exploration department to step up their efforts with an eye to increasing reserves. Dave Potter's fifth hole at Grasberg, more than 600 metres in length, was mineralized almost right the way through, 1.69 percent copper and 1.77 grams of gold per tonne of rock. It really was the motherlode, which was precisely what Moffett was hoping for. While Freeport speaks of Grasberg as a copper mine, it is also one of the world's top gold producers, with an estimated 80 million ounces of gold reserves. Grasberg set the mining world on its ear—there were still elephantine deposits out there, and they could be found in the unlikeliest of places.

The COW contract process won the approval of the international mining community, and the Indonesian government successively attempted to make improvements to the contract system through a series of so-called "generations." To companies that applied for COWs, the Department of Mines issued SIPPs, or Preliminary General Survey Period Licences (Surat Penyelidikan Pendahuluan), that granted the right to do early ground work—trenching and sampling—but stipulated early exploration expenditures in order to keep the SIPP in good standing. They were valid for one year only, but could be extended pending the operator's proof that reconnaissance work was ongoing at site. Quarterly reports on geological and geophysical investigation were to be filed with the Department of Mines, along with details of onsite expenditures, manpower usage and so on. The company had to place a bond, or what many called a "seriousness bond," with the government.

By the time it had an operating mine, Freeport, or any mining company for that matter, would be bound by the obligations stipulated in the COW and also burdened with royalties, corporate income tax, "dead-rent" for the land use, value-added tax on imports, stamp duties on documents, building tax, general administrative fees, "levies, taxes, charges and duties imposed by Local Government in Indonesia which have been approved by the Central Government." And on and on. The royalty tariff for gold was US$225 a kilogram for under 2,000 kilos, and US$235 for anything above.

There were smaller, more technical specifications. Should the company fail, for example, to recover minerals at the rate indicated in its feasibility study, the government would put the company on notice to improve its mining method.

Still, the terms were made appealing enough, as development of the country's copper and gold deposits was less advanced than that of coal and tin. In the case of coal, the country's production had been pushed by foreign interests after the departure of the Dutch: companies from Australia, Korea and Hong Kong. In 1986, the government announced that no further foreign investment in coal would be allowed.

The evolution of foreign development of at least one home-grown resource had run its natural course.

Gold was another matter. The price had run up, and investor enthusiasm was high. In North America, a staking rush had followed the discovery in 1981 of the Hemlo gold mine in northern Ontario. When Murray Pezim, the discovery's promoter, proclaimed the discovery—not on the fifth hole, or the tenth, but on the seventy-sixth —*The Northern Miner*, the Canadian mining paper of record, proclaimed it a crock. It wasn't, and the ownership battle that followed tied up the courts for eight years. Six years later, in Nevada, a heretofore unheard-of Canadian mining company called American Barrick, ruled by a Hungarian emigré named Peter Munk, came up with the Goldstrike Mine. Goldstrike was developed as a massive open pit, a "great canyon," Munk said. Many people had told Munk in the early going that he was full of bullshit. Major gold-mining companies had looked at this Nevada scrub before. There was nothing there, said the disbelievers, nothing but a stock promote. But it was real.

In Indonesia, that the Department of Mines was awarding contracts to small foreign outfits like Jason/Pelsart signalled, according to geologist Theo van Leeuwen, a significant change in government policy. "Previous contracts had been awarded almost exclusively to large international mining companies," he said. "This change reflected the Government's wish to promote development of smaller deposits, which were of no interest to the big companies, and at the same time to encourage domestic participation through joint ventures."

The COW process helped, too, to obviate some of the side-sum, under-the-table payments. Members of the mining community attest that SIPP approval could be got without having to grease numerous administrative palms along the way. Mining companies had an easier time getting their paperwork cleared with a minimum of administrative fees. Of course, such smooth processing did not apply to the local demands at a mine prospect's site—payments were needed for this, hands held out for that. And mining promoters with inside government access would be tipped off, for a fee, on the timing of property coming available. There were rumours that some within the Department of Mines received payments in the tens of thousands of dollars.

There was the smaller stuff, too. Want to clear some hammers from customs? Want the forestry department to grant access to their timber roads? Such clearances could cost hundreds of dollars, or perhaps thousands on a monthly basis. Not enormous sums, but companies were wise to factor "spreading around" money into their cost sheets. Companies would retain agents to expedite matters. Top-up fees to paper-handlers. In dealing with immigration and manpower, almost every company would use an agent. The mining community characterizes these as petty-cash payments, initiated and insisted upon by the Indonesians. Not the same thing at all as greedy foreigners eyeing a rich prize and coming in with offers of a million, or millions, to win it.

"In addition to the COWs approved for foreign investment," wrote van Leeuwen, "a large number of mining authorities ["KPS"] were awarded to Indonesian individuals and local companies between 1980 and 1987. However, few KP holders carried out serious exploration by themselves, preferring instead to sell or farm-out their tenements. In 1987, in order to reduce these activities, the Government imposed stricter conditions on obtaining and maintaining titles."

According to van Leeuwen, the gold boom was preceded by an increase in local mining. "Previously, gold mining by local people had usually been carried out by small numbers of villagers on a seasonal basis and had been largely restricted to alluvial mining by primitive methods. A dramatic change took place in the early 1980s when people flocked in large numbers to old and newly discovered gold fields, mostly in Kalimantan and North Sulawesi, to work on a full time basis." Oftentimes this local mining impinged on the rights of the COW holder, but it was up to the COW holder to resolve any disputes.

The country's export dollars were heavily weighted toward oil exports. Mining, outside of coal, had historically held the promise of riches but failed to deliver. The surge in the gold price had spurred locals to turn to small-scale mining, illegally, on property to which they had no title. For some it became a full-time endeavour, and a highly profitable one. In other lands—North America, Australia and Europe—there was another type of prospecting going on—mining the pockets of potential junior mining investors.

It was the first gold boom in Indonesia to be fuelled by stock markets, though it was offshore markets that provided the paper currency. The Jakarta Stock Exchange was still in its infancy, and penny mining stocks were unheard of. The junior mining game was old hat in Canada, where stocks had been underwritten on mining exchanges since the 1890s. Listing requirements then were startlingly lax, and the architecture of these small mining stocks was customized to favour a small group of insiders, the promoter or promoters and their immediate circle, who would take up privately issued stock, warrants, options, treasury shares, whatever was going, at, say, a penny, before the shares went to the public at two cents. Every so often, after a particularly brazen case of stock market manipulation, the mining exchanges (which merged and then eventually became part of today's Toronto Stock Exchange) would tighten their listing requirements, or their disclosure obligations, or would add more so-called "compliance" officers. It would take the next egregious case of bilked investors to prove that the regulations were still not stiff enough.

The penny promoters would argue that without such share issues there would never be a mine found. And, true enough, it was usually the little company that made the mineral discovery. If the discovery were real, that would send a siren signal to eager major mining companies, which in turn would buy out the little companies and the little men who ran them. Make the rules too tight, the little men would complain, and we won't play any more.

Then there were other promoters, the ones for whom a mineral discovery was not the objective. Mining money from investors was their game. Invariably these promoters had a tight group of confidants,

regulars keen to be first in on a share issue, knowing that a good promoter could pretty well ensure that the shares could be flipped for a
profit by, say, noon.

There is a predictable operating procedure. Advertisements would
be taken out in so-called tip sheets, which would be mailed to thousands of subscribers. Any mention in a trade newspaper of any type
would be blown up, copied and used as part of the tout. Long lists of
neophytes would be drawn up, and these innocents would be "cold-
called" by stock pushers virtually guaranteeing stock market winnings. More often than not, these were "area-play" stocks, companies
housing claims staked within hundreds of kilometres of a known discovery. This was the sell, the "we're right around the corner from Witwatersrand" pitch. Compelling disclosure of the trading practices of
principals was a long time coming. A promoter would tout the stock
as a fabulous discovery, but be "backdooring," or selling his stock,
at the same moment. Sucker.

As the North American regulatory authorities incrementally tightened the rules, other issues of supervision arose. The greater numbers
of small investors spurred the growth of brokerage houses, which in
turn retained analysts, often expert in a single sector—mining, or oil
and gas. The best analysts rigorously defended their independence,
their right, for example, to issue a so-called "sell" recommendation on
a company's stock, even if that analyst's employer, the brokerage house,
had underwritten that same stock. That is a risky position to take.
Underwriting a share issue puts as much as 5 percent of the total sub-
scription of the issue into the coffers of the brokerage house. Let's peg
that commission at $3 million, for example. Let's say the company issu-
ing the shares is in the waste management business. So the brokerage
underwrites Mr. Waste Management at $30 a share. The issue is fully
subscribed. The brokerage gets its three mil. Four months later, Bill,
the waste management analyst, figures Mr. Waste Management's business stinks and advises investors to sell. Shall we contemplate the message Mr. Waste Management has for the head of Bill's brokerage?

The Sisyphean task of retaining one's independence is perhaps obvious in this example. But there are more subtle problems at play when analysts get too close to a "story," the compelling narrative that the analyst's firm has backed in the marketplace. He can start to imagine that he holds a special place, that the company shares with him information that is not shared with the general marketplace. He becomes a believer. An acolyte. He gets "ahead of the story," as they say on the street. He loses his objectivity. If he is long on the stock, betting on a share price hike, he has to believe. And so, the walls between the untutored investor and the company's management do not hold.

Stocks run up all over the world, of course. Perhaps mining stocks more than most, built as they are on dreams, expectations that Mother Nature will this time offer up her riches. Many are the tales of geologists who scout a prospect and take a pass, making the judgment that nothing could be there. Then another geologist comes along, ten years later, or twenty, or one hundred, who sees it differently, who pushes and prods, drills this way and that and finds the mine hidden there. Canadian investors have come to know this well, and it has become part of the Canadian investing psyche—gambling on a natural resources score, gambling on Canada.

Mining plays are not a uniquely Canadian phenomenon. Trevor Sykes, author of *The Money Miners*, wrote of the mining stock boom in Australia in 1970. Australia had had a string of great mineral discoveries, which primed the investor pump and occluded innate skepticism. The events of the boom, known as Poseidon, were presaged, says Sykes, by a period of easy affluence, a bull market, and the discovery of "vast and previously unsuspected mineral wealth." And so, the leaders of subsequent mining plays got away with murder. "We don't need a geologist to prove there's a million tons of ore under this hill—you can see it," proclaimed the director of a company touting a tungsten discovery called Attunga. The director was right. He could see it, because the rock samples had been "salted," the minerals added to the rock samples after they were retrieved. Salting, said Sykes, "reached its height of popularity during the nineteenth century. A prospector would buy or otherwise obtain some gold dust, a shotgun and some cartridges. He would remove the buckshot from the cartridges and substitute the gold. When fired at a stope [the rock face] underground the gold would splatter widely, embedding itself as fine particles in the rock."

Salting, said Sykes, was primarily an American practice and, the tungsten caper aside, was most commonly employed in gold scams, for they were the easiest to salt. "With gold," he said, "a little dust can be injected into the laboratory bags after they have been sealed." Sometimes imaginative gold promoters did not even bother with the salting method. Sykes cited an Australian who simply swore he knew he had found gold. He said he could see it in the trees.

Poseidon was not a case of salting. The market was in the mood to support a mining tale unquestioned. The bull market; the prosperity; the previous discoveries. Happy investors eager to make another score. Disenchanted investors, who had missed out on the previous stock successes, were determined to ensure that it would not happen again. Together they presented a broad market of individuals who would throw their money at a company that had no earnings, no price/earnings ratios, that could not be measured in or by conventional business terms. Investors were betting on what might be there, and on what another company might pay to get it.

Poseidon was named after the racehorse that won the Melbourne Cup in 1906. It had been, once, a wolfram mine, till wolfram tanked. In the 1960s the company was destitute, but then bought an option that covered a couple of presumed nickel claims, and thus found new life. In September 1969, Poseidon was trading at $1.40 a share. The following month it released overstated nickel assays and by November a Poseidon share would cost you $50. In December, a Melbourne brokerage got behind the Poseidon tale and predicted that shareholders could expect $250 a share, minimum, in the next few years. On New Year's Eve the stock was $210. Myriad other mining companies staked plays around Poseidon, and their shares too advanced wildly.

Poseidon had only half the grade of nickel it said it had. "In this potpourri it was not always possible to separate the thieves from the optimists," said Sykes. "Not one major deposit was discovered on boom money." He damned the egregious performance of the investment companies. "The only rationale for these companies is that their management possess superior skill or knowledge which enables them to invest shareholders' funds in mining stocks and situations more wisely than the small investor could by himself. On all the evidence from the boom, the small investor has a better chance on his own."

In December 1986, President Suharto, on behalf of the government of Indonesia, signed 103 cows for mineral projects in Indonesia. The boom was on. Maps of Kalimantan showed a psychedelic array of mineral claims, each displaying its territory using a different coloured block. The markets had been eagerly pumping money into these gold-seeking companies.

Pelsart was pumping funds into its Jakarta-based operations. The company had the classic architecture of a young, hopeful mining outfit. Officers and directors were awarded cheap stock, making them the first to the stock trough and the first to score if the share price ran up. Similarly at Jason, the insiders were gambling on share winnings to make their fortunes. Prior to June 30, 1986, John Felderhof had 272,500 shares in Jason at 20 cents, and he was granted options on a further 300,000 shares in the months following, set to expire at the end of July 1989. Standard penny mining procedure. There was a basket of properties to be evaluated and promoted by the Jason/Pelsart partnership. There was tremendous opportunity for Michael de Guzman, Pelsart employee, to make it big at last.

The culture of Pelsart was light-years removed from Benguet. The money flowed as freely as the booze that was always in plentiful supply in the boardroom of the company's grandiose quarters. Cost controls were all but nonexistent. And for any expatriate, the tropical life was terrifically alluring: the women were beautiful and enamoured of western men, the food was exotic, the evenings sexily sultry, and the booze cheap.

As a Canadian, John Felderhof was odd man out in the group that de Guzman came to meet in his new Indonesian life. There was Mike Novotny. And Mike Bird, who had come to Indonesia in 1983, having left the Bond group, run by the dangerously profligate tycoon, Alan Bond. Bird had married a woman whose father was a police officer, and thus was seen to be well connected, or as well connected an individual as the Pelsart group could muster. And there was Laurie Whitehouse. Bird, Novotny and Whitehouse had already been part of a number of stock mining runs, including Tropic Endeavor, a uranium prospect in Australia that ultimately went belly up. With Kevin Parry financing this latest gambit, the boys at Pelsart had hit the big time. The accountant at Pelsart was a friendly Indonesian named Bernhard Leode.

From Jakarta, de Guzman headed out to the bush, to carry out the mapping and sampling that he had proved so adept at in his training in the Philippines. He had, as yet, no discoveries to his credit. The extension of the gold deposit at Acupan had stalled. He had no reputation internationally. For all anyone in this new crowd knew, he was just another Filipino geologist. Michael de Guzman knew he was much more than that. He was very smart, saw himself as an original thinker, and he had theories, rock theories. Michael de Guzman was here to make himself a geologist of world renown.

The Jason/Pelsart partnership had a piece of a number of projects. Between them the companies had 30 percent of Mt. Muro, a gold prospect in Central Kalimantan. But they were not the operators, nor the controlling shareholders. Like the entire parcel of prospects, Mt. Muro was defined as a gold-silver property in a volcanogenic epithermal type environment. Epithermal systems are commonly associated with volcanic activity in which the magma has reached the surface of the earth, but the ore zones have remained rooted in the subsurface volcanic rocks, generally not more than 1,000 metres deep. Because of the shallow "regime" of epithermal deposits, they tend to be diffuse, a broad network of veins, rather than strong, wide, singular veins.

Local miners were mining the quartz veins in the area, the first tip-off that there was gold in this prospect. But with their unsophisticated technology, the miners could excavate only the top twenty metres of these veins. "Unauthorized local miners," Jason called them in its reports, meaning they did not have mine title in the eyes of the officials at the Department of Mines in Jakarta.

Another prospect was Muyup, also in Kalimantan, a five-million-ounce gold mine later taken over by Australia's mighty CRA mine house. At Muyup the locals were mining both alluvial and hard rock in these altered volcanic rocks. John Felderhof would one day claim it as his discovery. But Umar Olii had done the early work at the site, having been notified by a previous field worker that there was gold at Muyup comparable to that at Kelian. Olii did the reconnaissance work. Given the gold workings by the locals, however, it is arguable whether either man was entitled to claim the "discovery." The timber roads that had cut into the interior had exposed the "alteration halos" in the first place. Jason had 90 percent of Muyup.

Muyup's contract of work was signed in the fifth generation, in 1986. Felderhof signed on behalf of the offshore operators and Umar Olii signed for the local partner, East Tara Malawi Minerals. There is a picture of this ceremony. Felderhof was slighter then and is seen pulling a pen out of his breast pocket, about to sign the contract. He is wearing a light-grey suit and a dark tie. His hair is slicked to the side, though a schoolboy cowlick has escaped and juts over his forehead. Umar Olii is bent over the paperwork, inch-thick agreements. Two officials appear to be directing him toward what to sign next. Umar's hair is moppish, and he wears a batik jacket that appears astonishingly vibrant, despite its shades of brown.

Olii had resigned from Rio Tinto and joined PT Mincon Abadi as a senior geologist. Mincon was a consulting outfit, and Olii, on Mincon's behalf, was put on various files. Assignments included an alluvial gold reconnaissance survey along the Kahayan, Kapuas and Lower Barito rivers for Jason Mining. Olii hooked up with Jonathan Nassey. The two had gone to school together in Bandung. Nassey was Irianese, from the island of New Guinea that was carved in two to become Papua New Guinea (which declared independence in 1975) and Irian Jaya (which Indonesia claimed). Nassey served as president and director of A.C.A. Howe's Indonesian affiliate. The mining community in Jakarta is small. Everyone, it seems, knows everyone.

As Jason's representative, Felderhof would visit Muyup, tooling about on a motorbike. Cesar Puspos took up his post as a geologist there. Felderhof and Olii would talk about styles of mineralization and exploration targets. Olii respected Felderhof's geological expertise, but, in 1988, he resigned from Muyup. He did not like the situation, he says. He had only a 10 percent share. No power. No voice. But he held on to his friendship with Felderhof. He would take on part-time consulting for Jason, and other outfits, including the Tara Group, an outfit run by Adam Tobing, a Batak from North Sumatra. Tobing was well connected, or was seen to be. It was said that his father had been close with Adam Malik, who had been so key in the consolidation of Suharto's power in 1966. Olii too had his connections. His uncle, Dr. Katili, literally wrote the book on tectonics in Indonesia and had been director general of geology and mineral resources.

Olii targeted what came to be called the Jambi cow, named after the Sumatran province of that name. Umar selected the area. Tobing invested through Target Petroleum, Felderhof through Jason, in what became PT Target Mas Perdana. Cesar Puspos was named senior geologist, then project geologist. Ultimately, the project was terminated. Later, when Tobing tried to reapply for KPS on the same property, he found that someone had beaten him to it. Tobing wanted to be part of this mining game. He would retain these contacts for future use.

Meanwhile, Jason had a third gold prospect, this one called Mirah. Mike de Guzman took over responsibilities as the site's exploration manager, but it was Mike Bird who called the shots. One day he told de Guzman to stop drilling at Mirah. It was over. Drilling is an expensive proposition, and on any virgin exploration site, the men in the office, counting the pennies, are deciding day by day to keep pushing on, five holes, maybe ten, trying to decide when to stop the cash flow to the site. When stock promoter Murray Pezim kept the drills running at Ontario's Hemlo prospect to hole seventy-six, it was absolute madness. Certifiable. Yet Hemlo hit on that hole, a multimillion-ounce gold reserve still in production today.

De Guzman was not pleased by Mike Bird's directive. He had seen some geochem kicks, or "gold spikes," in assay results that he liked the look of. He could smell gold. Just smell it. He dreamed it. The fantastic images of Acupan, spawned in those nights of high revelry in Baguio, had proven to be accurate, hadn't they? Here he was. The golden boy. How dare Bird question what he knew, what he felt, what he could intuit? What do they know, these Australians who spend most of their time in offices and bars? De Guzman had more on-the-ground expertise. He reminded himself of that. How dare Bird stop him dead in his exploratory tracks? So Mike de Guzman ordered another hole drilled, ignoring Mike Bird's call.

Mike de Guzman trusted his instincts. The hole hit, and Mirah started to look very promising. It certainly added to the lustre of Mike de Guzman. Gold would come to him in his dreams. It really would.

John Felderhof was impressed by Mike de Guzman, whose talents extended beyond the on-the-ground survey work. Investors needed to be wooed. Analysts too. That meant producing academic-sounding treatises, to present at "gold shows," where junior companies set up booths and make their pitches, hoping to get investors to take the bait. De Guzman could provide that. As early as February 1987, Felderhof was putting together what would become a staple paper on the "geological setting of epithermal gold and alluvial prospects in Kalimantan, Indonesia."

Based on field observation, Felderhof said he assessed two kinds of gold structures in Kalimantan: breccia pipes, of the kind that de

Guzman had studied in the Philippines, and maar volcanoes, which Felderhof described as "shallow level structures produced by the explosive interaction of an ascending magma body with ground-water.... Maar volcanoes are generally located along major regional fault structures and form by the eruption of ground water explosively flashing to steam when coming in contact with ascending magma." Kelian, Mt. Muro and Muyup, he said, were deposits of this type. Felderhof cited the work of Dr. Katili, Umar Olii's uncle, in his study. The most promising areas of Kalimantan were in the eastern regions "where the Triassic-Jurassic volcanic pile and sediments are still substantially intact. These ore deposits are very rich," said Felderhof, "and are commonly referred to as bonanza deposits." De Guzman, meanwhile, produced mounds of internal reports, piles of maps.

Felderhof had a rare knack for a geologist. He was great at hype, at pushing stock, and his grizzled "I've been there" appearance, his tales of years in the bush and his work at Ok Tedi made him a believable, charismatic stock-pusher. Finding the ore is only half of the circle. Finding the money to continue finding the ore makes the circle whole. Gold exploration is a cash-consuming game. To watch a million dollars disappear in a month would not be unheard of.

It did not hurt that the Indonesian government was moving to develop its domestic capital markets. At the end of 1988, there were just twenty-four companies listed on the Jakarta Stock Exchange (JSE), the country's securities markets having bypassed both the global explosion in capital markets in the mid-'80s, and the stock bust of Black Monday, October 19, 1987. The year-end market capitalization of the twenty-four companies was 449 billion rupiahs, or $350 million. The few companies that were listed had taken a place on the JSE principally to satisfy requirements of the Foreign Investment Law and its insistence on selling shares of companies operating in Indonesia to Indonesian nationals.

Felderhof and the rest of the crew started doing very well for themselves. Felderhof purchased a million-dollar house in Perth, Australia,

and when he and his second wife, Ingrid, attended a mining conference in England, it was self-evident that Ingrid not only enjoyed the
company of furs and diamonds but had the wealth to obtain them.
The men on the Kalimantan sites were drilling very fast, hoping to
extract 1,000 metres of core quickly, then swiftly release the subsequent assay results to the investing public.

For a brief period it looked as though life could only get better. The
government announced a deregulation plan aimed at promoting the
JSE as an alternative source of financing. Deregulation meant making
the JSE a more appealing home to foreign stock market players, the
kind that had had such a heyday in the Australian markets. The rules
of listing, underwriting and trading would be loosened. No longer
would the exchange restrict the amount of daily share volume allowed
in any one stock. And foreign investors could take much bigger pieces
of any stock traded. The changes, in other words, were just the ticket
for the kind of junior penny mine promoters who flourished in places
like Vancouver, Calgary and Melbourne. By the end of 1989, there
were fifty-six companies on the JSE with year-end market capitalization of 4 trillion rupiahs, or $2.6 billion. The exchange's governing
body was the Badan Pelaksana Pasar Modal, or BAPEPAM.

Ultimately the stock market bust did come to Australia, and
Indonesia, too. The Parry Corp. foundered, and in 1988, Hang Lung
Developments Co. of Hong Kong bought into the Australian company. As it controlled a range of properties, Pelsart had some appeal,
and through Parry, Hang Lung found itself in the position of trying
to turn Pelsart around. The company's staff had ballooned to three
hundred. Hang Lung moved a man named Bruce Kennedy in to try
to get Pelsart in shape. Some task. When the money machine dried
up, the company closed up the Mirah prospect. Amphalit, for example, had eventually produced some gold, at a cost of US$700 an ounce.

Rachman Wiriosudarmo, an employee with the Department of
Mines, had his eye on Amphalit, and he did not at all like what he
saw. One day he met with Mike Bird and Mike Novotny. The Amphalit

project had been delayed, and Rachman wanted to know why. "Technical problems," was the brief answer.

In Java there is an expression: *Angin*, literally "the movement of wind." It means, "I don't believe you. You are blowing air." *Angin*, thought Rachman as he stared at Bird and Novotny.

Rachman had twenty years' experience with dredging operations. He had little use for what he called "zero dollar companies," and Amphalit certainly fit that description. The company's technology, imported from Australia, was crap. "Toy technology" Rachman called it. "I cannot accept your reasons, sir," said Rachman, a slight, trim man with a very serious gaze. "Your exploration was not appropriate for alluvial gold. You must restart your exploration report, redo your infill drilling and recalculate your reserves. Rewrite the feasibility study and reconsider your choice of equipment and mining method."

Amphalit, in other words, was a disaster. Rachman made a site visit. He found very fancy houses there, or at least fancy by Indonesian standards. In one of these lived Michael de Guzman, when he was around. De Guzman had met a woman from Palangkaraya, the capital of Central Kalimantan. Her name was Sugini Karnasih. Michael called her Genie.

It was not uncommon for men in Indonesia to take a "contract wife," or two, or more. That practice dovetailed nicely with the miner's dilemma: gone from home for so long a stretch. Where does one find love? And for Mike de Guzman it was love he sought, something much bigger than sex. He found it with Genie Karnasih.

The cash control at Pelsart was so loose it was not a difficult task for de Guzman to outfit his new home with Genie. Furniture. Appliances. A fridge, a VCR, a television set made their way out of Pelsart's site premises and into de Guzman's riverside love nest. He could bill for an item for the mine camp, then appropriate it for personal use instead.

It fell to Bruce Kennedy, Pelsart's president director, to fire Mike de Guzman. On October 19, 1990, the geologist submitted his letter of resignation to Kennedy. De Guzman said he was seeking professional advancement, and said he was grateful to the company and its staff. Kennedy wrote a letter for the file. As project manager of the Mirah hard-rock gold project, he said, de Guzman oversaw all of the geological work that resulted in the discovery and eventual reserve definition of the Mirah complex of orebodies. "We wish Mike well in his future career." Felderhof weighed in too, with a letter of praise that was copied to de Guzman's file, dated October 24, 1990. "I have had the pleasure of knowing and working with Mike de Guzman over the period of four years," wrote Felderhof. "In my opinion as an international geologist over a period of 27 years of which the last 15 years engaged as managing director of an international consulting firm that Mike de Guzman is the best exploration development geologist I have encountered. His resignation as project manager PT Kasongan Bumi Kencana is a major loss to the company."

The letters were mere formalities. As a contract worker in a country with strict rules concerning foreigners working on their shores, a dismissal on de Guzman's file would haunt his attempts to find other work. And Pelsart did not want the grief of having to appear before an Indonesian labour tribunal should de Guzman try to contest his dismissal. So polite letters were issued all round, a mutually acceptable departure package was agreed upon, and Michael de Guzman was on his own.

The routing of the Pelsart boys took Mike Novotny back to Australia, where, in the summer of 1990, he brokered a deal on a mining property in West Australia called Karpa Springs. Karpa was a touted gold discovery near Mount Gibson, east of Kalgoorlie. Three prospectors—the Ireland brothers, Dean and Len, along with Clark Easterday—had claimed high-grade gold intersections in eleven of the nineteen holes it had drilled at the property. The property, they said, had a "strike length" of 1,500 metres and was "open in all directions." In other words, the Irelands and Easterday hypothesized that the riches of Karpa were vast, the property's horizon wide. The prospectors wooed

Novotny, who in turn formed an investing syndicate with two well-known Australian mining entrepreneurs, which they dubbed Aracus.

Aracus sold 50 percent of the property to a junior Australian mining outfit, Perilya Mines. Perilya, in turn, struck a deal with Canada's mighty Noranda Inc., which had invested in a number of Perilya prospects over the years. Noranda took a 30 percent interest, at $6.15 million, and retained an option to acquire a further 20 percent for an additional $4 million. Ultimately, Noranda would be free to raise its stake to 70 percent of the property.

According to the *Australian Financial Review*, it was Warren Batt, a Perilya executive, who first became apprehensive about the Karpa investment. The drill samples had been locked in a warehouse in Kalgoorlie. It was Batt who got a key to the warehouse and, when he opened it, found no samples there. Payments to the three prospectors were quickly frozen, and check holes were drilled at site. In August, Perilya issued a press release stating that the holes showed a "complete absence of gold." The *Review* said stockbrokers were horrified by the results. "One said investors had been enthusiastic about Perilya because of its links with the conservative Canadian miner Noranda Inc. 'Noranda just doesn't make those mistakes,' one broker said." The prospectors were convicted of spiking, or salting, their samples.

The Pelsart premises today are as grim as the Benguet digs. Fong Fatt Chong, now general manager of Pelsart Resources, takes a slow drag on a cigarette, then a sip of coffee. "Embezzlement, fraud, theft, these are far too heavy descriptions," he says. Though the corporate residence is very down at the heels, Fong appears very smartly turned out in his blue striped shirt, his Pierre Cardin tie. He keeps a small silver lid on the top of his water glass. The company shut down the Amphalit mine in 1994 but has kept a small alluvial operation in production on that site. The Mt. Muro investment was sold to the Pennzoil group: Pelsart could not carry its piece of the project financing. In January 1997, illegal miners outnumbered the Pelsart employees. The Indonesian military was called in, and they seized the locals' equipment. The company hasn't made a dime in years. As for Mirah, attempts have been made to restart the project. Fong gives de Guzman credit for discovering the extensions there, and says the geologist's maps are still much in use. He came in contact with Felderhof after his Jason days, when Felderhof was seeking a joint venture with a company he had hooked up with, Bre-X Minerals. Pelsart had hired a Filipino metallurgist named Rudy Vega, but de Guzman, who was then working for Bre-X too, pinched him before he could even settle in. Six months later, Vega inquired as to whether there might still be a position for him at Pelsart. There was not.

He summons de Guzman's red personnel folder. There is no information concerning health troubles. There is a copy of his passport. And there is a Valentine's Day card that de Guzman had given to Rod Pangilinan, another Pelsart employee and a fellow Filipino.

According to members of Michael de Guzman's family, he was worried when he left Pelsart. He had a family to support, no clear prospects, and Indonesia was in a slump. Work permits had to be renewed on a regular basis, and without an employer, de Guzman was naked. He returned to Manila, taking a job with United Paragon Mining Corp. United operated the Longos open-pit gold mine in Parapale, in Camarines Norte. Output was small, 11,000 or 12,000 ounces a year. Pedro Oyam hired de Guzman as a geologist. De Guzman showed workers how to do mapping work, supervised the project's drilling and worked on structural projections on gold vein extensions. He was paid 25,000 pesos a month, which meant a U.S.-dollar salary of $1,100. Paltry by Indonesian standards, where salaries were easily twice that.

After just three months on the job de Guzman went back to Oyam and said he wanted to change the terms of his employment. He wanted his position converted to a contract that required him to work just two weeks a month. Oyam said no. According to Oyam, de Guzman did a good job while he was there.

Returning to Indonesia, de Guzman jumped from job to job,

consulting for Bakrie Nusantara Corp., then moving to John Nainggolen's company, PT Hunamas Putra Interbuana. He went to Hunamas as project manager and took Cesar Puspos along as his senior geologist. But Hunamas's mineral prospects did not pan out, and Puspos and de Guzman left, unpaid, realizing at last that Indonesia had not quite worked out as expected. In fact, it now looked like a royal bust. De Guzman had Tess and their family to support back in Manila, and there was Genie too. For the golden boy of Acupan, life was looking pretty damn grim. And it was not looking much better for his very good friend, John Felderhof.

Salvation arrived in the form of a French-Canadian mining promoter, Armand Beaudoin. He had a plan to float a junior mining company on the Jakarta Stock Exchange, a full underwriting, the whole show. None of this offshore senior partner stuff. The company was called PT Minindo Perkasasemesta.

The most predictable cast of characters gathered round. Umar Olii took on the job of translating the documents to be filed with the JSE. De Guzman was "Chief Geologist—Consultant." Puspos was "Senior Geologist—Consultant." And Felderhof sat above them.

Minindo had a variety of promising prospects. Lateritic nickels in Irian Jaya. Oil in Central Kalimantan. Gold on the upper Woyla River in Sumatra, and a small-scale alluvial project in the river's lower regions. But that was secondary. Of primary interest was the share play, the chance to load up on the very cheap stock at the outset, the same stock that others would surely buy at far higher prices. Oh, they would be millionaires. Or that is what was assumed. A Filipino metallurgist named Jerry Alo was operations manager at a company called PT Ara Tutut, one of the Minindo interests. Alo had transferred to Indonesia after spending three years working in East Africa as plant superintendent at Dar Tadine Tanzania Ltd. Before that he had spent more than a decade working in the Philippines.

Alas, Minindo came crashing down. The issue was undersubscribed. The company ran afoul of the JSE. Felderhof's contract with

Minindo, which had the company paying for his house in Bogor, fell through, and he was on his uppers. One of his daughters was suffering recurring bouts of diarrhea. Umar Olii and his brother, Tommy, talked Adam Tobing into helping out. Felderhof stayed with Tobing for a time at his house in West Jakarta. By the beginning of 1993, wrote Theo van Leeuwen, "12 foreign companies had active exploration programmes compared to more than 30 during the gold boom." Van Leeuwen surmised that junior companies were unlikely to make a reappearance "in force" within the foreseeable future, for several reasons. "For one, their overall disappointing performance has prompted the Government to tighten the screening process of new COW applications by increasing the foreign contractors' financial obligations during exploration. By contrast, involvement of large Indonesian business groups in gold and coal has been increasing significantly during recent years, and this may lead to a broadening of the domestic mining industry."

Many of the former Pelsart boys found themselves on the bones of their asses. Felderhof spent a great deal of time in the Captain Cook Bar at the Marco Polo Hotel, a short-stay hotel with a flashing outdoor sign: "29,000 rupiahs." He would drink enormous quantities of beer. He purchased a pen for his daughter one Christmas—it was all he could afford. He tried to land a job, at one point knocking on the door of PT Ingold, an Indonesian subsidiary of Canada's Inco. Ingold needed workers for a project in Irian Jaya, just 30 kilometres from Ok Tedi, the mine that had made Felderhof famous. Why should we hire an old geologist for a place like Irian? was the internal response to Felderhof's query.

Felderhof was, he would say later, "very fucking broke." Not only was he very fucking broke, but he seemed to have no prospects for being anything other than very fucking broke.

PUTZ

IN THE COURT OF QUEEN'S BENCH of Alberta, Judicial District of Calgary. Bankruptcy Department.

I, David Walsh, make oath and say.

1. That I reside at 6 Varbay Place, N.W., in the City of Calgary, in the province of Alberta, which property I jointly own with my spouse.

2. That I am employed by Bre-X Minerals Ltd. and Bresea Resources Ltd.

3. That my prospects for income in the immediate foreseeable future are as follows: At present I am taking no draws from the above companies but it is my intention to take approximately $1,000 depending on the availability of funds from either of the two junior resource companies.

4. That my wife earns approximately $2,500 before taxes per month performing secretarial services for Bre-X Minerals and Bresea Resources Ltd.

5. That my wife and I have two dependent children. Sean T.D. Walsh, 22, student and Brett R.D. Walsh, 20.

6. That I do not own a motor vehicle.

7. That I have acquired no assets subsequent to my assignment in bankruptcy.

8. That the reasons for my bankruptcy were low income from self-employment, lawsuit and over-extension of credit.

The affidavit was signed March 15, 1993. David Gordon Walsh was seeking discharge from bankruptcy. He was forty-seven years old and, ostensibly, penniless. But in relative terms Walsh's life was on the upswing. The year before the phone had been ringing a great deal—not potential investors eager to buy into Bre-X promotions, but rather creditors seeking payment. Walsh had run-of-the-mill debts: the mortgage on his house on Varbay Place; a couple thousand to the income tax people. But a recitation of his credit card debt was as long as a grocery list, and much more serious: Bank of Montreal MasterCard $6,521.85; a second BMO MasterCard at $6,833.70; two Visa cards with the Bank of Nova Scotia for a tally there of $6,382.66; the Royal Bank's Visa department had issued three Visas, for $15,921.36; a couple of Royal Trust MasterCards and a Visa from Central Guaranty. Oh, and one MasterCard each from the National Bank and the Canadian Imperial Bank of Commerce. Throw in the paltry $1,681.73 he owed to the Canadian Tire Acceptance Corp. and David Walsh's credit card debt was $52,492.43. The phone at Varbay Place would ring all day long. Walsh tried to cut deals. Creditors refused. He was robbing Peter to pay Paul, he would say later.

Walsh's ability to juggle so many creditors started to collapse in the Christmas season of 1991. When the creditors could not be held back, they threatened to sue. Then, in January, the Bank of Montreal followed through, filing suit, followed by the CIBC the following month. Walsh did not bother filing a statement of defence. In addition to the $52,000 owed on credit cards, RBC Dominion Securities Inc. said it was owed $48,227.76. In the summer of 1991, a judgment was issued against Walsh, which he was still fighting the following winter. A declaration of bankruptcy promised to vaporize not only the charge card people but RBC Dominion too. On the day when he could at last say to his creditors "Call the trustee," he felt a huge weight had been lifted from his shoulders.

Throughout the grim days, Walsh held tightly on to the one thin thread that promised him, if not salvation, then the hope of salvation: his corporate listing on the Alberta Stock Exchange. He had many calls about that, too, pressure tactics from the exchange to get him to give it up. But it cost him just $1,000 annually to keep his stock alive, and by holding on to his listing, Walsh maintained his connection to a pot of gold of sorts: penny stock investors perennially willing to take a punt on a stock in the hopes of big winnings. "Peter went bankrupt. Paul survived," he told *Fortune* magazine's Richard Behar. "I didn't just lie down and suck my thumb."

The penny share trick lends itself particularly well to the mining game, a game fuelled by the dream that under a much-trod piece of pasture could be a hidden cache of nickel, copper, silver, diamonds, gold. "As long as you've got a drill turning you can turn the world upside-down," a mining executive once told me. There was no way Walsh was going to give that up.

On April 13, 1993, the court discharged David Gordon Walsh from bankruptcy.

In the life of a promoter there is never really one last chance, a last big gamble for that last big score. Oh, he may think he's getting to the end. That his time is virtually up. That if this punt fails, the jackpot might never be hit. But that is not the way it works. Promoters are eternal optimists, just like geologists. A penny stock deal can go right down the crapper on Monday, and on Tuesday plans are being laid for deal number two, or deal number one hundred, or deal number one thousand. Some are more deft at the game than others. David Walsh was in the "others" category.

Walsh grew up in Montreal, at 489 Grosvernor Avenue, Westmount. His father, Vaughan, was a stockbroker, and cut a dashing figure. The home, however, was modest: semi-detached, two-storey, nothing fancy. Walsh's grandfather, too, had been a broker. David was one of five children: three girls, two boys. He would say he learned perseverance from his father, but if he had a mentor it was his grandmother. "A doer," Walsh would say of her. A positive thinker. She ran a summer camp for girls.

A photograph of the family, taken sometime in 1955, shows the prototypical family of the day. David Walsh, aged 10, stands to the photographer's left, his dungarees rolled thickly and unevenly up from the ankles, a very small blazer on top. Young David appears to be squinting, his face furrowed in a manner that would become familiar to friend and foe.

When Walsh was in high school in Montreal, he never made the football team. Acquaintances joked that he could not remember the twelve plays. He took night courses in finance and, in 1970, went to work for Eastern Trust, later Canada Permanent Trust Co., where he worked as a trust officer and investment officer. He had already married, to Jeannette Toukmanian, and the newlyweds had moved into the Grosvenor home. A small scandal wafted through the company in the 1970s, when a broker at Yorkton Securities used various trust accounts, including one in Walsh's purview, to wash stolen share certificates, in other words, to create the appearance of stock market activity by trading shares through fictitious accounts. Walsh appears not to have asked any questions. Walsh told the *Globe and Mail's* Karen Howlett that when he was informed the shares had been pilfered, he called in the Montreal Fraud Squad. "I met with the officers once, gave them a statement of [the broker's] account and was interviewed. I never was contacted again." Walsh left Canada Permanent in the spring of 1976.

Walsh's bible was *Think and Grow Rich*. Written by Napoleon Hill, it was a 1960s motivational primer. The book had been given to his mother by his grandmother, and thence to Walsh himself when he was in his teens. He read it over and over and over. Fifty times, he once said. "All achievement, all earned riches, have their beginning in an idea!" Hill declared. Walsh's idea, in the aftermath of Canada Permanent, was to set up his own trust company. It was ultimately rather too grand an idea, and instead he turned to institutional equity sales for the brokerage firm Midland Doherty Ltd.

Walsh ended up working for Midland out of Calgary, oil and gas land. His mandate was to open up the territory for the brokerage, which had flourished in the east. Calgary should have been easy pickings; he would be rousing the investor interests of a clientele who had known, ever since the days of the oil discovery at Leduc in 1947, that a resource discovery could change the world. But Walsh was less interested in other people's mining prospects than in his own. It was the influence of Napoleon Hill again, the get-rich-quick guru who would quote Thomas Edison: "When a man really desires a thing so deeply that he is willing to stake his entire future on a single turn of the wheel in order to get it, he is sure to win." Just as well, for Midland determined that Walsh's performance was sub-par, and thus chopped his pay, which Walsh took as constructive dismissal. He sued, Midland settled out of court, and Walsh, for once and for all, was buck naked in the world of mining promoters and now desperate to prove he knew what the hell he was doing.

Walsh had formed a company, Bresea, named after his sons, Brett and Sean. In 1983 he met John Felderhof in Sydney, Australia. Felderhof was managing director of A.C.A. Howe International, and Walsh was interested in mineral properties. A chum of Walsh's had leased office space from Peter Howe and so he came to meet Felderhof. Felderhof invited Walsh to join him on a trip he was about to take to Kalimantan. He was hoping to find a partner to invest in the Mandor property. Perhaps Walsh was that someone.

Walsh and Felderhof flew to the site by helicopter, landing on the football field of the local school. The camp housing was a converted store, the sleeping accommodation hand-made cots under mosquito nets. Walsh was merely another prospect, another fish, albeit a rather large white one, startlingly out of his milieu. Felderhof, the grizzled river-walker, seemed right at home, of course. He had tried to offload the property onto Rio Tinto, which had led to his association with Umar Olii. That had failed. Walsh, out of his hometown and his own modest surroundings, could have been a con man for all Felderhof knew. And did he really care? Not likely.

The two walked some trails, hacking through the bush, and Walsh got his first nose-full of how different a mining proposition in Indonesia is from one in, say, Arizona. But Walsh was in no financial position to take up a piece of the property. More important, with no one paying attention to Indonesia as a mining prospect, Walsh's own prospects of rousing investor enthusiasm on this play looked frightfully thin. Nevertheless, something must have clicked between the two. They stayed in touch, and Felderhof visited Walsh in Calgary from time to time.

Walsh occupied himself in the oil town by pushing penny stocks, trading through a dozen brokerage accounts. In 1987, the year of the big stock market crash, $48,227.76 showed up mysteriously in one of the accounts he held at Pemberton Securities. He must not have been too puzzled by the newly arrived securities, for he sold them off, even though he did not own them. Pemberton, which became RBC Dominion Securities, would eventually sue.

Walsh needed to build a penny mining shell game and for these purposes he incorporated a company called Bre-X Minerals. The "X" stood for exploration; the "Bre" represented Walsh's son Brett. The new company became a sister company to Bresea. On May 24, 1988, Walsh and Bre-X Minerals (aka Walsh) signed a deal whereby Bre-X would take up an option on Walsh's forty-one mineral claims in the Mackenzie District of the Northwest Territories. Three months later, Bre-X announced a deal with Bresea (Walsh, again) whereby Bresea would earn a 28.5 percent interest in the same forty-one claims if it spent $285,000, presumably on exploration, by year's end. If Bresea (Walsh) were to sign the claims back to Bre-X (Walsh), 1,140,000 Bre-X shares would go to Bresea. The washing of shares to and fro said very little for either company's sincere intention to plumb for minerals.

Early in 1989, Bre-X shares were trolled to insiders, including Jeannette Walsh, who paid a buck for 125,000 shares, exercisable at 30 cents a piece. Geologist William Timmins, the company's vice-president, took 60,000 shares, the same 30-cent deal. Joel King, a Montreal lawyer and long-time Walsh associate, ditto. Walsh himself was in receipt of 229,000 shares.

In May, Yorkton agreed to a private placement of a million common shares at 30 cents a share, with a 10 percent commission going to the brokerage. The pitch was this: that the claims had the type of favourable rocks that host gold in the area; that Echo Bay's Lupin Mine, a gold producer, was just a hiccup away. The standard claims map was printed up, showing Bre-X/Bresea rubbing shoulders with the likes of Noranda, Cominco and Echo Bay, of course. Fine upstanding companies all, and producing ones at that. How could an investor resist when Bre-X was keeping such highfalutin company?

The share issue was finalized in July 1989, and on the tenth of that month, the company issued a press release concerning its hunt for gold. On September 15, the escrowed shares were released, and three days later, the company made this announcement: "Three gold rich ore zones in iron formations each extending over 2 kilometres in length were discovered.... The area of the discoveries are located 80 miles southeast of Echo Bay's Lupin Mine.... These three discovery zones, considered to be highly significant, produced numerous anomalous gold values with a highlight assay of approximately one ounce gold (.899 per ton).... Negotiations to provide major financing will commence immediately."

Oh, and the company was moving into northern Quebec, to a "highly prospective property" near Joutel, gold country. A year later, in the spring of 1990, the company was in negotiations to acquire a majority interest in forty-five claims in Mohave County, Arizona. "The claims include three past producing mines and cover prolific gold bearing vein systems," said Bre-X. Proven, probable and possible ore reserves totalled, it said, 1,383,387 tonnes grading 0.21 ounces of gold per tonne. "This property is an excellent opportunity for Bre-X to make a rapid transition to being a gold producer," said Walsh.

Well, need we say that nothing much happened? The company's 1991 annual report was a fiscal horror, though not uncommon fare for a penny mining company. No revenues, a loss for the year of $540,739. The RBC Dominion lawsuit still loomed, and the credit card bills were mounting.

Ultimately, the RBC suit became the proverbial last straw. The Walshes filed for bankruptcy, knowing that the horror of the credit card balances would be washed away in the tide with the monies claimed by RBC. Opportunity, wrote Napoleon Hill, "has a sly habit of slipping in by the back door, and often it comes disguised in the form of misfortune, or temporary defeat." Perhaps Walsh viewed his bankruptcy in this way. Perhaps he just had to *think* his way to riches, to convert defeat "into stepping stones to opportunity." "Every adversity, every failure and every heartache carries with it the Seed of an equivalent or a greater benefit."

Walsh read, over and over, Hill's account of the fellow who caught gold fever in the days of the gold rush. He made a discovery and scrabbled together with friends and family to finance its extraction.

"The returns proved they had one of the richest mines in Colorado! A few more cars of that ore would clear the debts. Then would come the big killing in profits.

"Down went the drills! Up went the hopes of Darby and Uncle! Then something happened. The vein of gold ore disappeared! They had come to the end of the rainbow, and the pot of gold was no longer there." They sold off the equipment to a junk dealer, who called in a mine engineer to reevaluate the gold discovery gone dry. "The engineer advised that the project had failed because the owners were not familiar with 'fault lines.' His calculations showed that the vein would be found *just three feet from where the Darbys had stopped drilling! That is exactly where it was found!*"

It was so tantalizing, the prospect of winning for a change. And Hill made a promise: "When riches begin to come they come so quickly, in such great abundance, that one wonders where they have been hiding during all those lean years. . . . When money comes in quantities known as 'the big money,' it flows to the one who accumulates it, as easily as water flows downhill."

Walsh merely needed to become "success conscious," to "magnetize" his mind "with intense desire for riches," to "visualize" himself delivering the goods, whatever the goods might be, and receiving the money in return. When he tumbled into bed at night, Walsh was to repeat aloud his desire for the amount of money he hoped to accumulate, and a description of the service or merchandise he was to deliver in return. Stocks. Diamonds. Oil and gas. Over the years Walsh must have had a panoply of propositions floating through his brain, a Disneyesque parade of goods in abundance and millions received as recompense. It was his private little money mantra. He had to slay skepticism, to beware intemperance. "The bottom," said Hill, "is a monotonous, dreary, unprofitable place for any person."

Walsh believed he could sell anything that he believed in, a nostrum nicely complemented by his ability to believe in anything. The Napoleon Hill psychology is very much in sync with that of promoters: that the pot of gold is waiting just around the bend, if only one would apply oneself. Hill did warn, however, that "Money without brains is always dangerous."

Bre-X's first-quarter report in 1992 showed a grand total of $15 cash on hand. By the spring of 1992, Bre-X had changed course. It was now on the hunt for diamonds in the Northwest Territories, following on the success of a junior company called Dia Met Minerals in the Lac de Gras area, northeast of Yellowknife. In March, in what appears a desperate move, Walsh sold 175,500 Bre-X shares at 10 cents a share.

Two months later, the company got a significant boost when Kennecott Canada Inc., an offshoot of the Australian company Felderhof had worked for years previously, optioned eight of Bre-X's Northwest Territories claims. *The Northern Miner* ran a story on May 25. "Kennecott options Bre-X diamond bet," ran the headline. "If a production decision is made," said the story, "Bre-X may elect to surrender its 30% undivided interest in return for a 6% Gross Overriding Royalty [GOR]." Readers of the *Miner* should have read these words with caution. These were not facts unearthed by a *Northern Miner* reporter; rather, the text was lifted word for word from a Bre-X press release.

The Dia Met tale had already become the stuff of Canadian mining legend. A slight, fidgety prospector named Chuck Fipke had gambled his last gallon of gas on one final flight over the wilds of the Northwest Territories near Lac de Gras. The idea that Fipke would find a trail of mineralization that would eventually lead to the construction of Canada's first diamond mine looked too absurd. But the diamonds were real, and Broken Hill Proprietary, the mighty Australian copper miner, took an option, then control. Those first in— Fipke and his pals, then a small circle of believers—made out like bandits. Fipke became a multimillionaire. The conventional business press took a cautious approach. Another penny push, they figured. Diamonds in the Northwest Territories? Not bloody likely.

Funny thing was, the diamond tale was true. A mere 320 kilometres from Yellowknife, the prettiest, clearest diamonds outside South Africa were buried in the tundra.

In January 1992, *The Northern Miner* ran a story on the diamond play. Since the previous fall, when Dia Met announced its discovery, thousands of square kilometres had been staked in the area, one of the largest, if not the largest staking rush in North American history. The activity was exciting enough to spur the involvement of Monopros, a division of De Beers, the diamonds-are-forever people. In its January article, *The Northern Miner* made mention of "a few fortunate juniors, including Argus Resources (ASE), Bre-X Minerals (ASE) and Tanqueray Resources (ASE)," who "hold nearby gold claims secured long before the diamond discovery." The *Calgary Sun* ran an early piece on Bre-X and Argus in the Northwest Territories. Dorothy Atkinson, then a geologist with the federal government in Yellowknife, expressed the general hope that the area excitement would prove to be "one of the most important mining finds in Canadian history." But Atkinson added a note of caution. "It's still early," she advised.

Bre-X/Bresea was no slouch when it came to making sure investors caught every mention made of it in the credible press. Nor was manufacturing such mention beyond the talents of the company's investor relations people. And so, after *Northern Miner* writer Virginia Heffernan wrote studiously about the geology of the region in a second article on Lac de Gras, someone at Bre-X decided to give Heffernan's piece a new closing sentence in the copies prepared for their own shareholders: "But a few fortunate juniors, including. . . . " You get the picture.

Heffernan continued to follow the diamond story, writing in April that 22,800 square kilometres had been staked around the discovery. "Ontario's Hemlo gold rush of 1982 pales in comparison. That year, 2,700 square miles in northeastern Ontario were staked solid after geologist David Bell made the discovery of his lifetime. Three mines now producing a quarter of Canada's gold emerged from the land grab and subsequent exploration." Bre-X, as any junior mining company would, ran off claims maps of the Yellowknife area, showing the Dia Met discovery surrounded by the likes of Aber, Argus, Tyler, Puregold, Commonwealth and so on.

A handful of heavyweight fund investors got behind the Dia Met story in the early going. Frank Mersch, a legendary investor at Altamira, one of the country's largest mutual fund companies, was in. Most fund managers remained disbelievers and so suffered the wrath of investors who would have liked to see such high returns show up in their portfolios.

The Kennecott arrangement was badly needed good news for Bre-X. In April, the company had released its annual report, opening with a bracing introductory sentence: "Yes, we are still in business and are proceeding with a sound strategy to develop your Company into an intermediate size natural resource company as expeditiously as possible." Walsh promised a joint venture signing on diamonds (which turned out to be the Kennecott deal), a positive working capital position, "enhanced value of marketable securities," and the funding of oil and gas limited partnerships. Yet, despite the diamond prospect, Walsh announced that the company was undergoing a change in corporate focus, looking now to oil and gas in western Canada.

The Kennecott arrangement was too little too late for David Walsh. Bre-X stock was at 6 cents. He was bust, broke, flat. Three months later he resigned as director. Five months after that, the company notified the Alberta Securities Commission that the company had relocated, from its offices at 1 Palliser Square to a post office box. Walsh was working out of his basement.

Yet through that alchemy so adeptly practised by junior mine promoters, as David Walsh was telling the courts that he was taking no draws from his company, that his prospects were dim, he was on the phone to John Felderhof, sniffing out the possibility of tying up a prospect or two, in Indonesia.

On April 2, 1993, Walsh contacted Felderhof. "With Canadian companies exploring in Latin America, Africa, etc., and getting Canadian investors attracted and some big upside stock moves, I thought I would see what is up in Indonesia as I have always felt there is great potential since I went to Borneo with you 10 years ago," he wrote. "I want to put some romance into both companies [Bre-X and Bresea] ASAP. We have a great speculative stock market going in Canada now."

Typical punter. Romance, as soon as possible. There is something contradictory there. What Walsh meant was the need to inject the companies with some sex appeal, immediately—to sprinkle the musk scent upon the investor, the irresistible allure. As one mining executive remarked: "We all know somebody who knows somebody who made a fortune somewhere." That's it. That's the junior mining addiction.

What better way to accomplish that but in the wilds of a relatively unknown place half a world away, in "the middle of ruddy nowhere," as one analyst would come to put it? Walsh was tired of being at the end of the line, the last guy in, the penny hopeful to nose in on the area play, banking on the belief that the appeal would rub off on his stock, too. Walsh wanted to lead the pack. Why, he had been back of the line for years.

His missive to Felderhof contained the operative phrase "speculative stock market." Romance or no, the eager stock market was the key.

Felderhof informed Walsh that he would put together information on some properties. Felderhof himself had no other prospects; Ingrid and the children were staying with other Felderhofs in Nova Scotia. "I plan to go back for a month around the middle of May," he wrote Walsh. "I need to make some big bucks again and hold on to it."

In late April, David Walsh took his airline seat in economy class alongside his son, Sean, and a local geologist named Kevin Waddell. Waddell had known Walsh for years, liked him, and agreed to

accompany the Walshes to Jakarta to size up the parcel of properties that Felderhof had lassoed. It has become part of the Walsh lore
that he was down to his "last $10,000," which, safe to say, the
courts did not know about.

The three checked in to the Sari Pan Pacific Hotel in Jakarta. Sean
and Kevin bunked together, while the promoter stayed seven floors
above.

Felderhof consulted Adam Tobing, who had put Felderhof up for
a time in his Jakarta home and who offered him office space at his
own. There would be a dinner. Yes, of course. Formal, in the Sari
Pacific Hotel. Tobing would host. Umar Olii would be invited, of
course—he was a natural for this project, should it fly with Walsh.
Tobing would also bring along his youngest brother, and a brother-
in-law. Mike Bird would attend.

It was a pleasant enough evening. Walsh was given the impression
that Tobing was well connected to the government, that he would be a
powerful ally to have on board. Waddell was left to study relatively
scant information on a number of prospects. He reviewed a report on
a site called Busang, which had been drilled, nineteen holes, by a previous owner. This company had taken a flyer, drilling another hole to
the southeast of the original nineteen. Waddell was not provided with
any signed assay sheets to back up the information. Still, he told Walsh
that Busang was worth more work. He recommended a second
prospect, called Singhe. He was, in fact, more keen on the latter. Singhe
was the only property for which airborne geophysics surveys had been
done. But Busang, having already been drilled, was the more advanced
of the two. There were assay results, and though they suggested little,
perhaps they could be reinterpreted.

Felderhof told Walsh he believed that Busang had a million ounces
of gold. It was a ready-made promotion. Instead of shilling muck with
no proof of mineralization, Bre-X could start its Busang tale by convincing the Canadian public, first, that a mine was guaranteed. Mines
have been built on fewer than a million ounces. Unlike the old-style

Walsh prospects, which invariably tagged on to some other company's discovery, this promotion had a built-in level of credibility. Felderhof said he was not interested in promoting any old "crap." Walsh said he was not interested in pushing any old "crap" down investors' throats either. Busang was in play.

Busang, in fact, was already getting rather long in the tooth as a gold prospect, at least as far as the Department of Mines in Jakarta was concerned. Jonathan Nassey had conducted a reconnaissance survey in East Kalimantan in late 1986 for PT Westralian Atan Minerals. The following year, in December 1987, as John Felderhof was signing his contract of work for Muyup, two COWs were signed covering the area, one of which was called the Muara Atan COW. By that time a field camp had already been set up at the project's site on the Atan River.

The foreign, and majority, partner was Westralian Resource Projects Ltd. (WRPL), a publicly listed Australian company headed by Warren Talbot Beckwith, who based his operations in Perth. The local partners, each of whom had 10 percent, were Jusuf Merukh and Haji Syakerani. The 10-percenters' interest was "free carried"; they did not have to pay up front for their pieces.

Few Indonesians recognized mining as a good business to be involved in. One who did was Jusuf Merukh. Merukh was born on the tiny island of Roti off the southwest tip of Timor, a place subjugated and converted by a German Protestant. Merukh became a member of Parliament, but his business affairs involved the lassoing of hundreds of properties in the mining sector. Merukh had made excellent arrangements within the Department of Mines.

For the purposes of operating in Indonesia, a new corporate moniker was adopted, PT Westralian Atan Minerals. Henceforth the operation would be known as PT WAM, or just WAM. That same year, 1987, Jonathan Nassey was dismissed for what PT WAM would describe as unethical behaviour, having sold prospective properties to companies other than Westralian.

In January 1988, Graeme Chuck, an expatriate from Australia, joined Westralian as exploration manager. Three months later Chuck and senior geologist John Levings headed for Kalimantan. The duo set their base of operations in Balikpapan, and from there they would visit what they referred to at first as the Atan site.

The WAM COW was initially a series of seven blocks, T-shapes and oblongs, not all of them connected. Chuck and Levings determined that Block V, what would later be called the Central Zone, was the prospect's most promising piece, ten kilometres away from the existing Westralian camp, just to the south of the Atan River. The Dayak were panning the rivers everywhere throughout the region: the Atan, Menyoh and Klinjau, the Telen to the north. In Block V Chuck and Levings observed alluvial mining operations and hypothesized that the gold was shedding northward, off a so-called intrusive.

The Westralian crew found abandoned gold-sluicing operations, where the Dayak had washed surface muck through sluice boxes and then patiently panned to retrieve the gold. Active sluicing operations were still ongoing at the base of the property and a kilometre to the north. At the southern site, workers had cut a massive sluicing operation into a ridge, levelling trees and clearing the land. This was serious business and far more industrious than the tarpaulin-covered riverside set-ups that the villagers would sporadically construct. There was every indication that there was a gold-mineralized system at Busang.

Chuck and Levings theorized that what they had come upon in Block V was an intrusive complex. The rock was brecciated, further advancing the belief that the rock was mineralized. The duo established a new field camp adjacent to a spit of a creek called Busang. Henceforth, the gold pursuit would be called the Busang Prospect. Jerry-built shacks became the temporary homes for site workers. The life they would lead there would be spartan as they commenced the age-old geological contest: man against nature.

The surface sampling at site was encouraging. Assay tests returned values of between 6.6 and 27.3 grams of gold per tonne. Chuck and

Levings suspected that the gold mineralization ran southward, down the eastern boundary of Block V. A target zone for the drilling was set 2.5 kilometres from the active alluvial operations.

Before the operators commenced the drilling program, another Australian outfit, Montague Gold NL, struck a deal with Westralian to earn the right to "farm into" the property, in other words, to take an equity interest in exchange for funding the exploration effort. In this, Montague worked through a private subsidiary, Montague Pacific. Westralian, in turn, held a majority stake in Montague. Graeme Chuck thence moved officially to Montague as exploration manager, with a US$600,000 budget to plumb the depths of Busang.

In the spring of 1989, a company called Mintech started the drills turning at Busang, nineteen holes in all, pulling just shy of 1,500 metres of core. The core was scrupulously split, lengthwise; samples from one half were shipped to an assay lab where they would be crushed and tested using the fire assay method.

The site was Montague's prime exploration project. All but two of the drill holes intersected gold zones. In hole one, or BUD-1, a five-metre section assayed 4.29 grams per tonne of gold. In BUD-3, a one-metre piece assayed 6.82, the highest assay in the nineteen-hole program. But the intersections were all short—there was no great run of gold through the core. The gold was deemed to be nuggety, as a way of explaining why one sample taken from a metre of drill core could produce impressive gold, while another could be virtually barren.

Still, the project might have been sellable. And Montague, drill results in hand, certainly tried. The Australians were pitched: CRA, Rio Tinto, BHP (Broken Hill Proprietary) were all approached, as was PT Ingold. But investors had lost interest in Indonesia after the crash, and with no funding prospects, the site was shut down late in 1989. The crew left behind a pile of discarded core splits.

PT WAM sat on Montague's books with a smattering of other COWs: Gunung Bijih in Irian Jaya; two others in Kalimantan. The company was eager to farm the things out. Indonesia was dead.

In 1991, geologist Ian Wollff wrote up a field report for one inquiring outfit, the Marunda Group. The Busang area, he wrote, "shows encouraging signs of high level epithermal alteration, along with panned silvery gold on its steep slopes." Small-scale gold panning, he noted, was active over a large area. Wollff inspected the discarded core at the abandoned Busang camp site. He noted the local mining area, one kilometre downstream. Had the gold been shed from Busang? Or was there an undiscovered epithermal source? Wollff was more interested in prospects for alluvial dredging. The hard-rock potential of Busang, he concluded, "requires an assessment of all drill and mapping data before conclusion can be reached satisfactorily. Some potential may exist for other epithermal targets."

In January 1992, Willy McLucas, a Scottish fund manager, took over Montague, replacing Warren Beckwith. McLucas's fund group, Waverley Management, had been buying up shares in Montague's parent, Westralian, until Beckwith was out and McLucas was in.

McLucas immediately refocused the Montague portfolio of mineral prospects, claiming as its chief interest a group of mineral prospects in Central Alaska, properties known as the Doyon Lands. According to Montague reports, Doyon held the promise of everything from small-lode gold finds to large base metal prospects. Kalimantan, in contrast, held little appeal for McLucas. In the company's Indonesian portfolio, the Gunung Bijih prospect in Irian Jaya took precedence. Muara Atan was dismissively lumped in with the two other less-interesting COW areas in Kalimantan. Precisely what interest Montague held in Muara Atan appears to shift. Reports have the company with a 90 percent interest, then an 80 percent interest. At one point the interest is qualified as "reducing to 60%," though there is no explanation as to when and under what terms this would take place. While the Australian records appeared muddled, one aspect of the Muara Atan tenure was clear: the COW approved in December 1987 had been set to expire in December 1991. PT WAM applied for, and was granted, a two-year extension. Willy McLucas had twenty-four months to offload the PT WAM COW if he wanted to make any money on the deal.

The fund manager turned to John Felderhof. Felderhof was a talker, a believer. The Ok Tedi fame had stayed with him, even through his down days when he was begging money and favours from friends past and present in Jakarta. The discovery gave Felderhof credibility still, and he could accurately claim in the company of interested purchasers that he had a more than passing acquaintance with Kalimantan and its geological hopes.

Felderhof in turn hired Mike de Guzman, who was working then for a geological consulting firm called PT Surya Veneutasakti. The proposition was to get de Guzman to make a site visit, probably eye-ball those split discards, draw some fresh surface samples, walk the property, figure out how to sell it.

November 1992. Where were all these riches that Indonesia had promised? At thirty-five years of age, with a scattershot résumé and no great discovery to his credit, about all Michael de Guzman had to show for his adventure was a recurring familiarity with malaria and the repeated heaving vomiting that came with it. Can't sleep. Can't think straight.

There was Genie to support. And Tess back home with the six children. Hunamas and Minindo had both been busts. And Pelsart—what a fine escapade that had been.

Now there was Busang. What the hell was that about? Yet another gold prospect, 58,000 hectares of low-lying jungle brush. Still . . .

Michael de Guzman headed out on the Mahakam River, bound for Busang. He would trek for 32 kilometres, accessing the site through a local company's timber road. For four days he conducted his survey. Day-long rains. He studied the drilled horizon. He perused the previously-arrived-at data. He retrieved six surface samples with the plan to have them assayed.

He said he then spent three days making representations to local mining offices in the town of Banjar Baru and the city of Samarinda. Bre-X would later say that a "three months [*sic*] detailed data consolidation and review was conducted," though this seems unlikely.

On December 8, the day after his return from Busang, de Guzman faxed a memo to David Hedderwick in Australia. Hedderwick was acting on behalf of Montague. "Surface impressions confirm favorable features related to gold mineralization," he wrote. "Five (5) altered—weathered rock and soil chip samples and one (1) pan concentrate . . . was collected at Busang Prospect. Visible fine-grained hypogene gold observed at the concentrate." The surface samples were taken from the area surrounding the "collars" of the drill holes sunk by Montague. The pan sample came from rejects from Montague's fourth drill hole, which de Guzman crushed by hand and panned. "Fine grains of visible gold observed," he said to Hedderwick. All the samples were assayed at Indo Analisa Laboratorium in Balikpapan, known in the industry as Indo Assay. The lab was a well-respected outfit run by an Australian named John Irvin, who had done the test work for Montague.

De Guzman said follow-up field work was "*necessary*": "to upgrade the geological viability of the cow in preparation for a Joint Venture or Farm-Out of this concession to other parties." The follow-up, he said, would take two or three months and would cost, he expected, us$40,000. For an additional ten grand, de Guzman said, a small drill could be got to drill four eighty-metre holes.

"In summary, the Muara Atan cow potential should not be focused mainly at Busang Prospect," de Guzman said. Busang was but one of three similar zones, he said, in what he identified as a "Maar-Diatreme geological environment." He saw implications of "economic viability" in other areas of the cow, specifically Block II, which abutted the headwaters of the Menyoh River, and Block VI, which sat to the southwest of the area zeroed in on by Chuck and Levings.

De Guzman compared the geological environment to that of Acupan, and he attached a copy of the presentation he had given at

Melbourne, which itself had been spun from the presentation he had given at the Pines Hotel in Baguio, 1977. An accompanying diagram illustrated the diatreme breccia at Acupan, and the G.W. orebodies, as they were called, named after Grover Whitney de l'Mari. The implication was clear. De Guzman had seen something very like this before, and it was one of the longest-lived mine producers in the Philippines. Surely that would help either revive Montague's interest or reinforce the project's saleability. Those who did not know de Guzman would have missed the more subtle message. He had been deprived of the kudos that would have been sent his way had Benguet mined the mineralized extensions he had discovered at Acupan. Busang offered an opportunity to earn the worldwide recognition that he thought he deserved.

In his Busang analysis, de Guzman audaciously gave resource estimates for both surface and underground mining, depth, tonnage and gold content, with a "mineability confidence factor" in the first instance of 40 percent and in the latter 20 percent. He estimated the total resource at 20 million tonnes of more than two grams per tonne gold content.

The numbers were an extrapolation of Montague's work. Realization of the potential, de Guzman conceded, was dependent upon the rate and scope of exploration activities. Even with that caveat, de Guzman's brazen expectations for the overall mineability of the project were outrageously beyond the standards of the industry.

There was just one year remaining in the exploration period of the Busang COW. Whoever took on the property had until December 1993 to make a "discovery" at Busang. Otherwise, the COW would lapse, and the property would return to the database of the Department of Mines in Jakarta. Montague went on to report de Guzman's findings in its quarterly report.

In a more comprehensive report filed later, de Guzman says the intensive exploration work program was scheduled to commence in January 1993. "In-depth laboratory studies and testworks have to be initiated to establish the detailed features and characterization of the mineralization and establish deposit type with respect to metallurgical parameters." De Guzman budgeted $2.7 million for work to cover four blocks of land, the majority of which was to be devoted to Block V. He carefully detailed a breakdown of costs. Forty-eight trips by speedboat at US$200 per trip. $28,000 in helicopter time. "Camp facilities and maintenance and hygienics": $50,000. "Government liason [sic] and representation": $10,000. It certainly sounds as though de Guzman was hoping that this would be his meal ticket for the next little while. And he had a theory: "The over-all geologic environment of Muara Atan and its immediate vicinity manifests a Maar-Diatreme setting"—citing again the Acupan comparison.

Apparently McLucas had other ideas. Why should Montague throw more money at Busang? It was not worth it, not until a partner was found to "farm in" to the property, carrying Montague along for a small percentage.

There was, however, a fish on the hook, and his name was David Walsh. On April 25, John Felderhof wrote to Hedderwick, informing him that he had a potential buyer lined up. He urged Hedderwick to set McLucas's financial terms while Walsh's interest was still high.

Felderhof figured he had found a well-placed financier in Walsh. Walsh, who knew nothing about the dire financial straits that Felderhof had so recently been mired in, in turn probably thought he had found something more than a tropical bum in Felderhof.

On May 3, Walsh faxed Felderhof asking him to proceed with arrangements to purchase the Muara Atan COW. The next day, Felderhof faxed Hedderwick: "I strongly suggest that you accept US$80,000 as the COW is not in good standing and it will take some work to convince the mines department that serious work will soon commence. There is a real danger you will lose the COW." Felderhof was right. The COW had been extended, but time was running out, and the Department of Mines liked to see work progress at a steady pace under such title. This was not an exploration permit, not a SIPP, with which the tenant can do only superficial site work. Under a COW, the Indonesian Department of Mines expected to see full-bore exploration. Deep drilling. The delineation of an orebody.

Hedderwick faxed Walsh, confirming that he was "prepared to accept your offer of US$80,000 for 80% of PT Westralian Atan Minerals with Montague retaining a free carried 10% to bankable feasibility." It was standard mining-speak. Montague got to stay involved in the project, for free, up to and until a mine was deemed feasible on the basis of defined ore reserves. In a later corporate report Montague stated that it had given an "option over the shares held in PT Westralian Atan Minerals for the period of twelve months for the sum of US$80,000 to a Canadian company, should the Canadian company exercise their options the shares will be transferred for US$100."

As far as David Walsh was concerned, Felderhof was in charge of Indonesian operations. It was Felderhof who was to tie up the transfer of title, deal with the government, hire the workers. In turn, Felderhof committed to trips to North America every month or so, to sell investors on Busang, to weave the tale of the jungle struggle for gold.

Thousands of kilometres away, across an ocean and fifteen time zones, the beer was very, very cold. It was cold at Hy's, and at Caesars which would later become the Three Greenhorns. It was even cold at the bar in Smitty's Restaurant & Lounge in Market Mall.

These were the places where David Walsh lived when he was not in his basement. And he was often joined by Barry Tannock. Tannock had made a career working for Shell Canada. In due course, he should have retired in that fine house in Calgary's Pump Hill that he shared with his wife, Marilyn, and his two boys, John and David.

Instead Tannock had left Shell, and some of the days that followed were as threadbare as Walsh's. But neither the threat of insolvency nor the prospect of bank foreclosure deterred David Walsh and Barry Tannock from heading out for dinner and drinks. Mostly drinks.

Post Shell, Tannock had started working the junior mining gambit. Hooking up with his cousin, Stan Hawkins, he was sussing out a prospect in Casa Berardi, in the bushland of northwestern Quebec. Tannock even shipped his son John out there for a summer of working like a dog, riding on the back of a drill platform, crashing through the forest, sampling, slinging ore bags. The bosses would helicopter a couple of investors in from time to time, keep them snorkelling drunk in their tents, then ship them out again.

Tannock drove a '76 Chevy Impala in a muted shade of puke green, the hood of which presented a smooth expanse so vast it looked as though it could host a hockey playoff. He was arrogant, smart, and knew how to make a market. During the day. When he was not immersed in share swings he could get ragingly drunk. He would stumble down the basement stairs, to where his sons would be playing Atari, and blindly pee into the bookcase. The family was utterly and completely broken when, on December 23, 1983, David Tannock killed himself in that fine house. It seemed as though nothing would ever go right again.

Barry Tannock hooked up with Walsh on a company called Ayrex. In February 1986 it went public on the Alberta Stock Exchange. Ayrex promised platinum and palladium in its Ungava property, gold at Casa Berardi.

Together Walsh and Tannock mastered the fine art of the "promote:" find a small, eager group of investors, ones who won't mind being tapped time and time again. Get at least one broker on side. And try to find a favourable analyst who will publish timely and compelling commentary on the latest opportunity.

The pair drifted apart, then came back together in the summer of 1992. Walsh needed someone to help promote Bre-X. Tannock would do.

Tannock worked out of the kitchen at Varbay place. The Walshes took over the dining room. The objective was to push the stock. Tannock established a computerized contact system, a master list of investors. Gradually, his system grew more sophisticated. The list grew longer, was cross-referenced and ranked brokers and investors alike.

Tannock kept running diamond information to investors, though it was the excitement of Dia Met, primarily, that he was reporting. He liked to throw in general, though tantalizing, tidbits. "Large fancy pink diamonds—the top of the line—have auctioned as high as $us300,000 per carat." This had precisely nothing to do with Bre-X, which had made no diamond discoveries. Tannock ran advertisements in *The Bull & Bear*, a tip sheet based in Longwood, Florida, to rouse investor interest. An "article" in *The Bull* said Bre-X appeared to have been overlooked in the diamond euphoria. "A consulting geologist to Bre-X, Mr. Kevin Waddell, president of Willow-Q Explorations Ltd. suggests perhaps a new cluster of [kimberlite] pipes is in the Bre-X vicinity." Someone had started a rumour that a "g-10" garnet had been found on the property. Garnets are common indicator minerals for diamonds. It seemed not to matter what the rumours were. Investors did not bite.

The tipster system had potential, but the winnings were small. In May 1993, 23,000 Bre-X shares were sold at an average price of 51 cents, for proceeds of $11,790. Get rich quick it was not.

And David Walsh could not even get a credit card, which might explain why he took Sean to Jakarta that spring; Sean took along his own American Express card.

On May 6, Barry Tannock issued a press release, dateline Calgary, Alberta. Bre-X Minerals Ltd. is pleased to report that it has entered the Pacific "Rim of Fire" as a potential gold and base-metal miner. He gave the spiel about the volcanic setting. In a nice touch, Tannock assumed the role of reporter. "In his first interview since returning from Jakarta, Indonesia, Bre-X president, David G. Walsh, stated: 'We have targetted Indonesia which is particularly attractive by virtue of its geological setting, a favorable investment climate, and political stability.'" Walsh went on to say in this "interview" that Bre-X had found just the man to spearhead these efforts, one John Felderhof, co-discoverer of the Ok

Tedi mine, who is "also credited with the discovery of four mineral properties in Indonesia of which one is in production, two scheduled to go into production and one at the feasibility stage." Tannock was building up a broadcast fax line. He wanted to ensure that every interested party received the critical corporate information instantaneously.

Felderhof, meanwhile, had picked his team of geologists, though they went unnamed in the release. A separate "fact sheet" identified Felderhof's "hand-picked" geological team: Umar Olii, Mike de Guzman and John Nassey.

It took a great deal of haggling between Walsh and Felderhof, but Felderhof finally secured a five-year employment contract with a net salary of $60,000 per annum, and an agreement to pay him $500,000 should his services be terminated, or should there be a change in company control. Michael de Guzman would be paid $3,400 per month.

The Walsh press release described the prospect as a "deposit," which it was not, the presumed gold resource as "reserves," which they were not, and said that drilling on the property by the previous tenant had yielded numerous intersections of more than two grams of gold per tonne, which was a lie. It also projected the potential of the property at 20 million tonnes at more than 2 grams per tonne of gold, which was absurd, with mining and processing costs of US$155 an ounce. Everything Walsh signed off on ran counter to industry practices. The discovery of mineralization, for example, should be stated as a "resource." Only when the orebody has been defined— that is, the mineable scope of the deposit has been determined—do credible companies release "reserve" figures, usually stated in three categories: proven (the stuff the company knows it can recover); probable (the stuff it stands a good chance of retrieving); and possible. Only then does the project become a deposit, and only then do recovery costs come into focus.

Based on all of the above, Bre-X breezily touted a real live gold mine with net annual after-tax cash flow of $10 million. At the time of writing, Bre-X had yet to retrieve even a single surface sample from

Busang. Its projections and elaborations were a crock. In predicting a million-ounce gold mine at a minimum, it was promising, without so much as setting foot on the property, what in the minds of most mining analysts would be a darned good sized gold mine.

A subsequent Bre-X report referred to how "important" it was in its Indonesian operations to have a partner there, and that "Adam Tobin [sic]," a "prominent businessman in Jakarta," had agreed to be Bre-X's domestic partner. "This association will greatly assist in dealing with the government and acquiring mineral properties." That would have been news to Tobing, who, according to Umar Olii, took a pass on Bre-X.

Bre-X was still a lousy 49-cent stock. True, 49 cents was better than 6 cents, the territory the stock had visited not all that long ago. But now David Walsh had John Felderhof on the line from Jakarta saying he had no money in the till and a quarter million in payables. Send more money.

He did. In the early going, the company kept afloat by having Bresea buy Bre-X shares. "Bresea would sell Bre-X shares in the open market," explains Tannock. "Bresea would advance funds to Bre-X and periodically, at an advantageous time, take a private placement of Bre-X shares with warrants attached. For example: Bresea sells a share for $1 in the market. Bresea privately buys a share of Bre-X from Bre-X for $1 and also has the right, by means of a warrant, to buy another share for $1.20. Sort of perpetual motion."

For the six months that ended on May 31, 1993, Bre-X's cash position was $249. Not bad. The year previous it had been $8. In mid-June, the Calgary Herald ran a story called the "Glitter Gamblers," in which Waddell, Tannock and Walsh are photographed staring at a map of Kalimantan. "I'm looking for the bucket of gold at the end of the rainbow," Walsh told the reporter.

Felderhof was general manager of the gold search, and as such made all management decisions regarding the Indonesian operations. Or at least that is what he would say in an affidavit years later. "I have undertaken the 'hands on' management of all of Bre-X's Indonesian operations. I have been the person who has made all decisions regarding which further properties to apply for and invest in, who our joint venture partners were to be, what surveys, exploration and development should be undertaken, what expenditures should be made and what information should be acquired and disseminated." He would go so far as to say he "did not permit others to be involved in the management of Indonesian operations."

In June, Felderhof flew to Vancouver and made a presentation to brokers there. Andrew Muir of Pacific International was present. Yorkton Securities' Doug Leishman. None of those gathered had ever heard of John Felderhof. Walsh liked to say they did not know where Indonesia was either, which was his attempt to dismiss witheringly the analysts' lack of interest. Felderhof pitched this balanced portfolio of properties, as he saw it. Fact was, no house wanted to hold David Walsh's stock. The competition for speculative money was fierce. There were far better punts than Walsh's.

There was no money in the company. Walsh had 512,000 stock options, exercisable at between 8 and 20 cents, held by himself and Jeannette. Walsh asked for, and got, the approval of the Alberta Securities Commission to increase the exercise price to 40 cents. Walsh exercised his options for a net of $200,000. (He would later say that $80,000 of that was used to buy the option on the Central Zone.)

Bre-X had $70,000 in the kitty with which to begin the exploration of Busang. A sad little bit of money, when the cost of drilling a single hole, if all goes well and the hole is a clean drill, can run to $50,000. Walsh and Tannock tried to get an investment banker to underwrite a Bre-X issue, but no one would touch it. So Walsh found himself going back to the same people who rode with him on the Louisiana oil and gas proposition, and on the diamond play in the Northwest Territories. Bre-X had never come close to "commercial values," as Walsh politely termed it.

The company announced that on July 15, Bre-X had opened an

office in Jakarta. Well, not exactly. John Felderhof was still working out of Adam Tobing's digs. Nevertheless, life was looking up. But the Bre-X boys had a tight time-line in which to make good on their promise of confirming a couple million ounces of gold at Busang. In outlining the work program to investors, Felderhof stated that field activities would start August 1, that the site would be mapped and sampled, that six or seven holes would be drilled, and that "should this diamond drill program be successful, the company will have established drill indicated reserves and will then proceed on a major definition diamond drilling program in early 1994." Again, the time-line was dictated by the limited life of the COW that the geologists were working under. Felderhof and de Guzman had just five months to make Busang real.

THE DREAMS OF MEN

THE OCHRE GROUND IS LIKE clay, and when it is wet, which it often is, it is as slick as ice and can suck the boots right off your feet.

The monkeys screech. Such beautiful butterflies. Do not let them land on your arm for they will start to lunch. Scorpions. Fifteen-centimetre moths. Two-metre lizards. Pigs standing waist high. Pythons slithering, six metres long. Orangutans with feet as big as a grown man's. Poisonous snakes, leaping three metres from the trees. The duri vine, a thin tendril with a garotte's potential to maim, is camouflaged by the comely, fan-shaped leaves that grow upon it. A driller lost part of a hand to the vine once.

It is August 1993. Umar Olii is headed for this place, now familiarly know in the geological community as Busang. Umar knows the territory and what is expected of him. The pageantry of nature is commonplace, even comforting. He has Zufrein to keep him company, another Indonesian geologist whom Umar does not know well. About his neck Umar wears a hand lens, a geologist's prize possession, metal-rimmed, smaller than a quarter, which he can tuck into his eye socket to peruse pieces of rock, as a gemologist would a precious stone.

Base camp is just off the Busang spit-of-a-river, by a bulldozer road that runs off the main timber road thirty-three kilometres to the east. Umar's task is to survey the area and retrieve surface samples. Perhaps some would see drudgery in the task; others, like Umar, see it differently. Man and nature. Freedom and self-governance. He believes he can take his time. John Felderhof has given him this assignment. There seems to be no urgency. Felderhof has suggested that Umar take two months to carry out this part of the project. Umar supposes he would not need so much time. A month might be sufficient.

The Department of Mines map Umar has with him shows an area perhaps fifteen kilometres wide at the top, stretching to perhaps twenty-five just below its middle, then narrowing again. The length of the area runs approximately twenty-five kilometres. It is the same block that Chuck and Levings assessed for Montague, and which Michael de Guzman analysed not a year earlier.

On his map Umar sketches rough shapes, ovoids of perhaps a kilometre in diameter. Using a code, he marks the presence of mercury found in stream sediments. He marks these high on the block, north of the Menyon River. He draws smaller, connecting ovoids indicating where mercury is found in the soil alone. To the south is the Atan River and the town of Mekar Baru. The Busang is a tributary of the Atan, which in turn is a tributary of the Kelinjan, which springs from the upper part of the Mahakam tributaries. To the southwest of Mekar Baru, Umar sketches a large area, crossing it with straight lines, affixing "au" to the legend—the chemical symbol for gold. Gold in pan concentrates is plentiful here. Umar sketches its presence. There are many locals panning in the area, setting their tarpaulins by the riverside, migrating to this hobby for a brief time, when there is no work to do elsewhere. Even amateurs would not be surprised to find gold in their pans.

For Umar, geology is not simply a science. It is an art, an amalgam of the concrete and the ephemeral. The mystery of the unknown.

Busang looks like an exciting prospect. He studies the brecciated rock, knowing that breccias are a good trap for mineralization. The Aussies found their gold here, smatterings of it. De Guzman's dramatic extrapolation, if it proves to be accurate, would transform this ground into a million-ounce gold mine. A million ounces. Mines in the million- to five-million-ounce category are considered large. Mines larger than that are considered rare. Anything above twenty million ounces is deemed not only rare, but a monster deposit.

Umar can see a future for himself here. All is going well. Better than planned. He makes a traverse to the southeast, investigating, wondering if de Guzman's casting of this gold-bearing structure might trend in that direction. He does not see any indication that it does. He theorizes that Busang is a small, contained target, the Central Zone. A company called Magnum Minerals had held part of this territory to the east. But Magnum geologists remarked to Montague representatives that there was nothing there to offer much encouragement. The gold values were lower than those that had been recorded by Montague.

Umar meticulously bags his surface samples, rock chips taken from an outcrop, which appear to signal the gold mineralization. He labels each with BS000 and a specific number. He ships the first fifty to Indo Assay in Balikpapan. Umar signs the dispatch sheet, recording the corporate sender as PT Westralian Atan Minerals.

On August 27 the samples arrived at the Indo Assay office. Umar requested that the lab analyse the fifty-gram samples by fire assay, which the laboratory did, testing for gold, copper, silver, mercury, lead and zinc.

The previous month, John Felderhof had produced his first "overview" of the Bre-X holdings in Indonesia. "Bre-X's selective acquisition programme has resulted in a portfolio of high quality mineral projects within favourable geological mineralized belts for large tonnage open pittable resource," he wrote. The company's "portfolio," he declared, "consisting of diamonds, gold and copper, is appropriately balanced and are extremely attractive both from mining and financial considerations."

Felderhof sounded like a Bay Street investment fund manager who might, within a single resource fund, balance an investment in a high-risk junior exploration company with the stability of a mining company long in production. To suggest that Bre-X's various virgin prospects provided any sort of asset balance was simply comical. Felderhof in his reports sounded near-professorial: "I expect the price of gold to remain within US$380-400 range until mid 1994 before there be another upward trend." So now he was a gold price prognosticator, too—an expert on global events.

David Walsh and Barry Tannock immediately set to work pumping out press releases on the "Rim of Fire" from David Walsh's "office." This Rim-of-Fire business had such a nice ring—a volcanic arc bursting with gold in countries many investors had only dreamed of. Walsh, too, adopted a certain air of authority in his writings. It was the opinion of "your management," he said, that gold, then trading in the area of $370 an ounce, and copper, at 75 cents a pound, were at or near bottom. Walsh did not bother to share with shareholders why he thought this was so.

Bre-X was in the business of touting properties, not propagating economic theory, and it now had two prospects: Busang, or the Muara Atan prospect, and Taware Valley, on Sangihe Island in North Sulawesi. The island is 225 kilometres north of Manado, the capital of North Sulawesi. The company was also in negotiations for a third property, the Sable prospect, in North Sumatra.

Taware had been Waddell's top pick, and in the early Bre-X paperwork, it carries more weight than Busang. In mid-August, in another "interview," David Walsh proclaimed that a "mirror image of the Taware Valley prospect is the Kingking porphyry copper-gold deposit in Davao, Mindanoa, Philippines which has drilled reserves of 105 million tons at the main ore body containing 0.55% Cu and

0.75 g./tonne Au and is being brought into production at present."
By "Mindanoa" he meant Mindanao, but at least he spelled "Philippines" correctly this time. Describing a deposit as porphyry might
catch an investor's eye. Such deposits, if they truly are deposits, are
often huge in volume, mined at surface as open pits, from which hundreds of thousands of tonnes of rock are excavated daily. "Porphyry"
denotes the rock type, often created by a volcanic eruption, in which
magma, or molten rock, pregnant with minerals, is shot to surface.
Most porphyries are exploited for copper; gold is often a byproduct
in copper porphyries.

As for Busang, it was compared to Benguet's Acupan mine, which,
safe to say, few would have heard of. Michael de Guzman had not yet
been introduced to shareholders, yet his influence was already much
in evidence.

Walsh would repeatedly refer to the extrapolation of the drilling
of Montague's nineteen holes as an exercise carried out by company
personnel. This was not precisely the case, for the reassessment
exercise had occurred under the previous title-holder, before Walsh
had ever heard of Busang. "Visible fine grained gold was observed
in the concentrate," he said, referring to a sample taken by de Guzman in his 1992 trip, again pre-Bre-X. Umar Olii had not yet arrived
on site.

As Felderhof and Walsh primed the share pump, the media started
to get its first sniffs of Bre-X. On August 9, *The Northern Miner*
reported on the company's acquisition of an 80 percent working interest in Busang. "The sampling, coupled with a reinterpretation of
existing data . . . suggests the property could contain about 20 million
tonnes at two grams gold per tonne, mineable by open pit. To substantiate the reserves, Bre-X is planning geological mapping and sampling . . ." The wording was sloppy. There was the presumption of
reserves again, though no such thing had been proved. Other mining
companies might refer to their reserves in three categories: measured,
indicated and inferred (equivalent to proven, probable and possible).

The "measured" category being that which the company had assessed after defining the property, having drilled the ground in closely spaced holes (twenty-five metre spacing is industry practice) and having carried out a complex series of calculations. Umar Olii had not even set foot on Busang to retrieve rock chips.

Sometime in early September, John Felderhof flew to Kalimantan. On the seventh, he personally delivered the second batch of Busang samples to Indo Assay, where it was recorded that they were hand-delivered. On the ninth, the assay results from the first set of samples were faxed to him in Jakarta.

There was nothing to surprise the assayers at Indo Assay. The samples showed some interesting levels of gold, as they had for the previous tenant, Montague. Indo Assay had done the lab work for Montague, and there had been gold values in those samples and in the subsequent drilling. In the files at Indo Assay, Felderhof's name appears, as does that of Umar Olii. There is no mention of Mike de Guzman or his number two, Cesar Puspos.

To Umar, it appeared that the Busang survey program would take another few days. There were no telephones on site, no disturbances save for that made by the wildlife. He had no idea that twelve thousand kilometres away the phones were ringing.

David Walsh's phone rang at Varbay Place on August 9. It was Paul Kavanagh on the line, calling from Toronto. Kavanagh was vice-president of exploration at Barrick Gold Corp., a very big, very mighty gold-mining concern. Kavanagh had spotted the *Northern Miner* piece, the Bre-X self-promotional press release. He was interested, and in his position he was well placed to pursue junior mining prospects.

Kavanagh arrived at Barrick in 1993, after holding down a series of highly placed jobs at major mining companies. Kavanagh had a Ph.D. from Princeton and was seen in the industry as a stellar geologist. But he had been hobbled by the decree of Peter Munk, Barrick's founder and leader, that the company find growth in the gold-mining industry at home, in North America. However, in early December 1995, Munk announced that Barrick had had a change of heart. Now, he said, he wanted to be the biggest gold miner on the planet, and he did not seem to care where the gold might be found. The company arranged a US$1-billion line of credit with the Royal Bank of Canada to advance the new strategy. For a geologist like Kavanagh, the new corporate strategy was a gift, if a short-lived one. He was two years away from retirement. What were the odds that something sexy would happen before then?

Kavanagh was widely admired for his geological expertise and the analytical rigour he brought to the profession. His licence plate read "ROC DOC," and he had done well enough financially to live near to Paul Reichmann, when Olympia & York was still a stellar real estate play, in Toronto's upscale Forest Hill neighbourhood. But Kavanagh, gruff and arrogant, had a reputation for rubbing even admirers the wrong way.

During that first conversation, Walsh told Kavanagh that Bre-X was not yet seeking an association with a senior mining company. He said the company had just started drilling, by which he presumably meant the Taware property. He said the management team wanted to see some drill results before taking any partnership steps.

Days later, Walsh changed his mind. A breakfast meeting was set for August 20, to be held at the Royal York Hotel, the aged but still relatively stately railway hotel in downtown Toronto. Perhaps the thought of discussing the Indonesian prospects with someone with forty years in mineralogy to his name did not warm the heart of David Walsh. He took John Felderhof along. At that meeting, Walsh told Kavanagh that he would welcome a $200,000 investment from Barrick. Bre-X was cash poor. Barrick was the biggest gold-mining company in the country, and the continent, and one of the biggest in the world. Cash was not an issue.

Kavanagh was impressed by Felderhof, who was well-enough known in the geological brotherhood. His Ok Tedi work was widely

recognized, though most people had little knowledge of what Felderhof had been up to in the intervening years. His jungle days had added
an entrepreneurial edge to his reputation, and Kavanagh would likely
not have been aware of the weak validity of his claimed discoveries
in Indonesia. He appeared to be hard-working. And he was aggressive. To Kavanagh, this was a positive attribute.

Kavanagh reported to Allan Hill, who headed Barrick's exploration and development team. Hill was in charge of this new international expansion. Kavanagh recommended to Hill that Barrick
partner with Bre-X. For a mere $200,000, Kavanagh figured, Barrick
would gain a cheap entry to Indonesia. Felderhof later said he would
talk with his chief geologist, Mike de Guzman, about site visits to the
properties. Very shortly thereafter, Felderhof was headed back to
Jakarta, thence to Kalimantan.

In early September, Umar Olii saw five days of work ahead of him.
Then it would be back to Samarinda. His contact had been with John
Felderhof exclusively, but he could feel Michael de Guzman waiting
in the wings. He sensed that de Guzman would emerge as a key player.
But he had no idea it would happen so quickly.

It was quiet at the site that September day, the sun searing straight
overhead. Umar had begun his work much earlier, in the comfortable
pre-dawn hours. Suddenly, Michael de Guzman hove into view. He
had come upriver, then travelled to the site by the timber road. He
was attired in his favourite jungle wear, which included a funny floppy
hat that gave him the appearance of an explorer turned drag queen.
There was nothing humorous about his manner. De Guzman often
had the attitude of a man who did not much enjoy life.

Umar stayed quite quiet, not out of deference, but in keeping with
Indonesian sensitivity: to be polite even in the face of unpleasantness.
Which this was.

De Guzman did not have many words that day. He turned to Umar.
"I want you to stop work right now. There's some paperwork I want
you to attend to in Samarinda. Government matters."

De Guzman had made himself perfectly clear. He did not want Umar to have any association with the site work. To put a geologist onto paperwork hundreds of kilometres away was to put him out of business. Zufrein would last another month before de Guzman sacked him, too. Umar's brother, Tommy, was doing administrative work for the company, but that was in Samarinda, out of harm's way. From that point onward, the Busang camp would be ruled by Michael de Guzman and his right hand, Cesar Puspos. Tommy Olii disliked de Guzman enormously and would keep Umar apprised of the goings-on at Busang for a long time afterward.

De Guzman did not need Umar Olii. The geologists' sampling was a waste of time in his view. Rather, he wanted to get a drill rig hauled to site posthaste. There was little money. He would have to make do with inadequate machinery. At least initially. But that would be short-lived. He could feel the gold in the area. Just feel it. He expected to hit his dream target very quickly.

Mike de Guzman approved the proposed Barrick site visits. Paul Kavanagh intended to make the trip with Allan Hill, but Hill bailed, and Larry Kornze stepped in in his place. Kornze was not an expert on the Indonesian scene. None of the Barrick types was. But he had a stellar reputation as a geologist. Kornze, like Hill, had been integral in the development of Barrick's famed Goldstrike mine, a great gold canyon that Peter Munk had ordered dug along the Carlin Trend in the state of Nevada. Under Barrick president Bob Smith, Hill and Kornze had built Barrick's reputation as a world-class gold operator, almost solely on the basis of Goldstrike. They were top-class miners, and it was largely to their credit that the derision of skeptics, who would not believe Peter Munk, the entrepreneur with the roller-coaster past, had been ultimately overcome. The gold along the Carlin Trend was so fine-grained it was rarely visible to the naked eye. The rocks on the trend look like any old rock—a bit bleached, with a smattering of sulphides. Panners had passed the area over in the

1920s and '30s. Skeptics in the '80s initially misunderstood the Carlin geology as much as they underestimated Munk. Kornze had co-discovered the Betze deposit at Goldstrike, and it was named partly in his honour, the "ze" representing Kornze. When Betze was developed, it was an open-pit mine producing approximately two million ounces of gold annually.

As Barrick readied its posse, Bre-X went about the business of getting investors hooked. *The Bull & Bear*, the investor newsletter out of Florida, proved particularly suitable for this purpose. On September 2, an article appeared in the newsletter entitled "Indonesia: A Brief Mineral History and Outlook." Its author was John B. Felderhof, P. Geol. The piece offered a touch of politics, a taste of geology. Felderhof even threw in some average rainfall figures. Such template material would be recycled over and over again by Bre-X, as it acquainted the share-buying public with this place called Indonesia. In the original essay, Felderhof praises the contract of work system, declaring that a mine can be brought into production "without any additional interference." The last leg of the story takes a curious turn, with Felderhof, the author, suddenly turning into the interviewee, being asked for his stock picks in the Indonesian gold scene. His choices: Freeport-McMoRan and Bre-X.

There are pockets of penny mine promotion in the United States, and anyone who has ever attended a "gold show," in which a couple dozen juniors set up booths littered with pamphlets and rock samples, can understand why this is so. Troops of investors, many sporting grey hair and expensive sneakers and toting give-away bags stuffed with promotional material, wander through speeches on one gold company's prospects in Khazakstan; another's in Uzbekistan. The seekers represent a delicious prospect of their own: investment dollars.

There are myriad tales of penny mining outfits that have crapped out, and the flow of investors at gold shows would know this better than most. The North American public now is eager to invest in the market, and the media has pumped them full of buyer-beware advice.

So hungry for information are these investors that papers such as *The Bull & Bear* are in high demand. La Jolla Securities Corp., of Phoenix, Arizona, publishes another. One of the cardinal rules for cautious investors, if the term cautious can be applied at all given the high-risk nature of these baby equities, is Know Thy Management.

Outfits such as La Jolla addressed precisely these concerns. Les Reid, writing for La Jolla, was an early Bre-X follower, when the stock could be had for 35 cents a share. In the fall/winter newsletter, Reid, writing from "The Mining Desk" at La Jolla, introduced David Walsh, forty-eight, president of Bre-X Minerals. A past vice-president of a large Canadian brokerage. A past fund manager for a Canadian trust company. A founder or co-founder of three public companies. "Mr. Walsh's vision and courage, decisive and not easily discouraged, has brought the company to where it is today."

John Felderhof is introduced as an "upper echelon executive" with "five mines currently to his credit." "In addition to his technical prowess, he is said to have a remarkable 'feel for the ground.' Mr. Felderhof's role will not be restricted to identifying potential world-class mining properties. In his part of the world, contacts are extremely important. His prior experience with local governments in Indonesia will be invaluable." In a later report, in October, Reid would trumpet Felderhof's support crew: "Mr. Michael T. de Guzman, Dr. Jonathan M. Nassey and Mr. Umar Olii, all exceptionally well educated and experienced, are part of Bre-X's Indonesian team." But Umar Olii was long gone.

For La Jolla, the "bet" (their quotations) was that Bre-X was capable of finding one or more mines. That, said the company, "would imply a stock value in the $10 to $50 range." Major mining companies were interested. "One company has already sent two of its three top officers to look at the properties this past October. Reports are that they were most favourably impressed. Negotiations are currently underway with them and with others." Kornze was not an officer of Barrick, but Hill was. There were certainly no media reports of either Kornze's or Kavanagh's impression of any of the Bre-X properties. These "reports," therefore, must have been coming directly from Bre-X. La Jolla predicted that Walsh would strike an agreement with a joint venture partner soon. Walsh, meanwhile, was telling Barrick that other majors were keenly interested in joining forces.

La Jolla's conclusions were positively operatic. "*Enterprise*, that's what you have to call it. This daring leap by Bre-X Minerals into far-off Indonesia is no ordinary feat. No other small company has yet had the vision or the daring to do it. It is the type of drive and ambition that will pay off in the way that Placer Pacific has been so well rewarded for its jump into New Guinea, and Freeport-McMoRan, with its rich and productive Grasberg/Ertsberg complex in Indonesia."

Bre-X occasionally mentioned the ownership issue at Busang in its own early reports. In an internal overview of the company's operations, dated July, John Felderhof said the Muara Atan (Busang) contract of work was signed on December 21, 1987, between PT Westralian Atan Minerals and the Department of Mines. "Shareholders' interest in the Joint Venture company include 80% Westralian Resource Projects—Montaque Gold NL based in Perth, and 10% to production each to the Indonesian companies PT. Krueng Basui and PT. Krueng Taungah." Investors could surely pull themselves through the mangled composition. But how were they to know that "Montaque" was really a company called Montague, that "PT. Krueng Basui" was really PT Krueng Gasui. Bre-X said it had obtained the "right" that same month to acquire 80 percent from "Montaque Gold" for a nominal sum should Bre-X be successful in delineating a potential orebody.

The company was just getting going in Indonesia and already its ownership status was as clear as mud. The company issued a press release, dateline: Calgary, Alberta, July 19, 1993; 9:30 a.m. MDT: "Bre-X Minerals Ltd. is pleased to announce the successful acquisition of an 80% working interest in an advanced gold project in East Kalimantan." But was the seller Montague or Westralian? And was the 80 percent actually acquired, as stated here, or had Bre-X merely struck terms on the right to acquire the 80 percent? Bre-X's annual report offered this version: "The company purchased an option for US$80,000 to purchase 80% of the outstanding shares of PT Westralian Atan Minerals (PT WAM), at an exercise price of US$100."

The contractual relationships seemed sloppy from the get-go. In entering into this agreement, whatever it was, David Walsh took on two Indonesian partners he did not know. One was Jusuf Merukh, who had 10 percent. The other was Haji Syakerani, who had an equal share. The minority interests would, if standard practice were followed, expect their interest to be "free carried" to the production stage: that is, neither Merukh nor Syakerani would be expected to put up any capital. Over time the foreign party's interest, that is Bre-X's, would be reduced, thus allowing for the escalation of Indonesian national interests. Training programs for national workers would be required, as would the eventual introduction of Indonesian nationals into the management of the company.

Bre-X investors had no means to assess the validity of such statements. Merukh and the Australians had formed these companies in 1980 and 1981 respectively, as Indonesia was entering its gold boom. Merukh had turned the prospect of being the Indonesian partner for foreign mining interests into a veritable industry. The foreigners, compelled by law to find an Indonesian partner, had often found themselves sidling up to Merukh. But the crash of 1987 and the Minindo debacle had seen such enterprises fall dormant, as had WRPL's interest in Busang.

Years earlier, in 1986, Merukh had partnered with the Syakerani family in creating an Indonesian company called PT Sungai Atan Perdana. It was Merukh's sole company, PT Krueng Gasui, and the Syakerani company, in which Merukh had a minority interest, that, with WRPL, had secured the COW. The easiest way to follow the corporate alliances was to reduce all these operations to their initialisms. And so PT KG (Merukh) was in business with PT SAP (Syakerani) and the Australians (WRPL). PT KG + PT SAP + WRPL = COW. And the COW was still tenanted in name by PT Westralian Atan Minerals, or PT WAM.

One of the few elements of the Bre-X architecture that was crystal clear was that John Felderhof would be running the show "over there," while David Walsh held the fort at home in Calgary. Walsh made the statement that while Bre-X would be the operator of its exploration and development projects in Indonesia, the projects would be managed "under the supervision of Bre-X's General Manager–Indonesia Operations, John B. Felderhof, P. Geol."

Having dispensed with the impenetrable ownership business, the Bre-X team back in Calgary could return to more urgent matters: pushing the stock. Barry Tannock drove a stake through the heart of that wonderful diamond proposition. "On the Northwest Territories diamond front we are stalled," he said. "Kennecott has not initiated the program of ground geophysics and till sampling previously announced. We are seeking clarification." Indonesia was it. The hot thing.

Tannock busied himself with what was dubbed "Fax Facts," a grab-bag of voodoo prognostications that were faxed to Bre-X shareholders. "Gold is strong and diamonds are weak," he proclaimed. "Gold gives real promise of entering an extended bull phase." Tannock's idea of running through Bre-X's economic prospects consisted of comparing the Bre-X "projections" with Freeport-McMoRan's proven numbers. And so, Grasberg/Ertsberg tonnage was quoted as 6.8 million in 1988 and 20.8 million in 1992. Alongside these ran estimated tonnage for Taware—8 million ounces; and Busang—2 million ounces. Operating income for Taware: $94 million. For Busang: $20 million. Tannock would do up a page called "Bits and Pieces." "The sheer size of Indonesia is mind boggling," he told investors helpfully. "In general, the local climate is reasonably hospitable (e.g., doesn't get cold) and the overall business climate is very reasonable—tax regime, political stability and business orientation."

The intention was to widen the net, to draw in both individual investors and those who penned investor newsletters, such as Ted Carter, of Calgary. Since 1992 Carter has published *Carter's Choice Newsletter*. "I rarely trade on the Alberta Stock Exchange and usually recommend against it," said Carter that September. But, he added, Bre-X was peculiarly compelling. There was the Rim of Fire business, and Felderhof's presence. "His accomplishments include discovering four mineral properties in Indonesia.... I have taken a stock position in this company and perhaps there are some of you who may be interested as well."

Like any sales job, pushing a mineral property comes down to numbers: the more insiders pushing the stock, the greater the potential for hooking the fish, aka the investors, to the bait, aka Busang. Steve McAnulty, an erstwhile chum of Walsh's from the Midland Doherty days, reintroduced himself to his old pal, and before he knew it he too was working the phones at Varbay Place, talking up potential investors, talking up brokers.

The time-line for Busang was run by Felderhof, the man in the middle between the money in Calgary and the site guys, represented by de Guzman. In August, he was plotting the timing of the drill plan. The pressure was on. The COW was due to expire in December, and Felderhof had to get holes sunk and rock assayed, both to woo the markets (the Walsh end) and to satisfy the Department of Mines. "We better make sure the holes are well sited and come up with the expected results," he wrote in a project report. "Should the porphyry Cu-Au be positive [the presence of a copper-gold deposit be confirmed], Bre-X will have no trouble finding a partner as several international companies are looking for advanced porphyry targets."

The big news—that is, the drilling results—would be issued via press release and "Fax Facts." On October 7, Tannock announced that drilling had commenced at Busang, saying yet again that the objective was to delineate a 1-million-ounce resource. Taware, the company predicted, had two and a half times the potential of Busang. Throughout most of the fall announcements, it was drilled into the minds of investors that Taware was the bigger play. In the October 7 release, Tannock teased investors with this: "A ten day field trip by senior personnel, of one of the many major mining companies who have expressed an interest in our activities, commences October 15, 1993." This was not strictly cricket. Such early stage meetings are meant to be kept in confidence. But Bre-X had other interests. The stock had closed the month of September at 70 cents. Tannock in his "Fax Facts" said that a "successful mine at Busang" would imply a US$10 a share value to BXM. "The potential net to BXM of Taware is 2.5x that of Busang." There was much work to do to boost shares to that level. Teasing investors with the attentions being paid by a major mining company could only help.

Kavanagh liked what he saw at the site. He packed up some surface samples and, with Kornze, returned to Toronto at the end of October. He summarized the trip for Allan Hill and, in a memo dated October 28, recommended that Barrick make an investment in little Bre-X. "Bre-X has an excellent, motivated exploration team, very experienced in Indonesia, with a successful past record there. With meagre funding, Bre-X has already acquired, during only a few months, three exciting properties in Indonesia." Kavanagh noted Montague's work: "Some 19 former diamond drill holes yielded inconclusive results because of poor recovery and poor reproduction of assay results, indicative of coarse or spotty gold mineralization." Perhaps Kavanagh had been shown the assay sheets from Montague. Indo Assay's John Irvin had given de Guzman copies. Somehow he had convinced himself that Montague's unspectacular results might have been understated. If gold in a deposit is coarse, or nuggety, it will not be widely dispersed throughout the rock. Geologists liken the phenomenon to a raisin pudding: an intersection of core might hit a raisin, or it might not. Perhaps Montague missed the raisins. Perhaps the raisins were there.

At the end of the month, David Walsh said that "negotiations concerning joint venture possibilities continue with various major mining companies who have expressed an interest in our activities including one company whose senior personnel recently completed a ten-day field trip to the BXM properties."

Felderhof had retained a drilling outfit in Jakarta to start the site drilling. PT Drillinto Tiko had offices in the Cilandak Commercial Estate, an industrial complex on the outskirts of Jarkarta where many of the foreign mining outfits took office space. The company was one of a handful of well-known drilling outfits in the city. Not the top flight, but reputable.

In October, the first drill was pulled on site at Busang. Richard Galbraith, a big Aussie, was the first driller. Felderhof had requested a different drilling procedure. The previous owners had used the wet drilling method. If there's free gold, Felderhof said, water might flush it out, and the recovery would be poor. Galbraith had met with the Bre-X boys, specifically de Guzman, in Jakarta in the summer. He knew de Guzman from the Pelsart days and had drilled at Mirah. Busang looked like any other drill job.

It was not. The rig was antiquated, and as Galbraith and a group of Indonesians set to work, they had a devil of a time pulling clean core. It was slow, tedious labour—surely far too slow for David Walsh, anxiously awaiting the first hard news to fatten a Bre-X press release. The job of the drillers was to try to get the core out as cleanly as possible, lay it out in wooden trays, then hand it off to the geologists. The geos would then study the core, number and log it, creating a permanent record of what was drilled where and when and at what depth. As soon as the core was handed off by the drillers, it would become the geologists' charge.

Michael de Guzman was the chief geo, but he was supervising three properties. Cesar Puspos was initially assigned to Taware. On October 5, de Guzman instead named him senior geologist in charge of all field operations. Henceforth Cesar Puspos would spend most of his time at Busang. The twosome drew a third Filipino into this close relationship. Jerry Alo had taken up the job of consulting metallurgist to PT WAM that fall. Alo had started his career working as an assayer for the Manila Mining Corporation in the late 1960s. He had worked for a number of Filipino mining outfits for a decade and a half before suddenly moving to Tanzania in 1985 to work for a mining firm there. Three years later, he was chief metallurgist for PT Ara Tutut, part of the Minindo Web. From there he jumped to PT Westralian Atan Minerals.

Jerry Alo was practically standing over Galbraith's shoulder. Would've been standing on his head if he could have. Alo wanted to be very close to the drilling action. He quickly became the guy who more or less ran the camp, and he was helping to "spot" the drill holes, working up the plan for where they should be situated. That he was a metallurgist by training seemed of little interest.

It was a typically miserable site existence. The food was limited and dreadful—prawn crackers and tea. Galbraith lost eleven kilograms in nine weeks. The Indonesians were coming out with their trousers dropping off them. Tin upon tin of canned corned beef—that was the life. But the pay was good, and the foreign workers were supposed to be spelled off every six weeks.

As the core was hauled to base camp it was logged before one-metre pieces were cut, broken up with geo-picks, bagged and made ready for the trip downriver to Samarinda. The entire piece of cut core was sampled in this way. Industry practice is to split the core lengthwise and retain half the rock in a core library, but the Busang crew was instructed to adopt this alternative method. The whole core would be crushed at Samarinda. The gold was too coarse, too nuggety, to run the risk of splitting the core, they were told. What if all the raisins were in the other half of the split?

Cesar Puspos supervised the logging, then the bagging. The work was not going well. In November, de Guzman spent a day and a half on site, and he was not at all happy. The rig was a piece of crap, and with so little time to pull core and get the stuff assayed to keep the project alive, de Guzman did not need a glitch like this one. "Drill machine at site turned out to [be] LY-34!! Again a 'Big Shit.'. . . Even driller on site is complaining about this worn-out rig."

Galbraith sweated over the holes, under bright plastic tarps strung above the shaft to fend off the merciless sun. The weight dropped off him. Puspos, as custodian of the core, monitored its journey by river to Samarinda, and thence to Balikpapan. Galbraith made that trip with Puspos once. The sample bags of core were loaded on a truck as soon as they arrived at Samarinda. There were no pit stops.

The lab guys at Indo Assay put the core through its normal paces, crushing the rock in successive stages until very fine. "Fingers crossed," said de Guzman to Felderhof.

Fire assay is the oldest method of sampling the presence of gold in rock, and is still, by a wide measure, considered the definitive method for gold analysis. In fire assay, a sample of rock is crushed, thence ground, and "split" into a smaller sample. On average, 30 grams of the ground material is placed in a crucible, then mixed with various "fluxes," which, once the sample is fired, or smelted, in a furnace, will assist in the melting of the sample. The molten mass is poured into a mold. The lead in the mixture, which contains the gold and silver, sinks to the bottom of the mold. When cooled, this forms a "prill," or button, at the bottom of the mold. The prill is then fired in a furnace, the oxidization leaving behind a precious metal bead. The bead is then heated in nitric acid, which dissolves the silver. The final gold bead is weighed and the result is related back to the initial weight of the sample.

If the gold in the rock is characterized as "nuggety," a nugget or nuggets might be present in the sample, which would spike the assay results, or might be entirely absent, so that the assay sample would fail to be representative of the presumed orebody. The presence of nuggety gold would likely encourage a company to conduct both fire assay and cyanide leach test results on its rock samples.

BRH-1. Hole number one from Busang. Samples 0001 through 00016. The odd base-metal kick. The odd gram of gold. One sample that kicks to two grams. Very similar to the showings found by the previous tenant. BRH-2: anomalous base metals. Lead and zinc showings. Gold? Barely.

So where was this gold that Michael de Guzman had imagined? Where was the dream target? On November 15 he sent a memo to Felderhof: "Disappointment! No continuity. Unbelievable!" Memos from the time indicate an urgency to get information on the project's progress: "Will wait 12 noon info from Cesar Puspos for latest update."

Investors did not know Cesar Puspos. They had only just learned the name Michael de Guzman. At the end of October, in a report to shareholders, Walsh refers to Felderhof, his Ok Tedi success, and the "experienced team of four senior geologists" he had brought on board, "including Mike de Guzman co-discoverer of the large Dizon porphyry copper/gold deposit in San Marcelina, Central Luzon, Philippines." Perhaps it should have fallen to David Walsh, corporate overseer of these foreign activities, to ensure the veracity of the material he was releasing. Had he bothered, David Walsh could have learned in a five-minute phone call that Dizon was discovered in 1933, and that while reserves were later increased in the 1980s, de Guzman was at Acupan at the time. Co-discoverer? A straight lie.

The shortness of time was torquing up the stress levels. The next batch would come up gold rich, de Guzman was sure of it. On November 22, Indo Assay received the last samples from BRH-2. The project had just weeks left to live. The proving of a mineral discovery is a process that requires enormous patience. De Guzman had none. The results came back: Arsenic here and there. Lead. Zinc. Again, the odd kick to a gram of gold. Nothing dramatic.

There is a map, dated December 1993, compiled by Cesar Puspos and checked by Michael de Guzman. "Busang Prospect, Surface Gold Geochemistry," it says. Across an 800-metre area Puspos has sketched a line that swoops east to west across the entire area, nipping and tucking here and there, outlining what might look like a lake, with bays and inlets. Within this Puspos has drawn smaller shapes, many of them ovoids, that he has marked showing "0.5-1.0 g/tonne gold." Within these are smaller areas yet again, which are dotted, indicating more than one gram of gold per tonne. Small boxes are drawn outside this lake-like area, indicating the various surface sample results, running as high as 15.2 grams/tonne. Fifteen grams. Mike de Guzman would have been happy with a fraction of that. Instead he was facing, after two holes of a four-hole program, a dud prospect, a bust.

Hole three was straightforward drilling. No complications. At hole four, Galbraith stopped short. It was December 3. Mike de Guzman shut the drilling down at Busang. He was not happy with the rig; he was not content with the speed of progress. Galbraith, Puspos and a load of samples later left the site and made the river journey to Samarinda. It became Galbraith's job to find another rig in town. This one had to go.

Mike de Guzman would later say that Felderhof was putting the pressure on to shut down the project after the second hole, because the site seemed not to be prospective after all. Yet Walsh and Tannock were telling investors and tipsters that they hoped to conclude the Barrick deal by December 18. Expiry of the land title was just days away. In order to move beyond the exploration period, the company had to prove a discovery to advance to the next permit phase.

There are days missing. The samples from hole three and hole four did not arrive in Balikpapan until December 9. The submission sheets were signed by Cesar Puspos. Irvin was asked to fax the resulting data to Mike de Guzman in Jakarta. On December 11, Cesar Puspos sent a fax to Indo Assay, to John Irvin's attention. "Please take note of the following sample numbers where possibly visible gold was observed megascopically," he said. He referred specifically to 00264 and 00266 on the fourth hole.

Megascopic. Visible to the unaided eye. Suddenly the samples were exhibiting vastly different characteristics. In hole three, drilled about seventy metres from Montague's ninth hole, the gold started kicking as high as 10, while the lead and zinc and other metals were in keeping with previous results. Hole four was even better. Sample BRH-4 00264 graded 16.3. BRH-4 00266 graded 17.3—the equivalent of half an ounce of gold per ton. At $300 gold, that is $150 worth of the precious metal. Retrieval costs might be $7.50 a ton. Nice profit.

Indo Assay had observed the presence of coarse gold in the Montague samples, but nothing, nothing on this scale. John Irvin sent an acknowledging note to Bre-X: "I suspect there are some pretty large pieces of gold in the system."

Who would ever suspect its provenance? Would anyone ever wonder whether this was anything but nature's alchemy? A file was taken to a piece of gold, perhaps jewellery, methodically shaving off tiny, tight curlicues of the precious metal. A small deceit, perhaps. To sprinkle a shaving or two into the sample bags, to become crushed with the core.

Indo Assay noted the poor reproducibility of the results on samples three and four, echoing Paul Kavanagh's earlier comment. If the lab recorded a particularly high grade on a sample, they failed to reproduce that grade in a follow-up test. That supported the view that the gold was coarse gold, and not fine-grained.

The Dayak have not been here long at Mekar Baru. Fifteen years ago they migrated from the Malaysian border.

Houses on stilts have been washed grey, but other bungalows sport splashes of colour. Salin has set to work with his pan, not at the riverside but rather at what appears to be an outcrop. He has taken a tool that has the look of a shovel-head stuck at a right angle to a long hammer handle and carved the earth away. He has a makeshift pump drawing water to his miniature mine site, making a soup of ochre muck, which he swirls in his pan—stage one. Stage two is getting the concentrate to a finer and finer form.

Salin has a moustache and a goatee and is handsome. He is missing part of his forefinger and thumb on his left hand, cleaved at the knuckle. Still, he is a dexterous panner. The nuggets that emerge at last are irregular in shape, similar to seed pearls. They vary in size, resembling the Klondike-style bubblegum that children used to buy in cotton pouches. Salin is prolific. And he will sell his gold to anyone who comes by. Sometimes he finds large pieces of gold. Sometimes he uses a broker.

On December 14, Mike de Guzman informed Jonathan Nassey of the exciting gold showings. "Busang hit a 'Golden Pot' at hole 3, 4!" He also issued an inter-office memo, restricting site access and reaffirming his control over operations. The circle was tightening.

A Golden Pot. That had taken some ingenuity. The gold in hole three was not Mother Nature's work. Careful filings had been added. Possibly from a piece of jewellery. Finicky, slow work. Particularly when one wants to prove a gold mine. By hole number four the strategy had changed. Lovely rounded nuggets had been added to the core, placer gold, their edges softened by the rocking of water.

Michael de Guzman had failed to keep the dream alive by keeping a drill rig turning. He had failed to divine his motherlode. As time ran out, he had turned to desperate measures.

In the third week of December, David Walsh wrote to Alex Davidson, Barrick's senior vice-president of exploration, referring to a meeting three days earlier that had included Felderhof and Allan Hill. Walsh advised Davidson that Bre-X was in general agreement with the Barrick proposal: Munk's company would take up 500,000 Bre-X shares at $1.25. "We require your written offer by January 5, 1994, which is just prior to John returning to Indonesia," wrote Walsh. "The US$500,000.00 equivalent of Canadian dollar equity funding will be expended to continue drilling and exploration of our three properties: namely, Busang, Taware, and Sable, and to commence review of additional prospects which may have joint venture possibilities."

The following day, Davidson sent an internal memo to Hill. "Since the visit, Bre-X have been reporting success from both the drilling on Busang and the trenching and sampling on Sable," he said. Davidson cited the assay results from six samples from the third hole at Busang. "The use of selected private placements in certain junior companies [the Teck method] in return for down the line 'back-in' rights and rights of first refusal on future financings can be an effective way to gain exposure to targets in other areas for minimal exposure." Davidson recommended proceeding with the offer.

Over subsequent weeks, however, the offer was derailed. The particulars were not smoothing out. The Barrick offer initially suggested a split in the 65 to 75 range—in other words, that Barrick would take 75 percent of the venture should they decide to proceed down the road. Bre-X was prepared to cede to Barrick as much as 70 percent, but then Barrick did an about-face in seeking an 80 percent interest.

In late December, Bre-X released the assays on its initial drilling at Busang, six sample results from hole three, and the general comment that the fourth hole intersected "significant gold values of 10.43 g/tonne." The drill program, it announced, would continue in February. The day after the release, PT WAM entered the next feasibility stage at Busang.

As the New Year passed, Barrick still had not made an offer in writing. Were they waiting to squeeze the company, till it was so desperate for cash they would accept any deal at all? Busang was shut down in this period. In the third week of January, Gregory Wilkins sent a letter to Walsh with the Barrick proposal. The following day, Barry Tannock sent a fax back. Bre-X needed clarification. But there was no follow-up from Bre-X. Felderhof had sent a memo to Walsh: "American Barrick is a bullshit proposal.... Under the American Barrick terms you would be selling the company at basement price."

On January 14, de Guzman faxed Irvin, asking him to please prepare sample splits from the drill core stored in the lab from hole BRH4. "Cesar or myself intend to pick up same at the earliest 24 January, 1994." At about this time, John Felderhof had discussions with Irvin's laboratory team about testing methodology. With the reproducibility an issue, perhaps a cyanide assay would be the more comprehensive approach. Cyanide leach was a cheaper route: $10 a sample, versus $24 for fire assay.

On January 22, driller Richard Galbraith headed back to Australia. Busang was going to be "down" for a time anyway. The company's activity was now more corporate than exploration-oriented. It was time to turn up the heat on Barrick. On January 24, Walsh made a public announcement that a deal with Barrick was in the works. And to make sure the public got the message, Bre-X bought space in *The Bull & Bear*, saying it was "in receipt of a proposal by American Barrick offering to acquire a minority equity interest in BXM and secure property joint venture options. Terms of the offer will be released upon execution of final documentation and various approvals."

As the two companies went back and forth on the proposed joint venture, all was quiet at Busang. On February 11, Walsh announced that the deal with Barrick was off. That same month, the Syakeranis, partners with Bre-X in the Central Zone, claimed the ground next door, what would be called Busang II, or the Southeast Zone.

On February 22, Bre-X rebooted its efforts at Busang. The drillers headed back to hole number four and "twinned" it, mirroring the aborted, but tantalizing, hole that Galbraith had drilled in December. On March 24, the company announced that BRH-4A had intercepted an average 3.99 grams per tonne, and that it ran as high as 6.6 grams per tonne.

At the same time, Paul Kavanagh, who had retired from Barrick, formally stepped aboard the Bre-X bandwagon, to sit on the company's board of directors. The introduction of Kavanagh gave the company the prestige in its home market that it badly needed. The comments made by *Global Stock Report*, published out of Casper, Wyoming, were typical: "Dr. Paul Kavanagh, formerly senior vice-president of exploration at American Barrick, is impressed enough with the company, that after a visit to the properties in Indonesia has accepted an invitation to join the board of directors. Dr. Kavanagh's wealth of experience and knowledge will add another level of confidence for investors to own Bre-X Minerals."

Kavanagh's postgraduate degree from Princeton and the corporate positions he had held took the company to a higher plane. All of a sudden Busang was not so far away. Now, a corporate executive who had walked the same corridors in downtown Toronto as the leaders of some of the richest mining companies in the country had proclaimed himself a believer. Busang must be real. In March 1995, the stock was trading in the $3 range.

The company was certainly gaining a higher profile, and Barry Tannock, in David Walsh's view, was not doing much to enhance the Bre-X image. On April 1, Tannock met with Walsh at Varbay Place, complaining that he was being financially screwed, that Walsh had reneged on bonus promises. Walsh offered to continue paying him $2,000 a month, and threw in a bunch of share options. Tannock pitched a fit, Walsh fired him, and part of that glitter team the *Calgary Herald* had been so high on was gone. Tannock sued, for $54,818.17, a sum of money that would seem laughably small in the months to come. Walsh denied that he owed Tannock a penny. In his statement of claim, Tannock explained how his job had been to create a good market for Bre-X shares, so that Bresea, or the Walshes, could sell their shares in the marketplace, then advance funds to Bre-X for exploration. Bresea would replenish its Bre-X shares by taking private placements for the funds advanced. The private placements had warrants attached, so the Walshes—and David Walsh did much of his trading through accounts established in the name of his sons Brett and Sean—were able to increase their Bre-X position geometrically over time.

By now Bre-X was drilling its tenth hole at Busang. Late in the month, samples were shipped to Indo Assay. Instead of being signed by Puspos, as they normally would have been, these worksheets were signed by de Guzman. This bit of paperwork is a curiosity for the simple reason that, of the twenty-nine samples submitted, only two showed gold values, and these were spotty, between one and four grams of gold. The rest of the batch was a dud, under a gram of gold throughout, consistent with Montague's results.

On April 7, Felderhof wrote to Walsh. "We are confident that Busang is in the bag so to speak. Now it is just a matter to determine how big it is. Don't discuss any deals with interested parties until you and I have sat down in Vancouver. Have you let Paul Kavanagh know?"

In early May, Puspos was back on paperwork duty, and the performance of the bogus gold rose again to its previous high showings. Were the previous month's samples salted, just unenthusiastically so? Had de Guzman tried to do the salting himself but botched it? Did de Guzman prefer a more modestly orchestrated scam, one less eye-catching? There is another, plausible theory: that Michael de Guzman still believed that the gold would show itself to him. It was still early days.

The company closed a private placement with Loewen, Ondaatje, McCutcheon Ltd., Nesbitt Burns Inc. and others in Toronto on May 20, 1994. The share sale put just shy of $5 million into Bre-X's coffers. In announcing this to the public, the company tagged on some new assay results and, as a capper, repeated the now shopworn statements of "20 million tonnes of +2gm/tonne . . . the processing cost of US$155/oz . . . the after tax cash flow of US$10 million."

Brian Fagan, whose *Asian World Stock Report* specializes in penny exploration stocks, reported that an underwriting by such high-calibre brokerage houses was a positive sign. They "do not finance junior companies without doing a lot of due diligence," he said. Whatever did he mean by that? "Due diligence" normally applies to companies assessing a potential acquisition target: searching land title, drilling fresh holes, seeking independent assay verification.

That same month, a surface exploration team under the supervision of Cesar Puspos concluded, or so Bre-X told shareholders, that the Central Zone trended northwest to southeast, and that further land applications should be made for adjoining territory.

On July 22, Rob van Doorn, Loewen's mining analyst, put out a "buy" recommendation on the stock in a report entitled "Small hunter in elephant country." In bold type on the report's front page, van Doorn said that "early results on Bre-X's Busang project indicate that the project probably contains in excess of one million ounces (Moz). In addition, the first indication at the Taware project points to a multi-million ounce discovery. BUY." Van Doorn touted Bre-X's management, Walsh, Felderhof and Kavanagh, "a valuable hands-on board member."

Van Doorn appended drill results to his report. That Busang had vaulted from dross to pure gold between holes one and four does not appear on van Doorn's chart. The Bre-X team redrilled hole two. The new, improved BRH-2A showed 7.96 and 7.43 grams per tonne of gold. Thus van Doorn's chart showed a wide range of good, often fabulous, gold values, ranging from 1.17 on hole eleven to 16.03 on hole seven. Van Doorn did not include hole ten in his chart, which had come up dry, but rather confined his report to what he termed "significant drill results." In a footnote, the analyst said that check assays, wherein samples are run again and their results compared against the first assays, "returned 7.5 percent higher results than original values."

He set a target price of $4 for the stock. "Backed by superior knowledge, Bre-X is scouting for additional projects on Irian Jaya (New Guinea). At the same time Bre-X is studying projects in the Philippines. . . . Bre-X's senior geologist is from the Philippines and has excellent knowledge and contacts."

Two months later, van Doorn issued another "buy" recommendation on Bre-X. The stock was quoted at $2.60. Van Doorn set a target of $5. "Ore reserves are still estimated between 1 and 2 million ounces," he said, "although Bre-X is currently postulating a resource of 2.7 to 4.5 million ounces." To postulate: "to assume or claim as true." On what basis did Bre-X make this postulation? And to whom did it postulate? Van Doorn does not say. And why did he refer to the numbers coming out of Bre-X as "reserves"? Van Doorn should have known better. He did say that the company "aims to be listed on the Toronto Stock Exchange by year end." Increasingly Bre-X analysts were letting "the story" get ahead of them.

That Loewen would promote Bre-X was no surprise, given its earlier role as underwriter. While a firm's departments of equity research and corporate finance are meant to be independent of one another, with the integrity of research unsullied by the undertakings of finance, this is too often not the case. In fact, the reverse is more often true. Once a firm has taken a role in financing a company, the firm's analysts are expected to support the company in question. Certainly it is the expectation of the company's officers that "buy" recommendations will follow. Should an analyst turn negative on a firm's prospects, the analyst is more likely to clam up than issue a "sell" recommendation.

Interestingly, van Doorn said that results from the company's Taware project in North Sulawesi suggest that it "promises to be even larger than the already sizable Busang." Assuming that Busang held a million ounces, van Doorn extrapolated Taware's potential on the basis of fewer than a dozen holes drilled.

On September 20, a day before van Doorn's report, Bre-X had issued a press release with the drill updates for Busang and news on Taware. "In an interview from BXM's Jakarta office, Mr. John B. Felderhof, General Manager, Indonesia, and Mr. Mike de Guzman, Exploration Manager, stated: 'We are confident that an open pittable resource ranging between 30 million tons to 60 million tons at an average grade better than 3g Au/t (.09oz Au/t) can be attained at Busang.'" The company announced that "a potential underground mineable resource will be tested with 3 deep holes of 300 m each during November 1994."

On August 4, Felderhof wrote to Walsh: "Things are looking very, very good. Don't worry—Bre-X shareholders are going to be a very happy bunch by Christmas. We be big time."

ALL THAT GLISTERS

DZIA UDDIN—SMALL, WIRY DZIA, a devout Muslim—hopped up from his morning prayer and made preparations for yet another river journey on the mighty Mahakam. His family owned a pleasant house in Samarinda, bleached white with a wrought-iron gate, a house with a cool, polished interior. He lived there with a sturdy, stately wife, who towered above her elfin spouse.

Dzia had worked in Australia for a few years but had come back to Kalimantan to take up a job as field project co-ordinator for PT WAM. He would regularly check in at the company's modest offices on Jalan Gajah Mada, #89, in Samarinda. A simple place, unprepossessing, the white clapboard siding of the Bre-X mess was offset by maize window trim. Gajah Mada had more the look of an alleyway than a promenade, but it was handy, just up from the wharf. From his home base in Samarinda, Dzia would head to the Busang site for weeks at a time.

Cesar Puspos was still sequestered in his private quarters and would not be making this trip. Perhaps he was asleep, at last. He was often up all night, his light on, his door locked. Two o'clock in the morning.

Puspos was not a sleeper. He had motivation and energy in awe-inspiring quantities. Anyone who worked with him could see that.

Puspos insisted that all the bags of rock samples, shipped down-river from the Busang site, be humped up the street to these premises, up perilous gangplanks hitched at a forty-five-degree angle, over the detritus swept to shore by the city's logging industry. Puspos would order that the fibreglass bags be opened, to let the samples dry. The sample bags would be taken upstairs to his private quarters. He always kept the door locked. He would study the longitudinal sections of the drill holes. He might also have the drill logs of the guys in the field, so he could study the core while making comparisons to sections marked by the geologists as mineralized. He would enter data in his computer. Two days later the samples would be shipped to John Irvin's lab at Indo Assay in Balikpapan.

The building that Bre-X rented for its mess was owned by Achmed Maulana, who lived next door at #87. Maulana was a wary, even suspicious man. He had a doctorate in economics, was said to be related to the governor, and through a company called Sapulidi was a supplier of many things to Bre-X, including the boats that would carry the samples to Samarinda and then the Bre-X workers, along with the site supplies, back upriver again. When Michael de Guzman was in town he did not stay at the company mess but rather at the Hotel Senyiur.

Dzia had been hired by Bre-X to attend to administrative matters: camp set-ups; travelling and work permits for foreigners; government paperwork. The paying of administrative fees, or side sums, would also fall to Dzia—the local police, the governor, whoever. People had to be paid off along the way. Such was the way of life here. Perhaps something had gone awry with a work permit; perhaps a Bre-X employee, a foreigner, had only a tourist visa. Twenty-five thousand rupiahs could fix all manner of troubles. An expense report from the Sable project lists payments to the *Camat*, the police, the military and a "Donation for the New Year," which likely went to some threatening official.

Dzia had had his run-ins with de Guzman, notably a fight over wages for some local staff. De Guzman was copied on all administrative matters. Mess expenses, telephone charges, electricity costs—there was nothing that escaped his notice. "If you pray five times a day, you're still a liar," de Guzman screeched in a faxed memo to Dzia. "You're like my father." Dzia would try to deal with the boss man civilly, quietly. "It's dangerous, Mike," Dzia would say of this belittling of the Muslim faith. The local military were just looking for excuses to oust the foreigners. Dzia had spent some of his time handling administrative tasks at the company's Sable project, in the ultra-Muslim Sumatran province of Aceh. There, the top military man in the nearest village toted a high-powered rifle and was always looking to make some easy money—expecting payoffs if work permits had not been renewed at the precise time they had lapsed. "If I show this to the government," said Dzia of de Guzman's fax, "it's out from Indonesia for you."

Anyone who ran afoul of de Guzman ran the risk of receiving a similarly flaming fax. "Get your ass back to camp," he messaged one of the few foreign geologists to become part of the Bre-X crew. The geo had been trying to renew his work permit.

Dzia would accompany de Guzman back upriver to Busang. They would stop at Eddie's floating prawn shack for lunch. Everyone would listen up when de Guzman was around, yet he was not one for sharing information. When a new geologist arrived, the new guy would reasonably anticipate an initiation session with the boss—not Felderhof, but de Guzman. The new guy would expect to be able to shadow de Guzman for a few days, pick up the nomenclature, learn to see what the boss man saw in the rock. De Guzman did not do that.

De Guzman would, however, turn to Dzia during those early site visits. His voice was high and tremulous, bordering on feminine. "Pray, Dzia," he would say. "Pray to open the gold. Show me this gold at Busang."

To dream of gold. To pray for its recovery. Such wishfulness recalled Acupan. Months had passed since those first holes. The drilling program was escalating. Either Michael de Guzman was a very good actor or he still believed somewhere inside himself that his geological divination would be validated.

Practices at camp conformed with local custom. Dzia would sacrifice a chicken every time the driller prepared to sink a new hole. He would neatly slit its scrawny throat, splattering the blood quickly about the place. It was believed by the Dayak that this would appease the gods. If de Guzman spotted something promising, if the rock offered a tempting impression of gold mineralization, he would cry: "Dzia! Dzia! We've got gold! Delicious!"

Site work was hard labour. The crews would take the first shift out at 7:00 a.m. by tractor, the wheels wrapped in chains for traction in the muck. The drill rigs worked two shifts, trying to pull core as deep as four hundred metres. Depending on where they were drilling, the core would be retrieved in varying states. If the rock were particularly vuggy, it had the appearance of termite tunnels running through it. If it were highly fractured, or brecciated, it would likely crumble in spots. Other Busang rock would come out as clean as a whistle, smooth and hard, a pale grey.

The core would be placed in wooden boxes, built by Indonesian workers on site. The boxes were slotted, and into these the core fit almost snugly. The core trays would be transported back to base camp, then deposited on a flat, wide, concrete pad, rather like a bas-ketball court. With eighty metres of core drilled each shift, and with each core box holding roughly five metres, sixteen boxes a shift were being ferried back to camp. The drilling rig operations multiplied from one to two, thence four.

The loggers at base camp would try vainly to keep up with the core, numbering, recording. The loggers were geologists, and so they would study the core, selecting two-metre sections that were deemed mineralized. Only these sections would be advanced to the sampling and assaying stages. By de Guzman's rules, these were not jobs for the Indonesian geologists, who would instead be employed in the temporary fly camps in the outreaches of the projects, or conducting topographic surveys, trenching and mapping. Filipino geologists, and the occasional Canadian, were in charge of the core handling. Perhaps once every twenty-four hours one of the foreign geologists would make a visit to one of the drill sites.

The concrete pad was entirely exposed. There was no protection from the sun. Workers in track shoes or rubber thongs would slap across the rapidly multiplying boxes. Then, after removing the samples, they would take a steel-bristled brush to the core boxes, sweeping whatever tiny grains might have been left behind onto cardboard so they could be added to the rock to be sampled. One never knew— there might be some raisins there. Bobby Ramirez, a Filipino who had spent thirteen years at Benguet, logged hundreds of metres of core, sometimes bagging at midnight and shipping at 2:00 a.m. One geologist who logged core at Busang never, ever saw visible gold in the core he was logging.

De Guzman would spend a couple of days a month on site. Those who went on a traverse with him noticed that he favoured one leg when walking downhill. He said he had been beaten up on a basketball court years before, in the Philippines.

With Puspos spending the majority of his time at the company's premises in Samarinda, the site's top man was Jerry Alo. Alo would live at Busang for three months at a stretch, taking two-week leaves to break the pace. Alo was in charge of many things. He had overseen the construction of mine camps before, and at Busang he was overseer of plans for new buildings, much more comfortable than the digs inherited from the Montague crew. The main mess was built around a comfortably furnished verandah. When visitors came calling, Busang seemed a well-appointed place relative to other exploration sites. When the decision was made to expand the camp, Pebit, the Dayak village chief, ordered that a pig be sacrificed.

The foreigners' buildings could not, of course, hold a candle to the Dayaks' own creations. The community centre at Mekar Baru was intricately painted in swirling patterns of turquoise, yellow and red. Two carved figures with elongated heads stood sentry at the base of the wooden ramp that rose to its entranceway, while a totem pole rose as high as the roof of the centre. Men in soccer gear regularly commandeered the adjacent field for a game; others preferred to organize a pickup game of volleyball on a nearby court.

And when Sean Walsh and Steve Felderhof, John's son, paid a visit that fall, a grand affair was arranged. The Dayak honoured their guests with a traditional dance at Mekar Baru. The women danced with their sprays of black-and-white hornbill feathers, their costumes intricately sewn with sequins of pink and copper and gold.

Life was good at site. Not only was there beer in the fridge, there were parties, too. The prawn crackers had been replaced by much more substantial fare. This was a welcome development for the ruddy, large Aussie drillers who towered over their co-workers. Jim Rush was one of these. The change in fortune meant only one thing to Rush: lamb chops.

Alo was a chatty camp companion. And he was tremendously preoccupied. He would make more visits to the drill sites than the geologists—often two a day. He oversaw the sampling procedure with meticulous attention. He would visit Indo Assay, flexing his metallurgist's muscle, making suggestions to John Irvin, who knew very well how to do his work. Irvin had to tell him to buzz off.

Those who spent any time at site came to know Salin, who in the Indonesian manner went by only one name. The handsome panner ran a mixed goods store in Mekar Baru. His reputation for prolific panning was well known. Some Busang site workers tried to buy Salin's pannings, but he would turn them away. His gold, he said, was for Pa Cesar, Pa Mike.

Mike and Cesar were regular Salin clients, buying five grams at a time, sometimes ten. A young Indonesian worker at Busang named Min, who aided Dzia in office affairs, would often be the one to tool off on his motorbike to make the pickup. "It's for a sample," Mike told Dzia. "So I can show the people in Canada and the Philippines." The gold, of course, was alluvial, fetchingly round and smooth. It did not, or should not have had, the characteristics of gold buried deep, that which had not come in contact with the reshaping effects of water. What would be the point of showing this gold to investors? It could not prove the possibility of a mineable gold deposit. How curious, that given how nuggety de Guzman said the gold in the Busang core was, there was none visible, or visible enough, to show the eager investors.

De Guzman was buying Salin's gold. That was on one side of the ledger. On the other side was the fact that he was not making as much money as he needed to. He started working up some businesses on the side. Any outfit that wanted a piece of Busang's commerce faced the prospect of paying kickbacks to the boss man. Some say de Guzman took seven dollars for every metre drilled by PT Drillinto.

October 1994. More than a year had passed since David Gordon Walsh had announced his stewardship of this parcel of Indonesian properties. A full twelve months had passed since Larry Kornze and Paul Kavanagh had traversed the site on behalf of Barrick Gold. Perhaps it was time for Walsh to make a Busang visit too. Cash was terribly tight. Still, as the company's top corporate officer, Walsh was signing off on all the press releases. Perhaps he should see what it was he was promoting. On the other hand, what was the point? Walsh could carry his five-foot, nine-inch, 250-pound frame up and down the Busang site and understand precisely nothing of what he was being shown. There was that furrowed look again. The man appeared perpetually puzzled.

The following month the company placed an advertisement in *The Bull & Bear* offering to send information to interested investors. "Noteworthy, upon completing an inspection of various mineralized zones and drill core awaiting shipment to the Assay Lad [sic], Dr. Kavanagh commented 'What Bre-X has in Indonesia is a jewellery store.'" Of course, he meant tremendous riches. Kavanagh was not on the Bre-X board in those December days when someone filed those gold curlicues into the sample. Still, his analogy seems amusing, given the character of the gold investigators later found there. And it does invite the question: just what was Kavanagh seeing in those zones, in that core?

At the same time, Walsh was trying to reel in the conventional business press. "Bre-X Minerals Ltd. says recent drilling at its properties in Indonesia will soon lead to gold reserves of more than 2 million ounces," ran the first line of a Dow Jones story on November 24. And there was that word "reserve" again—the one that mining reporters are supposed to be so cautious about using. "We reckon that we'll have a drill-indicated reserve of two to two-and-a-half million ounces by year end," Walsh said. Busang would be "one super open pit."

Walsh cast ahead to plans for drilling in 1995. "We intend to have two rigs drill off another kilometre, 'another two-and-a-half million ounces' by the fall of 1995. 'The surface mineralization of the areas to be drilled next year is identical to what the company is currently drilling,' Walsh says." It was interesting that Walsh managed to double Busang's "reserves" based on the size of the areas to be drilled, that he could play God in this way. The Dow story appears to make the first mention of Bre-X building a laboratory on site. Numerous media outlets picked up on the Bre-X news.

Key changes were taking place. The same month that Walsh visited Busang, a decision was made to switch to cyanide assay. Perhaps this method would help smooth the wild variances. The request to shift to the cyanide method was made by Felderhof and de Guzman. Indo Assay was now undertaking a bottle roll assay for the samples. Sometimes the laboratory would have as many as 150 bottles rolling at a time, lined up conveyor-belt style, and the bottles would be mechanically turned for thirty-six hours, dissolving the gold.

The sheer volume of samples presented Indo Assay with other problems. Thirty tonnes of cracked rock would be arriving at the lab every few days. The Bre-X sampling program had progressed so dramatically that Bre-X was often Indo Assay's number-one client. Thirty tonnes of material is a huge quantity for any lab. Worse, the delivery was sporadic. On occasion, someone from Indo Assay would phone the Bre-X office in Samarinda. We're empty, Indo Assay would say. Can you send more samples? "We can't," was the answer. "Cesar's not here." No samples would get past Samarinda unless Puspos or de Guzman gave clearance.

The American tip sheets were trying their best to get investors to see the errors of their ways. In November, *The Bull & Bear*, quoting the *Global Gold Stock Report* announced that the drill-indicated resource of Busang was as high as fifteen million ounces. At a minimum, Busang appeared to have five million ounces. "Five million ounces of gold worth $100 an ounce in the ground gives us a value of $500 million. Divide this by 18 million shares, fully diluted, and we get $27 per share." *Global Gold*, at least, was using appropriate terminology.

Global Gold's editor, Michael Schaefer, had many reasons to recommend the stock. David Walsh, he said, was "one of the sharpest executive officers that we have ever encountered in this business. He is also one of the most honest and dependable." The tipsters like Schaefer started exhibiting the mind-set that appears to have temporarily taken hold of management after Barrick was rebuffed. "Management has every intention of taking Busang all the way through to production, on their own, without a senior partner." And there was more good news. A long-term bull run for the gold price was due, figured Schaefer. "The market will not support a gold price below the $340 oz. area for any sustained period of time."

Investors were getting a full brief on Bre-X, but how credible was the information? At the bottom of Bre-X's press releases ran the standard disclaimer: "The Alberta Stock Exchange have [sic] neither approved nor disapproved the information contained herein." At the bottom of Loewen Ondaatje's buy recommendations: "The accuracy or completeness of the information is not guaranteed." While the

Global Gold Stock Report was shouting "BUY BRE-X MINERALS!"
the smaller type at the bottom of the page suggested that "subscribers
should not view this publication as offering personalized legal or
investment advice." With some members of the media now repeating
the Bre-X line, everyone was singing from the same songsheet. But
where were the checks? Where were the balances?

Felderhof, meanwhile, had turned to Roger Pooley, a chum from
his Pelsart days and a mine engineer, to write up a report on a mine
plan for Busang. That seemed a touch ambitious. Bre-X was drilling
its holes at a 250-metre spacing, at least five times the industry average. Only after holes were drilled in between those now existing, at
a distance as tight as 25 metres, would the company be near to
defining a mineable deposit.

As it happens, Pooley provided what may have been the first cautionary note in the Busang tale. He told Felderhof that, based on an
estimated million ounces of gold, Busang was unlikely ever to become
a mine. He told Felderhof that Busang needed at least a million and
a half. What he saw was too ill-defined, too low in grade and too
small a resource to become viable. Nor did he observe the free coarse
gold that Felderhof and de Guzman insisted was so plentiful in the
Central Zone.

The association with Pooley did not last long. The Alberta Stock
Exchange informed Bre-X that his credentials were not up to their
standards. Felderhof sent a message to Walsh: "Please tell the
exchange that I take this as a slur against me as a professional." Slur
or not, Bre-X was going to have to find another engineering firm.

Felderhof knew the area to the southeast, a block of land that
would come to be known as Busang II. His previous employer, Jason,
had had the COW in that area. In fact, Felderhof had initialled a contract on the area in the mid-1980s, but the best pieces had been taken
up by a company called Magnum, so he had recommended that Jason
forget it. The Magnum folks subsequently told the Montague folks
that they had not found much on their turf.

In the fall of 1994, the government cancelled the Magnum COW, citing the tenant's lack of progress. Felderhof knew the COW was on the road to cancellation. So did everyone else in the mining community. Such deductions don't take much sleuthing. Most of the players in the mining game would have their sources within the Department of Mines in Jakarta keeping them apprised of land cancellations. The department then had no computerized system for mining tenancy.

Felderhof wanted to put in a claim, but as per the rules of Indonesian mining law, the application had to be made under the auspices of an Indonesian joint venture partner. So the Syakeranis, who shared office space with Bre-X at Rasuna Said because of their partnership with Bre-X on Busang I, made the application. In Busang I, the Syakeranis' local company was PT SAP. For Busang II they constructed a new company, PT Askatindo. Jusuf Merukh, who sat on the board of PT SAP, was apparently not informed of any of this.

From Felderhof's perspective it was purely speculative, time for some quick exploratory work. He would later say that there were mineralized outcrops in this Southeast Zone. In November, Bre-X commenced ground reconnaissance work at Busang II.

Periodically, Felderhof would take to the road, giving dog-and-pony presentations on Bre-X. He looked appealingly haggard and worn and sounded like a man who had walked up every damn creek in the entire country. There was something tremendously appealing about Felderhof. Investors could not help but be impressed by his history. The audience would readily believe that if there was a mine to be found in Indonesia, this was the man to do it.

De Guzman, meanwhile, was constantly on the go, travelling between Jakarta and Bre-X's other two sites: Sable and Singhe. At Sable, a rough-hewn L-shaped building cut from wooden planks served as a miserable home for geologists and support crew. The armpit of the world, they called it. A hose was run from a nearby creek to the concrete bathroom. The menu was salted fish with chilies and rice. Spotting elephant tracks and the paw marks of tigers was not uncommon. The wild pigs were insufferably noisy, and the orangutans could swing through the trees as fast as a grown man could run, travelling high in the canopy, so that if a branch were missed the great ape would dip and catch one at a lower level. For the Indonesians, the pay was not much more than a rice allowance, and when a worker from Java was asked how long it had been since he had been home he said he had not seen his family in a year. The Indonesians were afraid of being fired.

But of course the exercise was not about making money for the people who performed the work. The exercise was all about making money in the market. Bre-X Minerals saw out 1994 as the seventh most active stock on the Alberta Stock Exchange, trading more than nine million shares that year, though it came in leagues behind the ASE's leading volume trader, Abacan Resources, with 56 million trades. Bre-X closed the year at $2.85.

Early in 1995, John Irvin recommended that Bre-X establish a prep lab on the Busang site. He suggested that such a lab would greatly reduce the enormous load of core being shipped to Balikpapan.

As part of this arrangement, Indo Assay would supervise the prep lab to ensure the work met the high standards set by the company. Irvin's suggestion seemed not all that peculiar given the remoteness of the site. Freeport-McMoRan, for example, had a prep lab at its site near Timika in Irian Jaya. But there was a rather large difference between the two: Freeport was working an established mine in Irian. The company was years beyond having to prove the validity of its deposit. For Bre-X to have its own sample lab on site was unorthodox, at least by North American standards, even with Indo Assay's supervision.

The lab was constructed under the watchful eye of Jerry Alo. Visitors who drove through the main gate at Busang would, on their left, pass a small bridge that led walkers to the main mess. If the driver kept to his right, the road connected with the prep lab, sitting at the top of a slight hill. It was a building of simple construction, in front of which someone would come to plant the name Bre-X Minerals in garden greenery that was visible from the air.

Propitious timing. Busang was about to grow exponentially. With the Southeast Zone under geological surveillance, Bre-X now had a far, far greater chance of becoming something very large.

Cesar Puspos had been softly whispering in de Guzman's ear—or so he would later lead the world to believe. The Southeast Zone. The gold mineralization extends there. He said he wanted to step out aggressively into this area. If he took a big leap, and gold were there, then connecting the dots between points A and B . . . well, the potential was unfathomable.

Puspos and de Guzman were spelling one another off in the zone. De Guzman, sweating, the stress building. Psychological pain can sometimes be so great that it hurts physically. Napoleon Hill once wrote that "[t]he ease with which lack of persistence may be conquered will depend entirely upon the intensity of one's desire." Michael de Guzman desired this thing intensely.

David Walsh must have desired this thing intensely also. But for all the good news that had come from the project since its inception, and despite all the very hard work done by his "investor relations" people, the stock was still in the doldrums.

May 1995. It is time for Busang to tell a different story. It cannot be the story of a one-, or even two-million-ounce gold mine. A $4 stock meant insignificant rewards for Walsh and his many stock options. And Felderhof's hard-fought-for employment contract was not going to make him a rich man. De Guzman was even less well paid.

And so, perhaps it was time for a fable. The golden boy would say he had traversed the Southeast Zone on that hobbled knee of his, spotted what he deemed to be a potential mineralized outcrop, perhaps the thumbprint of something very large. And so he had left a note for Puspos there. Check this out, it said. And when Puspos did, and came to the same conclusions as his very smart boss, he wrote checkmate on that piece of paper.

One night de Guzman woke Puspos up and asked him to draw a circular picture of a diatreme, to predict its widest extent. This Cesar did. This, they would suggest, was the moment of scientific discovery: their realization that Busang was a massive diatreme, only slightly present in the Central Zone but expanding widely into this new adjacent territory. Was it a dream?

Busang had to move off the Central Zone, whether to real or imagined minerals. It would not have washed in the mining community in Jakarta to have discovered a huge gold resource in territory previously drilled. The Southeast Zone was relatively uncharted ground. There was no existing dossier to contradict what the Bre-X team might find there.

That same month, Loewen led private placement at $3.75 a share. Nesbitt Burns Inc. was another brokerage to support the sale. Was Brian Fagan being naive or disingenuous when he wrote that a national brokerage house would not finance junior companies without doing a lot of due diligence?

The Bre-X tale had now reached the top rung of investment analyst coverage. And its promoters had done it without the aid of Barrick. Felderhof's distaste for Barrick reached new heights when Barrick, in partnership with a company called Mutiara, made an application to acquire the land next door to Bre-X's project in Sumatra's Aceh province. Bre-X charged that Barrick had used proprietary information, obtained at the time of the Kavanagh–Kornze visit. Joel King, an old pal of Walsh's and then a Bre-X board member, sent complaining letters to Barrick from his Montreal office.

Soon, Bre-X would pay scant attention to such irritations. PT Drillinto Tiko was hauling drills onto that Southeast Zone, and sure enough, in the spring of 1995, the gold started assaying out of those holes, too. At the end of May, Michael de Guzman was granted 20,000 Bre-X stock options. He had five years to exercise the options, at a strike price of $5.05. Nassey was given 10,000. As was Puspos.

Michael de Guzman compiled a simple map in June. Within the

outline of Kalimantan he spotted a series of deposits, including Mirah, Muro and Muyup, running in a soft arc, up and to the right, at the top of which sat Busang. This tertiary period volcanic corridor "is traceable toward the Zamboanga Gold District in Southwest Mindanau Philippines," he wrote, citing his own data file of 1986.

A meeting of minds, Felderhof would say, the synchronicity between himself and de Guzman. The theory, said Felderhof, was developed in the Philippines in the 1970s. Then he would say it was developed in New Zealand in the '70s. But what was this theory, precisely? On this Felderhof was never terribly clear. He would try verbally to sketch a diatreme, to explain explosive intrusions, but it occurred to more than one who had this conversation with Felderhof that he did not quite grasp what it was he was attempting to describe. The orebody grew larger in the Southeast Zone, he would say—less erosion, and gold occurring near to the earth's surface. But if that were the case, then surely the mineral should have been visible to someone somewhere in the Southeast Zone.

Spells were being cast. They must have been, for too few questions were being asked. The company started pumping out drill hole location plan maps, showing the drill lines, or fence lines, running at a ten-degree angle through the Southeast Zone. In June, Bre-X reported that it was confident the Central Zone would yield three million ounces by October. "It is noteworthy that extensive check analysis by a second independent commercial laboratory has given a 5% higher grade result using a fire assay method of analysis." The same month, the Alberta Treasury bought 400,000 shares of Bre-X at $3.75 a share.

The following month, the drillers were instructed to "step out" a full kilometre from their existing drilling. Such a practice is unheard of. No company would make a jump like that from its current drill. Delineating an orebody is a methodical business, you step out in baby steps to ensure that the gold runs through. This, surely, was folly. But sure enough, not only did the hole, BSSE-1, run gold, it ran gold through more than 200 metres of the core drawn from it. And the grade averaged 3 grams of gold per tonne. The hole was on line 24, or SEZ 24. Because of the depth of the interception, and the grade that came with it, Bre-X insiders and the analysts who followed the stock called this the discovery hole.

The stock was on wheels, and the price quickly quadrupled. In September, Egizio Bianchini, gold analyst at Nesbitt, one of the Bre-X underwriters five months previously, started coverage of Bre-X. He set a target price for the stock of $21. A month later, Scotia McLeod, which was also part of the underwriting, set a one-year target price of $62. By the third week in November, Bianchini's stock price expectation had moved to $70. Workers monitored its performance via the radio-telephone on site.

The company did not yet have its COW. Felderhof had started the ball rolling on the application months before, but as of the summer of 1995 action on the Southeast Zone at Busang was supposed to be restricted to surface soil sampling and hand-auguring and trenching.

But who would know? Not only would the Canadian analysts not have a clue about the title procedures in Indonesia, but they were very likely still grappling with de Guzman's geological explanation for how the mineralization occurred in the first place. Felderhof phoned Walsh with very big news. "This thing's a monster," he would say. Or perhaps, "We've got a monster by the tail." The operative word-image was *big*. David Walsh did not know what it was, this maar diatreme something or other. The boys at Busang were given a free exploration mandate. Carte blanche. Drill wherever you want to, as deep as you want to. David Walsh would keep the money coming. Funny thing was, somebody ordered that the drilling on that twenty-fourth fence line be aborted. The drillers kept leapfrogging across the property. This would prove to be a mistake. Even analysts with limited experience, and certainly other mining companies monitoring Bre-X's progress, would question this decision.

Life within the Busang camp was not focused solely on the Southeast Zone. Geologists were spotted into the western region of the

Busang area, near the Semeden River, carrying out reconnaissance surveys, initially identifying a northwest-trending structural zone. There were no volcanic or intrusive bodies, but the zone was gold-bearing. There was evidence of extensive placer gold mining. Rock samples and stream sediments were retrieved and sent to Indo Assay for testing.

The community of geologists in Jakarta knew of the stock run-up, of course, but they had seen little of the Bre-X team. Many had made requests of the company to pay a site visit and had been refused—an ungentlemanly act in a business where, once a discovery is made, the finders tend to want to show off their discovery.

On October 17, 1995, a group of Canadian mining analysts arrived at site. The visit was a breakthrough in the Busang story, as far as outsiders were concerned. De Guzman, intensely secretive, had tightly controlled all aspects of the operation. He was furious when he found out that a staffer had supplied Busang's co-ordinates when asked. "You should never give co-ordinates or positions to anyone," he snapped.

The analysts were helicoptered in from Balikpapan, and they stayed two nights at the guest houses, walking across the core pad, spying the drill holes, listening to the spiel, having a beer. Cesar Puspos showed off his own personal piece of core, with a nugget of gold near the drill cut. The nugget was perhaps three millimetres in diameter, and those who saw it swear that the nugget was present naturally in the core. No doubt about it.

The company issued a press release that day. "In an interview from Jakarta, Indonesia, Bre-X's senior vice-president, John Felderhof, stated that the central zone pales in comparison to the potential of the southeast zone and the Busang project in its entirety has the potential of becoming one of the world's great gold ore bodies."

Steve McAnulty, who had taken over investor relations after Barry Tannock, told the Reuters news service on October 18 that the company "was comfortable with the estimates that Busang could contain more than 30 million ounces of gold." Before the month was out, a single share of Bre-X would trade at $59. A stunning 7.5 million shares would change hands. Michael de Guzman's options were worth $178,500.

Egizio Bianchini was one of these visiting analysts. After the site visit he circled back to Canada by way of Australia, where he stopped in at Sydney to meet with David Baker, who manages one of the biggest gold funds in the world, for Mercury Asset Management. Bianchini had a boating date with Baker. At the Sydney Park Hyatt Hotel, Bianchini ran into Pierre Lassonde, the handsome Euro-styled head of a Canadian mining outfit called Franco Nevada. The two met for a drink in a lobby bar with the reserved atmosphere of an English gentleman's club. Lassonde had not asked for it, but Bianchini offered it up anyway. The Busang pitch, that is. "This stock is gonna be 100 bucks," said the analyst, predicting that Bre-X would nearly double. Lassonde should have known that, with Bianchini getting in back of this thing, it was going to fly.

David and Jeannette Walsh were already enjoying their good fortune. Earlier in the fall they had packed their bags and headed for Nassau. The Walshes had always wanted to live in a warm clime, and Calgary, at minus-70 with the wind chill, was not to their liking. They had found an old plantation house, built in the 1920s, that was just the ticket. The previous owner had chopped it into three units. The Walshes wanted it restored to all the glory its 550 square metres would allow. By Christmas time the Walshes would be admiring the fabulous returns on their stock and revelling in their experts' pronouncements that Busang was a ten-million-ounce gold resource.

But there would be no peace. If the company wanted to follow the path of successful juniors that had gone before, including Dia Met and Diamond Fields Resources, the time to seek a partnership with a major mining company was at hand. Juniors lack the capital base, the financing capabilities and the technical expertise to take a mine into production. Major mining companies in the gold game are not all that plentiful. Placer Dome, Newmont, Anglo American. Bre-X's earlier insistence that it would take this project to production solo was now wholly discounted.

One company was more obvious than all the others. Australia's CRA Ltd., one of the largest mining companies on the planet, owned 90 percent of the Kelian mine, just 120 kilometres away. The company had taken the mine into production in 1992, and it became the standard-bearer for gold-mining operations in Kalimantan. CRA also owned and operated the largest coal mine in Indonesia, which happened to be in the same area, and the company had a reputation for bringing enormous projects, with major environmental considerations, on stream. All of which made for a compelling package: it knew Indonesia and how to operate effectively in the country; it knew size; and it knew gold.

CRA is one of the biggest explorers in Indonesia. As such, it was one of the myriad companies that took a look at Busang years before, when it was up for sale but appeared too marginal, even with an $80,000 price tag. Geologists are as fallible as the next guy, and not only was CRA prepared to admit it had underestimated Busang, it decided in November 1995 that it had to have it.

At the time, CRA was on the verge of merging with mine house RTZ Corp. to form Rio Tinto. Rio Tinto's chief geologist in the country is Theo van Leeuwen, who had not only written the textbook reference on mining in Indonesia but had twenty-five years' experience in the country and had been a friend of Felderhof's for years. He had seen Felderhof through his hardship, through the Christmas when he bought his daughter the sad little gift of a pen. When CRA was invited onto the property, the company swiftly, and not unreasonably, assumed it was the preferred partner. Felderhof implicitly conveyed the message that he trusted CRA.

In November, van Leeuwen flew to the site in the company of John Craig, CRA's managing director of gold development. Craig and van Leeuwen became CRA's project leaders on the Busang evaluation. At site they met with Walsh, Felderhof and de Guzman. CRA was told that Bre-X wanted a partner, one that would take a minority position rather than insisting on control.

As the sun rose over Busang that November, as Walsh and Felderhof dove very early into quantities of alcohol, the atmosphere was convivial. Felderhof, the man wary of big-company attitude since his Kennecott days, particularly liked the fact that CRA had paid for his airfare for this visit. And the friendship with van Leeuwen seemed to confirm that the Australian mining house was in the preferred position.

The CRA representatives toured the site, with de Guzman showing off the discovery. They were filled in on site practices, which raised two peculiar problems out of the Busang muck. First, Bre-X was not splitting the core, as is common practice, but rather was crushing whole core. Second, the drillers had been instructed to drill the holes in one direction only. CRA had had tremendous difficulties assessing the grade of its resource at Kelian. It was imperative, they knew, to drill "scissor holes" at an angle to the existing holes in order to get a fuller picture of the orebody.

It quickly became apparent that there was little point in tackling John Felderhof on these issues. Craig and van Leeuwen had brought along a technical SWAT team, and though they put questions to Felderhof they failed to elicit clear answers. In fact, the mystic geologist's responses were so garbled one could have been forgiven for assuming that he did not know what the hell he was talking about. Walsh, meanwhile, was completely out of his depth. That he did not understand this strange place he was temporarily camped out at was not a huge concern. But as the chief corporate executive, the man who would presumably spearhead negotiations in any deal, he had not retained a financial adviser, nor did he have a chief financial officer. Walsh gave the company no credibility at all.

De Guzman talked mostly with van Leeuwen. Otherwise he hung back. He seemed not to want to come in contact with Craig, the suit. More than unassuming, de Guzman was extremely quiet, withdrawn.

The geological issues were not of tremendous concern. Any mining company interested in striking a partnership with another is going to insist on geological due diligence, and that would mean fresh drilling overseen by CRA, and CRA's control of the subsequent assaying. We'll fix it in the due diligence, was the CRA view.

CRA had already commenced the early stages of due diligence: running down profiles of the people involved; checking the legals; checking the title. The procedure was standard, but the results were alarming. Without a COW, Bre-X did not have title to this Southeast Zone it was touting. CRA was of the view that no company in its right mind would drill on the basis of an exploration permit. This was a fundamental problem. Felderhof was supposed to have been in charge of this business, but his paperwork was in complete disarray. John Craig had been in the mining game a long, long time, and he was not far from retirement. He certainly knew the wily ways of Indonesia. He saw the inevitability of Bre-X losing the Southeast Zone unless it married up with a major power of political capability.

Craig, Walsh and Felderhof gathered for a cold beer. Craig had the politics of Indonesia on his mind, and the vulnerability of Bre-X. His chosen words carried a menacing, though not inappropriate, tone. He turned to address Walsh. If you do not do a deal with a major mine house, he said, "Another will come and put his hand on your shoulder and say, 'I am your brother.'"

Craig's comments would have sounded cryptic only to the uninitiated. If Bre-X did not choose a partner, Indonesian interests would step in and force a resolution. Craig chose a metaphor, a "black hand," he called it. If David Walsh started then to see large shadows lurking in the woods, he did not show it. Rather he seemed utterly dumbfounded, turning, puzzled, to cock his head at Felderhof as a puppy would at his master.

Felderhof agreed with Craig. "This is why I want you to do a deal with CRA quickly," said Felderhof. Craig said one word: "Right."

THE BLACK HAND

MICHAEL DE GUZMAN, DRESSED in a tan suit, appeared ill-at-ease standing before a gathering of mining analysts and investors in a sepia ballroom in Toronto's Royal York Hotel. De Guzman was neither an elegant nor an eloquent speaker; his voice was soft, high and slightly tremulous. But it had fallen to him to make this presentation, describing what, to North American investors, was this newly fabulous gold find.

It was March, commonly a hideous month in the city, caught in the wet, grey gloom that precedes spring. Years before, the men and women who organized the Prospectors and Developers Association (PDA) annual convention purposely chose this time for their get-together, a pick-me-up and a drink-em-up before the prospectors' return to the bush in April.

The PDA every year draws thousands of industry participants and inquisitive investors from across the land. It is something of a mating ritual, wherein companies hope to marry their mining shares with the pockets of risk-takers, catch the eye of more established companies interested in partnerships and maybe pull another analyst or two onside to start selling "the story." Bre-X had planned to make the most of the affair. Not only would the company set up its exhibition booth, passing out reports and maps and such to the curious, but de Guzman, jungle conqueror, transported straight from the heart of Borneo, would give a presentation on the geology of Busang. As an added bonus, the company would hold its annual meeting in a day's time in the same hotel. If Busang had escaped the notice of anyone in the Canadian investment community, that was now about to change.

The stock had exploded. In mid-January, John Felderhof, ever the promoter, had advised the public that "[a] resource of 30 million ounces can be readily attained in view of the recent results and visuals of the outstanding four holes." Core from "the four holes" had not yet been analysed "due to the large number of mineralized samples." The company had not released "resource calculations" that were anywhere near such numbers, but no matter. Felderhof had manufactured a gold deposit that, by a sliver, exceeded the gold reserves at Barrick's Goldstrike Mine. Bre-X stock struck a new landmark that month, hitting a high of $100 a share. *That* was the point.

The mood in the Jakarta office had been celebratory that winter. The company had hosted a Christmas dinner for its employees. De Guzman chose to squire Genie, who looked lovely in black that evening. Everyone at the Bre-X office knew that Michael had two wives.

As Michael de Guzman took his place behind the podium that March day, a single share of Bre-X was trading at $167. "Without further delays, ladies and gentlemen," de Guzman said awkwardly, "I will lead you through this talk with emphasis on the exploration history and discovery of the Busang gold deposit." With the aid of overhead transparencies, de Guzman moved slowly through the Busang spiel. There were already two producing gold mines in the area, he said, including Kelian, just 250 kilometres to the southwest. The site had long held the interest of John Felderhof, who had surveyed the area more than a decade before. A group of Australians had drilled the site previously in a limited way. "The results of that," he said, "yielded narrow intervals of gold intercepts graded better than one gram."

In this way de Guzman built the credibility of the project. The trouble with the Australian efforts, he said, was their "inadequate understanding of the surface mineralization and its subsurface counterpart"; they assumed that the gold existed in structurally controlled quartz veins. His red laser shakily pointing a bead across a hunk of rock, the geologist, whose fame in Canada was just beginning to grow, said that when he laid eyes on this "exposure" there was no doubt in his mind "that the area is within a diatreme or within a maar diatreme complex."

This description might have been obscure to the majority in attendance, but they would leave it to others—their brokers, or their brokers' analysts—to understand the geological specifics. What they got a taste of was the exotic allure of the locale—de Guzman showed an appropriately jungle-like image of the spartan thatched shack he said he had inhabited when he had done his site survey—and its potential. Ninety percent of the discovery, he explained, lay in this newer zone to the southeast. There were four drills running continuously, and the entire project was "much more sexier" than the transparencies let on. The potential of the Busang gold deposit "seemed to be like a moving target. It is highly probable we may be crossing the borderline in the very very near future." The geologist did not bother explaining what he meant by "borderline."

If there were any doubters in the audience, de Guzman had a convincing array of numbers to dazzle them. Under the heading "Resource Calculations," Bre-X listed its own internal resource estimates against a "geostatistical evaluation" worked up by Kilborn Engineering. And so for the Central Zone, Bre-X's figure was listed as 3 million ounces, against a "measured and indicated" Kilborn number of 2.88 million ounces, and an "inferred" figure of .25 million ounces. As for the Southeast Zone, "Kilborn's figures come up to be this time better than we are. Looks like I'm sleeping a little bit on that one. I will compensate better next time." There was a smattering of laughter from the audience. De Guzman seemed so self-effacing, hardly the push-push promoter type. And Kilborn had put its stamp of approval on Bre-X's calculations. Or at least that was certainly the way it appeared, and that was certainly the message the company intended to convey to the crowd.

The following day, Bre-X shareholders crammed a Royal York ballroom to overflowing for the company's annual meeting. Steve Fox was sitting in the front row. Fox was an early Bresea/Bre-X investor who had invested in the stock in its penny days. Now he was worth roughly $14 million and drove one of the many cars in the province that sported a BRE-X licence plate. Because he had invested early and hung in, and because his investment was of considerable size, Fox had moved into the inner circle of Bre-X acolytes. This was the group that was in regular, often daily, contact with Bre-X operations in Calgary, getting the lowdown on the next big good news coming out of Kalimantan.

Many of Fox's co-workers at Bell Canada were investors too, even the bigwigs. He could recall a particular boardroom meeting during which the participants repeatedly took "washroom breaks" in order to check the Bre-X share price. The stock had danced from $20 to $58 that day.

Bre-X and its Busang find had become national news. Leaping from the pages of *The Northern Miner*, the tale of the now fabled discovery had made its way into the mainstream business press. Greg Chorny was in the audience too. Chorny was a onetime lawyer, raised in the heart of mining country in northern Ontario. His law practice had taken him into civil litigation—motor vehicle accidents and the like—but his real passion was investing in the mining game. Chorny had watched the hubbub over Hemlo in the 1970s, and he had made his first big personal score with the Stikine gold discovery in northern British Columbia, which had hit gold at a place called Eskay Creek on hole 109. When Placer Dome Inc., a major mine company, bought out Stikine's shareholders at $67.38, well, that cheque was enough to pay Chorny's mortgage, his debt and taxes on the capital gain, with a nice piece of working capital left over. He had invested in Diamond Fields, but that was a relatively small play for Chorny, just enough to buy a sports car. At Christmas time 1994, Chorny made his first investment in Bre-X, purchasing 10,000 shares at $1.75, a Christmas present for his kids. Bre-X was his biggest bet. He was now up 1.2 million shares: 2 percent of the entire float of the company. Chorny was such a "size investor" that he was close to the Bre-X loop: he could get David Walsh on the phone anytime, and the company had invited him to its Christmas party.

The night before the annual meeting, a number of Bre-X boosters were hanging around on bar stools at the hotel, cooking up a deal that they would call Bro-X, a Bre-X spinoff that would become the corporate home of the Sable and Singhe exploration sites. Bre-X now would be a one-deposit play—Busang. If all went well, Bre-X shares would split ten for one the next day. Michel Mendenhall, a Nesbitt Burns broker in Ottawa, who was rumoured to be holding $45 million of Bresea and Bre-X, was one of the participants. As was Donald Carter, also from Nesbitt in Ottawa, who handled accounts for Walsh. Walsh himself was there, of course. Jeannette, on whose small salary Bresea had been carried in the dire days, had gone to bed early.

Spirits were still revving high through the official business of the meeting. John Felderhof faced the Canadian media en masse for the first time when he narrated a slide show on Busang. His presentation was painfully stiff and, for such an exciting discovery, tedious and even incomprehensible in parts. At the dais with Felderhof sat Walsh and de Guzman, and a new team member, Rolly Francisco, who had just taken on the post of chief financial officer.

Most if not all of the reporters that day would have known him from his days as CFO at Lac Minerals Ltd. He was unassuming and unfailingly polite. That he had committed his career to Bre-X was reaffirming. Bre-X, as it appeared to the outside world, had acquired a veneer of professionalism. Felderhof now said that Busang had 30 million ounces in her—"plus, plus, plus." Even the journalists could do the quick math. Bre-X was now sitting on a 100-million-ounce gold mine, the single largest gold resource in the whole wide world.

There was a buzz in the crowd that day, people eager to meet Felderhof, de Guzman and Walsh. Walsh was looking freshly Brylcreemed, as usual. For a man whose beer consumption was legendary, he had the youthful, scrubbed glow of a little boy being sent to have his school photo taken. After the formalities, as investors far smaller than Greg Chorny made their way to meet their mighty leader, Walsh asked the same question over and over: "What did you get in at?"

One shareholder told him he had bought at $30. "Not bad," said Walsh. "It's $168 now."

Paul Kavanagh, the ex-Barrick explorationist who had moved onto the Bre-X board, was beaming that day. His great bald head looked finely polished, his grin stretched his face from ear to ear as he posed for newspaper photographers. Part of the day's presentation had been a slide of the Bre-X executive team loping through the jungle, taken months before. In the picture, these now very rich men are walking away from the camera, along a sun-dappled road. Kavanagh and Walsh are walking last in line, side by side, sporting soft cotton hats to keep off the sun, which is soaking through the jungle greenery. The image is practically poetic, Kiplingesque.

Mike de Guzman said the gold ran along the veins at Busang like fine brown sugar. And the team, he said, had drilled only a quarter of the property. It sounded so tantalizing—as though, if one could simply find one's way to the heart of Kalimantan, one would be bedazzled by the sheer beauty of all that gold. David Walsh announced that he had an idea. He would sell 25 percent of Busang. Come and get it.

The unstoppable good news from the exploration site had further spurred the mining majors to find an in at Busang. Barrick had kept an eagle eye on the property, and, in a decision that seemed pragmatic given the distrust that had arisen between Barrick and Bre-X, decided to do an end run around Walsh and his crew by getting at Busang through Haji Syakerani. Syakerani had 10 percent of the Central

Zone, but, more important, he held an equal stake in the Southeast Zone. By the terms of the joint venture arrangement struck the year before, Syakerani was the only Indonesian partner in the southeast. The Syakeranis made no secret of the fact that they thought they were not being treated well by Bre-X. They complained that they were not getting feedback from Felderhof and de Guzman. They had been expecting monthly status reports, which were not forthcoming. In December, Barrick had commenced its due diligence on the Busang land title. In January the company had reached an agreement in principle to buy out Syakerani's stake.

Bre-X, meanwhile, was trying to patch up its sloppy paperwork, to put it charitably, on the share transfer on the Central Zone. In mid-February, de Guzman and Felderhof sent a letter, on PT Westralian letterhead, to Kuntoro Mangusubroto at the Department of Mines. The letter explained that Bre-X had purchased Montague, which in turn owned 80 percent of Westralian. The joint venture on Busang I, the duo explained, consisted of 80 percent Westralian, 10 percent PT Krueng Gasui (Merukh) and 10 percent PT Sungai Atan Perdana (Syakerani).

The Bre-X board had relied primarily on Felderhof and his much-touted Asian expertise to steer the company through the government approval process. But Felderhof's paperwork, if it existed in the first place, was wholly disorganized.

Busang was now such a huge prospect, it was more than odd that Felderhof and de Guzman were bothering themselves with ministerial missives. Where was the internal legal counsel to handle such matters? Where were the finance men and the investment advisers? With a property the size of Busang, Bre-X should have been up to its snout in professionals of the billable-hours variety. As David Walsh continued to pump the stock, he had failed to create a head office infrastructure with any degree of professionalism to look after such matters. Bre-X's Calgary office was little more than a calling room for investor-relations types. With the appointment of Francisco, the company at last appeared to be doing the right thing.

The share transfer was only half of it. On the Southeast Zone, which was already being touted as fabulously rich, the company held a SIPP. The SIPP is a reconnaissance permit, awarded by the minister of mines and energy. It is stated clearly in government documents that a SIPP is not a contract of work and is "prohibited from being used for objectives other than the purpose of the SIPP." The SIPP allows the permit-holder to take rock samples, dig test pits and trenches, to make geophysical surveys and geological maps, and to carry out shallow drilling, which is not defined.

Bre-X, for months, had been aggressively drilling off the Southeast Zone, totting up the gold resource statistics, touting those numbers to investors. The Department of Mines initialled the contract of work for the Southeast Zone in March. "An excellent and progressive piece of mining legislature," said Bre-X (perhaps meaning "legislation" there). "The COW provides the foreign company [Bre-X] with the assurance that when economic mineralization is discovered, the Government of Indonesia guarantees title to the deposit." But Bre-X did not yet have this COW, and the company had taken a risk in transgressing the SIPP rules. Perhaps the government would be unconcerned with this lapse. On the other hand, perhaps it would be keenly interested. Without a signed COW on the property, Bre-X had to know it was at risk. Further, David Walsh might have been interested in selling a minority stake, but would any company sign up without confirmation of clear title?

There was at least one interested mining company with a very clear view on this: CRA. John Felderhof was still interested in negotiating with the Australian mine giant. In the early spring he rang up John Craig, inviting him out to the property again. He wanted to show off how big the project had become. It had doubled in size. "You guys aren't making a big enough offer," he said. Bre-X had provided CRA with a copy of its drill hole database, a computerized model. The gold was widely distributed, and the grade did not chop and change. To the company's internal analysts, Busang and its gold were bewitching. The company kept up the hunt.

In April, Craig returned to site, this time in the company of Rolly Francisco. Rio Tinto chief geologist Theo van Leeuwen made the return trip as well. Craig was pleased to see Francisco on staff. He had advised David Walsh that the company needed someone with credentials to begin to package a sale. Francisco had that. In Craig's view, neither Walsh nor Felderhof had the credibility to steer a deal of this size. Craig pushed Walsh to bring a Wall Street financial adviser on board, but by April, Walsh still had not done so. J.P. Morgan had plenty of Indonesian experience in structuring and financing mine projects. Craig suggested to Walsh that he give the firm a call.

Craig and Francisco got along well. CRA had been stalking Busang for six months now, putting a great deal of energy into the conquest. Craig being a finance man, the two had something in common. So perhaps it was no surprise that Francisco, fresh to the company, would share his early assessment of the file he had been handed, that is, clearing up the share transfer on Busang I and getting up to speed on the status of Busang II. "It's a mess," Francisco said in his soft way. "An absolute mess."

In Craig's assessment, no company in its right mind would drill like this on an application only, because of the risk of losing land status altogether. In Indonesia, things happen. The "black hand" image seemed to have been clearly understood by Felderhof, and perhaps even by Walsh, yet still Craig made no progress. By April, he had tabled at least one offer, but Walsh was always trying to wangle a sizesum up front—a "deposit," he would call it, a "sign of good intent." Walsh raised the idea of the Australian company taking down a private placement, an equity stake in Bre-X. But CRA had no interest in this. The company did not want David Walsh's shares. CRA was adamant that there would be no funds without due diligence, and by due diligence they meant drilling their own holes at Busang.

Craig was left scratching his head as to why Walsh would reject the biggest mining company in the world, one that happened to have expertise in Indonesia. But the larger CRA's proposals became, the

larger the "deposit" grew. CRA was still willing to be a minority partner and finance 100 percent of the project, which should have seemed
a dream come true for David Walsh, who must have known that many
mining companies would jockey instead for majority control. Yet still
he would not budge. As CRA saw it, David Walsh was about to get
crucified, murdered, taken apart. Why would the company choose to
run the gauntlet?

As CRA struggled with what seemed the corporate dementia of
Bre-X, Jusuf Merukh was beating paths to the doors of numerous
mining companies. He said he had a piece of the Southeast Zone to
sell, and his 10 percent interest in the Central Zone would naturally
be carried into the bonanza. He approached Barrick. He approached
Placer. He appeared to have no preference. The Busang saga already
had enough characters. Now Merukh wanted a starring role for himself. It was, just as Francisco had said, a mess.

On February 18, a month prior to Bre-X's star turn in Toronto, Dale
Hendrick held a lunch meeting in Jakarta at a Japanese restaurant.
Gathered on that day was a field group retained by the junior company Hendrick was consulting to, Pacific Amber Resources Ltd. John
Levings was among them. Levings was now a geologist and director
with PT Mineralindo Rejeki Alam (MRA), mineral and mining consultants. Levings had worked alongside Graeme Chuck on the Busang
property in the Central Zone in the Aussie days. They had been the
ones to call it Busang in the first place.

Hendrick was bullish on Busang. Levings was not. He had lived
Busang, he told Hendrick. He had supervised the drilling of the nineteen holes and had left a pile of rock splits deep in the jungle.

Hendrick had heard that the new boys were not splitting the core.
For Hendrick, with more than forty years' experience in the mining
industry, this was near heresy. This was against all the rules of exploration. Why would the company not comply with industry standards—particularly a company still at the exploration stage, whose

deposit was ultimately still undefined and who as yet had no partner to take the project into production? On the other hand, Hendrick was holding 5,000 Bre-X shares and had thought, until this moment, that it was a great story.

Hendrick was supremely keen to get on the Busang site. He showed up at the Bre-X Jakarta office trying to connect with Felderhof, or de Guzman. Greg MacDonald was walking about in a sleeveless, insulated hunting jacket, which certainly looked uncomfortable in the 90 percent humidity. Hendrick was, sensibly, wearing shorts. "You're looking at my jacket," said MacDonald. "I guess you think I'm strange. I'm field testing them. Going to sell them to the natives in the mountains."

Hendrick was slack-jawed as he cast his gaze across the sparse Bre-X corporate digs on Rasuna Said. This, Hendrick wondered, is a $4-billion company? He was told that Felderhof was in the bush. De Guzman was reportedly playboying up and down the Jakarta waterfront in some manner of expensive car. Hendrick went back to his Australian friends. The fact that the office set-up seemed cockamamie did not prove a thing. There must, he said to Levings, be something there, referring to the gold motherlode. "Dale," said Levings, "there isn't diddly squit."

As he does every year, Dale Hendrick made the rounds at the PDA. Hendrick is an old-timer in mining terms, a grey-haired geologist in his sixties who did his time working at major mining companies before turning to a private consulting practice. He was not, however, in his dotage; he was instead intensely involved in the launch of junior mining companies, and this time round that meant Indonesia.

Hendrick knew John Felderhof's brother, Will, who was also a geologist. At the PDA that spring Hendrick introduced himself to John. "Hey, I'm going to be working in Indonesia," he said to Felderhof. "Great," said the Bre-X geologist. "Come on over. Pay us a visit." It felt to Hendrick as though he had just made a new best friend.

Hendrick mentioned his meeting with Levings. "John, the Australians told me there was nothing in the holes," he said. Felderhof sputtered. "Those doughheads didn't know how to assay. They didn't know what they had there. It's all free gold. Erratic gold. When you split it, you leave all the good stuff." Hendrick tried repeatedly to make good on Felderhof's promise of a site visit. It would never happen.

On April 19, Dale Hendrick faxed a letter to John Felderhof requesting a site visit. On May 20 he received a curt fax reply from David Walsh: "Please be informed that it is company policy that independent mining consultants are not invited to site visits of our various projects. Nevertheless thankyou for your interest and kind comments."

While the mining industry was whooping it up at the PDA, back in Jakarta it was nearly Ramadan, the annual Muslim holiday, a time of fasting. Haji Syakerani said he wanted to shut down negotiations for the duration; there would be no business discussed now. Barrick's agreement in principle to buy out his interest sat, unresolved.

Syakerani's son, Ahmad Yani, also at the PDA, was keeping very busy. Barrick did not know it yet, but they were about to be blindsided. Ahmad Yani, on behalf of his father, made a different deal altogether: he sold part of the Busang interest to a mining company in Toronto that most had never heard of, Minorca Resources.

John Felderhof was steamed that such a small mining outfit as Minorca had waltzed into Busang in this way. The Indonesian Foreign Investment Review Board had not had an opportunity to study the agreement, he warned. And the board's written approval was a requirement. "I understand that the agreement has been approved by the Montreal Exchange; however, in Indonesia this agreement may have more holes in it than a lobster trap." Felderhof certainly made himself sound like an expert in Indonesian share ownership.

At Barrick, Peter Munk was steamed too. He had thought his people were dealing with the Syakeranis. Who was Minorca? The men representing Barrick in Jakarta had been dealing with Haji. How were they to know that Ahmad Yani was in a position to sell the family's stake? By April, Munk had decided on a takeover, and a draft offering circular. Forget the Syakeranis. The company's long-time outside legal counsel, Davies Ward & Beck, were called in. Barrick started to ready itself, to move into position, should it decide to pull the trigger on a takeover bid. Barrick's corporate culture was very clear on one point: should Peter Munk pull that trigger, the company must win. There would be no embarrassments in the marketplace.

The company had paid handsomely, perhaps too handsomely, for Lac Minerals in the fall of 1994. That acquisition, won after a prolonged bidding war, had cost Barrick $1.9 billion. And that was for a company with established, producing mines. Bre-X was a company of promises still, but Walsh and his team had done such a masterful job of pushing the stock up, assisted by the bullish reports of some of Canada's premier gold-mining analysts, that a takeover of Bre-X would be pricey. Barrick's style is never to take a minority. Control is essential. That is the Peter Munk way.

Now the ground was starting to shift under Bre-X. Busang had become far too dazzling. CRA was still on the hunt, even after the wholly discouraging site visits. Barrick had been shut out by Syakerani, which merely heightened the company's resolve to get Busang somehow. Placer of Vancouver, having struck no deal with Merukh, was trying to find its own access point. Merukh, meanwhile, having been shut down by all the majors, sought a new ally. He found one in Warren Beckwith, the Australian who had been part of the previous Montague foray into Busang. It was getting as noisy in certain corporate corridors as it was in the Busang bush.

As if Bre-X did not have enough issues to contend with, that same spring, journalist Peter Kennedy wrote a story in the *Financial Post* querying Bre-X's assay methods. Dale Hendrick was Kennedy's anonymous expert. Felderhof snapped back that he did not have time to educate such simpletons as to the ways and means of assaying. Sample splits were assayed, declared Felderhof, side-stepping the point that the core was not cleaved in two. And furthermore, while cyanide leach testing was being used on the first runthrough, check fire assays were being carried out by Bre-X and an independent laboratory. "Metallurgical testwork" conducted by Kilborn had concluded that "current and previously reported gold assay results are in fact understated by as much as 12.9%." There was the validation again. This was not just Bre-X's word, this was Kilborn's. Bre-X beat a hasty retreat. From this point forward, the company adopted a bunker mentality, favouring only those members of the press who favoured Bre-X with complimentary coverage. The circle was growing smaller.

In April, Bre-X was listed on the Toronto Stock Exchange. The Alberta Stock Exchange had served its purpose—getting the stock up and running—but institutional investor respectability came from the TSE. In its filing document Bre-X claimed "reserves" based on the Kilborn feasibility study of the previous February. It was not compelled to file a prospectus. In fact, the only prospectus Bre-X ever filed was back in 1989, long before it had invested in Busang.

Bre-X was such a high-flier that it automatically moved onto the TSE 300, the stock market index that is compiled by market capitalization. Because of the calculation used, high-fliers like Bre-X could move onto the index to keep company with some of the bluest-chip firms in the land. But these relatively green additions were not seen as high-fliers in the conventional sense. The high-fliers, the companies touting suspect discoveries, had been banished from the Toronto marketplace in the aftermath of the Windfall scandal of 1964. In November 1963, the Texas Gulf Sulphur Co. had announced a copper-zinc discovery near Timmins, which had created a wild area play, with the usual penny mine suspects promoting their worthless land claims as tag-along claims. The rush was so fat with share price run-ups that local ministers had sermonized about tithing stock-market winnings to the Church.

One of the biggest winners was Viola MacMillan, the self-named Queen Bee of Canadian mining. MacMillan had staked two of her companies, Windfall Oil & Mines and Consolidated Golden Arrow

Mines, onto the Texas Gulf discovery. Windfall went from 50 cents to $5.70 on rumours that the company's drill core had shown encouraging assay results. They hadn't, the stock collapsed to 23 cents, a royal commission was struck, and many investors were left much the poorer. Mrs. MacMillan had been trading for fifty-two accounts in six different brokerages. She served a short jail sentence for "wash trading," trading shares through fictitious accounts. In the aftermath, the Toronto Stock Exchange tightened its regulations and would be home no longer to the penny mine punt. Those companies would have to go west, to Vancouver, to find a listing. The TSE would list only credible mining juniors. Or at least that was the promise. Bre-X was now one of these.

A month later, in May, Bre-X filed its Form 20-F corporate disclosure documents with the Securities and Exchange Commission in New York. In its filings, Bre-X submitted the share transfer agreement, between Westralian Resource Projects and Bre-X, for the ownership of Busang I. The copy filed was a duplicate, "replacing original lost document dated July 20, 1994." Similarly, the option deed filed was a duplicate. That could be attributed to sloppy paperwork on the part of Felderhof, a trait for which he was legendary. The contract of work, signed by Suharto, looked appropriately official on the first and last pages, but those pages book-ended seventy-five pages of unoriginal text. Any company doing title due diligence would find this filing curious, to say the least. Combined with the botched share transfer, and the machinations of Mr. Merukh, Bre-X seemed to be hauling a heap of dirty laundry. On the other hand, rare is the mining project that does not face at least one title challenge along the way.

Busang had turned Kalimantan into a massive area play. Tanqueray Resources, Mindoro, South Pacific—dozens of companies had piled on, refashioning a map of the island into what looked like a children's board game, with distinct blocks of colour to represent different corporate interests. International Pursuit, run by Stephen Dattels, who had started his career at Barrick long ago, was joint ventured with

Barrick on some of its properties and had chosen Armand Beaudoin, the roguish Canadian-born mining promoter, as its Indonesian partner, and ran their Jakarta affairs out of Beaudoin's offices initially. International Pursuit was purple on the maps. Busang was red, with a pretty yellow star in the middle.

Positive articles were being written in Indonesia about what an accomplishment this was. *Petrominer* magazine wrote that "in only five months, January to May 1996, the Government succeeded in approving no less than 140 contracts of work in general mining, thus placing Indonesia fifth in the world ranking of mining investment target countries." By contrast, between 1992 and 1995 only seventy COW permits were issued. The piece also lauded the new computerized structure for the Department of Mines. "Formerly it took three to six months to process a Contract of Work up to the signing of the permit in principle, but now it takes only 10 work days."

The fifth-place ranking reflected a risk assessment, carried out by an Australian mining journal. Sovereign risk (expropriation), red tape (and green tape), civil unrest and other considerations were part of the grading process. Chile ranked number one with the lowest risk level. Argentina was second, Australia was third, followed by Canada, then Indonesia. The United States was eighth. Papua New Guinea was fifteenth.

"Being ranked higher can be accepted as a measure of how attractive Indonesia is to investors," said *Petrominer*. "The new ranking will have a positive effect, because without foreign investors Indonesia's mineral resources will never be extracted. Domestic investors cannot as yet be expected to extract minerals in Indonesia not because they are unwilling, but because of limited funds to finance mining projects." The chairman of the country's banking association noted that "on top of everything else the national banks are actually not very knowledgeable about mining," an industry seen as high-risk, and terribly long-term. The still relatively unsophisticated banking sector preferred the quicker returns offered by other industrial and commercial ventures.

Foreign companies, said the magazine, "have the capability of mobilizing funds from the public through stock exchanges, a practice which is not yet popular in Indonesia." There were few mining companies listed on the JSE at all, and there were no young exploration companies. The stock exchange rules did not accommodate their listing: companies had to now prove three years of profitability before they could secure a JSE listing. "The Canadian companies now in Indonesia have in general already been listed on a stock exchange, even though they are still at the exploration stage. In Canada it is no problem whatever, because mining companies are routinely submitting factual reports without any manipulation for evaluation by the shareholders and authorities concerned. If there is any question of deceit, the reporter involved will be immediately penalized without any compromise." While the phrasing was somewhat strangled, the message was clear: Canadian authorities would not allow these small Canadian companies to get away with any unethical practices.

More than once the magazine mentioned that Busang had made its discovery the previous January, 1996. The run-up in the stock and the continuous disclosure of reserves had gone unremarked in the host country until then. Now there were innumerable Canadian mining companies hoping to duplicate what Bre-X said it had found. "They all hope that venturing into mining in Indonesia will crank up the price of their shares on the stock markets and have got the idea that there are many more locations in Indonesia like the one discovered by Bre-X," geologist Umar Sirait told the magazine.

Government workers in Jakarta were clearly unprepared for the enormous volume of work that had landed on department desks as a result of the Bre-X "discovery." Seventy contracts of work, including Bre-X's, comprising what was termed the sixth generation of COW, were awaiting approval from Suharto. More than twice that many had been applied for in the seventh generation. The department had only four teams of inspectors to conduct on-site evaluations. And, at least on paper, it had stated its intention to conduct a dialogue with heads of local governments, addressing issues from community development to environmental concerns.

Perhaps it was due in part to Bre-X that local panners took to the rivers in greater numbers. In central Java, villagers flocked to the Arus River in the summer of 1996. The locals were allowed to pan without a permit; anyone coming in from the outside had to get local government clearance. All panners had to pay a "contribution fee" before they set to work, 500 rupiahs for the locals. A small stipend given that panning for these people, most of whom earned their living as farmers, could take their daily income from 5,000 rupiahs to 180,000.

On June 7, Michael Fowler, an analyst with securities firm Lévesque Beaubien Geoffrion in Toronto, put out a report on rumoured title disputes at Busang. Two negative street rumours had surfaced, he said. The first had to do with ownership uncertainty concerning the Southeast Zone. But the cow there had been initialled, argued Fowler; formal approval was merely a "rubber stamp." cows, to the best of his knowledge, had not been cancelled before, and if the Indonesian government were to start now, the country would lose credibility in the eyes of the international mining community. The second rumour was the hint of a lawsuit over the Central Zone. On this Fowler was unconcerned, for should it materialize it would have nothing to do with the rich Southeast Zone. Investors should see Bre-X as a buying opportunity. "A resource calculation is due mid-June," he said, "and will likely be good news."

How would he know that?

At 3:36 in the afternoon of June 9, Egizio Bianchini, the Nesbitt Burns gold-mining analyst, pressed the play button on the videocamera he was holding and started to record a site visit of Busang. Rubber-thonged feet are observed slapping over a football field of core boxes. The drill core goes from a bluish grey and highly brecciated, and thus crumbled in some sections in the box, to smooth, beige-grey tubes with spidery, dark-green veins.

As the camera rolls, Bianchini's voice is heard; he's an enthusiastic, sometimes breathless storyteller. On Bay Street, Bianchini had become Bre-X's biggest booster. Now he was writing part of the script—Bre-X's very own Hollywood cinematographer.

De Guzman wears striped shorts, a blue T-shirt and runners. He seems comfortable in this setting, walking across the core boxes, picking up a piece here and there, hosing down a hunk of rock to get a better look at the indicator minerals.

De Guzman takes his videographer through the drilling to date. Bianchini asks to see a particular hole. "We have the assays I think," says de Guzman. "It's just about . . ." Before he can finish his sentence, Bianchini interjects: "Is it a good grade?" De Guzman laughs. "Quote unquote," he says.

Bianchini's lens finds a line of core that the analyst is particularly smitten with. "You haven't seen this hole yet, Mike? Oh, look at this. This looks good. Five grams. This is five grams right here." The core has not been assayed. Bianchini seems to have become expert in eyeball estimates. Rather than asking the site participants what conclusions they are drawing, and why, Bianchini offers up his own. He makes many pronouncements for someone who should have been there to learn, who would soon return to Toronto to inform the sprawling network of Nesbitt brokers, who would in turn advise an even broader group of investors. His questions lack rigour. To suggest grades in unsplit core, to hypothesize what the gold, presuming there is any, will run, fulfils no duty of responsibility to the client. There is no due diligence here. At one juncture, Bianchini's narrative verges on the orgasmic. "The rock looks extremely favourable . . . Oh, yes. Mike, we're in good stuff here?"

In the background in many scenes, metallurgist turned site administrator Jerry Alo assumes his standard huge-shouldered pose, hands on hips, head sunk into his shoulders, Nixonesque, his jet-black hair perfectly shellacked. Sometimes he holds a file of papers. By this time, Alo had hired another Filipino, Rudy Vega. Alo knew Vega from their years working together in Butuan, in Mindanao. Alo had phoned Vega up, telling him that if he were interested in an adventure, Busang was the place to be.

De Guzman in some frames stands with his left shoulder close to the camera, and here one can see quite clearly a lump the size of a nectarine on his shoulder: a clearly identifying characteristic, perhaps, if one were ever needed.

Mike de Guzman's drill map shows kilometre after kilometre of white space beyond the existing drill grid. He waxes poetical about the potential that lies out there. But for now the company is doing in-fill drilling between the existing lines, having stopped expanding the periphery of the drilling. "What made you guys stop at [line] 69?" asks Bianchini. "Is that a decision that was made corporately?" "Yes," answers de Guzman. "It is a corporate decision."

In one scene, de Guzman goes on at length about some form of mineralization in a barely audible tone. He is addressing an unidentified westerner—perhaps an institutional client; possibly, though less likely, an analyst. The westerner favours backward-turned baseball caps, and in the unrelenting burn of Busang he takes off his cap, scratching his head like Stan Laurel wondering what Ollie was up to. He appears on the verge of fainting. He asks not a single question.

Jerry Alo leads the walk-through of the sample-preparation facility, pointing at the rock-crushers, explaining the procedure. He outlines what size of sample gets bagged for Indo Assay and explains that check samples are sent to another laboratory, called Inchcape. To the side sits a trolley for small pans of roughly broken core. Alo gives every indication that the on-site prep lab is being used to process samples from the current drilling of the mineralized core.

Yet this makes little sense. When the prep lab went up in early 1995, the facility spent its first months preparing stream samples. The crew did not start processing drill core until late in May 1995, and this, after being crushed to a pulp and bagged, was sent on to Indo Assay. For the next four months, the Bre-X staff, under the supervision of Alo and Puspos, sent these pulps to Balikpapan, along with bags of uncrushed core. The on-site lab did prepare all the so-called "infill" core.

In August and into September of that year, Indo Assay encountered severe reproducibility problems with the samples. Very soon after that, the site preparation of the mineralized core was stopped. Two years later, John Irvin would test a coarse crusher residue from one of the site-prepped samples. The sample itself had been high grade. The residue showed no gold.

As the camera rolls, Bianchini asks de Guzman if the sample bags he is filming are to go to Indo Assay for checking. "Yes," says de Guzman. "Something like that." But the sample was not on its way to Samarinda, and thence Balikpapan. Samples from this particular hole, BSSE 75, had been tested long ago.

Warren Irwin stepped into the elevator of his waterfront condominium on a hot summer's day, 1996. He did not recognize the older gentleman he was to share the ride with, who seemed to be deeply interested in a front-page story in that day's *Financial Post* on Arequipa Resources. Irwin, well over six feet but not much past thirty, started up a brief conversation about the headline news, but conversation quickly turned to the now hot mining tale, Busang. The gentleman reader introduced himself as Dale Hendrick. He was, he said, a skeptic. Warren Irwin was fabulously long the stock. This was the first negative word he had ever heard about the discovery. He wanted to know more.

Two weeks later, the gentlemen met for lunch. Hendrick has seen so much in his years in the business. He filled the head of Warren Irwin with fantastic but true tales of the scandalous side of junior mining. Salt jobs, particularly. Hendrick knows just about all the salting stories that have been told in Canadian mining. Warren Irwin had never heard of a company called New Cinch. Dale Hendrick could recall just about every detail.

It was the fall of 1980. Shares in New Cinch Uranium Ltd. vaulted from $1 to just shy of $30 on the Vancouver Stock Exchange. The property, in southern New Mexico, was called Orogrande, and the company said it had found gold big time.

New Cinch was using an assay lab in Texas, El Paso Chem-Tec Laboratories. It was El Paso that produced the high-grade values. When an independent company was called in to reevaluate the samples from two high-grade holes, and the samples came up with bare trace amounts of gold, the stock collapsed to 20 cents. The independent investigation concluded that gold had been added to one of the agents used in the assaying of the samples.

The tale took a turn worthy of Dashiell Hammett when Michael Opp, a lab worker in El Paso, took a bullet in the temple in his El Paso apartment. The FBI, the RCMP and Scotland Yard moved in to investigate. Budding mining executive Peter Allen had been buying up New Cinch shares in the hopes of taking over this great gold discovery as part of his mining empire, which he would build into Lac Minerals. Writing in *Maclean's* magazine at the time, Tony Whittingham remarked that the caper featured promoters in far-off places, the familiar circle of stock market promotion and frenzied share-buying on flimsy evidence: "the whole panoply of spontaneous irrationality largely eliminated from the stock market in recent decades with increasing regulation designed to protect investors and promoters from their own stupidity and greed."

Peter Allen sued, and the case went to court in 1984. One of the key witnesses was Bert Applegath, a onetime Toronto penny promoter resident in New Mexico, who had shopped the Orogrande property. On the witness stand in the spring of 1984, Appelgath wove a great tale. "Perhaps the greatest tragedy of all," he said, "other than the human frailty, is that none of us in this room, or any room, might ever know who concocted this whole damn thing."

I attended a gold-mining conference in the spring of 1996. "Conference" is often too staid a word to use for such gatherings. Some of these, like the big ones in New York and San Francisco, offer presentations by the top mining companies in the world, as well as giving smaller but promising outfits a chance to sell themselves to legions of investors. The one I attended was actually a smaller affair, in Atlanta, in Buckhead, to be precise. Booths were set up in the hosting hotel to display the corporate literature of a dozen or so small mining companies—the standard set-up. Such conferences are usually a fair representation of the area plays and the exploration countries deemed, for whatever reason, to be in vogue. The exploration targets *du jour* were the former Russian republics. The CEOs of these junior mining companies were anxious to proclaim that mining the tailings of copper in Mongolia was the next big thing, though last year's big thing might have been diamonds in the Northwest Territories.

The guest of honour at the Buckhead soiree was Robert Friedland, who had the kind of checkered past endemic to promoters. Friedland had backed a heap leach gold-mining project in Colorado's San Juan mountains in the early 1980s. Heap leaching is a mining technique whereby the ore can be sucked from the rock using a cyanide solution. Friedland's mine was called Summitville, and it proved to be not only an economic dud but, worse, an environmental mess, for which Friedland took no responsibility. I remember before the fall how Friedland had been the darling of a big American gold show, and how, after the fall, at a gathering in New York, no one wanted to have much to do with him.

In the spring of 1996, however, he had risen again. Friedland had been the promoter behind Diamond Fields Resources, which was on the hunt for diamonds—until it found nickel in Labrador instead. The discovery was called Voisey's Bay, and it was the largest single nickel deposit known on the planet. After the discovery, Friedland started giving speeches about the uses of stainless steel, and how nickel was a good investment bet because, once the Chinese caught on to stainless-steel forks and spoons, why, the demand would skyrocket. Friedland bears the typical promoter trait of being able to sell a listener on his belief in whatever it is he is selling at the moment. He's a preacher, dexterous in his ability to sell soup one day, nuts the next.

Not only was Voisey's Bay real, it became the focus of a takeover battle between two of Canada's largest mining companies: Inco Ltd. and Falconbridge Ltd. Friedland took to wearing a Falconbridge tie and went on a road show with Falconbridge management, championing the marriage between Diamond Fields and Falconbridge, till Inco upped the bid and the game board changed again. That, of course, was Friedland's objective: to get the top dollar for shareholders, of which he was a rather large one. Friedland, even his critics would have to admit, played the battle for Diamond fields like a winning general. David Walsh would study Friedland's masterful negotiating skills with much interest.

The Buckhead gathering seemed perhaps not quite as swish as one Friedland would now be willing to give time to. But the investors here—Republicans, big gold-jewellery lovers, fans of home boy Newt Gingrich—had been loyal to Friedland and had loaded up on Diamond Fields stock, which had made some monstrously rich. These are precisely the investors who flood conferences such as this, eager to find the next penny share that will become a hundred-dollar stock: the one in a thousand, one in ten thousand punt.

At the "gala" dinner I sat beside Paul Stephens, managing director and chief investment officer of Robertson Stephens & Co. in San Francisco. Stephens talked fast and was very high on Friedland. And no wonder, Stephens had made something like a gazillion dollars for his investment funds by betting heavily on his friend Robert.

Stephens complained that Canadians use the "promoter" label for people such as Friedland. It seems so dirty, suggesting someone who wants merely to fleece sneakered retirees. Good promoters, he said, are venture capitalists, not unlike the guys in the software business. "The jerks in Vancouver who buy the cheap stock, take it public and sell their stock as the public is buying into the promote, that's what's wrong with the Canadian gold business."

Stephens said promoters like Friedland had been forced out of North America by the environmentalists. Good promoters played an important role, he said. Discoveries such as Voisey's would not be made were it not for his ilk. Big mining companies rarely make discoveries such as this.

I had heard this speech from others many, many times before. Part of me agreed with it. But the other side of these promotions was the lax regulations that allowed the insiders to belly up to the trough, devouring huge amounts of cheap stock, while touting the stock's merits to the uninformed, who buy the stuff. The insiders then sell and make their profit. The game is rigged, really.

Unless the mine find is real. And then it becomes a different game. When Friedland realized Voisey's Bay was real, he had to be very careful in his handling of the property. "When the stock was $15 I think his biggest fear was that someone would bid $30 and take it away from him," said Stephens. "He knew it was worth a lot more."

Friedland stood on the dais, the lights low to allow for his Voisey's Bay slide show, and neatly tripped through the "knives and forks" business for the hundredth time. I turned to Stephens. Voisey's Bay was really yesterday's story. The hot news of course was Bre-X. Was he invested? Were his funds in? Stephens's contrarian fund alone was worth a billion dollars, and his clients included the likes of Fidelity, the largest commission-generator in the United States.

Stephens surprised me by offering a very clipped "No." Well, he had been in, earlier, but sold out suddenly. How come? Stephens smiled. It had been 1993 when Ed Flood, a geologist who then worked with Stephens, had talked up the theory of investing in areas that had not seen much exploration for the past half century. Zaire. Angola. They talked of the Rim of Fire, one of the great untapped areas. Nobody there but the Australians and a little company called Bre-X with a pretty good geologist. Robertson Stephens had bought 400,000 shares at 40 cents. They had summoned Bre-X management. "We'll take twenty times that," said Flood to Walsh, "but we'd like to get to know you better."

Walsh flew to San Francisco with Jeannette and Barry Tannock. The men in the crisp cotton shirts at Stephens & Co. were less than impressed by the look of this trio. Walsh talked about his past exploits: oil and gas and real estate. Stephens did not want to hear about his hopes and dreams. Sulawesi was the company's number-one prospect then. "None of them had any clue what was going on in the field, or what the money was being spent on," says Flood. Stephens & Co. had been pondering a private placement. Instead, the company sold its stock straightaway. They had bought in initially at 68 cents and were pretty pleased with themselves that they had tripled their money before the rest of the world found out what putzes these people were. In stunned amazement they watched the shares rise and rise and rise.

Months later, under different circumstances, I spoke with Stephens again. Bre-X had gone to very nearly $300 a share. "I left $300 million Canadian on the table," he said. "All these people would call from Canada and say how great Bre-X was, and I would say, 'They're drilling illegally. They don't have title. If they find something really phenomenal, that corrupt government down there will just take it away from them.'"

Stephens had instead become a big investor in Robert Friedland's Indochina Goldfields, with exploration interests ranging from Kazakhstan to Indonesia. The lead underwriter on the Indochina issue was a Canadian brokerage, Nesbitt Burns. Stephens figured Nesbitt had done a lousy job of pricing the issue, which went out at $15 and sort of just hung there. Then the Sumitomo scandal hit and commodities prices cracked and Indochina tumbled. Well, crashed is more like it, down $6 a share. Some analyst named Egizio Bianchini had gone around to clients, according to Stephens, advising them to sell their Indochina. "He blew everybody right out of the company right after they got a fee to take it public," griped Stephens. "He basically did his clients a horrible service."

Friedland had invested, too, in a company that would heap leach copper from gargantuan waste dumps in Mongolia, which sounded like an environmental threat that the western media might never get a chance to analyse. Investors watched their savings being funnelled into mining companies spinning farther and farther out across the globe, to remote and inaccessible corners. That same month, March 1996, the newswires were spitting out hairy stories about a mining operation in Irian Jaya. Friedland and I spoke of this, and he launched into a compelling narrative about tribespeople sporting penis gourds stuffing westerners into cooking pots. He was not being entirely fanciful. Penis gourds are still worn in Irian. Tragically, rioting in Tembagapura and Timika resulted in the deaths of three people, while more than a dozen were seriously injured. Thousands of immigrants had flooded to Timika over the years, drawn by the prosperous glow cast by the rich foreign mining company that was pulling so much copper and gold from the land. Resentments had quickly grown: between the immigrants and the locals; between both those groups and the mining company. The indigenous groups wanted better employment opportunities; more input into social development; and wanted the forces of Jakarta, the army men who control the site, out. The mine was Grasberg. The company was Freeport-McMoRan.

Within the month, Freeport's chief executive officer, Jim Bob Moffett, was pledging myriad improvements in the social contract between the mining company and the Irianese. Increased training of native Irianese; a doubling of the number of Irianese in management positions in ten years; a distribution of 1 percent of the mine's profits. But why had it taken such horrific circumstances to compel this mighty company, so smart and rich, a member of the Fortune 500, to offer up the most obvious concessions?

SINEWS OF WAR

THE HOT WIND STIRS THE SENSES, raising an intoxicating mixture—the scent of cloves, the smell of smoke. Advertising balloons lift
in the air, their soft drift somehow making their slogans less aggressive. They are lit after dark, and so even at night in the heart of downtown Jakarta visitors cannot escape their messages of commerce.

The landscape is a jigsaw of glittering highrises. But the swish real
estate cannot disguise the *kampong*, the slums potted throughout the
city, their shacks of Javanese, the suffering poor, for whom Indonesia's Pak Suharto has done little. The sludge they call water can hardly
move through these walled villages within the Great Man's Great City.
Suharto says he is not an almighty leader, but rather a father, and these
people are his family. But the Asian miracle has made the rich very
rich. The car dealers cannot keep $480,000 Mercedes-Benz ragtops
in stock. Demi-actress Demi Moore had recently opened a Jakarta
branch of Planet Hollywood, the restaurant chain that bizarrely begat
a public offering and a stock exchange listing. The markets had gone
mad. They would support all manner of foundationless endeavour.

FEVER

Melanie Griffith, Sylvester Stallone, Danny Glover and Bruce Willis joined in the Planet Hollywood celebrations. They took over the two penthouse suites at the Grand Hyatt Hotel at US$5,400 a night. The walls surrounding the penthouse patios are cloaked in greenery, and with the high hibiscus, palm fronds and white, wood-slatted venetian doors shutting out the stark realities of Jakarta twenty-six floors below, this scene could be Raffles before the war.

Not a block goes by without offering a reminder of Suharto's power. From the trip to the city centre from Sukarno Hatta International Airport, the management of which is contracted to companies owned by Suharto's children, through the toll roads built by companies controlled by Suharto's number-one daughter, Siti Hardyanti Rukmana (or Tutut), to the shopping condominium galleria that was a particular pet project of Suharto's wife, Madam Tien, before she died in April 1996, the Suharto aroma, indistinct from the aroma of graft, is everywhere.

Along the roadways, the Timor car, son Hutomo Mandala Putra's favourite commercial enterprise, is well advertised. In early 1996, Hutomo, known as Tommy, entered into a car-manufacturing arrangement with Kia of South Korea to launch a "national car." The autos would, at first, be imported, then gradually shift their manufacturing base to Indonesia. Tommy was granted special import concessions for the Timor that effectively conferred duty-free status on the imports, giving the little sedans a yawning market advantage over all other autos, which carry duties as high as 125 percent. To ensure sales, it was decreed that any government car purchases would be of Timors only. This is how the Suhartos make a market.

The Timor deal did not sit well with brother Bambang Trihatmodjo, whose group had bid for the same gold-plated contract. When Bambang was shut out, he announced the development of two cars of his own, tagged Cakra and Nenggala. Indonesians got the point. Bambang had named his autos after weapons used by brothers battling in the *wayang*, the nation's lacy shadow puppetry. In the *wayang*, whose most popular tales are taken from the Hindu epic poems the *Ramayana* and the *Mahabarata*, taloned, beaky creatures enact sonnets of ecstasy and treachery. Their shapes shadow on a linen screen, a midnight-to-sunrise battle of good against evil.

Some of Bambang's interests have a thuggish air, including Rajawali, his real estate venture, which aims to be part of a luxury hotel development on the island of Lombok. The local villagers have suffered repeated raids by army soldiers, who burn houses and loot what little the villagers do have, trying to force them to leave. The people of Indonesia have been swallowing the growing enterprise of Suharto's children for two decades. The car escapades have become the symbol of a corrupt regime gone over the brink.

There is now a mounting unease, a sense of dislocation, a foreboding that might sound overdrawn to those who have not come here. But this is a dictatorship, and the military is in force throughout. The country has 300,000 active military troops. Suharto is seventy-five. Those who keep a watching brief on his "presidency" note that, despite the jaunty pictures of Pak Suharto astride a motorcycle, or the anecdotes of regular golf games and fishing adventures with his various good friends, his health is not as strong as his public relations.

In the months following the passing of Madam Tien, Suharto's offspring, six children who have advanced their interests in myriad corporate entities, engaged in a rent-seeking bacchanalia. If Fellini had been a 1990s filmmaker looking to capture a grotesque example of engorged commerce, he would have come here. The children's interests are indiscriminate: from real estate to oil and gas to the banking sector, they're there, their interest often "free carried," their equity paid for by the foreign operator, in order to secure business here. And it is not just the children who have behaved in this way. Various corporate tycoons have done well through their alliances with Suharto. They have taken up pieces of enterprise, no money down. They have built multibillion-dollar empires. The Suhartos have made the Marcoses look like pikers.

The country is comprised of a diverse group of Javanese, Sundanese, Madurese and Malay, speaking more than five hundred languages. More than 200 million people live on 6,000 of the country's more than 13,000 islands, the world's largest archipelago. Indonesia has the largest Islamic population in the world. Nine million Indonesians live in Jakarta. Traffic clogs the city: passengers hang out of double-decker buses that advertise the likes of Lipton ice tea; motor-scooters seem hitched like train cars as they weave through the congestion.

Suharto is the world's second-longest-ruling head of state, after Cuba's Fidel Castro. His defenders point to the progress that Indonesia has made under his rule. And it is true that he has lifted the country from wholesale despair. By many economic measures, Suharto's governance to the mid-1990s has benefited the country. The per-capita gross domestic product has risen to US$3,500; the per-capita income to US$960. The government uses these numbers to prove that the rising economic tide has lifted the smallest boats. But what western economist Kevin Phillips calls "the boiling point" in North American society, the expanding chasm between rich and poor, is obscenely pronounced here. At the same time, Suharto has failed to groom a successor, and he has taken his country to its own boiling point.

It was Bung Sukarno, the charismatic freedom-fighter in the ever-ready sunglasses, who brought independence from the Dutch after the Second World War. For years he was seen as brother, or *bung*, to the people. He introduced the concept of *Pancasila*, the five principles: a belief in one Supreme God; democracy through deliberation and consensus among representatives; justice and civility among peoples; the unity of Indonesia; and social justice for all.

Sukarno's charisma was initially the glue that bound the country's coalition of politics and armed power, of "amity and animosity," as one student of Indonesian history has termed it. But the military never saw its role as limited to the fight for independence. According to journalist Adam Schwarz: "As early as 1947, the military under the leadership of General Sudirman had begun setting up its own, parallel system of government so that each civilian official, from provincial governors down to district supervisors, would be matched with a corresponding figure from the military."

Many in the armed forces were drawn from a social caste that claimed near-aristocracy and higher education; many were connected to the leaders of political power. According to Schwarz, while the political and military systems were parallel in structure, "at each level of the bureaucracy the military counterpart wielded more power." The army assumed control of numerous Dutch enterprises in the 1950s. In 1958 the army's chief of staff introduced a new doctrine, clearly defining the role of the Indonesian army as both military and socio-political. The new ideology was called, initially, the Middle Way, and in the decades that followed it grew increasingly influential. In Bahasa Indonesia they came to call it *dwifungsi*: dual function. In the summer of 1959, eight of the country's twelve cabinet posts went to army men.

"The Indonesian army, having played a crucial role during the revolutionary period, began carefully to work out an image for itself and its mission," wrote Baladas Goshal, "and claimed itself to be an 'Army of the People.'. . . Posing itself as unique among the armies of the world, never having been created as an instrument of the state, the army claimed for itself a role which transcend [sic] the purely military and extend [sic] to all social, political and economic fields." There was, says Goshal, an ideological divide between the military and the country's western-trained academic intellectuals, in effect, a "competing elite," a challenge to the "civilian intelligentsia." Academics have argued that the growth of the Indonesian army was mishandled. Neglected and impoverished in the period immediately following the Second World War, the army wallowed in corrupt practices.

The country's revolutionary period was not confined to the ouster of the Dutch. In the latter 1950s, rebel uprisings in Sumatra and Sulawesi threatened Sukarno's attempts to consolidate power in Jakarta. According to historian Hamish McDonald, "[a]rms and advice were supplied to Sumatra, and CIA combat aircraft flew missions in support of the Sulawesi rebels from U.S. bases in the Philippines." The rebels were seen as anti-Communist, and they were fighting in territory, particularly Sumatra, that was rich with oil.

Sukarno's great accomplishment was the unification of Indonesia's thousands of islands—the peoples who were Muslim, Hindu, animist, Catholic—giving them one language, Bahasa Indonesia. He built a monument to himself at Merdeka Field, a tumescent obelisk with a six-metre gold flame spewing from its top, an ugly symbol of freedom. Sukarno, affectionately called Bung Karno, became increasingly less of a brother to his people, and the gold-topped freedom monument became a metaphor for that. "Palace Millionaires," as they were called, would regularly call on Sukarno and offer payoffs in exchange for special privileges granted to their businesses. The little man who initially aligned himself with the poorest of the Javanese, who embraced, ideologically, a socialist future, said "Let them eat rats" to the people when vermin ate the paddy crop in Java. In his overthrow of colonialism, Sukarno could not accept even the most moderate of free-market models. The centre could no longer hold. The people were starving, and Sukarno became increasingly megalomaniacal.

Ultimately, Sukarno's promises were proved a fantasy—"verbal flatulence" Tarzie Vittachi called it in *The Fall of Sukarno*. "Unfortunately, as Sukarno intoxicated the masses, so he intoxicated himself. He fed off the masses and fattened his ego to such gargantuan proportions that he could no longer see beyond the rim of his own self." The people were starving, yet Sukarno announced the launching of the Outer Space Health Institute to study the well-being of Indonesian astronauts. In 1965 he announced he was pulling Indonesia out of the United Nations. According to Vittachi, Sukarno told the Ceylonese ambassador that "living dangerously" in this way gave him a "sense of the eagle."

As inflation spiralled, as the Indonesian currency, the rupiah, was massively devalued, the price of sugar, and chilies to make the *tambal*, were increasingly beyond the reach of common folk. Sukarno adopted a new motto: 1965, he decreed, would be the Year of Self-Reliance. "He could make words sound as though they were the things they stood for," wrote Vittachi. "He could make people believe that the mineral wealth of their country was already bulking so heavily in their pockets that they could afford 15-story palaces rising out of the filth of Djakarta's slums."

Sukarno's representative government was called NASAKOM, and it was structured to embrace religious parties, the nationalist party and the Communist party. But by the mid-1960s, the country witnessed the growth in popularity of the Indonesian Communist party, the PKI. Mounting PKI support quickly caught the eye of western leaders, particularly in the United States. Foreign corporate interests feared shutdown and expropriation. Mounting destitution fed PKI sloganeering, and emotions turned against the imperialist influences, the *necolim*—the white-skinned neocolonialists. The West saw Jakarta taking its place in the corridor of Communist power: Jakarta, Phnom Penh, Peking. Sukarno issued a somewhat revised map of the world: the Indian Ocean became the Indonesian Ocean and the Greenwich meridian was moved to Jakarta.

The Chinese, who controlled a majority of the country's commerce, gave financial support to the PKI, perhaps to help turn local aggression away from their profiteering practices. D.N. Aidit, the PKI leader, proclaimed that the roots of the economic crisis lay in the "capitalist bureaucrats, economic adventurers and corrupters known as the three evils of the cities."

As the country moved toward its twentieth-anniversary celebration on October 5, 1965, Sukarno tried vainly to paint Jakarta as a new power, on par with Washington or Moscow. "We have now emerged from being a nation of coolies into a nation which determines the history of mankind," he said. But there were menacing noises rumbling through the capital city of a coup d'état. Rumour had it that the army, which had announced manoeuvres to coincide with the anniversary, was plotting the overthrow of Sukarno. For the PKI, the army was chief among the corrupters that had to be eliminated.

On September 30, as Sukarno was speaking in Jakarta Stadium, sporting his trademark black sunglasses, his black *pitji*, he fell ill and stumbled away from the microphone. Anguish started to swell through the crowd, a presumptive mourning for the death of the mighty Bung. An hour later a revived Sukarno was back at the rostrum. Aidit, says Tarzie Vittachi, "made for the exit and was never seen in public again."

The events that followed still seem, more than thirty years later, as haunting a play as the *wayang*, mysterious and unresolved. The commander of Sukarno's palace guard, Lieutenant-Colonel Untung, ordered the execution of a group of army generals; six were murdered. General Suharto was on Untung's list, scheduled for arrest at 2:00 a.m., but he was not at home when the marauders came. The story of his whereabouts quickly became woven into the mysticism of Suharto himself. His *dukun*, or guru, had prophesied that he should not be at home before 2:00 a.m., and so he had sailed to the mouth of a river and spent his time in peaceful worship, he would say. Suharto had remained in the *bayang*, the shadows.

By the time he returned home, the assassinations were well under way. The bodies of the slaughtered generals were dumped down a 36-metre hole. Hoary tales, later discredited, of genital mutilation of the generals by Gerwani, the PKI's women's movement, quickly circulated.

Sukarno needed the support of the PKI to keep the army at bay. After the night of the generals, Sukarno publicly supported the view that the Communists had readied themselves for a counter-coup in the face of their expectation that the army intended to seize power from Sukarno. Major-General Suharto and others, Sukarno charged, were complicit in this "generals' plot." This Council of Generals, Untung said in a communique, had plotted the mobilization of troops for October 5, Armed Forces Day. The September 30 movement was organized to prevent this counter-revolutionary coup.

Many historians support the view that Untung mistakenly assumed that Sukarno had passed away, or was at least permanently disabled as a leader, after exiting the stadium on September 30. That Sukarno seemed instead to appear in surprisingly good health after his attack presented a problem for all the participants. What role could now be written for Sukarno in this power play? The army version quickly cast Sukarno as a complicit participant in an Aidit-PKI overthrow. The *Times* of London reported this version of events. "The fresh but secret evidence," said the *Times*, "appears to have come from the Central Intelligence Agency."

At midnight, October 2, Sukarno announced that the initiative to restore peace to Indonesia had fallen to Major General Suharto. Suharto was a relative unknown. As a lieutenant-colonel in 1950 he had led the Garuda Mataram Brigade in the fight for independence, from which the East Indonesia Government was born. Suharto's commander was Colonel Gatot Subroto. Years before, Subroto had adopted an ethnic Chinese boy whose name was The Kian Seng. After his adoption he was named Mohamad Hasan; to westerners, just plain Bob. Under Suharto's command, the army shrewdly moved into commercial enterprise in Central Java. They inserted themselves into the governance of nationalized Dutch enterprises, and they pursued what Hamish McDonald calls "direct entrepreneuring." Chinese partners, says McDonald, would provide the capital, and the *baju hijau*—literally "green shirt," the army man—would grease the wheels of bureaucracy and taxation. One of the Chinese businessmen allied with Suharto was Bob Hasan.

Suharto also established what were called *Yayasan*, or foundations, which, when the veil was lifted, were mechanisms to funnel profits into army pockets. "These foundations became partners in companies directed at taking over marketing and distribution of key commodities," says McDonald. "Suharto gained a reputation as an efficient money-maker. His reasoning was that where commercial opportunities existed it might as well be authorities who benefited."

The people rose up against army corruption, and the army's top commander, General Nasution, ordered a housecleaning. McDonald says an investigation unearthed a sugar-smuggling deal, in which Suharto played a part. In October 1959, Suharto was relieved of his command. "According to sources close to Nasution, Nasution and his deputy, Gatot Subroto, took a conscious decision 'because of the political climate' not to take further action. Suharto was assigned to the army's Staff and Command School (Seskoad) in Bandung." He was thirty-eight. The setback would not last long. Subroto was in charge of army promotions, and his beloved son, Bob Hasan, was now in deep with Suharto. Suharto was named head of the Kostrad, the Army Strategic Command.

The days and weeks that followed Suharto's ascension were of horrific slaughter. Under the guise of an anti-Communist cleansing, hundreds of thousands of men, women and children were murdered. Historians have argued their numbers. They cannot be known finally, but the estimate that put the deaths at 500,000, which once seemed high, now occupies the middle ground. The tally might have been twice that. It was under Suharto's new leadership that this slaughter swept through Java and Bali. The army participated in the massacres and provided arms to other perpetrators.

As Robert Cribb notes, inefficient record-keeping contributed to the darkness that surrounded the mass killing, as did the fact that the murders were dispersed, nocturnal and carried out by small groups. The Indonesians named the moonlight assassinations Stormking executions, after imported lanterns of the same name. While the mutilation of the generals was disproved after their exhumation, there are numerous accounts that the military-supported beheadings of PKI, or presumed PKI, included genital mutilation and rape. Beheading with a broad-bladed knife was a common form of killing. Bodies heaved into the Brantas River would beach along the shore and be thrown back in again. The reason for the extermination was never made terribly clear; the slaughterers' agenda lacked a strong ideological force.

Says Cribb: "If anything, the Indonesian killings have been treated as if they fall into an anomalous category of 'accidental' mass death."

The rise of the PKI presented a clear opportunity for the army, what Michael van Langenberg calls the "management of violence." The manufactured demonism of the PKI, particularly in the assassination of the generals, fuelled the violence that set the course for the military to form the foundation for Indonesian nationalism. The deemed urgency of the restructuring suited Suharto's purposes. Again, early accounts make this seem accidental—that Suharto more or less fell into power.

The violence was allowed to proceed unchecked by the military, which virtually licensed the massacre, thereby highlighting the need for the army to restore order. The violence, wrote Kenneth Young, "[w]as a political choice deliberately taken by the military commanders who controlled perhaps the only instrument of State policy that could be relied upon—the army itself." Years later, Bertrand Russell would write that "in four months, five times as many people died in Indonesia as in Vietnam in 12 years." The CIA reported that the killings ranked "along with the Soviet purges of the 1930s, the Nazi mass murders during the Second World War, and the Maoist bloodbath of the early 1950s. In this regard, the Indonesian coup is certainly one of the most significant events of the 20th century."

Writing in *The New York Times* in June 1966, James Reston said, "There was a great deal more contact between the anti-Communist forces and at least one very high official in Washington before and during the Indonesian massacre than generally realized." He said it was doubtful that the Suharto coup "would ever have been attempted without the American show of strength in Vietnam or been sustained without the clandestine aid it has received indirectly from here."

Vittachi, who also used the numbers of dead in the Vietnam War as a benchmark against which the horror in Indonesia could be compared, put the number of orphaned children at two million. Would they one day rise up to protest what had gone on in the dark, waning days of 1965?

The western world was given a cinematic taste of this time when Christopher Koch's novel *The Year of Living Dangerously* was adapted to cinema. Koch's hero was Guy Hamilton, a handsome Australian newsman new to Jakarta, a city in squalor and increasingly disaffected with Sukarno. "Most of us, I suppose, become children again when we enter the slums of Asia," wrote Koch. "We re-discover there childhood's opposite intensities: the gimcrack and the queer mixed with the grim; laughter and misery; carnal nakedness and threadbare nakedness; fear and toys. This was now happening to Hamilton, who found that the puzzling clove-and-nutmeg scent, like the smell of the heat itself, had intensified; it suddenly became very important to know what it was."

Koch's Billy Kwan, a dwarf cameraman, is the book's moral core, who initially idolizes, then comes to despise Sukarno. If *Dangerously* were a *wayang* play, Kwan would be the *dalang*, the storyteller who stands to the side of the linen *wayang* screen.

Kwan adopts a biblical mantra—"What then must we do?"—which he takes from Luke, chapter three, verse ten. John the Baptist says to the crowds who come to be anointed by him: "'You brood of vipers. Who warned you to flee from the wrath to come? Bear fruits worthy of repentance.'. . . And the crowds asked him, 'What then should we do?' In reply he said to them, 'Whoever has two coats must share with anyone who has none, and whoever has food must do likewise.'"

In this, Sukarno was a failure. He could free his people from the Dutch, but ultimately he could not hold this democracy, for he could not advance its domestic economy, or the well-being of its people. Sukarno failed, says Vittachi, "to develop the vast potential wealth that lay under its feet."

On March 11, Sukarno, still shakily in power, was chairing a cabinet meeting when he was handed a note: "The palace is now surrounded by irregular troops." Ostensibly, the troops had circled the palace to keep a mounting student movement at bay. The true intention came clear with this memo, which might have been written by

Suharto. Sukarno quickly exited the palace by helicopter and flew to Bogor. He was presented with no choice but to agree formally to the empowerment of Suharto. At midnight, Suharto's voice was transmitted over radio: Sukarno had transferred all authority to him to restore peace and justice to Indonesia, and to bring economic prosperity.

Bung Karno now rests in history as a multi-titled lover of many, many women, Sole Interpreter of the Revolution, ultimately a self-aggrandizer. At Crocodile Hole, where the bodies of the generals were dumped, the Suharto government erected a monument to *Pancasila*, the five principles, the code by which the new Indonesia would live.

One of Suharto's first acts was to ban the PKI. But he did not appear to cleave personally to any one ideology. As a motivating national creed, *Pancasila* sounded like a 1960s version of the kind of vaporous inspirational material that business in the 1990s would come to expect from management gurus. Indonesia was henceforth deemed a "paradise for investors," and the military, the intelligentsia and the business elite were to work toward the common goal of economic development. Commerce became the compelling force.

Yet Suharto himself never appeared a man of business. He maintained the air of mysticism that he brought with him from the Night of the Generals. People said he was the lost son of the sultan of Jogjakarta, the great ancestral city to the west of today's capital. It would be many years before Suharto would share his true history. He had grown up in a small village, the son of an irrigation official. His father went through various name changes, which is not uncommon in Indonesia; it's a practice used when one wants to shed a particularly bad spell in one's own history. Both his father and mother had various marriages, and numerous children from these. His mother, Sukirah, seems to have fallen into a state of deep despair when Suharto was a child, and so he was taken to live with an aunt, returned to his mother at three, then taken away again, this time by his father, at the age of eight. Then back to his mother. Then back to his father.

Suharto was said to see himself in Semar, one of the many popular clown characters in the *wayang*. Semar lives in the caves of Java. He is the father of the Javanese, and he protects the island. The Indonesian people see their history as the highest order of civilization. The great surprise is that Semar is so powerful, yet a small buffoon, too.

Suharto dubbed his regime the New Order, and under this the notion of *dwifungsi* flourished. Indonesian army officers were trained at American army bases, including Fort Bragg. The objective: to mould an army elite into economic and ideological ambassadors. Having accomplished that, "[t]he military leaders discard their titles and don civilian clothes and even 'conduct' elections at regular intervals." It is a dictatorship, nonetheless. The army presents itself as an agent of economic progress.

The structure became increasingly shaky, as the army tried to micromanage economic sectors for which it was entirely ill-equipped. Quoting from a U.S. Military Assistance Program: "A primary goal of future American military and economic assistance programs should be to encourage the new military elites to assume greater responsibilities in promoting economic progress." Goshal calls the "bayonet and the ballot box" an interesting "technique," but one with dangerous consequences, including the demise of democracy, the rise of authoritarianism and mass repression.

Adam Malik was a trusted friend of Suharto's and one who provided close counsel. A former newspaperman and diplomat, Malik, in Suharto's new cabinet, would be awarded the governance of nine ministries, including foreign affairs. Malik would play a key role in rebridging Indonesia to the outside world; during his term the country rejoined the United Nations and the International Monetary Fund.

In October 1966, the Suharto government introduced a new economic policy that was aimed at securing the approval of the West, in general, and the International Monetary Fund (IMF), in particular. In *The Army and Politics in Indonesia*, Harold Crouch observed that "[t]he new policy reflected the outlook of the IMF, emphasizing stabilization and liberalization as essential prerequisites for development.

It involved balancing the budget, a tight credit policy, reliance on market forces, the setting of a 'realistic' exchange rate through de facto devaluation, and, finally, encouragement to the private sector and especially private foreign investment."

Suharto was seen by the West as a moderate, relative to what had gone before, and the leader himself became a standard-bearer for modernization and development. He was fond of the unofficial title "Father of Development"; in Indonesia, the term father (*bapak*, or *pak*) is a sign of great respect. The advancement of civilian technocrats, often western-trained economists who had attempted to rehabilitate the economy under Sukarno, was part of the pro-business strategy.

Harold Crouch explains that the military leaders "hoped that the technocrats would formulate stabilization policies, creating a favourable climate for business and the restoration of confidence on the part of the Western states and Japan, which were expected to become major sources of capital—both public and private—for the government's program of economic development."

To western leaders, this introduction of "stability" neatly fit with their Cold War, anti-Communist ideology. *Time* magazine called it "the West's best news for years in Asia." U.S. Defense Secretary Robert McNamara noted that the U.S. programs for training Indonesian military at American universities were "significant factors in determining the favorable orientation of the new Indonesia political elite," aka, the army. To promote this economic growth of Suharto's, foreign investors would be welcomed with open arms; these investing countries would then in turn welcome Suharto to the anti-Communist fold—yet another member of this grand compact—turning a blind eye to the rather more grassroots issues of human rights atrocities and the plight of the poor. Henceforth western leaders would satisfy themselves that by advancing economic engagement over confrontation, the Indonesian people would ultimately benefit.

Economically, the country was in crisis. Foreign debts totalled $2.5 billion. Trading relations were strained. People were starving. "Indonesia abounds in natural resources which, developed, would make it one of the wealthiest countries in the world," wrote Vittachi. "But it lacks technical and managerial skills in sufficient depth and quantity for the best intentioned government to be able to make a visible impact for many years."

From the early days of March 1966, Suharto exhibited a wiliness that seemed stunning, even for the famously indirect Javanese. This was not a coup, he told reporters. And please do not mistake it for a new government. To myriad questions Suharto would answer, *Belum*, meaning "Yes, but not yet"—which, because it meant "Not yes yet," could equally be interpreted as "No." This oblique posture was not entirely cultural; rather, Suharto found it a convenient means by which to accommodate diverse, oftentimes competing, groups. To wit, the presumed adoption of the economic platform that pleased the IMF was not entirely adopted after all. As Harold Crouch points out, "The widespread involvement of army officers and army units in commercial activities had created powerful interests that would have been impeded by a strict implementation of the new economic program." Similarly, Suharto kept the ground shifting under his reformers, the technocrats, stalling their proposed advances if they threatened the two constituencies that were deemed more important: the military, and a small group of increasingly powerful, and wealthy, businessmen who owed their success to their apparently unfettered access to Suharto himself. Suharto became the country's most masterful puppeteer.

The richness of the economic prize seemed inversely proportional to the progressiveness of the reforms. The country's richest resource, oil, has been a case in point. The oil reserves of Kalimantan helped spur the creation of Peusahaan Pertambangan Minyak dan Gas Bumi Negara, or Pertamina, bringing small Indonesian oil companies together into one mighty state company. According to Crouch, the army in the 1960s raised at least half of their operating funds from Pertamina and other commercial enterprises that fell under their control. Later, when Suharto's children were old enough to get in line for

Pertamina rewards, they scooped up marketing and distribution contracts that, according to Schwarz, have netted them many hundreds of millions of dollars. "Corruption in our country," Suharto himself once said, "is not the result of corrupt minds but of economic pressures."

Schwarz points out that corruption in Indonesia "was a prominent part of the scene prior to the arrival of the Dutch." Low-level corruption was, and remains, endemic. Foreign business became used to the reality that side sums, or small payments, needed to be made for all bureaucratic movements—of paper, of equipment—a practice as common as tipping in North America. There was a time if you wanted a letter out of a minister's office, you would be hard pressed to see the thing typed unless the secretary was paid a small sum. It might cost fifty cents, it might cost tens of thousands of dollars. The law is irrelevant, says an Australian who has lived here for decades. "You can't go to court without paying a judge."

From the time of Sukarno, says Crouch, "most if not all government departments operated their own 'welfare funds' or 'foundations,' which allocated supplementary salaries to civil servants from money raised through a wide range of legal, semilegal and illegal activities. Although the 'official' budgeted salary of cabinet ministers in 1970, for example, was only Rp 17,000 per month, their actual remuneration was estimated to be between Rp 80,000 and Rp 100,000, and similar 'unofficial' supplements were made to the salaries of officials at all levels, as well as such perquisites as housing and automobiles."

"Examples abound," says Schwarz, "of ministers, provincial governors, regional military commanders, district chiefs and others operating miniature patronage networks based on the model used by Suharto."

The West moved in eagerly, turning a blind eye in 1975 when Suharto's army, outfitted with American arms, overran East Timor as the former Portuguese colony moved toward self-determination. The United Nations called for withdrawal. Henry Kissinger, who had just come from a state visit to Jakarta with then U.S. president Gerald

Ford, did not protest the plan, but rather encouraged that it be under-taken "quickly, efficiently and don't use our equipment." Many thousands of Timorese died after the invasion, from starvation and by execution. In 1989, Australia signed the Timor Gap Treaty with Indonesia, and thus by act, if not by declaration, affirmed Indonesia's rule of East Timor.

The technocrats made various stabs at reform in the mid-1980s with the opening up of the Jakarta Stock Exchange, and the shutting down of some of the country's most outrageous monopolies. But Adam Schwarz paints a picture of a technocracy that, toward the end of the decade, became increasingly handcuffed as reforms were pushed aside in favour of the tried-and-true Suharto cronyism and rampant corruption. Some argued that the technocrats' reforms were too loose, and that they too exhibited favouritism toward certain business people. Deregulation in the banking industry in 1988 took the number of Indonesian banks from something on the order of 120 to double that in seven years. The army was unstoppable. Says Schwarz: "By the 1990s, the army had used dwifungsi to push its way into the soci-etal fabric to an extent that would have been the envy of several Latin American states."

Suharto, at least for public consumption, supported the growth of nationalized corporate interests. Indigenous Indonesian enterprises were called *primu bumi*, or *pribumi*. Yet the president has aided and abetted the phenomenal financial growth of two non-indigenous entrepreneurs: Liem Sioe Liong, the Chinese chairman of the multi-billion-dollar Salim Group, and Bob Hasan, the country's billionaire timber baron.

Hasan built his first fortune through a plywood monopoly, then spread his interests to insurance, shipping, soymeal and car manu-facture. He heads Nusantara Ampera Bakti, or Nusamba, an invest-ment company that represents his own interests as well as those of Suharto. Since the 1950s, and throughout Suharto's presidency, Hasan has retained the status of favoured partner; in more recent years he has often been seen alongside one or another of the president's off-spring in myriad enterprises.

Oftentimes, the ethnic Chinese tycoons and the Suharto clan worked the same side of the same deal. Foreign companies coming in would strike a partnership with a local operator, who in turn would seek out his favourite Suharto, for a consideration of some sum of money, with the implicit understanding that having the Suhartos on side would guarantee stability of operations. There were a number of Suhartos from which to choose: the aforementioned Tommy, who in addition to his car interests and half a dozen other enterprises held the distribution monopoly on cloves; Tutut, whose Citra Lamtoro Gung Group is big in construction; Bambang Trihatmodjo, whose holding company, Bimantara Citra, is into just about everything, and who was crowned in an *Asiaweek* cover story as the most successful of the lot; Sitit Hediati Prabowo, known as much for her marriage to a high-ranking army general as her construction interests; Siti Hutami Adyningsih, who seems peculiarly not to be involved in much of anything; and Sigit Harjojudanto, Suharto's eldest son, who, among other holdings, has a 10 percent stake in Nusamba.

The country's state-run banks bulked up on loans to all manner of Suharto sibling enterprises, unfettered by any of the standard requirements of due diligence. Tommy Suharto's clove monopoly was a fine example. Ninety percent of Indonesian smokers purchase *kretek*, the clove-scented cigarettes that infuse the country with that incomparable air. Tommy sought from industry minister Hartarto, and was ultimately granted, a monopoly by way of the creation of a so-called association that, like Bob Hasan's plywood association, is merely a thinly disguised way to gorge on profits under the auspices, in Tommy's case, of a group that was seen to aid the clove farmers. It did not, of course—it was merely an attempt to inflate the price of the commodity, an effort that wholly failed, left the association with bloated clove stocks and had Tommy turning to the farmers to suggest they burn off half their crop. What was most repugnant about the clove fiasco was Tommy's ability to get the country's central bank to finance the mad enterprise to the tune of about us$150 million.

The Suharto creed insisted that anything that exists on, or in, Indonesian soil belongs to the Indonesian people, and in the Suharto interpretation, the "people" are first and foremost the Suhartos themselves. They appear to make these commercial claims as if by divine right, the obvious benefits accruing to the Suharto royal court. Until she passed away, Siti Hartina, Suharto's wife, known variously as Madam Tien, or Madam Tien Percent, in recognition of the 10 percent stake she would regularly siphon off, was the most high profile of the money-grabbers. In the wake of her death, the children have pressed their greedy fingers in so many pies it is virtually impossible to document. Should any business deal of size appear on the horizon, the siblings are bound to begin lobbying quickly to be chosen as the "agent" to help facilitate a successful deal. Schwarz maintains that "hardly a single major infrastructure contract has been awarded without one Suharto relative or another having a piece of it."

The children, taken as a group, very likely became the country's largest *pribumi* business leaders. The exponential growth in the country's business enterprises required the support of the banks, which, throughout the 1990s, set a pattern of profligate lending practices. As a result, the banks racked up enormous levels of bad debt, much of it resulting from the commercial endeavours of the Suhartos.

Through more than three decades there was little to test the authority of the senior Suharto. The country's ruling party, or "functional group," as Suharto prefers, is Golkar (Sekretariat Bersama Golongan Karya). More than 120 million Indonesians cast ballots at election time, but the DPR (Dewan Perwakilan Rakyat) that is named as a result does not function as a western-style parliament or legislature. Ostensibly, it is empowered to pass all laws, but it never actually creates legislation. It is the MPR (Majelis Permusyawaratan Rakyat), the country's assembly, that elects/anoints the president, aka Suharto, a year later, for a five-year term. Seventy-five members of the MPR come from the army and are appointed by the president. Though the Suharto children in the main remain outwardly apolitical in the conventional sense, Tutut sits as vice-chair of the Golkar executive board. Of all the children, only Tutut seems in any position to aspire to take over from her father, but given the presumed need to see another military man take the presidency, the political power of Tutut has been widely discounted.

As Suharto's presidency moved toward its fifth term, western observers were asking how long he would last, how he would provide for succession, and whether his "unity in diversity" was finally crumbling. Amnesty International, which has had Indonesia on watch since the 1970s, charged that "a clear and persistent pattern of human rights violations has been practised by the Indonesian authorities as a means of suppressing political dissent." On November 12, 1991, Indonesian troops marched on Dili, the capital of East Timor, and shot and/or stabbed an estimated one hundred people in a funeral procession. Young people, mainly students, were killed at Dili as they honoured a political activist who had been in hiding in a Dili church, till the army found him and killed him. General Try Sutrisno was then commander of the armed forces. "These ill-bred people have to be shot, and we will shoot them," he said. Sutrisno would later be named vice-president, and his portrait would hang alongside Suharto's in every corporate office throughout the country. Though, constitutionally, Try was Suharto's successor should anything ill befall the Great Leader during his time in office, he remained a relative unknown in the West.

The human rights violations are not restricted to East Timor. It is estimated that in Aceh and North Sumatra two thousand civilians were murdered in a five-year period starting in 1989, largely in an effort to put down the pro-independence Aceh Merdeka movement. Amnesty International records that "[d]uring 1990 villagers in Aceh and North Sumatra reportedly found scores of unidentified corpses, some of them still blindfolded and with hands and feet bound, in shallow graves, ditches and rivers. According to reports many of the corpses bore signs of torture and had bullet wounds in the head. In October 1990 the Indonesian weekly, *Tempo*, provided details of eight people who had been found dead in plantations and along the roads in North Sumatra and Aceh. Some of the bodies were said to have had mutilated genitals and no ears."

The repression extends to Irian Jaya, where rebel groups have risen up against Jakarta. The various flashpoints gave rise to speculation in the mid 1990s that Suharto might not stand for a seventh five-year term, in the spring of 1998. But he did. And, surprise, he won. Prior to the reaffirmation, his children were gobbling up chunks of corporations with a vigour and urgency that suggested they figured the timeframe in which to do so was limited. Until the death of Madam Tien, Suharto seemed unfazed by their activities, though their antics were becoming increasingly transparent, and an emboldened media in Jakarta was becoming increasingly willing to criticize.

After Madam Tien's passing in April 1996, political observers said Suharto seemed at a loss as to how to manage Tutut and the gang, particularly the reckless Tommy. He seemed to rely even more on his close association with a select group of powerful business leaders, particularly Bob Hasan, who would regularly play a round of golf with the president or visit him at his beloved cattle ranch in Tapos, West Java.

That Hasan was elevated to top status did nothing to introduce transparency, or a rules-based structure, to Indonesian enterprise. Someone said the regime seemed bereft of the ideas, mechanisms and skills to adapt to the rapid changes engulfing the archipelago. Yet Suharto, as he moved in to start up his new term of office, remained impassive. Writer Karl Jackson captured this pose: "The truly powerful man is the one who sits motionless while his enemies energetically posture and exercise their power, giving the evidence that they are so weak that they are forced to make the first move, dissipating their power rather than concentrating it."

Hartojo Wignjowijoto has welcomed me into his home. Hartojo is president director of PT Aspecindo Kreasi, an economic consultancy based in Jakarta. He is Indonesian, with a Ph.D. in economics from Harvard, a member of the World Gold Council and adviser to numerous corporations, including major mining ones. "Of course Indonesia's internal situation is very weak, and very greedy, and very corrupt," he says. Surveys have, in fact, placed Indonesia at the top of the list of the world's most corrupt countries.

But Hartojo makes the point that it is the corrupt country that attracts the corrupt country, that tests the ethics of foreigners. How will they behave here? Can they get through the system with side-sum payments only, or will they choose the route perhaps presumed faster, but increasingly more perilous: free equity partnership with the Suhartos? "I don't know if you have a Foreign Corrupt Practices Act in your country," he laughs, knowing that Canada does not.

Hartojo's concerns extend far below the greedy family. "I don't want to see Indonesia be like Africa. They cannot eat. They have minerals. Just suck it in, suck it out, you know. I don't want that to happen to this country."

He has witnessed the sometimes comic battles over ownership in interests as diverse as telecommunications, construction and certainly cars. Oil has been a big feeding-ground all along. But mining less so. Mining has been the less-prominent part of the Department of Mines. Yet it holds the promise of development that could, if handled well, benefit the nation, the real people.

A brawl is now brewing over a very big pot of gold—Busang—and Hartojo is wonderfully Javanese in his take on the issue. "Gold is made of fire and fire is the raw material of gold. But fire is also the material of Satan."

Of course, the politicians are getting into the muck.

Ida Bagus Sudjana, a three-star general, is the minister of mines and energy, including oil and gas. Sudjana had had his eye on the department, was seen to be inordinately ambitious. His predecessor, Ganaja, was western-educated, well liked and exhibited a comfort and ease with foreign businessmen, the prime investors in this portfolio. By contrast, Sudjana was seen as piggish and, worse, stupid.

"For politicians, it's always the short term," says Hartojo. "What do they have to gain? If the foreign multinational companies bring cash their eyes turn green, you know. Politicians are like mushrooms. Keep them in the dark and keep them in shit and they will grow like a mushroom."

GRASPING AT THE SHADOW

THE BLACK LIMOUSINES PULLED into the traffic circle at 47 Wimpole Drive in north Toronto on the evening of Thursday, June 13, 1996. It was sticky, humid, the typical too-early summer soup that would go on to stew the metropolis well into September.

The half-moon of asphalt that swept past the front door at Wimpole sent the right sort of status signal. This was a home of some grandeur. The Indonesian consulate had made it the residence of its consul general. The Honourable Bas Soetarto had nearly come to the end of his term as the country's top representative in the city. This was one of the last big dinners that he was to host.

The guests were ushered to a reception room to the right of the centre hall. As they swept through the foyer, they passed a statue of a grand garuda, mythical bird of Indonesia, the requisite nationalistic touch. But there was something amiss with the ambience. The lighting was wretchedly harsh—so bright, so stark, yanking eyelids back into sockets, that it gave the gathering throng eyeball-burn. And where in the world was the guest of honour, the Balinese prince, the minister of mines and energy, His Excellency, General Ida Bagus Sudjana? Late, again.

At last the three-star general arrived. Perhaps he had been hand-some once. He was tall for an Indonesian. With an oil slick of black hair and a moustache to match, he had the look of an Asian movie star gone to flesh, and a bit to seed.

The attendees moved across the hall to be seated for dinner. Eight tables of ten. All eyes, of course, were fixed on table number one, as they always are at such affairs. Seated at twelve o'clock was Scott Hand, president of Inco Ltd. The positioning of Hand was a no-brainer. Inco is a powerful nickel miner, and the company had been operating in Indonesia for close to thirty years. In 1967, just months after assuming power, Suharto had invited bids from foreign mining operators to explore for nickel deposits in Sulawesi. Inco had first explored south Sulawesi in the 1930s, when the Dutch still ruled Indonesia. When Suharto opened the investment gates, Inco bid to develop the Sulawesi deposits. In 1968 the company signed its first contract of work.

Beni Wahju was an Indonesian geologist who worked for the Direc-torate of Geology in the 1960s. "One day, sometime in the late '60s, I was struggling through the mangrove swamps when all of a sudden I was confronted by a canoe full of rebels," he later recounted. "They looked pretty hostile so when we met them I immediately looked at my watch and said, 'Time to pray.' You see that's another advantage to being a Moslem." Wahju worked for Inco in the early days at Soroako, loading up water buffalo with rock samples to take to the riverside docks en route to the Bay of Bone. When the water buffalo proved too fond of bathing en route with their sample loads, the camp workers switched to ponies.

By the late 1970s, Inco was producing 36 million kilograms of nickel matte from its mine near Soroako, a highland village on Sulawesi's Lake Matano. A 165-megawatt hydro-electric power station had been built, along with an airport and port facilities. In the spring of 1977

President Suharto himself officiated at the dedication of the processing plant at Soroako. The initial capital investment of US$1 billion was the largest single start-up approved by Suharto and, Inco hoped, would become a model of international business co-operation. It would be years before Soroako would be profitable. Like all miners, Inco was hostage to swings in commodities prices, which were hostage to economies everywhere. An upswinging North American economy meant an increased demand for stainless steel, which meant an increasing demand for nickel. Drooping economies had the opposite effect.

Just as Inco's operations had virtually created the northern Ontario town of Sudbury, its mine in Sulawesi had spawned housing in Soroako and nearby Wawondula, a hospital, schools, post office, a mosque, a sewer system and a nine-hole golf course. Scholarships had been endowed. In the spring of 1990, Inco took PT International Nickel Indonesia (PT Inco) public, floating 20 percent of the company on the Jakarta Stock Exchange, thus accommodating President Suharto's eagerness to develop the country's capital markets. Just two years earlier the JSE had a scant two dozen companies on the board. By 1990, that number had grown to more than 120, but still the market was illiquid and had not caught on with retail investors at home. PT Inco was precisely the kind of company the JSE needed.

In accordance with the terms of the contract of work, Inco had gradually replaced expats in managerial functions with Indonesian nationals. And the company had brought Indonesian nationals onto the board, including Sutaryo Sigit, the past director general of the Department of Mines. After Jim Bob Moffett's Freeport-McMoRan, Inco had the highest profile of foreign mining operators in the country. Penny operators like Minindo had left a bad taste in the mouths of stock and mining officials in Jakarta. PT Inco and Scott Hand, its president commissioner, knew the importance of being seen to be doing the right thing. Still, Inco had had its troubles at the site. Twice when the company conducted worker layoffs, the military had to be brought in to ensure site security.

The Sulawesi operations were vitally important to Inco. In 1993, when the crew at the company's corporate offices in downtown Toronto were assessing how to build the company, Soroako's efficient, low-cost facilities seemed a logical focus. But the contract of work was due to expire in 2008. Expanding Soroako would require a capital investment of close to US$600 million. Inco needed assurances that its investment would be secured, which meant negotiating an extension on the COW. That job fell to Scott Hand, a lawyer who had joined Inco in 1973. It took Hand three years to negotiate the COW extension. In the interim he met Suharto only once, at a United Nations gathering at which the president was giving a speech. "Ah Inco! Great company Inco," said the Almighty Leader. "I attended your opening." In January 1996, the new COW was signed.

During the negotiations, Indonesia had been represented by Kuntoro Mangusubroto, a technocrat who worked directly under the minister and who was well liked in the mining community. Kuntoro and Hand had come to know one another well. When Kuntoro was elevated to director general of mines, the community of foreign miners was comforted by his intellectual presence in a department where mining was seen as second-cousin to the mightier part of the ministerial portfolio, oil, and where the appointment of minister would traditionally go to military men, some of whom were more competent than others. Mining companies had complained of the overly long waiting periods that attended COW and KP approval, and of the absence of a modern, computerized mapping and claims-recording system. Kuntoro was working on all of that. In a speech he gave in the spring of 1996, Kuntoro acknowledged that his government needed "to lure more foreign capital to explore and subsequently develop our mineral resources in competition with other countries in the Asia Pacific region. . . . We are also aware that Bre-X's Busang gold discovery, believed to be one of the world's richest, on Kalimantan, is generating so much interest that junior exploration companies in Canada are getting attention just by announcing property acquisitions near the find. And shares of such companies have soared significantly in the stock market. Such development is encouraging provided that these companies invest the capital they have raised into their exploration projects in Indonesia."

Kuntoro's portfolio included the restructuring of the state mining companies, PT Aneka Tambang and PT Tambang Timah. He was also steering the de-bureaucratization of the Department of Mines. Perhaps most significant in the view of foreign mining companies was that Kuntoro was the ministerial representative who signed the COW applications before they were sent up the line to receive the signature of the president himself.

Scott Hand made it his business to call upon Kuntoro whenever he was in Jakarta. He knew as well as anyone the importance of building relationships with the company's Asian host and had an appreciation for the Javanese mind-set. It was not about "doing business," per se, but about the subtleties that surround the business. So when Inco was informed that an Indonesian ministerial tour of duty was taking place in the early summer of 1996, with the minister himself due to attend OPEC meetings in Vienna and then meet with the Chevron people in California, they proposed a Toronto stopover.

That sticky evening in June, Kuntoro took his assigned seat to Hand's left. On Hand's right was Bas Soetarto and, beside him, Ida Bagus Sudjana. Sudjana was roundly disliked in the Indonesian mining fraternity. It was a given that the army, the centrepiece of Suharto's rule, had its representatives in key posts. But Sudjana was focused first on Sudjana, was inordinately ambitious and was fixed on his personal star within the Indo hierarchy. He was not bright, and he had had a nasty run-in with parliament over 50 billion rupiahs (US$23 million) of misappropriated funds that had mysteriously ended up in his personal bank account. It was all a misunderstanding, he said, the money was merely making a pit-stop on its way to its rightful depository. He had, however, ordered the transfer personally and had fired the directors of the state-owned coal company in question when they transferred only half the funds requested. Worse, in the eyes of the foreign mining community in Jakarta, Sudjana knew squat about mining, was a loose cannon and did not get on with his number-one lieutenant, Kuntoro. To visit the minister was, in the view of those who played the game in Jakarta, a waste of good fresh air.

Sudjana was a problem. There had been at least two occasions on which contracts, not in mining but in other areas of his purview, had been cancelled after they had been signed. In one case, he had preferred to grant a contract to a company close to him; in another, he had dictated the addition of new partners.

Still, as minister, he was to be accorded the highest respect, and so red carpets were rolled out. Sudjana had brought his son, Dharma Yoga, along, and his economic adviser, Adnan Ganto. Sudjana never went anywhere without Ganto.

Beside Sudjana sat Allan Hill, the Barrick Gold executive who, almost three years previously, was supposed to have conducted a site visit of Busang for his employer. After Bob Smith, Hill, a Brit, was key to Barrick's stated ambition to become the biggest gold company on the planet, to spread like magma through South America, China, Indonesia. Especially Indonesia. Hill made an aside that night to one of the other diners. He really could not believe that the grade of gold Bre-X was claiming at Busang was for real.

Still, the Bre-X story had been getting better and better. By June, Busang was promising a 30-million-ounce resource, and John Felderhof had done a convincing job of getting admirers to view the prospect as three times that, without any resource calculations to prove it. The stock had been split ten-for-one the previous month, so any investor once holding 100 shares was now holding 1,000, each valued at one-tenth the single share price on conversion day. With the split, a Bre-X investment, which once would have seemed stratospheric at more than $200 a share, could now appeal to a whole new tranche of investors. In the summer of 1996, the most interested buyer was

Barrick chairman Peter Munk. The Barrick leader had made it very clear to his lieutenants that his company must take Bre-X somehow.

As the diners settled into their appointed spots, David Walsh himself, all 250 pounds of him, loomed into view. An outsider here, and until recently an insignificant gnat, it is unlikely that Walsh was familiar with the Canadian corporate representatives from the likes of Nova Corp., TransCanada PipeLines or Noranda Mining and Exploration. Still, he was the man of the hour, in a way, for as president of Bre-X Minerals he was corporate steward of what he was now touting as the largest gold discovery in the world. So naturally Walsh had been invited to the consul's home, and had been assigned a seat not in the outfield but at the best table, directly across from Sudjana. Beside Walsh was Rod Scribben from SNC Lavalin, the Montreal-based parent company to Kilborn Engineering, which was doing contract work for Bre-X and that was counting on the engineering contract to build what was starting to appear to be a billion-dollar mine. Beside Scribben sat Kuntoro.

Introductions were made all round. Walsh was stiff, not at all relaxed. His discomfort seemed the natural baggage for an erstwhile bankrupt who preferred his familiar Calgary watering holes to gatherings such as this one in Toronto. Scott Hand introduced himself to Walsh. "That's quite a discovery you made in Indonesia," he said. "Congratulations." Walsh was very quiet.

What came as a surprise to more than one person at the table was the need for Scott Hand to introduce Walsh to Kuntoro. The fat man with the fattest gold mine ever, who was running the company that ran the payroll of hundreds of workers in Kalimantan, had not, after three years of operating in Indonesia, so much as set eyes on the gentlemen with the power to determine his company's fate. For men who had worked hard at honing their companies' cultural skills in Indonesia, this was more than an oversight. It was not only stunningly graceless, it was, potentially, extremely dangerous.

Few paid much attention to the egg soup, the gado gado, the chicken dish that servers brought around as the main course. A representative from Canada's external affairs department made a short speech about the hope that the latest round of contracts of work would be signed soon. So many Canadian companies were moving into Indonesia on the heels of Bre-X, and their fate rested on the signing of the COWs. Billions of dollars were floating through stock exchanges in New York and Toronto, thanks to Bre-X.

If only they had known. Known that Barrick had been suddenly shut down by Syakerani in March, making the company that much more determined to move in on Bre-X. Known that as of April Barrick had decided to craft a takeover bid instead, its outside counsel at Davies Ward & Beck working long days and sleeping short nights to make that happen. Known that an offering circular had been drafted and Munk, who had conquered Lac Minerals and did not take well to losing, could taste victory even then. There is, after all, nothing quite like the smell of a multibillion-dollar takeover.

David Walsh's hate for Barrick was, of course, already finely honed. There was the collapsed deal of January 1994, negotiations in which Hill had been key, which Bre-X insiders had worked up into a tale of corporate balls-squeezing on the part of Barrick. There had been the threatening legal noises over Barrick's acquisition of its Aceh property, cheek by jowl with Bre-X's Sable property there. Bre-X had howled that Barrick made its acquisition based on insider knowledge acquired over the course of the 1993–94 deal-making. Even after Bre-X, in the summer of 1995, had suspended communications on this matter, John Felderhof and Michael de Guzman had never missed an opportunity to recall the incident as another example of Barrick's storm-trooper tactics. As the Busang "resource" grew, Barrick had tried, and failed, to reconnect with the company.

Barrick was not the only company in this position. From the beginning of 1996, Placer Dome Inc. of Vancouver had also been closely monitoring the increasingly fabulous tale. Placer saw itself immediately as a good fit for Bre-X. The company was mining its Porgera deposit in Papua New Guinea, so it could rightfully claim the construction of a mine operation in an area not entirely dissimilar to Kalimantan. In March, the tailings dam at Placer's 40-percent-owned Marcopper mine in the Philippines burst. "Tailings" is the sludge that remains after the concentrate is extracted from the rock. A breached tunnel at the Marcopper operation on Marinduque Island, south of Manila, spewed tailings into the Boac River, infecting fish life, the water and adjacent plantations. The company found itself facing an environmental, and a public relations, nightmare. Executives were temporarily barred from leaving the country, and threats of criminal charges were being made in high government offices in Manila. The Marcopper mess was a significant blight on Placer's heretofore blue-chip reputation.

John Willson, Placer's chief executive officer, had repeatedly attempted to contact Walsh to pursue marriage talks. He wanted to get to know the company's principals. And Placer certainly wanted to get on site. The company's geologists in Vancouver watched every Bre-X drill hole as it came out. They calculated resource estimates over and over and over. Oh, they wanted Busang badly.

Meetings would be set, only to evaporate. Calls would go unreturned. Placer was the second-largest gold-mining company in the country, yet Walsh could not be bothered. Walsh had indicated at the time of the annual meeting that selling a quarter interest in Busang would fetch a fancy figure: $2 billion. The companies in the world big enough to cope with such a project could be counted on the fingers of two hands. Yet Walsh did not take John Willson's call. Bre-X was intending to bring in financial advisers and an investment banker in the fall. Perhaps the company would consider tenders then.

By the time of the Indonesian delegation's visit to Toronto in June, Barrick's strategy had wholly changed again. The erstwhile two-bit company that claimed to have found the motherlode was, at least in the view of Barrick's legal advisers, in a heap of trouble. In the earliest Bre-X press releases, Walsh had said that the company had acquired an option on the Central Zone at Busang for US$80,000. The option had a one-year term, by which time it had to be exercised for a price of $100 or it would expire. Walsh had certainly left the impression that the option had been exercised and that 80 percent of the Central Zone was held by Bre-X through PT WAM. Two local partners, PT Krueng Gasui, owned by Jusuf Merukh, and PT Sungai Atan Perdana (PT SAP), owned by the Syakerani family, each had 10 percent.

But the ownership transfer was not as clean as all that. Bre-X understood that PT WAM was legally owned by Montague, a company that was owned, in turn, by Willy McLucas. Walsh said all along that he had made the acquisition by buying the Australian company (Montague) that owned the company (PT WAM) that owned the property (Busang)—sort of like the House that Jack Built.

Control of the Central Zone had actually sat with McLucas's Westralian Resource Projects Ltd. When Westralian's focus turned to Alaska, McLucas very likely did not expect to pay any further attention to Kalimantan, where the contract of work had been set to expire back in December 1993. By the spring of 1996, with the unfounded rumblings of the 100 million ounces beneath Busang, Willy McLucas was sitting on a virtual gold mine of his own. He started to bleat that Felderhof had not acted in good faith, that the geologist-turned-promoter had had an obligation to cut McLucas in on the prospects for Busang back in 1993. He threatened to sue. Unfortunately for Walsh et al., they had the wrong company targeted as the owner of Busang I, and, worse, there had never been any conveyance of shares from the McLucas group to Bre-X. Legally, Bre-X had no title to Busang I.

That had become Rolly Francisco's problem. When Francisco arrived at Bre-X, his first task had been to clear up the McLucas-Montague-Westralian mess. It was clear to Francisco that Bre-X was going to have to pay up to get rid of the wily Willy, that the much-touted association between McLucas and Felderhof was worth approximately zero. Francisco did not know quite where to begin. There were documents everywhere: Edinburgh, Sydney, Perth, Jakarta, Calgary. The record-keeping was a shambles; the title had not been properly transferred. In May he flew with Felderhof, Felderhof's wife, Ingrid, and Peter Howe to London, where they met McLucas. McLucas said he wanted $10 million. Bre-X offered $6 million, pending completion of the due diligence that would then be carried out by Bre-X lawyers. No money was going to change hands until the title was proved to be clear and fully Bre-X's. McLucas accepted. Bre-X saw it as a payoff. Its troubles were not over.

Getting clear title was crucial. In the absence of ownership of PT Westralian, Bre-X would be unable to sell that 25 percent stake—if that ever truly was the plan. Nor would it be able to sign up a joint venture partner. Bre-X had followed John Craig's advice and had tentatively engaged National Bank and J.P. Morgan, both in the United States, as financial advisers to steer a joint venture. But the bankers too were wait-listed on this assignment, pending the removal of the McLucas menace.

There was some urgency to fixing McLucas. CRA was still in the wings, Placer was trying to gain access, and there was always Barrick. If Bre-X wanted to choose its own destiny, it had to be in control of the process, and it could only be in control of the process if it controlled its properties. And Bre-X had no contract of work covering the majority of the gold that Felderhof and de Guzman claimed they had discovered.

Barrick was making calls to Bre-X. But the carry-over effect from the botched first deal seemed to have invaded the pores of John Felderhof, Michael de Guzman and very likely David Walsh. The association with Barrick had less and less to do with business and more and more to do with thin skins. It certainly seems as though no one at Bre-X felt compelled to take the calls.

Francisco had a different view of Barrick. Only a handful of companies would be able to take on a project of this size, and Barrick was certainly one of those. True, it had not built a mine in jungle lands like Busang, but that hardly seemed a sensible reason to exclude it. In May, flying back from the London trip with McLucas, Felderhof and Francisco met with Walsh in Miami, which seemed as convenient a spot as any. Francisco turned to the cowboys and expressed the view that it would be a disservice to exclude Barrick as a potential partner. It was agreed that Francisco would make an approach to Barrick on Bre-X's behalf.

After his return to Toronto, Francisco contacted Munk through Bob Fung, an investment banker at Gordon Capital, a boutique brokerage in Toronto. Gordon had backed Munk in his early mining days. Munk was told that Bre-X wanted to meet. Sometime in mid-summer, Francisco presented himself at Gordon's highrise offices in downtown Toronto. Munk brought along Bill Birchall, a sleek grey fox who had worked at Munk's side for decades. The meeting was brief, meant only to convey that Bre-X was in the mood to talk. Barrick saw it differently. That it was the chosen one. The next move was Munk's.

Peter Munk called David Walsh in Nassau requesting a meeting. The two met at Walsh's home in late May. Walsh showed Munk the construction drawings for his planned renovation on his plantation house. Munk apologized for the way Bre-X had been treated in 1993, when Barrick had changed the terms of the deal of its proposed association for Busang.

At approximately 10:00 on the evening of June 13, His Excellency Ida Bagus Sudjana left Wimpole Drive in the company of Scott Hand and Kuntoro Mangusubroto to return to his Grand Suite at the Sutton Place Hotel in downtown Toronto. There was golf to be played at Glen Abbey in Oakville the next day. On the links, Sudjana shot 87; his son finished 10 points back; Ganto settled for 108. Barrick reps picked up the party by van soon after lunch, ferried them to a regional airport nearby, then took them on a fly-past over Niagara Falls. The sky was clear as the delegation was shown the American side, then the far-prettier Canadian side. Mr. Johnnie Hermanto, president of the Panutan Group, and Mr. Harsono, president of PT Panutan Duta, were very chatty with the Barrick folk, eager, it seemed, to sidle up to Barrick and its Indonesian pursuits. The controlling shareholder in Panutan is Sigit Harjojudanto, eldest son of Indonesian president Suharto.

At 8:00 a small group of business folk gathered at the Toronto Club, at the invitation of former Canadian prime minister Brian Mulroney, on behalf of Barrick Gold. Mulroney, three years out of politics, had taken a post on Barrick's board of directors and served as chairman of its International Advisory Board, along with honorary adviser George Bush, forty-first president of the United States, u.s. Senator Howard Baker, past Bundesbank chairman Karl Otto Pohl and, of course, Peter Munk. International advisory boards were much in vogue, lending the look of global reach and the lustre of power. Barrick's was more high-powered than most, and Mr. Munk expected board members to earn their keep, to open doors, to make connections, to assure the uninformed of Munk's business acumen and the global intentions of the company he led.

On this night in June, Mulroney played host, and, indeed, with Munk away he was the most powerful Barrick board member present. There were four tables. Bob Smith sat with Mulroney, as did His Excellency Ida Bagus Sudjana. Sudjana's son was there, as was Gunadharma Hartarto, one of the sons of one of Indonesia's superministers, the co-ordinating minister of production and distribution. It did not sound like much of a title, but in truth the senior Hartarto was one of the most powerful men in Jakarta, overseeing industry from telecommunications to forestry to mines.

Mulroney rose to address the gathering. There would be no big speeches tonight, he said, no grand pronouncements. Sudjana said a few words in his halting English. Kuntoro had already taken off for the United States, where his son was at university.

Brian Mulroney followed up with a letter to Sudjana. A simple letter of thank-you. Etiquette? Politesse? Perhaps. But Barrick had just raised the stakes. Bre-X had thought it was in control. That's the message that Walsh was trying to send to CRA and Placer and Barrick, too. It was wrong. From this point onward, Bre-X would be massively outranked.

There were other troubles. On June 25, Jusuf Merukh sent a letter to Kuntoro complaining that the Bre-X boys had shut him out of what was rightfully his. Through PT Krueng Gasui, Merukh had 10 percent of the Central Zone. But he claimed he had an option to increase his interest to 20 percent, and though he did not have the documents to prove it, there was a pesky reference to the 20 percent in at least one corporate document. Further, Merukh was insisting that his interest in Busang I should have been carried into Busang II. Bre-X would have none of it. It was PT Askatindo, also controlled by the Syakerani family, that had applied for Busang II, Bre-X pointed out. Therefore it had no obligation to include Merukh. Still, Merukh had the ear of some in the Department of Mines and was threatening to sue. He had met with a number of representatives from a number of mining companies, including Placer, convinced he had something to sell.

Felderhof was sufficiently concerned that he approached Ridwan Mahmud, a retired mining official in Jakarta, to advise the company on its position. Ridwan had spent thirty-seven years with the Department of Mines and knew Felderhof. In Sukarno's time, he had sat on Suharto's 1967 committee charged with modernizing the rules for foreign investment in Indonesian mining. Ridwan was smelling something, and he did not care for the odour. But he had no proof.

Merukh became the wild card, both because he knew how to make noise within the Indonesian Department of Mines and because his complaint served the purposes of another corporate entity: Barrick. Ultimately it would serve both Barrick's interests and those of Merukh that the department be pushed to investigate his land claim. At some point in the summer, Kuntoro carried a ten-centimetre-thick pile of documents to his top lieutenant, Rozik Soetjipto. The investigation of Jusuf Merukh's file was officially opened. But why? The view held by officials within the Department of Mines was that this was a commercial dispute between two corporate interests. Why had it become a political affair?

The politics had just begun. Barrick had surveyed the Jakarta landscape—the cronyism, the in-bred business practices. What to do? Form an alliance with one of the wealthy ethnic Chinese? The Chinese business community controlled 80 percent of the enterprise in the country. Forge an association with one of the Suharto offspring? There was already the view that aligning with any of the siblings could prove precarious, at least for long-term projects. At best, Suharto had one term left. Once he was out of power, there was bound to be a mighty backlash against the children. The way the kids were gorging themselves on partnerships with foreign companies, they seemed to have realized that the opportunities left to them had a limited life. Madam Tien had kept her puppies in line, to a degree. With her death in April, Suharto seemed at a loss to oversee their escapades. The children were now grabbing equity stakes recklessly, and very publicly. These were not the subtle ways of Indonesia. Suharto needed help in herding the rabble. He turned to Bob Hasan. Bob Hasan became, for these purposes, the new wife.

Barrick would not attempt to move forward without allies. The takeover bid had been scuppered, and, despite the seemingly friendly meeting between Walsh and Munk, someone was insistent that nothing would happen on friendly terms. Someone must have been, for CRA had been in talks long before Barrick, and they were getting the same treatment.

Sometime toward the end of June, Barrick made its move, striking an arrangement, not with the overeager boys of Panutan but with Airlangga Hartarto, brother of Gunadharma, another of the superminister's sons. One of Airlangga's companies is PT Garama Dhananjaya. It became Airlangga's job to advance the Barrick story within the corridors of the Department of Mines. Should Barrick be successful in getting control of Busang, Airlangga would participate, through Garama. Barrick had bought its fixer.

The following month, Barrick went one step further. It was one thing to have Airlangga moving through the department; it was quite another to feel assured that the deal would get done. Barrick secured what must have seemed the ultimate entree in early July when it struck an agreement in principle with Siti Hardyanti Rukmana, or Tutut. PT Sumber Hema Raya (SHR), a subsidiary of Tutut's Citra Lamtoro Gung Persada, was the partnering company. Should Barrick win Busang, SHR would be awarded construction contracts and a piece of the project, perhaps as much as 10 percent. The top-level negotiations were conducted by Peter Munk personally.

Munk shook hands on the arrangement. This was a pragmatic move in his view. Goddamned gold, he would say. It would be the same whether Placer mined it, or Newmont, or the Afrikaaners with slave labour. Barrick would have to distinguish itself as a company with an unblemished record, a company of quality, with the financial clout to carry Busang into production. But it needed ambassadors to ensure that the message would be heard. First came Airlangga. Then Tutut. This partner, deemed Munk, would provide contacts, credibility and, most of all, insurance.

John Felderhof, river-walker, the guy that, as the analysts liked to joke, had had malaria more times than most of them had had sex, readied himself for another group of Busang visitors. More analysts had been invited to the site. Some of them were top names: David Neuhaus from J.P. Morgan, Daniel McConvey from Lehman Brothers in New York.

Mike de Guzman was, of course, part of the squiring party, as were Cesar Puspos and Jerry Alo. Jonathan Nassey had moved over to Bre-X and thus spent his time at Sable and Singhe and not at Busang.

De Guzman was in high spirits, and he was keeping very busy. He had carried out, by helicopter, a site inspection of the old Mirah prospect. He had not given up his belief in the potential of the project, which had been revitalized under a joint venture with Mike Bird's Diadem Resources Ltd., with Bre-X taking the controlling stake. A long-time pal of David Walsh's, Stan Hawkins, had 30 percent through a company of his, Tandem Resources.

At Busang, de Guzman walked the visitors through the site, and his theory. This was the largest maar-diatreme dome in the world, he believed, and he estimated that the dome itself measured six by four kilometres. Like Muslims to Mecca, the analysts came to see de Guzman's discovery outcrop. He explained that all those swanky mining companies that had walked this ground before had retrieved surface samples that showed no or negligible gold. But the first ten metres was weathered, he said, and so leached of surface gold. There were clues to the presence of gold in this weathered rock, said de Guzman. He would not share what they were. That was a secret.

De Guzman spun intoxicating tales that mixed geology and adventure in ways that the western crew could only imagine. He had been held hostage by the Dayak once, he said. He had eaten dog brains to prove himself one of them, and in recognition of his joining their brotherhood they had given him a special blanket. He told tales of his malaria, crawling through the bush, the leaches, the maggots, the snakes.

On July 13, the analysts were taken to Indo Assay. Peter Kennedy's story in the *Financial Post* four months earlier had some of them seeking reassurances that Bre-X's methodology was credible. Jamie Ordona, who worked for John Irvin, provided the obligatory tour. Felderhof had provided his explanation for not splitting the core: that to do so would sacrifice the nuggety gold showings. As for the cyanide leach, the group could see that Indo Assay was a professional set-up, and they knew that other operations too used this methodology. Busang was clearly a geologist's dream: the recovery rate was as high as 90 percent. Not only was Busang a huge gold find, but the gold would fall from her easily and plentifully at an extremely low cost. The group was not shown the prep lab, which had briefly pulped the mineralized core on site. No one made any mention of it.

No one saw Cesar Puspos lining up the sample bags in the Samarinda office, lining them up in order. This meticulous practice discredited his assertion that the samples simply needed to be made dry. If that were the sole reason for the bag-opening, they wouldn't need to be so orderly, a pell-mell assemblage would do. To "salt" a discovery of this size, however, meant building a mine plan, a model orebody wherein the reported flow of the mineral would not cause alarm but, rather, would swell and then peter, an ore map that would make sense when the calculations were studied. It would not do to report enormous gold quantities in one two-metre sample, only to have the gold disappear in the next. Modelling required a more sophisticated calculation. This was science.

The bags would sit open for a day, perhaps two. Workers would have to walk on the bags to pass through the pool room. The Canadian geologists at site were Sasha Mihailovich, Trevor Cavicchi and Steve Hughes. Hughes, a twenty-six-year-old geologist from Nova Scotia, was new to the field. His wavy blond hair and cherubic face gave him the look of an innocent, but he knew enough about conventional field practice to query Puspos. "What the hell are you doing? Why are you opening the bags?" Puspos. Broad through the shoulders. Virile. A charmer. Thickening in the middle. A man who had taken Yennie, the administrative secretary in Samarinda, as a girlfriend, to share a bed with at the Samarinda offices. What was it Puspos said? Something about needing to ensure that only the good stuff, the mineralized rock, was being shipped to John Irvin's laboratory. The lab guys were pumping the numbers back to Bre-X in Jakarta, who were pumping them over to Kilborn at Cilandak Commercial Estate.

The analysts on that site trip retrieved pieces of Busang core. Some fully intended to have their samples tested when they got back to North America.

John Felderhof was on site at Busang, a rare event, save when groups of select analysts were hauled in and needed the geological primer on Busang that the river-walker would help give. Bre-X had just upped its resource calculation to 47 million ounces. Busang was offering up the equivalent of more than a gold mine a week. The company was now talking of a mine with a life of fifty years. Michael de Guzman had created a gold producer that would outlive the executive team and most of the investors. Bre-X said it expected to have its COW in hand in August. In the meantime, the government had granted Bre-X a SIPP extension.

A call came in to the camp for Felderhof that day. Not a run-of-the-mill office call, nor one from Ingrid, but a call from Kuntoro. Perhaps it did not come entirely as a surprise. Felderhof, with de Guzman, had been the point person with the department on the land issue. Francisco was on the verge of getting rid of McLucas once and for all, but there was still Merukh and the business of the interest carried into the Southeast Zone. Bre-X had assured outsiders, Placer for one, that the Merukh claim was wholly without merit. And some within Bre-X undoubtedly believed that to be true. Under normal circumstances. Which these were not. John Craig's warning had been listened to without protest by Felderhof. He had even agreed with Craig's assessment: that a black hand would land on his shoulder if he persisted in standing (figuratively) naked in the middle of the Kalimantan jungle.

Kuntoro proposed a breakfast meeting, July 22, at the Shangri-La. Felderhof regularly stayed there, a top-notch hotel without the hoity-ness of the Hyatt. The place glittered at night. There was always a lot of lobby action.

Kuntoro told Felderhof there was a company he would like him to meet later that day, 4:00 p.m., his office, to discuss Busang. Felderhof dutifully showed up. There was a new player for him to meet. His name was Airlangga Hartarto. Barrick's power base within the city suddenly became clear. By retaining Airlangga, Barrick had hitched its prospects to one of the highest seats of government. Sure enough, Felderhof was told that Bre-X was to work with Barrick. All those dreams of auctioning Busang to the highest bidder, of the company ruling its own destiny, calling the shots, suddenly collapsed.

Francisco was in Sydney finalizing the payoff of Willy McLucas.

McLucas had decided he wanted more money—surprise—and Bre-X was impatient to see the last of him. Francisco's next scheduled stop was Jakarta, where he was to negotiate shareholder agreements with the Syakeranis. Francisco was used to calling on the assistance of lieutenants, but this was not the case at Bre-X. Aside from support from the company's outside counsel, Francisco had found himself flying around and around the globe, utterly alone, conducting damage control.

Kuntoro made it clear that the talk about the future of Busang was going to have to go much, much faster. Felderhof protested that Francisco, the only corporate executive in a position to handle such negotiations, had not yet arrived. Kuntoro seemed impatient.

Francisco arrived in Jakarta on Sunday, July 27. He was already growing weary of the travel, and he had had enough of the heat. In May, his black leather valise had been pried open by airport security. He had glued it back together. That was only his second trip. His apartment in Calgary had been broken into, and he was sure a surveillance van had been parked outside his home. His garbage had been rifled. Walsh's home in the Bahamas had been broken into too, though he thought that the work of a local thief, who had stolen Jeannette's purse. But a break-in at Bre-X's Calgary headquarters was of greater concern. The company's computer hard drive had been taken; an entire window had been lifted out to allow the thief, or thieves, access. Puspos was complaining that an investigator had visited his family in Dasmariñas. He had said he was working for a major mining company and wanted answers. Puspos's family thought Cesar's job was in peril.

Bre-X had hired its own investigator, who informed his client that Kroll Associates was working on the Bre-X file. Kroll had been retained by Barrick. Kroll was the crème de la crème of corporate private eyes. Founded by Jules Kroll, a onetime assistant district attorney, the company had made its reputation doing due diligence on one corporation for another. Kroll officially operated out of a highrise on

Third Avenue in Manhattan, but its tentacles spread worldwide to places like Hong Kong and Singapore, where Kroll would put top ex-cops in charge of the company's doings.

Kroll once told me that 90 percent of the time, he takes cases for the defence. "We look into material to help our client understand who the invader is," he said, sucking on a very large cigar in his Manhattan office. "Second, we determine what information can be developed to help them defend themselves." At the time, he was trying to repair the public relations damage done to his firm, at least in the eyes of Canadians, as a result of his company's work on the Lac Corona case. Kroll had been retained by Lac to help it pull together evidence against Corona. Kroll in turn had retained an outside private eye. And as much as Kroll himself would protest that "dirt doesn't fly any more," that what really matters is a company's business ability, it came clear in a subsequent court case that the old standby practices of stake-outs and garbage-pawing had not gone out of fashion.

Hemlo was not the first time Lac had retained Kroll. In 1980, the company had hired Kroll to help explain how they had become royally swindled in the New Cinch salting scam. Kroll's docket also included due diligence work on a heretofore upstart company called American Barrick, which in 1986 had been accumulating stock in Consolidated Gold Fields, a move that Consgold did not much appreciate. Kroll's splashier cases included trailing the missing millions of Haiti's Duvalier regime. But its work on various mining battles in Canada helped ensure that when a Canadian corporation needed a private eye, there was a very good chance Kroll would be the company called.

Kroll explained to me how he always preferred to be retained by a corporation's outside legal counsel. That way, he could plead solicitor-client privilege if anyone demanded to see his evidence. When the Reichmann brothers wanted to hunt down how Toronto journalist Elaine Dewar had pulled together a piece on their operations (over which they launched a multimillion-dollar suit), the Reichmanns' company, Olympia & York, retained Kroll through their top outside law firm, Davies Ward & Beck.

In the intervening years Kroll had tried to give up his beloved Cuban cigars, restricting himself to one a month. He watched his weight religiously and his very expensive suits hung about his frame more loosely. Kroll's point person on the Bre-X file was Steven Rucker, a senior managing director with the firm.

On Monday, July 28, Felderhof and Francisco headed down to the Shang Palace restaurant, where the shark fin soup goes for 98,000 rupiahs and the Peking duck costs 75,000. The Bre-X twosome did not know precisely who would be there to greet them. As it turned out, it was a full Barrick posse: Neil MacLachlan, a former investment banker who was in charge of Barrick's Far East operations; Randall Oliphant, the company's chief financial officer; and Pat Garver, Barrick's in-house counsel. Garver had joined Barrick in 1993, after the company had commenced its first attempt at hooking up with Bre-X, but Garver was not new to Barrick affairs. He had been retained by Barrick years before to help the company acquire the Mercur gold mine near Tooele, Utah, and the Goldstrike mine. Garver was a University of Utah grad and had practised law in Salt Lake City at Parsons Behle & Latimer, running the firm's natural resource group. Barrick ultimately kept Mercur, but it had been a bitter battle. Garver had been key in the victory.

Airlangga brought his lawyer, a man named Dermawan. Airlangga was ostensibly the evening's host, but Garver took on the role of spokesperson. "We're here to negotiate Barrick's interest in Busang," he said. Francisco was flabbergasted. "Are you on drugs, Pat? You're a lawyer. You know the procedure. We don't have a mandate from the board to negotiate."

Was Francisco saying that Bre-X would cut out Barrick as a potential partner? Not at all, said Francisco. It was this "shotgun marriage" approach that he objected to. Francisco went on to say that, as far as he was concerned, the bidding for Busang was still an open process. There had been the talks with CRA, and Placer was still interested (though John Willson had been shut out). There was Newmont, the American gold miner that had another big project on the go in Indonesia. With a prospect the size of Busang, any major gold miner in the world was virtually compelled to at least take a look.

Garver had no patience for Francisco's equivocating. Perhaps this was a reflection of his boss, Munk, who had even less. Garver wiped his mouth with his napkin, then tossed it on the table. "All I want to do is write the cheque," he said. It was not in keeping with Francisco's character to offer the swift riposte, but he offered one up anyway. "Are you sure it won't bounce?"

Felderhof rambled on about how doing business in Southeast Asia was akin to courting a beautiful woman. "You treat her tenderly, not like in North America." Now who was on drugs? Garver was not completely insensitive to the peculiarities of doing business in a foreign land, but he was a pragmatist, too, and surely, given that the partners were both western, they could find a common language. He seemed cranky. Garver was a closer, and he was here to seal this deal for Munk. He had had a couple of drinks. He was fatigued. He said Barrick had been poised to make a takeover bid, but that the company's research had uncovered problems, principally the Merukh complaint. It was this, said Garver, that encouraged Barrick to change course and tack toward a joint venture. "I was told we would be negotiating," he said flatly.

In the main, the meeting was not unlike many in the corporate community in North America: acrimonious, but with a smile, the liquor lending a looseness to the discussions. Felderhof, of course, had had a few. "I'm not afraid of the Bambangs, the Tututs of the world," he said. All this crap talk about a Barrick takeover went down far less well with the emotionally aggressive Felderhof than the more pragmatic Francisco. There might be another takeover, jabbed Felderhof. A Barrick takeover. Yeah, that was the ticket. Bre-X would take over

Barrick. What did the nice-suited men from the big highrise in Toronto think about that?

They went to bed.

The following day the parties met again, this time poolside at the Hyatt for lunch. The setting suggested a sylvan Balinese getaway, with the pool lagoon weaving through palms and stone statuary of Balinese grotesqueries. One might almost believe that this was not downtown Jakarta. But there was rioting in the streets, and its echoes made a disquieting backdrop to the seductive scene. A novelist might invoke life in the Hotel Indonesia, circa 1965—a rich retreat for white westerners who would frolic in the pool, despised by the hotel staff, who watched, and waited, for an opportunity to get back at the *necolim*.

The tenor of the Bre-X–Barrick talk now was much more highstrung, the Barrick reps more formal, more businesslike. "We know what you've done incorrectly in this country," Garver said. He revisited Merukh. And this time the laxness of the dealings with McLucas.

There were two ways of looking at the McLucas business. Bre-X's way was simply to plead disorganization. Barrick figured Bre-X had amended its story on the share transfer to keep it out of trouble with the authorities. If ownership of the immediate parent of the Busang I cow had changed, the authorities in Jakarta should have been notified. Bre-X maintained that it was ownership of the über-parent that had changed hands, an offshore company and therefore beyond the purview of the government.

Francisco paused, then said softly, "I did think at first that this was another Hemlo." But he was now convinced that there was no fiduciary duty here to include Merukh. Still, Bre-X knew it was in danger of having its SIPP cancelled. It needed no reminders from Barrick. Francisco raised the "historical baggage" that came affixed to any Barrick discussions, meaning of course the aborted first deal and the dustup in Sumatra. Bre-X was left with a clear message from this meeting: if they did a deal with Barrick, their problems in this country would vaporize.

Michael Antonio Tuason de Guzman: photographed a month before his demise, when he was being championed as the co-discoverer of the richest single gold mine on the planet

Jennifer Wells

John Felderhof: the Dutch-born geologist had had his ups and downs. His pairing with de Guzman was, for a time, seen as a geological match made in heaven

Jennifer Wells

Felderhof (left) and Cesar Puspos (far right) aboard the same helicopter that would take de Guzman on his final journey

De Guzman's career commenced at the Acupan gold mine in the Philippine countryside, where bachelor accommodation was modest

*The hunt for gold leads to Indonesia: de Guzman
in his early days in Kalimantan*

*De Guzman's eldest son, Paul, leads the funeral cortege
with his mother, Tess, and his aunt, Diane (far right)*

Promoter David Walsh: the furrowed look on Walsh's brow was the same in his deal-making days as in his youth, pictured here with brother, Ricky

Walsh took Bre-X from the basement to a mini-Calgary highrise, then back again

Indonesian workers drill for core

Bobby Ramirez logging the core

De Guzman holds a smooth piece of Busang

Min (left) would fetch the Dayak gold for the Filipinos. De Guzman would ask Dzia Uddin (right) to pray for Busang to show him the gold

The rivers of Kalimantan are her lifeblood: highways to transport her rich resources; tributaries to wash in and feed from

Richard Behar/Fortune

*Busang site, 1996: most of the analysts who visited
did not get a tour of the sample prep lab*

*Warehouse, Loa Duri: the lab in Balikpapan would ship
loads of Bre-X reject samples for storage here*

Richard Behar/Fortune

Jennifer Wells

*Bre-X office, Samarinda:
bags of samples would
sit in the breezeway
before bing humped to
Puspos's quarters*

*Puspos at site, holding a
piece of Busang core.
No core was shipped to
Balikpapan without
Puspos's say-so*

The Indonesian workers at site were given rudimentary accommodation, sleeping under tarps

By 1997, a whole new village was being built for Bre-X labourers

A Dayak woman in the nearby town of Mekar Baru wearing the traditional dress

Pebit, the local Dayak tribal chief, saw many jobs created for his people at the Busang site

*Busang, fall
1995: a grinning
de Guzman
alongside
Felderhof*

*The gang of four:
Puspos, de Guzman,
Felderhof and
Jerry Alo pose for
mining analysts, 1996*

*Felderhof explains
Busang's geology to the
same Canadian analysts*

Jim Bob Moffett looks on as President Suharto helps celebrate the opening of Freeport's Grasberg mine. I.B. Sudjana, minister of mines, stands to the rear of the president

Sylvester Stallone on the green with Suharto and timber tycoon Bob Hasan, who would ultimately broker Busang's future

Barrick Chairman Peter Munk with board mate and former Canadian prime minister Brian Mulroney (centre) alongside the 41st president of the United States and Barrick advisory board member George Bush

In the town of Mekar Baru, Salin ran a general goods store. He was a most prolific gold panner, and would sell his pannings to Puspos and de Guzman

Salin would start to prepare his pan, weighing it down with the ochre mud at Busang

Dextrously swirling his pan, Salin would eventually retrieve the lovely rounded placer grains of gold

Strathcona Minerals' Reinhard von Guttenberg, looking at the gold that wasn't, with Greg Corbett (centre) and Terry Leach, who had been retained by a still believing John Felderhof

Freeport chief geologist Dave Potter at Busang, March, 1997, with Puspos (far left) and de Guzman

On August 9, David Walsh sent a letter to Kuntoro.

Dear Director General:

Thank you for taking the time from your busy schedule to meet with our Messrs. John Felderhof and Rolando Francisco on two occasions recently at your offices. Although your goodself and I only had a brief chat, it was a pleasure to have had the opportunity to meet with you at the Consul General residence dinner, June 13, on behalf of His Excellency, I.B. Sudjana, the Minister of Mines and Energy. I trust your son has enjoyed Boston.

I thought it appropriate at this time to advise you that Bre-X is in the final stages of engaging two international financial advisers to assist us in determining the most advantageous approach to bringing the Busang property into production as soon as possible.

Walsh told Kuntoro that he envisaged three possible alternatives. The first was a joint venture "with one or two" international mining producers; the second was for Bre-X to construct and operate the mine itself, a prospect that Walsh said was not at all unreasonable as "we have had very positive discussions with major world bankers"; and, last, that Bre-X could partially finance and operate the property on a joint venture basis with a senior mining house. "It is our continued intention to keep you abreast of activities as they unfold."

Finally, Walsh topped off his letter with Bre-X's interest in incorporating a foundation, whose mandate "would be to finance various commercial activities, schools and medical facilities in the regions of East Kalimantan and Irian Jaya. In this regard, I would like to listen to your valued comments on the Foundation proposal at a meeting with you, if possible, when I am next in Jakarta. Yours truly," and so forth.

Now who was on drugs? The letter was far too little and much too late. Even a bureaucrat in far-off Jakarta would have seen the absurdity in Bre-X's suggestion that it just might undertake a $1.5-billion construction project on its own, and simply hire the appropriate operating personnel.

On August 15, the Department of Mines cancelled the SIPP under which Bre-X was operating on the Southeast Zone, or Busang II. Bre-X was now naked on the Southeast Zone. It had at that moment no legal title to the property. The following day, Ridwan Mahmud, whose work Felderhof had cited a decade earlier for its substantial contributions to the country's COW legislation, met with Bre-X representatives. Ridwan held to the view that this cancellation was a technicality, that there was no merit to the Merukh claim.

If Bre-X held any hope that it still had some manoeuvring room, that must have evaporated days later, for Francisco was meeting in Jakarta, at the Department of Mines, with Kuntoro, Said, Ganto and Rozik Soetjipto, an assistant to Kuntoro. This "committee" expressed the view that it wanted the expedited development of Busang. Bre-X was unnerved.

Felderhof, meanwhile, had been a hyperactive stock trader. Through April, May and June, Felderhof had been selling small blocks every few days. One thousand shares, two thousand, six thousand. On May 16, he sold three thousand shares at a personal high-water mark of $229 a share. At the end of that month, after the ten-for-one stock split, he picked up 3.28 million shares, exercising options, to hold 3.6 million. Felderhof now was a size player.

On a single day in July the geologist sold 70,000 shares in five separate trades at between $24.45 and $24.85. On August 29, days after the SIPP cancellation, Felderhof picked up 1.1 million Bre-X shares by exercising options, and on the same day he unloaded 778,600 shares. It was John Felderhof's heaviest trading day yet. But he had not come close to cashing out. He still held more than 4 million Bre-X shares. David Walsh held roughly 8 million. Jeannette Walsh had 1.7 million.

Teresa de Guzman took a call at her Quezon city home that summer.

The man on the other end of the line said he was looking for information on Michael. Someone showed up at the house one day, saying he was from the American Embassy and was looking for background information on Michael. Had he ever been hospitalized? Did he have a police record?

THE FIX

THE GOLDEN CORONA OF TORONTO'S financial district rises up
Bay Street, casting an elliptical shadow across a grouping of highrise
towers within which live the big men who pull the big levers of the
country's big money. They are a corporate cloister, an order unto
themselves, and they believe that reverence is their due.

On September 4, 1996, Peter Munk, the self-anointed high priest
of Canadian mining, moved along the carpeted corridor of the shini-
est tower of them all, the Royal Bank Plaza. His eyelashes pale as his
colourless hair, his figure leaner as a bespoke-suited senior executive
than it was in his entrepreneurial youth, Munk made his way silently,
in the manner of the extremely wealthy. Keys do not jangle in his pockets. Nor coinage.

Munk glided past the brass wall sconces, their small candle-like
lights meant to lend these premises a welcoming, if palatial, air. He
moved past the dreadful black Chinese screen that stands across from
the boardroom of Barrick Gold, a leftover from the office's previous
tenant, RJR Nabisco. In the foyer, rock samples from Barrick's various

properties are situated in a glass display case, the lone evidence that this company hunts for minerals. It could otherwise be mistaken for, perhaps, an investment bank.

In the company of Randall Oliphant and Bill Biggar, a Barrick corporate acquisitions specialist, Munk descended the twenty-seven floors to the Bay Street corridor, where the country's brokerages and its über-banks, which own the largest of the brokerages, command the financial district's prime real estate. A stone's throw to the north are the headquarters of broker Nesbitt Burns, and beside Nesbitt is the Toronto Stock Exchange tower and its newly computerized trading floor. Scattered through the district are suitably overpriced restaurants with names like Canoe and Acqua, which welcome the brethren when they choose not to dine in their private clubs. Pocketed in the highrises above are rent-paying junior mining companies, ever hopeful rock-busters who imagine that one day they too will have a real mine house and the imperial cast of a Barrick Gold.

On the September day in question, Munk and his lieutenants advanced to the Crowne Plaza Hotel, a conference-centre-like hotel not far away physically, but astrally removed in character. Unlike the Four Seasons, or the King Edward, the Crowne was new, devoid of personality and functional. This was the point. As was discretion.

A small conference room had been booked. Lunch had been ordered up. Barrick had requested the meeting. Bre-X had decided on a slate of three directors to attend that day: David Walsh, John Felderhof and Rolly Francisco.

Bre-X was boxed. With the cancellation of the SIPP for the Southeast Zone, the company was, if momentarily, uncomfortably exposed, with no paper in hand to cover its exploration activities at Busang II. Other than Bre-X itself, and a group within the Department of Mines, no other player in the growing Busang saga was as aware of this vulnerability as Barrick.

The Bre-X players were feeling increasingly beleaguered, day by day. Michael de Guzman had been saying that he had grown so distressed by the hounding that he was planning to uproot his Filipino family and move to Australia. Kroll, he kept saying, was all over him.

Working out of Jakarta, Bre-X had attempted to address with the department the administrative problems over the Southeast Zone. Ridwan had been engaged to run interference. Felderhof was writing letters. But the company was clearly losing. And Felderhof's red heat after the meetings in Jakarta with Barrick had not cooled. Perhaps that was one reason why Barrick did not send Pat Garver in on this round.

Peter Munk had grown impatient with what seemed like interminable delays. Garver was supposed to have been the closer on Busang two months before, yet he had returned to Toronto empty-handed. Barrick had secured its entree to the highest levels of government in Indonesia. On August 23, Neil MacLachlan, Barrick's Far East executive vice-president, based in Jakarta, had informed the corporate office that Bre-X's SIPP had been cancelled. Peter Munk's golden opportunity lay before him.

Munk commanded the moment. "We have been invited by the Indonesian government," he said in his cultured accent, "to pursue a partnership with Bre-X." Munk, in the view of the Bre-X cast, was his typical arrogant, elitist, condescending self. Munk explained that Barrick envisioned a 60-40 split, with the 60 going to Barrick, of course. From its block, Barrick would then carve out 10 percent for the Indonesian government. As for the junior partner, Syakerani, well, he would have to look to Bre-X for his piece. Merukh, too, would be Bre-X's problem. The Bre-X team wanted to know what lay beneath their 40 percent. What charges would be loaded on? In the end, what would Bre-X's interest truly be?

If David Walsh had hoped to truly auction Busang, his hopes must have evaporated that day. The inability of Felderhof et al. to get any satisfaction from the Department of Mines, the presence of Airlangga in those earlier meetings, had finally convinced him that the fix was in. The jig was up. Or was it?

Bre-X moved quickly. The following day, September 5, the company at last announced publicly that it had retained Republic National Bank of New York as its corporate adviser, and J.P. Morgan & Co. as its financial adviser. No question, Bre-X was taking the blue-chip route here. Days earlier, Bre-X had hired Bryan Coates as corporate comptroller. Francisco had been swamped by his responsibilities and had been pushing for months to get some top-drawer help. Coates knew Francisco from their days together at Lac Minerals, and his advent, for Francisco, was a welcome relief.

Francisco quickly headed back to Jakarta. The Department of Mines had questions about title, and it clearly expressed the view that what it wanted out of Busang now was not more exploration, but rather development.

Haji Syakerani's help was enlisted. Without a SIPP, the company was technically prohibited from doing any work at all on the property. But being the local partner, Syakerani, through Askatindo, was able to secure a KP to cover activities in the Southeast Zone. The KP, a survey permit similar to its SIPP cousin, was granted on September 13. Bre-X was now exploring under the auspices of its senior partner. Felderhof and Walsh would later state that Bre-X had in no way misbehaved, that the KP cleared Bre-X to continue its full-scale exploration of the gold-rich zone.

The troubles seem not to have disrupted Busang camp life. That fall, Cesar Puspos took a contract wife in the town of Mekar Baru. Her given name was Augustine, but she was called Augus. She had worked as a radio operator at the Busang camp. The day Cesar married her, some of the workers at camp took the day off to attend the celebrations. "We must attend Mr. Cesar's wedding in the village!" they said. Augus was Salin's sister-in-law, and on at least one occasion she relayed money for his gold pannings that had passed to her husband from de Guzman. Twenty thousand rupiahs per gram was the going rate.

Michael de Guzman's behaviour was more high-strung. Greg MacDonald was supposed to be in charge of the Bre-X administration in

Jakarta, but de Guzman's flaming faxes would remind him from time
to time who was truly in charge. "Dear Greg. I have received a fax
from Rolly thanking me for an opportunity to review our 'paper' then
advice me about the rules!!! This is the 2nd time you really badly
screwed up on me. I suggest you clean up your act and behave properly.... I have not yet completed the draft you sent it out without my
knowledge. Upon completion, it is company standards which I 100%
sanely know—need to have permission from senior management. I
intend to send copies upon thorough review. I want an explanation
from you on the 30th August about this matter which you fucked-
up.... I will be at the office."

De Guzman was an unpleasant office presence. The mood would
tighten when he was about. Bathroom breaks would practically have
to be approved. De Guzman had an edgy, off-putting way of staring
at people, sideways glances that made the recipients feel ill-at-ease.
The office had become de Guzman's show to run, not John Felderhof's. He frequently reprimanded staffers by fax, signing his missives
in that unmistakable loopy scrawl of his.

The pressure was mounting. With the government leaning heavily
on Bre-X to form a partnership, the Busang prospect no longer offered
a limitless vista. The ownership mess had dropped an unexpected fly
in the ointment. If Bre-X had been able to secure its contract of work,
it would not have found itself in this predicament. Mike de Guzman
must have been spitting mad about that. That had not been part of
the plan.

There were other issues. A report prepared for Bre-X by a company called Normet out of Australia made mention of the physical
nature of the gold in the Busang samples. The gold observed was
beaded, rounded, as one would observe in a placer deposit. But 300
metres down—could the gold look like that? Naturally, no. The topic
came up at a Bre-X board meeting that fall. Kavanagh appeared to
be struggling with how to reconcile the gold and the property. John
Felderhof would smack the inquisitors down. This, he said, was a

common occurrence in at least three deposits in Asia. The discussion would go on and on, for an hour at a time, at a number of board meetings, with Felderhof on the phone from Jakarta. He was always the man to lay the curious concerns to rest. Felderhof would often cite the work of Terry Leach (born in Canada, trained in Britain) and Greg Corbett, a geological duo in New Zealand who had made their reputations through their groundbreaking work on epithermal gold deposits.

On September 17, at 7:55 a.m., George Bush landed in the spunky town of Elko, Nevada, aboard the deluxe Gulfstream jet owned by Barrick Gold. The residents of Elko, population 20,000, had only recently welcomed their first Wal-Mart and their second McDonald's. Visiting former heads of state were, safe to say, not common. There was a motorcade, and the requisite swarming security force. Not only was Bush arriving, so were former Canadian prime minister Brian Mulroney, former Bundesbank head Karl Otto Pohl and former u.s. senator Howard Baker, Jr.

It certainly seemed fitting for Barrick's high-profile advisory board to gather here, the nearest town to the company's base of operations at Goldstrike. The Barrick gold mines on the Carlin Trend had helped promote the state to the leading position in u.s. gold production, with more than 60 percent of the country's output. The state's gold days dated back to the mid 1850s, an era of prospectors, panners and pack horses. By the time of Barrick's arrival more than a century later, the Nevada Mining Association had deemed the mining renaissance the "invisible gold era." You could not see the stuff, in nuggets or veins. But it was there. Incredibly fine.

The mining association has a motto: "If it isn't grown, it must be mined." Nevada calls itself the Silver State, but in modern days, gold mining has been the area's big economic success. Tourists are drawn to Elko's Cowboy Poetry Festival, its casinos and its Basque culture. Basque shepherds arrived from the Pyrenees in the 1860s, and their descendants still frequent the two Basque restaurants in town, figures nearly as wide as they are tall, topped off with black berets. Prior to the advanced mining technologies introduced by Barrick, Newmont and the like, the city, a hangout for cattle ranchers, held fast to the label "the last real cow-town in the American West."

It was Newmont geologist John Livermore who identified the Carlin Trend gold potential in the early 1960s. Gold was still fixed, at us$35 an ounce. But the company pushed ahead with its Carlin mining plans, and by the mid 1990s it was annually producing more than a million and a half ounces of gold from its Carlin operations. The gold was disseminated and microscopic. Miners time and again took a pass on the portion of the trend that Barrick would go on to develop. A series of shallow drill holes were sunk in the early 1960s by other miners, who left, discouraged, in the face of uninteresting results. Claims were staked, and later abandoned. In 1987, Larry Kornze, working for Barrick, helped discover the 12-million-ounce Betze deposit. By the early 1990s, the combined operations of Newmont and Barrick made the Carlin Trend the largest gold-producing region in North America and the third largest in the world.

Mining became the strongest economic motivator in the state, followed by cattle ranching and gaming. The Barrick hit at Goldstrike had spawned the proverbial staking rush. In the summer of 1987, there was not a motel room to be had anywhere in Elko, and the Basque restaurants were overrun with hungry geologists. That same summer, Munk celebrated his sixtieth birthday at Cliveden, the old Astor estate outside London. Galen and Hilary Weston attended, as did Ted and Loretta Rogers. All Munk's close friends were there. The stunning accomplishment at Carlin had fed the astonishing turnaround of Barrick and the unexpected second coming of Peter Munk. No one had expected any of the above.

Thirty years earlier, Munk and partner David Gilmour had flown the high-swinging success of a company they had created, Clairtone Sound Corp. For staid Canadians in the 1950s, the urbane Munk—boyish then, rounded face, hair and eyelashes as pale as spun gold—seemed a curiosity. Having emigrated from Hungary in 1948, Munk lacked social connections, but he was sophisticated, smart, and when he hooked up with Gilmour, the better-connected son of the managing director of brokerage Nesbitt Thomson & Co., a partnership was born that would surely last two lifetimes. Gilmour called Munk "the most exciting human being I've ever met in my life."

Clairtone was, for a time, the beautiful marriage of the two mind-sets: Munk, the trained engineer; Gilmour, the design aficionado. Together they created the Project G sound system, the first solid-state stereo. Their advertisements featured the likes of Tuesday Weld, and their supporters included cool crooner Frank Sinatra. Dean Martin had a Clairtone too. Full-page magazine advertisements featured a Clairtone model outfitted with two globes as speakers, ground-breaking at the time and achingly un-Canadian. Munk and Gilmour were golden boys. When Munk made his first speech before the Establishment at a Canadian Club luncheon in Toronto, he was still in his thirties. He had arrived.

But the Clairtone vision was too grand. Munk and Gilmour took the company public, expanded too quickly, moved into colour televisions and relocated to Nova Scotia, with the assistance of that province's industrial development agency, Industrial Estates Ltd. IEL underwrote $8 million in Clairtone bonds and continued to pump money in after Clairtone started to sink. Munk and Gilmour stepped out of the company in the spring of 1967. IEL tried for a time to keep the company afloat without its creators, but in 1971 manufacture of the Clairtone sound system ceased (it became a much-coveted collector's item). The collapse would hound Munk for years: the monies the province of Nova Scotia flushed down the toilet, the jobs lost, contrasted less than attractively with the secure financial positions Munk and Gilmour had arranged for themselves.

By the time Clairtone died, Munk and Gilmour were well out of it and were into South Pacific Properties Ltd. One day, when Munk was in the Toronto law office of his very good friend Howard Beck, partner in the firm Davies Ward & Beck, he coined the name Beachcomber for the hotel the pair would build in Fiji. Munk and Gilmour based South Pacific Hotel Corp. in London, where they were unknowns and thus unburdened by Clairtone's dirty laundry. They hired Bill Birchall, a chartered accountant who had been based in the Bahamas and who had hotel expertise, and the threesome would be a threesome forever. One of South Pacific's biggest backers was Saudi billionaire Adnan Khashoggi. By the late 1970s, Triad International Corp., the Khashoggi family holding company, had a 28 percent, and controlling, interest in South Pacific.

As far as Canadians were concerned, Munk was long forgotten—until 1979, when South Pacific moved its headquarters to Toronto. Munk said he preferred to raise his children there. But perhaps there was another factor. In Toronto, Munk could be a bigger fish. He would consistently say he wanted to make a contribution, something lasting.

Two years later, South Pacific, then a fifty-hotel chain with a pretax profit of $20 million, was sold to Tan Sri Khoo of Singapore, and Munk and Gilmour moved on to other challenges. They formed Barrick Petroleum Co., knowing between the two of them precisely nothing about the oil and gas business.

Barrick Petroleum redefined itself as Barrick Resources—an event that went, for the most part, unnoticed. Barrick Investments Ltd. was the parent company, and Munk, Gilmour, Birchall and Khashoggi were the principal investors. Barrick moved into gold in 1983, making investors take notice two years later with the acquisition, from Texaco Inc., of the Mercur gold mine in Utah.

Mercur landed Barrick in court. American miner Gold Standard Inc. alleged that it had struck an earlier deal to purchase the mine. Barrick went in search of local legal counsel, bringing Salt Lake City lawyer Pat Garver into the fold to fight to keep Mercur for Barrick. Scott Smith was president of Gold Standard. He had a meeting once with Munk, attempting to explain to the new Canadian what Mercur meant to Gold Standard shareholders. "Who ever said there's any-thing fair in business?" responded Munk.

In 1986 Munk put on his financier's hat and proposed a share swap that would transform a shell company called United Siscoe Mines Ltd. into a new entity called Horsham Corp., which would take up the shares in Barrick owned by another Munk vehicle, Horsham Securi-ties Ltd. Horsham would end up with 30 percent of Barrick and Munk would retain a 63 percent voting interest in Horsham. Adnan Khashoggi's Triad International, and Elk International Corp., con-trolled by Adnan's brother Essam, would end up with 25 percent of the subordinate voting shares. The corporate presidency would be taken up by Tariq Kadri, a Triad executive. Munk would be chairman.

The offering circular seemed to last about a heartbeat before it was withdrawn and all traces of Triad, Elk and Kadri were erased. The Khashoggi brothers had been good friends to Munk in his trying days post Clairtone, but the Canadian market seemed to want to have noth-ing to do with the Saudi pair. The Khashoggi interest was clearly a loose cannon, and the media were making hay with suggestions that Khashoggi had used Barrick shares to finance Iranian arms. That accu-sation turned out to be untrue. But Triad, headquartered in Salt Lake City, was getting into financial trouble and would subsequently dissolve into bankruptcy. The revamped Horsham gave Munk 100 percent of the multiple voting shares, which in turn gave him control of Barrick.

The same year, 1986, Munk made his run for ConsGold, buying up 2.9 million shares at a cost of about US$56 million. He told the *Financial Times* of London that he wanted to make a "quantum leap." The company then was producing a quarter million ounces of gold annually.

The failed run gave Barrick a reputation in the U.K. that Munk would describe as "upbeat." "We're seen as a brash junior entry into the gold business that in three years was big enough to tackle their biggest institutional gold house," Munk told me a decade ago. It was more than that. The Clairtone baggage and the Munk arrogance, which rubbed some analysts the wrong way, meant that the company and its gold-mining prospects were not embraced quickly. Munk would have to do much better than Mercur to win the love of institutional investors.

Then came Goldstrike, which was initially met with truckloads of skepticism on Bay Street and Wall Street. "There are analysts who a year ago wouldn't touch Barrick," Munk told me in 1988. "There are analysts who don't like the colour of my hair." But Barrick overcame. Bob Smith was uppermost in the street's decision to back Barrick. Where Munk was perceived as a jet-setter with a spotted past, Smith had a solid reputation as a miner—big, solid and straight as a die—who, if anything, would underestimate the potential of a discovery.

By the time Munk made his second Canadian Club speech, twenty-five years had passed. He was at ease describing his earlier "uniquely unsuccessful" junior oil and gas foray, for he was now a bona fide gold miner. He gave his talk about South Africa, about the demise of Ian Smith in Rhodesia foreshadowing not blood in the streets but "a sea of change . . . a fundamental attitudinal change towards the whole of the South African economy." European institutional capital, funds that traditionally placed between 3 percent and 10 percent of their assets under administration in gold shares, would flee to other miners. Barrick was waiting. Investment in gold, he said, was not unlike an insurance policy, though the Americans, who had not suffered the ravages of war as the Europeans had, did not fully appreciate this. There was, he said, a "God-given opportunity" for Barrick to succeed.

And there was blood in the streets. And fund money did flee South Africa. North American gold funds that had seen a monthly inflow of capital of $40 million were, by 1987, seeing nearly ten times that. The average weighting of gold shares on the Toronto Stock Exchange went from 2.5 percent to 11.5 percent in two years. Munk talked of his conservative approach to running a gold house, particularly focusing on his belief in "hedging" the company's gold sales, selling its production forward at prices set today. Investors feared missing the big upside when the gold price was hot—and no one could forget the way it had spun through $800 an ounce in January 1980. But Munk would argue that selling forward allowed him to lock in a predetermined profit, and that as long as his operations remained low cost—in the $200 an ounce range—"It was Christmas all the way!" Even if gold fell to $300. Few believed the metal would ever do worse than that.

Of course, the stock market was having a heck of a run too. By 1987, Barrick's own market capitalization had grown to $1.5 billion from $100 million four years previous. Munk would spend the post-Christmas season at Klosters, where he and wife Melanie would ski in the company of Prince Charles; summer was for his lovely Georgian Bay getaway in the semi-wilds of Ontario.

Ten years later, Munk made it clear that he intended to take Barrick to the top spot of the world's gold producers, and not strictly on the back of North American reserves, but with mines acquired in exotic locales. There was the Lac Minerals acquisition, with operations in Chile. Later would come Arequipa, which brought in Peru. Now Munk had a problem. Should any other gold company get Busang, it would, with the resource Bre-X was touting, automatically become the world's leader. In Peter Munk's view, he simply could not allow that to happen.

On the morning of September 17, 1996, the Barrick advisory board gathered at Red's Ranch outside Elko. They visited the three properties that comprise the company's Goldstrike asset. "I'd thought I'd seen a lot of things in my life, but this was absolutely mind-boggling," George Bush said in a speech that evening, given at a do thrown at the local convention centre. "I expect that there is as much enthusiasm here for Barrick as I have in my own heart." He referred to Brian Mulroney as his "great, good friend" who "got me involved on this advisory board for Barrick that he heads." Bush said that being part of the advisory team was "one of the luckiest things to happen to me."

Two days later, Bush wrote a letter to President Suharto. He wanted to impress upon the president, with whom he had had an audience years before, his "highly favourable" impression of Barrick.

September 20, 1996

Dear President Suharto,

I want to thank you for your thoughtful letter. I hope that my travels will soon bring me back to Jakarta so that we might meet again.

Earlier this week, I was in Elko, Nevada for a meeting of the Barrick Gold Corporation's International Advisory Board (to which I am a Senior Advisor) and had the opportunity of touring the company's vast mining operations there.

Because Barrick Chairman Peter Munk advised me of their interests in a major gold development in Kalimantan, Indonesia, I simply want to take the liberty of telling you how impressed I am with Barrick, its visionary leadership, technological achievements and great financial strength.

I can recommend Mr. Munk and Barrick with no reservations whatsoever.

My respects to you sir and my warmest best wishes,

Sincerely,

George Bush.

Munk was lining up his ducks. Mulroney had ingratiated himself with Sudjana. Airlangga was successfully pushing his way around the department. Bre-X was attempting to come to terms with the cancellation of its SIPP and cover its nakedness in the Southeast Zone. By the first week in September, Rolly Francisco was hurriedly meeting with Said, Ganto and Kuntoro in Jakarta.

Tutut was on board for Barrick, having offered her hand to Munk in the SHR arrangement, so he had one of the most powerful siblings, and the one with the most political clout, onside. There was risk in that, too. In eighteen months' time, Suharto would stand for re-election. Or would he? He was growing old. Even if Suharto stood again, surely he had but one five-year term left, if he survived it. And political risk experts predicted a backlash against the greedy children once Pak Suharto was gone.

Munk now had Bush attempting to open a direct line to the president himself, who could not necessarily be counted on to endorse Tutut's adventures. Barrick had covered itself off with the existing regime. Or so it thought.

It was time for David Walsh to develop some military manoeuvres of his own. On September 26, he announced that Bre-X intended to "pursue all available opportunities to maximize the value of the Busang deposit." The maximization of value had become a popular euphemism in the 1990s. Busang was on the block. The Bre-X board, he said, was prepared to sell Bre-X, merge Bre-X, joint-venture Bre-X, or sell Busang. "Bre-X will shortly seek the participation of a major mining company to facilitate expeditious development of the deposit and enhance its value," Walsh said. The words "expeditious development" were just what the government wanted to hear. But could the handling of the development be handed to anyone other than Barrick?

There was CRA, but John Craig was starting to pick up the ill wind of political interference from Jakarta, and the company, which had initially seen itself as the favoured acquisitor, had been wholly frustrated in its attempts to get the Bre-X crew to come to terms. By September, CRA was no closer to having its standard-practice requirements met— full due diligence—than it had been ten months before. The prescient comments made to Felderhof, about the heavy hand of an unwanted suitor coming to rest on the company's shoulder, were starting to come true. On September 18, Bre-X had closed at $28.40, or $284.00 on a pre-split basis. By having failed to secure a corporate partnership, Bre-X, as CRA well knew, was headed for trouble.

Walsh, of course, had already found himself in a heap of it. From its perch in Vancouver's Bentall Place, Placer Dome had continued to collate the Bre-X results, building its own mine model. Placer's John Willson, repeatedly rebuffed by Walsh, had awaited the day when the company would officially tender. With the announcement of the Republic–J.P. Morgan team, followed by Walsh's comment to the marketplace that he was prepared to do a deal any which way, Placer's moment had arrived.

At the beginning of October, Willson was on the road when he took a call from his assistant, Leona. "David Walsh called and he wants a meeting," she said. After months of corporate slumber over the ultimate partnership of the fabulous gold find, the inquiring calls that were never returned, the scheduled meetings that would evaporate, Walsh was suddenly in a panic. He wanted to meet with Willson ASAP. To Willson it seemed rather dramatic, but he was not about to question an opportunity to meet Walsh face to face, to hear the Busang story first-hand, and to be invited in. Well, there was a God after all.

On October 2, a Wednesday evening, John Willson joined David Walsh in Calgary for dinner. As Willson flew to Calgary, he attempted to size up the situation. But he knew so little. Placer had not been on the ground at Busang, and certainly had not been apprised of the tightening political noose. As he headed into his meeting with Walsh, he decided that he wanted nothing more than an understanding of what Bre-X wanted to get out of an arrangement. Placer saw itself as supremely well placed to be the chosen partner. In 1990, the company had started up its Porgera gold mine in the highlands of Papua New Guinea. In its first full year of operation Porgera had produced 1.2 million ounces of gold. More significantly, the company had met the challenge, as Freeport-McMoRan had at Grasberg, of constructing a mine against seemingly insurmountable odds.

As Willson assessed the landscape of contenders, there was Freeport, which certainly seemed to have its hands full with Grasberg, there were the Australians, though he knew nothing of CRA's frustrations,

Newmont in the United States and Barrick here at home. But Barrick's success had come from Nevada. Not to say that the technological achievement of retrieving the gold there was unimpressive, but building a mine in Nevada was nothing like the wilds of Southeast Asia, Papua New Guinea and now Kalimantan. Jungle territory. The social and political issues, Willson knew, would be enormous. The company had learned much weaving its way in PNG. Yes, Placer had a leg up, at least as far as North American operators were concerned.

Willson, a Brit from Sheffield, had grown up in the mining community. His father was a mining engineer, and Willson had spent many of his early days in central Portugal, while his father was working at a tungsten mine there. Willson was well liked in the mining community. He had a reputation for being refreshingly blunt, for sprinkling his conversation with soft expletives, for enjoying a good beer. Peter Munk he was not.

The evening with Walsh was pleasant and did not seem to bear out the urgency of the Bre-X executive's call to Leona. Walsh took Willson through his background, his life, his attitude toward things. He discussed his early corporate experiences, his bankruptcy, Jeannette. He did not come across as a sophisticated financier—rather the opposite. Certainly his lack of success spoke to that. But Willson, who had met Walsh just once before, liked Walsh for his dogged nature.

Willson spoke of Placer and its accomplishments, how it was the viable and logical choice for Busang. But there was an undertow to the talks. Walsh had been followed. There had been break-ins. He was under immense pressure.

Placer had previously tried another way in to Busang. John Loney, Placer's political risk expert, had met with Jusuf Merukh and his new-found business partner, Australian Warren Beckwith. Merukh maintained that he had a 20 percent carried interest into the Southeast Zone. He was willing to sell. The Merukh group had approached Placer in the first place, sending, as it did to other interested parties, a very legal-looking letter stating its ownership claims and its belief that any company interested in coming into the process had better deal with them, too. Placer, in turn, was wary. Merukh was known as a wild card in the Indonesian mining establishment. Placer had held talks with Merukh on his interest in another gold project, Batu Hijau, controlled by Newmont. But Merukh had failed to deliver. Willson's preferred strategy vis-à-vis Busang was to work its way into favour with Bre-X. Now it appeared as though it had accomplished just that.

Back in Placer's offices on the Friday, Willson dictated a letter to David Walsh, telling him how much he had enjoyed the evening. It was October 4, and for David Walsh it was a very bad day. The *Globe and Mail* had run a story on the Busang title issues that morning. It was the first widely disseminated news the Canadian market had had that Bre-X's hold on this mother of a gold mine was not as strong as all that. It was the first mention of Jusuf Merukh. The next day, a million Bre-X shares traded in a single hour. The share price was given a severe haircut: down six bucks to $26.90. David Walsh and his crew were in big trouble.

Walsh tried to dismiss the matter as technicalities of an insignificant nature, and his men on the ground in Jakarta, Felderhof in particular, were likely telling him precisely that. But the news story sent the first hint of troubles in the golden tale to legions of investors who had bought in. Mike Fowler's comment three months earlier had largely gone unnoticed, but now Canada's national newspaper was starting to suggest that Bre-X was on shaky ground.

David Walsh was clearly a lot more worried than he let on to his share-buying public. On October 8, at 9:30 in the evening, John Willson picked up his home phone. It was Brett Walsh. "My father wants to talk," said the young Walsh. "He can't talk now. He's on a call to Indonesia. He'll call you." There was the urgency again. Hot and cold running angst. The conversation was brief. John Willson stood by, and waited. At 11:00 p.m. the phone rang. Again, it was not David Walsh but young Brett. "I'm really sorry... My father's still on the phone. Can you come to Calgary for breakfast tomorrow?" The whole affair was starting to feel rather cloak-and-dagger. David Walsh was spending hours on the phone to Jakarta, talking to Rolly Francisco.

When he met Willson the next day, Walsh was circumspect. "We've got a situation," he said. "I can't tell you about it." He was very close-mouthed and admitted to being under pressure. "I want to go with Placer Dome," said Walsh. He had been talking to the friendly analysts he favoured to get the word on Placer. He said he had heard some good things and some not-so-good things, but that the bottom line was he believed the guys at Placer to be straight players. His talks with Rolly had led to the clear conclusion that Bre-X needed an ally. "We've made a lot of money out of this thing," said Walsh. "We need a partner. We recognize that the partner is also going to want to make some money out of this thing." Then David Walsh said a funny thing. "You can only wear one pair of shoes at a time."

There was so much pressure, so much pressure. "I'll deliver a lockup of 35 percent of the shares, me and my friends," he promised. David Walsh had been chasing the end of the rainbow for more than three years. Latterly, so had John Willson. Now Busang was seemingly being handed to Placer. Willson thought he had died and gone to heaven. But he had an immense question that needed to be answered: why?

Willson asked many questions that evening that did not get answered. Why was David Walsh so unforthcoming? He pondered the possibility that Bre-X was under a confidentiality agreement with another company, presumably Barrick.

Placer immediately put its team into action. On the ground in Jakarta, Loney worked at finding out everything it could about the Busang play. What was happening behind closed doors? The news that started to trickle in was grim. Placer was late into the game. The ownership of Busang was practically a done deal, and Barrick was the partner. Placer was going to have to be extremely aggressive if it hoped to see the Barrick relationship undone. Willson believed he had Walsh onside. Felderhof, in October, continued his discouraging meetings with the Department of Mines. "Goddammit," Willson said. "There's got to be something we can do."

David Walsh was thinking the same thing. The boys at Panutan, Johnnie Hermanto and Mr. Harsono, had continued their pursuit of a piece of Busang on behalf of their controlling shareholder, Sigit Harjojudanto. Barrick had brought Tutut on board, and it had Airlangga in its camp, along with the heavyweight western political connections. What strength did Bre-X have against that? The company did not merely lack an offence, it did not have a defence. What were those plays again? Writing in the *Asian World Stock Report*, Brian Fagan bemoaned Bre-X's fate. "Title to the ground is paramount," he said. "Without it you have nothing."

If Bre-X had any friends left in Jakarta, their numbers were dwindling. On October 17, Ida Bagus Sudjana issued a decree cancelling Kuntoro's authority over the Busang affair, handing it over instead to Umar Said. It was devastating news. Kuntoro was seen as a straight-shooter, clean. Said was another type all together: shrill, unpredictable, suspect, much more the Sudjana type.

On October 28, Bre-X announced to the world that it had struck a "strategic alliance" with PT Panutan Duta, aka Sigit. Panutan, the boys who had so eagerly sought an association with Barrick a scant four months earlier, had found their access point at last. The group, said Bre-X, would "assist in administrative, technical and other support matters." It would identify "issues concerning the acquisition, exploration, development and production" of Busang.

It seemed a curious alliance. Of the Suharto boys, Bambang was the most powerful and the most successful. Sigit was a shareholder in Bank Central Asia, as was Tutut, and he had a chunk of brother Tommy's Humpuss Group, the controlling company that ruled Tommy's various business interests. But Sigit was seen as shy, and not the most effective Suharto to have in one's pocket. Sigit's son, Ari Haryo Sigit, had placed a levy on booze in Bali, which had gone over fabulously unwell with the business crowd there. Suharto himself had rescinded the levy the previous March.

Bre-X had been advised by Jakarta insiders not to release the news of the Sigit relationship. It was not the Javanese way, and as much as President Suharto supported his children's efforts to help build one of the world's richest fortunes, it was ill advised to draw attention to it.

Sure enough, the deal with Sigit blew a pungent aroma across the time zones, the trading desks of brokerage houses and the computer terminals of journalists. This son of Suharto would draw $1 million a month for forty months for these so-called services; and he would get a 10 percent piece of Busang I and Busang II, which, at the time, looked to be worth about $1.5 billion. Further, Sigit would get 40 percent of the support services company that Bre-X intended to establish, supplying gas and limestone and such to the site. The memorandum of understanding between the two parties was subject to, among other things, the issuance of contracts of work for Busang II and Busang III, a third property block that thus far had been the focus of little exploration activity. "We are delighted to have formed an alliance with a strong Indonesian partner," said Walsh.

Not strong enough. On November 5, Airlangga's father, the mighty Hartarto, sent a letter to Sudjana. "Regarding the Minister of Mining and Energy's report, and ours, to Mr. President of last November 1, 1996, about the problem solving efforts in handling the Busang gold deposit development, in East Kalimantan, herewith we convey Mr. President's guidancy." Barrick, said Hartarto, "should be given a priority to manage the Busang gold deposit... as a major shareholder so that the gold deposit exploitation can be implemented soon." Mr. President's "guidance," said Hartarto, was to split the mine 75–25, the 75 to Barrick.

On November 7, Rolly Francisco stared wearily at the latest missive from the Department of Mines. This one was from Kuntoro, requesting the company's attendance one week hence, at the ministerial headquarters on Merdeka Selatan, not far from the hub of downtown hotels.

Another damn meeting. Walsh would need to be present for this one. Perhaps with Sigit in their pocket they could dispense with this menace once and for all. The Bre-X group assumed that they would be the only corporate interest meeting with the department that day, November 14.

Daniel McConvey, a mining analyst then with Lehman Brothers Inc. in New York, commenced his Bre-X coverage in November. McConvey had worked for Barrick for more than six years, his time at the company roughly mirroring that of Kavanagh's. Bre-X stock was fourteen dollars and change the day McConvey put out his first report. His commentary, which was very likely the longest research report released to date and included much information that McConvey had culled from his site visit in July, initially struck all the right cautionary notes: that tenure and political uncertainties clouded the discovery; that it was "a high risk stock that is sure to see high volatility during the coming weeks." This was not a stock for the meek.

But, McConvey added, "for those investors who are able to accept higher risks, we would advise them to hold on to their shares in the hope of a major share price rebound when the issues . . . are resolved. We believe the issues will be resolved and that there will be a significant rebound in Bre-X's share price."

Under the heading "What is Bre-X?" McConvey wrote: "The Canadians all own it, the Australians know it but many don't believe it and, despite the fact that, the last time we checked, America's two best performing mutual funds were major holders of its stock, most u.s. investors do not know what Bre-X is.

"Bre-X's recent Busang discovery in the jungles of Kalimantan Indonesia has, so far, had every indication of becoming the gold discovery of the century. One would have to go back to the Klondike or the discovery of the Witwatersrand in South Africa a century ago to find anything that compares to the apparent size of Busang. In five years, Busang may be the largest producing gold mine in the world." The market capitalization of Bre-X stood at $3.7 billion.

Two days later, McConvey issued a different, more urgent message:

"Bre-X takeover may be imminent. Buy this stock today." McConvey had "sources," who went unnamed, of course. "Our sources indicate that a deal to acquire Bre-X may happen in the very near future with the support of the Indonesian government. Our guess is that pricing will be in the c$27 to c$30 range."

McConvey had not completely shed his cautionary mien. This was still a risk investment, he reminded his readers. "Not everything Bre-X has done administratively in Indonesia has been orderly. If there is no buyout offer made, Bre-X may be 'left out to dry' while it struggles to resolve its situation with Merukh and acquire its cow."

On November 13, at 3:22 in the afternoon, Peter Munk checked into the Grand Hyatt Jakarta. He did not take the Majapahit Suite, where the sultan of Brunei stays when he's in town and for which he pays us$2,700 a night. The Munk suite was more restrained, named after Sriwijaya, a hero of Indonesian folklore who saved the island of Sumatra. Grand suite #2406 was cool and polished, its floors with the look of marble, its tub chairs upholstered in sand leather, studded with brass. The kitchenette was stocked with complimentary packs of Lucky Strike and Fisherman's Friend.

From the vantage point of the rather small desk, outfitted with phone and fax, Munk could cast his gaze below to the maddening semicircles of Jakarta traffic sucking themselves around the city's Welcome Monument, a hideous concrete creation in the Stalinesque style featuring a man and woman reaching for the sky. The circular pool that surrounds the monument does nothing to lessen the thick clog of bad air. To do business in Jakarta is to stay in one's hotel room as much as possible.

Munk had not planned to be here at all. He had been in Budapest, officiating at the ribbon-cutting of a TrizecHahn megamall. Trizec Hahn is Munk's real estate empire, which, at this point in time, was intertwined with his gold-mining empire, Barrick. Munk's next stop after Budapest was meant to be Toronto, where the Barrick crowd was to fete Bob Smith, who had been central in making Barrick one of the most successful gold-mining companies in the world. But while in Budapest, Munk had been faxed a copy of a letter requesting his attendance at the Department of Mines, November 14.

By the time of Munk's arrival, Bre-X knew that Barrick was in town. In fact, Randall Oliphant had phoned up Rolly Francisco, and the two had had dinner at the Shangri-La. Over a quiet meal, Oliphant informed Francisco that Munk would be in attendance the following day. Francisco did not know that Barrick had also hauled in its Canadian investment advisers. And why was it that Barrick seemed always to know in advance of meetings that Bre-X assumed were set up to deal with its own special interests?

Bre-X had buttressed itself for the meeting. Doug McIntosh and Leslie Morrison were on hand from J.P. Morgan, along with Bill Edge from the Republic Bank. After all those months of unprofessional drift, Bre-X at last seemed to have its act together. Francisco, Walsh and Felderhof were the executive team representatives that day.

The group taxied up alongside the ministerial building, colonial in appearance, white-columned and slightly decrepit. As they entered the appointed chamber, their collective hearts sank. For there was Barrick, and not just any old Barrick rep, but Munk himself—the heaviest of all heavyweights. Munk was in the company of the Ibu Yoke ("Ibu" is a respectful term of address), an aide to Tutut, and Airlangga Hartarto.

The meeting ran an uneventful course. At least initially. Munk trumpeted his corporate strengths. Walsh offered up the Bre-X defence. It was all a set piece. Ida Bagus Sudjana took the floor and read from a prepared text. Here was what was decided, he said in his stumbling English. Barrick was the partner of choice and Barrick would take 75 percent of Busang. Bre-X would take 25 percent. He gave the parties a deadline of November 20 to reach an agreement on mine development.

There was now no avoiding the reality that Bre-X had been snookered. Munk, in his smooth way, had appropriated Busang's future.

Bre-X was cowed. What to do? The 25 percent was not really 25 percent, because once the pieces were carved off to other parties, Bre-X would have 22.5 percent; Barrick 67.5 percent.

The Bre-X folk tried to put on a brave face, meeting with Barrick's financial advisers from RBC Dominion the next day. Why, Munk even invited the Bre-X reps for a private dinner in his Hyatt suite, which Felderhof and Francisco attended, attempting to chat amiably with Munk, Oliphant and Bob Smith. Munk left Jakarta on November 16. The deadline was just four days away. Surely the lieutenants could close her up now. After leaving Jakarta, Munk was laid low, chills and fever, a five-day bad spell. Munk rarely fell ill. Perhaps it was a sign.

Placer had been making preparations, meanwhile, for a site visit promised by Walsh, itching at the prospect of actually walking across the gold-rich discovery, studying the drill holes, sizing up how the work had been done. Walsh phoned Willson. The trip was off. "Jesus, John, it's just too hot. We don't dare bring you in." Walsh feared that giving access to Placer would rile the government. The word expropriation had already passed the lips of more than a few observers. "Shit," said Willson. "Goddammit."

Discussions between Barrick and Bre-X became increasingly acrimonious, the atmosphere more and more bizarre. Calls were placed to the Shangri-La Hotel rooms of Francisco and Felderhof. Did they want a massage? A what? There were disconcerting, hissing calls to Francisco: "Mr. Francisco, Mr. Francisco, I will call you soon." Felderhof had been offered a bribe by phone, something like $9 million, though the terms were never clarified. Francisco had taken to cranking up the volume on the television in his hotel room whenever he wanted to conduct a conversation of any import. Having his room swept for listening devices would be next on his list.

On November 22, Secretary General Umar Said extended the deadline to December 4. "I expect to hear only one word from you," he said. "Agreement." Bre-X issued a mangled press statement to a stunned public. "The Indonesian Government is very concerned about the immediate development of the Busang Gold Deposit," it stated, adding that the government had "given guidance to Bre-X to finalize a joint venture between Bre-X and Barrick Gold Corp. on the basis of 25 percent to Bre-X and 75 percent to Barrick." Oh, and Bre-X mentioned that the government of Indonesia had suggested that the "parties should consider" handing over a piece of the project to the government. Say, 10 percent?

The Toronto investment community was split in its reaction. It appeared that Bre-X was being hijacked—an unseemly gesture on Barrick's part. Yet many analysts criticized Bre-X for their apparently illicit activities with no contractual control over the land they were exploring. In doing so, Bre-X had put the investments of thousands of individual shareholders and long lists of mutual funds at risk. John Willson took a highly public approach. Bre-X "bled for years in the jungle of Kalimantan," he said. The company had a "terribly natural right to pick its own partner." That Barrick was the best partner was "manifestly untrue."

In November, Mike de Guzman's old bosses, John Nainggolen and Takala Hutasoit, passed through Toronto, stopping long enough to meet with their new mining partner, TNK Resources. Jeff Green, a heavyweight partner at Gordon Capital, arranged a lunch at Gordon's offices. Through PT Hunamas, Hutasoit and Nainggolen held the COW on the property seventy kilometres to the north of Busang. There was much talk that day of Bre-X's title problems, and that the company was deep-drilling the site without the proper contracts. TNK had had its own frustrations: the lumber company that owned the access roads was holding the company to ransom. TNK had finally agreed to pay the timber company, owned by Bob Hasan, $2,500 a month for use of the roads.

TNK workers saw the Dayak panning the river on the property. They tried repeatedly to buy some of this alluvial gold, but there was never any for sale. It was all destined for another buyer.

David Walsh shared with John Willson, in graphic detail, the inside look of the November meetings. Willson went public. He had been negotiating with Bre-X, he stated, and the company had every right to pick its own partner. Willson made himself unendingly available to the media. He was panicked on two fronts. The political side was the biggest issue, but there was also his assumption that Barrick had been on the ground at Busang. That Barrick was muscling Bre-X out of the way lent credence to the assumption that Busang was as fabulous as Bre-X claimed. Willson badly wanted to break the process open. But how? And Placer had not been allowed to do any due diligence, so Willson was fighting blind. But Barrick had not got close to the Kalimantan prize, not since Kornze and Kavanagh made their site visit in October 1993. That was soon to change.

On December 1, John Carrington, Barrick's chief operating officer, and Allan Hill were the first Barrick representatives to set foot at Busang in more than three years. De Guzman was on site that day. Barrick wanted rock. The geologist handed over as many as 150 pieces of so-called "skeleton" core, ten-centimetre pieces that had been stored at site. These pieces had been split lengthwise, as standard mine operations would have done with all their core. In the video of the previous summer, Michael de Guzman had shown how these pieces had been kept—a library of core, if you will—so that if any mining company wanted to take a look-see later, the core would be waiting.

The skeletons had not been crushed or processed in any way; nor had they been shipped downriver to Samarinda. The samples were shipped to Lakefield Research in Peterborough, Ontario. The Barrick team was pumped. This was their first piece of Busang. Perhaps someone at site had been unwilling to let these pieces of Busang go.

December 4, deadline day. No deal. At the Mandarin Hotel, across the thoroughfare from the Hyatt, neutral territory, Francisco and Felderhof met with the now familiar cast of characters: Oliphant, Pat Garver, the Ibu Yoke, Airlangga, with Said and Ganto tossed in for good measure. The Bre-X people had come to call the trio of Ganto, Said and Airlangga the Gang of Three.

Umar Said called another press conference, and this time he issued a stern warning. If Bre-X and Barrick did not reach acceptable terms soon, the government would "take the necessary and appropriate action... to expedite the development of Busang's resources." He then condemned Bre-X for failing to report various project developments as a way of defending the government's own manoeuvres, which he bizarrely characterized. "No one can find any traces that the government had interfered," he said. "If there are problems, we try to bridge the parties concerned."

Busang was now claiming a 57-million-ounce resource. The political agitation had not deterred the company from keeping the drills, and the markets, turning. David Walsh told Reuters that his company and Munk's were still negotiating. "We need certain additional comfort in any agreements that would satisfy the regulatory authorities and our shareholders." As for Said's complaints of non-reporting, Walsh retorted that "we may have not crossed all the T's and dotted all the I's, but it was not intentional."

John Willson was still trying to find a way into the deal. Given the high level that the hijacking of Busang was operating at, there were few options, few helpers, who could lever Placer into a better position. Barring President Suharto himself, there was only one fixer. His name was Bob Hasan, alias Haji Mohamad Hasan, alias The Kian Seng.

Hasan's wealth had grown and grown and grown, as had his influence. As head of Apkindo, the Indonesian Wood Panel Producers' Association, Hasan led one of the country's richest cartels, and his own timber interests made up the lion's share of the cartel's business. Of greater importance than the many corporate interests connected to and separate from Apkindo—which extended from tea plantations in West Java to steel fabrication, banking, airlines, car manufacture, newsprint and urea formaldehyde glue processing—was the seemingly unbreachable relationship between Hasan and

Suharto. For photo-op purposes, the two were fishing and golfing pals. But to those who understood Hasan's corporate reach, and the depth of his relationship with the president, extending back before the coup, Hasan took pride of place in Suharto's circle above all others.

The goings-on at Busang had certainly not gone unnoticed within the palatial walls of Hasan's home in Menteng, where he conducts much of his business. In fact, Hasan had met with Suharto earlier in the month at the president's cattle ranch, where talk turned to the fact that Busang had become far too eye-catching, for one, and for two, was certainly a rich, rich prize. That the Suharto children were elbowing one another at the trough had not helped. Jim Bob Moffett, Freeport's corporate leader, was there also. The two men advised Suharto that this messiness must be tidied up, for the good of the country.

John Willson quickly sized up whom he should be going after: Bob Hasan himself. He tried to connect to Hasan through Gerry White, the Canadian who worked closely with Hasan at Apkindo and elsewhere. Willson believed from the get-go that his relationship with White was a good one, the chemistry was right. What Willson had going for him was the growing distaste held by Hasan for Barrick in general, and Munk in particular. Hasan had been grabbing equity stakes in businesses in Indonesia for forty years. Just who did this Peter Munk think he was, coming in and treating Indonesia like some Third World country? Willson and White had a number of get-togethers. But Willson grew increasingly frustrated, at one point rising from a table at which White was sitting and snapping that if Hasan wanted competition for Busang, "another runner," then Placer had to get on the ground. "We're not going to do a damn thing until we get on the ground."

Peter Munk, runner number one, was getting periodic reports, fed up the line in Toronto then over to Klosters, on the Busang results. And they were not good. Sample after sample turned up a dud. The rare sample, perhaps as many as 5 of the 150, showed a value of a single gram of gold per tonne or slightly greater. But there was nothing to indicate a mineable deposit, let alone the richest gold mine ever discovered. Peter Munk's patience is not his strongest trait, and he had just about had it with the Bre-X crowd. "They've given us the wrong goddamn samples!" Munk believed, if briefly, that Bre-X hated him so much that they would deliberately queer the results.

On December 14, Randall Oliphant provided Rolly Francisco with a copy of the Lakefield results. The next day, Garver contacted John Sabine, Bre-X's top outside counsel, who worked out of a blue-chip law firm in Toronto, Bennett Jones Verchere. What could it mean? wondered Sabine, who had acted in mining cases before but whose skills were courtroom and not geological. On December 15, Garver wrote Sabine, making reference to the proposed terms of the partnership. "As to the assay results, in accordance with the wishes of the Bre-X board that condition has been deleted and instead for signing we will rely on the public disclosures made to date by Bre-X. We understand that Bre-X has agreed to provide full access to the property and otherwise work with us so that we can promptly confirm Bre-X's view that the results that were recently obtained from Barrick's independent assays are anomalous."

At 8:00 a.m. Eastern Standard Time, December 15, the Bre-X board held a teleconference meeting: Walsh, Felderhof, Francisco and Kavanagh, as well as Lyons, Coates and McAnulty. The outside advisers were included too—Bill Edge from the Republic National Bank, Morrison and McIntosh from J.P. Morgan. And Bennett Jones's Michael Melanson and John Sabine.

Rolly Francisco, facing personal troubles on the home front back in Toronto, was getting pretty near the end of his rope. Oliphant had cornered him on the anomalous assay results in Jakarta, and the despicable little shit Umar Said was engaging him in screeching matches. Francisco wished for one small concession: that he might be home for Christmas with his wife, Dorrie, and their two lovely girls.

Progress had been made. The board was happy to hear the news that Francisco had, during one of his meetings with Oliphant, ratcheted the price of the deal up by another $50 million.

But what of the anomalous results? In the board meeting, Felderhof and McIntosh said they had no idea why the results were so disappointing. Felderhof suggested that after the Christmas break, Barrick representatives would be given site access. J.P. Morgan's Morrison insisted that Barrick had not required due diligence at the outset of negotiations and should not be permitted to add such a condition now. No one, it appears, suggested drilling a check hole. Who was protecting the shareholders?

The board was puzzled. Why wasn't Barrick simply making a takeover bid? Why were the two companies still dancing in this manner? Perhaps when the contracts of work were issued, concluded these men, then maybe Barrick would make its takeover play.

Panutan Duta would get its pound of flesh somehow. Though it had failed in nailing the contract of work, the board agreed that perhaps "some funds" could be paid to Panutan for its services to date.

Rolly Francisco read a carefully prepared statement. He outlined the "unfortunate sequence of administrative errors" that had befallen Bre-X, that the regulatory processes required to buy PT WAM "had not been followed." That had forced the company to "close the loop" by buying WRPL "at an unexplained and considerable cost," which had led to the Merukh claim, which had introduced the possibility of McLucas trying to "claw back a position to which he has no entitlement."

"It is hard to say what effect the Merukh claim had in precipitating subsequent events," Francisco continued, "such as the cancellation of the SIPPs, the threatened cancellation of the KPs and the imposition of Barrick. On the one hand, it may have been something allowing the Barrick 'set-up' but, on the other hand, it may have been a convenient diversion."

Bre-X now faced what Francisco politely termed a "difficult decision." "The choice, taking a pessimistic view, is between participating in the development of a great mine on the one hand and, on the other hand, explaining why you are not doing so."

There were three possible roads to follow: the first, for the company to throw its lot in with Barrick; the second, to throw its lot in with the government; the third, to wait it out. This was a choice? Barrick was it.

On December 16, John Felderhof and David Walsh signed what was termed a basic agreement between Bre-X and Barrick. Ten percent of Busang would go to Indonesia, 75 percent of the remaining 90 would go to Barrick, Bre-X would get the remainder. Bre-X would receive a 15 percent gross proceeds royalty, meant to provide some shareholder satisfaction for having ended up with just a quarter of the pie. A separate $200-million fund would be established to satisfy Merukh's claims.

Midday, December 18, John Willson arrived in Jakarta and checked into the Shangri-La. Immediately he met with the Placer team in the capital and connected with Gerry White from Hasan's offices. It was a good conversation. White said he was delighted to get Willson's call, and he had very good news. Bob Hasan was ready to meet, 7:00 p.m., his place.

Placer had been trying desperately to get a meeting with Suharto. The company had been trying desperately to get a meeting with anybody who would listen to a proposal from anybody other than Barrick. Placer had retained a public relations firm in Jakarta called Mercurindo, owned by none other than Bob Hasan. Willson kept trying to torque up the outrage over the handling of Busang, but up until this moment he did not have a sense of when, or if, he would be granted an audience with the man himself.

At the appointed hour, Willson arrived at Hasan's Menteng home and was ushered into the living room of the grand residence. The room was sparsely, though tastefully, furnished—magnificent pieces of sculpture; Indonesian carvings of the highest quality. Perhaps, thought Willson, he could fit an entire floor of his Vancouver home into Bob Hasan's living room five times over.

The men sat side by side on the same sofa, the pale Brit, the squat, super-tanned Indonesian. The non-golfer and the golfer. Would small talk be required? Bob Hasan wasted little time. He was eager to hear about Placer, about its abilities to take on a project the size of Busang. Hasan was friendly, cheery, conspiring. "Why should Bre-X have anything to do with this?" he asked his new friend. "Bre-X is a nasty outfit."

What was Hasan's strategy? To get Placer to declare war against Bre-X? As far as Willson was concerned, he was waltzing hand in hand with Walsh. "Bre-X has a right," said Willson. "They found this thing." Hasan tempered his view. "Yeah. They found it. Okay." But Barrick—he seemed not to care for Barrick at all, its predatory tactics, like a cat pouncing on a mouse. So Hasan was anti-Barrick and anti-Bre-X. Was there a company he favoured? Freeport-McMoRan might seem an obvious choice. Willson put that to Hasan. "What about Freeport?" "No," Hasan said. "Freeport's not in this. They're too committed."

Willson tabled the bare bones of Placer's view of how the ownership of Busang could be conceived. One aspect of the rough outline was key: the Indonesians would get 40 percent of the project, though the "proposal" was entirely unspecific as to how that 40 percent would be divided. Willson left two copies with Hasan, who in turn committed to getting one copy into the hands of Suharto. John Willson left Menteng feeling he and Hasan had had a great, great meeting. Anything was possible. The writing had been on the wall, and it had said Barrick. Now it wasn't, and it didn't. Peter Munk had not even met Bob Hasan. He was probably dying to do so.

The media's eyes were still on Barrick, Bre-X and the Indonesian government. They were listening, too, to Willson, though unaware of the progress he had made. Downtown Jakarta had heated up as the warring deal-meisters staked their preferred hotel positions. You could feel the power.

On December 17, Bre-X and Barrick announced the broad brushstrokes of a confidentiality agreement between the two companies. Under its terms, Bre-X was prevented from approaching any other

suitors. But that did not mean it was prevented from picking up the
phone. Placer became increasingly aggressive, dealing through Willson and its chief financial officer, Ian Austin, who had had meetings
with Francisco in New York and Toronto.

With the agreement in principle in hand, Barrick made preparations
for a return visit to Kalimantan. More samples would be retrieved,
this time a batch of fifty-one mineralized core samples that had been
routed through Samarinda, thence shipped on to Indo Assay in Balikpapan. John Irvin shipped the core samples, whose release was
approved by Mike de Guzman, on to Lakefield Research in Peterborough. It was the third week in December. De Guzman faxed
Felderhof on the twenty-third. Barrick could take all the data they
want, he said, and any rock samples from the storage files. But under
no circumstances would Barrick be allowed to do its own drilling,
"UNLESS the Bre-X/Barrick agreement is 100 percent accomplished
with gov't approval and a new COW is already in place." He said he
intended to sell his Bre-X options and "FIND A BIGGER BUSANG OR
ITS EQUIVALENT IN 1997."

Barrick, however, fully intended to carry out a drill plan. The company intended to drill three holes. Rene Marion, a member of the
company's exploration group, was to lead the project evaluation
team. Marion shipped his itinerary to de Guzman and to Indo Assay.
His plan was to arrive in Balikpapan solo, then, later, hook up with
Keith Bettles and Jay Hodgson, two other Barrick geologists. On January 3, Marion checked into the Dusit, which is as far as he got.
Felderhof had already faxed de Guzman saying that, as far as he was
concerned, Barrick had all the information it required. De Guzman
informed all staff that no phone calls or faxes were to be taken from
Barrick Gold. Marion got the word from Felderhof. No site visit
would be allowed, he wrote. This was not how Peter Munk had
intended to start the New Year.

With the pace quickening, John Willson kept up his pursuit of Bob
Hasan. Hasan was king-maker; all participants in the drama were

clear on that. On January 11, Willson and Austin, his CFO, tracked Hasan to the MGM Grand in Las Vegas. Hasan seemed pleased with this second meeting. The Placer people had been working on tuning their proposal, the timing of development and so on. The most crucial information from the meeting came from Hasan: he still had not met with Peter Munk, and the Barrick people, he knew, were doing everything in their power to arrange a get-together.

On January 14, chuffed by this second go-round with Hasan, Willson informed Walsh that he was putting out a press release. Placer was making a bid. He did not, of course, discuss terms. "Go for it," said Walsh.

When the release hit, the Bre-X insiders were as surprised as the street. Placer was welcome, of course. But the $6.4-billion proposal, which would effectively merge the corporate entities of Placer and Bre-X, would spin a full 40 percent out to Indonesia. Placer did not specify how the 40 percent would be distributed. That did not much matter. No one within Bre-X had been expecting such a big piece to stay with the home country. The reaction within Indonesia was predictably positive: it was as if God were giving the country back her gold. But it also set a new standard against which all other proposals would be measured. Nothing less than 40 percent to the nationals had a hope of flying.

There was an interesting twist to the Placer arrangement: should it win, David Walsh, erstwhile penny promoter, would become the largest shareholder in Placer, a blue-chip outfit. Elements of the proposal helped to explain Placer's math: the company planned to expedite construction and development, so that Busang would actually be producing gold as early as 1999. Placer also increased production estimates to four million ounces a year; three million had been the accepted figure. While Placer never did get its team on the ground at Busang, it was provided with 140 samples, shipped to Canada from Indo Assay at Samarinda. Of course there was a reproducibility issue. But, overall, Placer liked what it saw.

The same day that Placer took its bid to market, Jusuf Merukh took his lawsuit to the Alberta courts. He sued Bre-X and its various inter-related entities—Amsya Lyna, Askatindo, Montague, Westralian, the whole lot of them. Individually, he sued Syakerani and his son, Ahmad Yani, Walsh, Felderhof, Nassey and de Guzman. Alan Lenczner, made famous by the Corona victory over Lac Minerals in the Hemlo fight, was retained by Walsh, Felderhof, Nassey and de Guzman.

The Merukh suit provided a snapshot of the byzantine dealings at Busang. There was Felderhof as a director of WRPL and Montague; Nassey as the exploration manager of WRPL, Montague and a com-missioner and shareholder of PT Sungai Atan Perdana (PT SAP)—all prior to Bre-X coming in. No one could contest that Merukh's Krueng Gasui and Syakerani's PT SAP each held 10 percent of Busang I, or the Central Zone. Merukh insisted that he had a call option agreement with WRPL, under which he could increase his interest to 20 percent. It was true that in December 1986, Krueng Gasui, SAP and WRPL had formed a joint venture, WRPL taking 80 percent and the other two par-ticipants 10 percent each. But could Merukh prove this option agree-ment? And what of his greater claim, that his position in Busang I meant that the new majority partners had an obligation to carry his interest into the adjacent, reportedly gold-rich Southeast Zone?

Haji Syakerani unquestionably had his piece of the Southeast Zone, and 10 percent of the Central Zone, whatever that was worth. But there were rumblings that Syakerani felt he had not been properly treated by Bre-X, not with the proper respect. Syakerani was getting squeezed, and under the Barrick arrangement he was looking at a 2.5 percent interest in the Southeast Zone.

On January 17, the Department of Mines informed Bre-X and Bar-rick that they would be given precisely one month to fix their deal. Sudjana was asked if other investors would be invited in if Barrick and Bre-X failed to resolve their differences. "Surely, yes," he said. The political atmosphere in Jakarta was at a higher pitch. Rizal Ramly, who heads an economic advisory group in the capital, complained that the contract of work system was too generous to foreign interests, and that the revenues received from taxes and royalties were too low. This was such a great discovery. Why would just a slice remain with Indonesia?

Such a perfect, neat opportunity for Bob Hasan. He did not have to orchestrate this from the outside; he could manoeuvre it from the inside. And so, through PT Nusantara Ampera Bakti, or Nusamba, Hasan took 50 percent of Syakerani's PT Askatindo. Nusamba was just one of the many Indonesian foundations controlled by the Suhartos, and Hasan was chairman of Nusamba. Such foundations were established to disguise the enormity of the Suharto wealth, and because of their opacity they are much favoured as investment mechanisms.

Not only was Hasan now Suharto's proxy at Busang, trumping both Sigit and Tutut, but he was the power-broker that would determine its ultimate ownership, trumping Sudjana, Said and the whole gang of cowboys at the department. The rules of engagement had now wholly changed. There rose the brief hope that Hasan would take the honourable course of holding an auction for Busang; certainly the people at Placer clung to that chance. So Hasan's direct entry into the Busang game could benefit Placer. That was a possibility. But it could only damage Barrick. That was a certainty.

In the early hours of January 24, a fire broke out at Busang, consuming the survey office, in which the drill logs were kept, as well as an administrative office and a small mess. Three Canadian geologists were at site at the time, but by the time they woke up, the survey building was partially engulfed in flames. Hours later, Jerry Alo ordered that the charred remains be bulldozed, neatly circumventing any chance of a proper investigation. There was talk of an electrical short-circuit, of an inexplicable power surge at 4:00 a.m. Felderhof speculated loudly that it was more dirty tricks. Barrick must have had something to do with it. A chopper had been spotted circling overhead. At this juncture, Michael de Guzman was conveniently parked, having checked himself into hospital in Samarinda complaining of chest pains, murmurings of a heart attack. PT Drillinto driller Jim Rush paid him a visit, taking some reading material to the ailing boss man. He seemed surprisingly well.

Peter Munk, who perhaps never expected to suffer the squalor of downtown Jakarta again, found himself in the same damn city, same damn hotel room, on January 27. He was scheduled to meet with Hasan, finally, and, later, Walsh. The public mood had little sympathy for Munk. "Cowboyisms," they called his corporate style. "I haven't seen anything like it since the Chicago mafia," said a former mining official. The idiotic statements emanating from the Department of Mines were of less interest now. The only individual anyone wanted to hear from was Bob Hasan.

John Willson had had yet another meeting with Hasan five days prior. Placer knew it was ahead of Barrick in this relationship. But things were going awry. The very-public sniping match between Barrick and Placer was not sitting well with Bob Hasan. Now he had Munk to meet.

No sooner had Munk left Hasan's company than rumours began to fly that the session had not gone at all well. "It was Barrick's deal to lose," said someone close to the deal. "And Munk lost it for them." Hasan thought he was in charge, which he was. Yet Munk was said to have confidently expressed the plan for Busang on his terms. There was talk of cultural faux pas, that Munk had put his hand on Bob Hasan's knee. Munk is very continental in style. He will use endearments to address people he knows not at all well. It was later reported that Hasan spat that he was not about to do business with Munk.

Jakarta was a hell of a stew, and Walsh's presence was required. The ever-determined John Willson, apprised of Walsh's co-ordinates, proposed picking Walsh up at the airport, thereby getting his mitts on him before any of the other contenders had a chance. Walsh initially agreed, then sent a message to Placer's office: "Tell John not to pick me up."

The morning of January 28, John Willson was having breakfast at the Shangri-La. David Walsh was checking in. He was sporting a two-day stubble and looked like hell. Willson came up to greet him. He was in no mood to chat. "John," he said, "I think I'm being watched."

BOB, JIM BOB

IT IS THE BEGINNING OF FEBRUARY, the third to be precise, and David Walsh is a dishevelled, chain-smoking mess. He is continually sucking Dunhills. He has not exercised in forever. He seems depressed. He certainly does not have the demeanour of someone who found, what was it now, 58 million ounces of gold? Which would be, what, the second-largest single gold deposit on the planet?

Walsh has been housed in his suite at the Shangri-La Hotel for days, or is it weeks, who can remember? His life and the lives of his friends and his adversaries have been shaken by this hotel existence. Like a losing weekend in Vegas times ten, without the craps. Is it day or night? This hotel claustrophobia is punishing. Mind-bending. Does one dare venture out, only to spend a day in a traffic snarl? This business, this deal-making, becomes an exercise in hotel protocol, the fax machine one's most trusted associate. The early-morning wailing from a nearby mosque rises from behind the Shangri-La pool lagoon at 4:00 a.m. Other businessmen have taken to wearing earplugs.

Documents are thickly spread across the coffee table, a snapshot of how horribly, absurdly messy David Walsh's life has become. He cannot focus. Oftentimes he drops a thought altogether and stares out his hotel room window, his pale-blue gaze casting across the way to the Grand Hyatt, the Barrick hotel, polished, glitzy, a hard-hearted hotel in the steam heat of Jakarta. Randall Oliphant is there. And Bill Birchall. The Barrick posse. Oozing influence. Or trying to.

Ian Austin, Placer's chief financial officer, is here at the Shangri-La. Norm Keevil, the head of Teck Corp., has come and gone. John Dow, senior vice-president of exploration at Newmont Gold Co., has just left. Newmont, a subsidiary of Denver's Newmont Mining Corp., has also expressed its interest to partner on Busang and made its pitch to the government. Newmont is already knee-deep in a gold project here, a copper-gold mine called Batu Hijau, on the island of Sumbawa. Jusuf Merukh, who appears to pop up in just about every interesting Indonesian mining play, has 20 percent of Batu Hijau, which he sort of offered up to Placer Dome. John Willson could never pin Merukh down.

Newmont, like Freeport, understands the delicacy of undertaking corporate actions in this country, how to operate, the elaborate ways of co-existing without causing friction. Dow spent twelve years in Indonesia. He knows how important it is when delivering bad news to not let it seem to be bad news at all. With Teck Corp.'s Keevil, Dow talked up the possibility of a joint bid between the two companies for Bre-X. An approach was made to John Willson. Might he be interested in a threesome? No.

The foreign interests have each attempted to advance their cause, to wedge their way into the good graces of the men deciding the fate of Busang. Or rather one man. Bob Hasan.

All of which has left Walsh wrestling with one rather large question. Why can't this fucking deal get done? Tying up a partnership on Busang has turned into a goddamned nightmare. First came Barrick, or "those buggers at Barrick" ("buggers" being a favourite Walsh word). Then came mines minister Sudjana, a three-star general no less, who knows "fuckola" about mining. Walsh likes that word, too.

Fuckola. Sudjana was roundly vilified on his home turf. Forget all this high-caste Balinese stuff—members of the local mining fraternity gave Sudjana the nickname Brutus: big, plenty of brawn, a minister of very little brain. What about duplicity? Was there that in him, too?

Then came Sudjana's number two, Umar Said, "a despicable little shit," in Walsh's view. Then came Bob Hasan. The ever-grinning gargoyle appeared to be everywhere, in corporate terms. He was worse than the Suharto sibs, more subtle, maximizing the use of the shadow factor. Now, nothing is certain. Nothing seems remotely tangible. The Land of Lies: that's the tag Walsh has affixed to this country that knows fuckola about the mining game and the stock market game. David Walsh is oh-so-weary. Every day he is getting different signals from the power players, and every day he figures he must have misunderstood what he heard the day before. Like mercury. Everything seems like mercury. He cannot get a handle on it. There are other favourite analogies. Doug McIntosh, Walsh's top investment adviser at J.P. Morgan in New York, has likened the drama in Jakarta to reading tea leaves. Christ, Walsh thinks, it could all be wrong. Layer upon layer of obliqueness. Opacity. It is excruciatingly exhausting.

And there is a new goddamned deadline. February 17 is D-Day now. Do a deal by then or face losing the mine-to-be altogether. That is the clear message. Other deadlines have come and gone, but they did not involve Bob Hasan. This one is real. Everyone within the company is prepared to face that fact. There is that word "expropriation" again, out there in the ether. Is it possible? All that slogging, all that hard work? Not blistering, rock-splitting work on David Walsh's part, but phone-slogging. Shilling. Selling the story. The goddamned story.

Compare and contrast. Walsh was "Mining Man of the Year," had been crowned such, along with his pal John Felderhof, by *The Northern Miner* newspaper. That Walsh did not know jack about mining did not factor into his frequent rants about how Busang's destiny was being handled here in Jakarta. He had memorized the line being parroted throughout the global mining community: that Peter Munk had single-handedly mucked up thirty years of Indonesian mining law. From Walsh, the bleating never seemed to carry much weight. Perhaps because of his past. Perhaps because of his refusal to take inquiring calls from many of the mainstream media.

But there were legions of other observers in Indonesia who now stood against Barrick and whose voices were very strong. Amien Rais, a political science professor whose leadership of a staunch Muslim political faction was rapidly growing, complained bitterly about the secret deal between Barrick and the Indonesian government, the corrupt game that he knew the bureaucrats were playing. The nationalist temperature seemed to rise daily. This was not just about a hole in the ground.

Other mining companies, Placer chief among them, were winning points, at least on the international political stage, by claiming to take the high road, fighting for transparency and an outright auction for Busang. On February 3, Greg Chorny faxed a letter to Gerry White. "We are advised that Indonesia is about to award Busang to Barrick and that senior executives from the other bidders are leaving today for Canada. . . . We are outraged by this and we do not intend to be forced into a marriage with Barrick. You and I should talk this evening about these issues so that our point of view can be fully presented to Mr. Hassan [sic] and to Mr. Suharto. If we are not granted these audiences & if the Barrick monopoly is mandated by the government, then certain consequences will flow. These include an immediate closure of our financial and capital markets to any company doing business in Indonesia & civil lawsuits against all Indonesians involved in granting the monopoly to Barrick." Arif Arryman, managing director of the Econit Advisory Group, was calling for a greater than 10 percent interest. After all, the people of Indonesia owned the resource, not David Walsh, whether he had misbehaved or not. "The Indonesian government has the right to decide on the size of share ownership without allocating any funds," Arryman said in a local daily newspaper.

"The product that is in the ground is the right of the people. The 90 percent that Bre-X says it owns is not true." The nationalist view played right into Bob Hasan's hands.

Still, David Walsh figured there was no way Peter Munk was not going to win this. He believed that, in Peter Munk's mind, Busang was already won. "It's ego," he would sigh, "not money." Walsh's assessment of his smooth adversary pinpointed why Munk appeared so fearsome. "He wants to be the world's biggest," he would say of Munk, meaning the world's biggest gold miner.

Walsh disliked Munk's continental manner. Munk called him "Darling." What is this? Zsa Zsa Gabor? Munk was too smooth by half. Always wore the latest tie. Actually used the handkerchief that rose from his breast pocket. "Bloody hanky," thought Walsh. "Butter wouldn't melt in his mouth."

On February 1, a pack of local reporters had returned from Elko. Barrick had flown them out, to check out the company's Goldstrike operations, to attempt to prove what a very good company they were. Walsh had to admit, that had been a shrewd move on Barrick's part, at least as far as the Indonesian media were concerned. They liked Barrick now. They certainly had enjoyed the Beverly Hilton in Los Angeles, and while Barrick described the accommodations in Elko as rudimentary, the Indonesian reporters felt very lucky. A journalist in Jakarta, a green journalist, could expect to make $400 a month. His more experienced co-workers, $600 to $800. Taking a private jet from Los Angeles, just getting to Los Angeles for that matter, would not be a realistic vacation plan. The cowboy poetry reading, the casino in Elko, why, that just wasn't an everyday kind of entertainment experience. Barrick was now viewed, at least by some of the reporters, as a good, qualified company. Luc Lavoie, for many years the right-hand man to Brian Mulroney, had taken up arms with the Barrick battalion at the Hyatt. While Hill & Knowlton worked the public relations from New York, Lavoie was Barrick's biggest gun on the ground in Jakarta.

The outlook for Placer had started to change. Didn't Placer have financial problems? the local reporters asked. A fax had been distributed pointing to Placer's tailings spill at the Marcopper mine in the Philippines, damning the company for its involvement in a mine that failed to meet environmental standards. Barrick was engaged in a slander campaign. Big investors like Greg Chorny smacked their chops at the risks Barrick was taking. These antics only made their case against Barrick stronger. Houston lawyer Tom Ajamie had been holed up on the club floor of the Four Seasons Regent tracking every rumoured indiscretion, building his file up for a class-action suit against Barrick.

Placer's Willson had blundered too, referring to President Suharto in a press conference as "the old man," and he would wonder for a very long time whether that faux pas had cost him what he had thought, after that December meeting with Hasan, was his first-place position in the starting gate.

Earlier on February 3, Walsh had met with Bob Hasan, at his home in Menteng. "You will set the mining industry in this country back a century if we do not get our COW," Walsh told Hasan. The two had met for the first time just days before. Walsh had tried to explain what his objectives were, how he had got to Indonesia in the first place. Bre-X was eager to emphasize its good works, the kindergarten they had started, the scholarship awarded to a local Dayak youth.

Terribly late, again. If Willson had met Hasan fully six weeks earlier, why was David Walsh just finding his way to Bob Hasan's door? True, David Walsh seemed, well, the wrong guy to be meeting Bob Hasan. He did not have the smarts, the commercial acuity, to put forward the Bre-X case. But then, who did? The bushwhackers? Hardly. Internally, Francisco was Bre-X's best bet. Hasan had made it clear, if his statements could be taken as fact, that he disliked the erstwhile penny company from Calgary. Walsh, being the outsider, should have been trying to ingratiate himself long before now. But as with his tardiness in connecting with the Department of Mines, his belated appreciation of Mr. Sudjana's "good self," David Walsh simply did not seem to get it.

Bob Hasan was not restricting his involvement to granting an audience to those who came around to his Menteng home. While stringing Willson along, he had sent at least one emissary out to other companies trying to find another suitable partner for the project. One of those companies was Yamana Resources, a young mining outfit in Vancouver that had lassoed huge tracts of Kalimantan land, largely through a financing arrangement struck by Barrick. The emissary said he represented Hasan, that big money was in it for him if he could find a suitable partner other than the grouping already listed on the dance card. But Yamana? Yamana was a junior too, had no producing mines, and had a financial relationship with Barrick in Kalimantan that would have made the company appear to be nothing more than a front for the bigger company behind it. Brokers were swarming everywhere, claiming to be Hasan emissaries.

David Walsh might not have known that. What he did know was that he was drowning, gasping for air. Whatever Hasan told Bre-X they were going to get was what they were going to get. Period. Bre-X had no control over the situation. None.

The morning of February 4, Walsh sat in the restaurant of the Shangri-La. He liked the mornings. A fresh day. New hope. Randall Oliphant was breakfasting nearby. Oliphant has the look of a college boy, a soft round face, a soft voice and a soft handshake to go with it. He passed by Walsh's table.

"How's Jakarta treating you?" he asked Walsh.

The king of Bre-X looked way up at the well-over-six-foot Oliphant. "I'd rather be home," said the beleaguered CEO.

"Wouldn't we all," said the Barrick executive. Oliphant turned and walked away.

Walsh had one more word, which Oliphant did not hear. "Asshole."

Just days earlier, January 29, Munk, from Jakarta, had taken a conference call with mining analysts. "I think that Barrick is the company that is going to be involved in Busang's development," he had said. "Not because somebody writes a letter, not because somebody calls somebody, not because somebody's got a better partner or worse partner, but only because Barrick is the company that has the most outstanding credentials to do the right job for Indonesia." Munk was, for the most part, correct. The partnerships, the connections and the letter-writing had ultimately done Barrick no good. While David Walsh still feared the persistence of Peter Munk, the *Jawa Pos* ran an article calling Munk "a member of the Jewish connection." And Hasan was king-maker. Munk had not counted on that. He had thought, as he would eloquently put it, "that the Department of Mines was the steward of this resource."

Barrick had just inched past Gold Fields to become, at least for the moment, the second-largest gold producer in the world, after Anglo American of South Africa Ltd., which was still ahead by a wide margin. Barrick produced 3,148,801 ounces in 1996, 23 ounces more than Gold Fields. A small victory in the eyes of outsiders, perhaps. Here he was, a decade later, now bigger than his onetime acquisition target. True, Barrick's production was only half that of Anglo American's. If Munk could get Busang, though, Barrick just might pass 5 million ounces a year in production.

There were some within the Bre-X fold who believed Barrick was likely now out. Mike Bird was one. The president would now decide, he knew. And Indonesia would get a bigger cut, that much was certain.

Bre-X stock had closed the day before at $22. The company now had a market capitalization of $4 billion. Barrick's was $10 billion, but Barrick had eleven producing mines. Bre-X still had nothing. And everything. Walsh figured if this monster deposit had been discovered in North America he would be sitting on a $40 stock right now. And if this were not playing out in Indonesia, he would be watching a trading volume of five, maybe six million shares a day, instead of this relatively anaemic one million. The crew of young, scrubbed stock-pushers he had hired for the Calgary office had not counted on having to work at damage control around Bre-X.

On the other hand, it could have been worse. If Walsh had disclosed to the market every time Bre-X was having a bad day in Jakarta, his stock would have been all over the place.

Fidelity, the largest mutual funds dealer in the United States, held 8 percent of Bre-X's shares. Walsh himself had something on the order of 10 percent. Felderhof was sitting with 5. Neither knew what would ultimately happen to their interests, how large an equity stake they would have once Suharto had had his say. With the stock trading at half where he had hoped it would, Walsh was in a state.

Felderhof had made millions twice, and lost them twice. That, at least, was not going to happen again. With the profits from his summer share sale in August, near to the time of the SIPP cancellation, a Cayman Islands palace had been purchased, at last offering Ingrid the surroundings she believed she deserved. And Felderhof at long last was winning the respect that he felt was long overdue. On February 11, his brother Marius, a professor at a college in the U.K., faxed John at the Shangri-La. Marius knew that John was about to be honoured by the Prospectors and Developers Association of Canada with the Bill Dennis Award, for prospector of the year. He offered congratulations on this recognition by John's peers. "Such judgment is to be treasured," he wrote. The Felderhof clan was immensely proud. In the Canadian mining fraternity, the Bill Dennis Award is a notable accomplishment. Solid gold.

Bre-X had drilled more than 170 holes at Busang II so far. For a very long time, too long a time, David Walsh's plan had been to drill as many holes as his financing would allow. The so-called step-out holes, taking drillers a kilometre or more beyond existing drill targets, had allowed Felderhof's wild resource extrapolations to pass more or less unchallenged. The camp of Bre-X believers, which had now grown to a veritable investment army, accepted the thesis that the gold extended as far as the eye could see.

Under professional management, Bre-X would have pursued a

much narrower hole spacing, would have advanced more slowly, would have carefully built the blueprint of an orebody. But Bre-X never did shed the personality that it had adopted under David Walsh's leadership: that of a stock promote.

A lifetime ago, when Busang was still just a gleam in John Felderhof's eye, Walsh had faxed his prized geologist the news of a five-cent rise in the price of the stock, to fifty cents. He had drawn a little happy face by the stock price. It had been tough to get the market rolling on this stock. It had taken a year, from the spring of 1993, to ignite investor enthusiasm.

In the beginning, as Busang was being born, or reborn, Walsh was barely out of bankruptcy. Now he was a millionaire many times over. Who knew how many pairs of shoes he had? He had even flown first class to Jakarta this time.

Now Bre-X was a full-fledged member of the Toronto Stock Exchange, the volume leader, and number one in price appreciation. Reflecting on the Busang ride, Walsh figured his biggest error, one that he now feared might be fatal, was in not developing a partnership early on. He had had his chance. Relative to CRA, Barrick had been late to the game. Very late. Barrick had not commenced its second run at the property until after the aborted special meeting in March 1996. CRA had already spent six months trying to get a partnership agreement. "Fuck," said Walsh reflectively. "We didn't have time to catch our breath." Bullshit.

If one looked past the byzantine corporate structure that overlay the Bre-X inter-ownership chart, it was not as complicated as all that, and Busang was really the only prospect that needed tending by David Walsh. All of the company's assets lay here in Indonesia. Walsh would say he liked it that way. "Putting all one's eggs in one basket," he would say, "helps keep you focused."

Beneath the windows of Walsh's high-priced suite, garbage heaved through a polluted stream, emblematic of the ever-present dichotomy of Jakarta: richly appointed hotel accommodation that cannot entirely distract attention from the fact that millions in this city live in squalor. The Javanese were shitting, drinking, washing in the city's creeping waterways, a life cycle no more advanced than that of the Dayak in Kalimantan. "Busang's a better place than this fucking city," thought Walsh.

Still, Jakarta had changed in the fifteen years since his first visit to Kalimantan. There were more and better hotels. The new airport was very traveller-friendly. Business people could have a comfortable stay. Walsh had not made many visits. After he had struck the deal with Felderhof in the spring of 1993, it was another year before he had got back to Jakarta. He couldn't afford to make the trip.

Walsh was plagued by a rattling wet cough. His belly was his body's advance man, standing far out above his chinos. His left eye was bothering him again, and it was rheumy and wet. A cataract operation four years earlier had not salvaged his sight entirely, and now he had a torn retina. When he got home, if he ever got home, he would pursue reflexology, good for the circulation. Until that time, Walsh was but a hapless schmuck who knew he was out of his depth, but who could not imagine how far out of his depth he truly was. Over the previous months, bagmen had been drawn to Bre-X like bees to honey, men with promises of power and influence. Most were flakes. It was so hard to know who was on the level. Three weeks earlier, Jeannette had seen someone pawing through the couple's garbage in Nassau. The stealthy garbage-picker drove off when he saw Mrs. Walsh. Mr. Walsh sent a memo to the Calgary office ordering the shredding of all sensitive materials.

Was Walsh being followed? He had that shadow-over-the-shoulder feeling. There were so many shadows here. The whole damn country was full of them. Even people one met face to face seemed shadowy. Everyone appeared to have an agenda.

Francisco had the creeps too. He had had his room and phone swept the other day. Paranoia? Perhaps. Francisco had the heebie-jeebies. He missed his family, had seen his life messed up because of this Bre-X business, and more than once he had envisioned his body being shipped in a bag to the Philippines. Indonesia can have that effect.

The company's supporters in the community of analysts were growing more nervous that this deadline, February 17, must be met, or else. "We were cautioned last week by a source we respect concerning our optimism that Bre-X's Busang interest would not be expropriated if the February 17 deadline were not met," wrote Lehman's Daniel McConvey.

The tension was running very high, yet Mike de Guzman appeared to have other matters to attend to. He scribbled out an itinerary. "Finale," it said across the top, before specifying that he and Genie would be flying to Singapore February 7. De Guzman would spend two days in Singapore with Genie before going on, solo, to Manila. Then back to Singapore on February 11, where he would reunite with Genie, the two of them flying back to Jakarta on February 12. De Guzman had booked his series of health tests at the Mount Elizabeth Hospital. He would have his many aches and ailments looked into. The corporate deal-making could be left to others.

It was almost Idl Fitri, the Muslim New Year's celebration. Jim Bob Moffett would be arriving in town soon, as he does every year, asking forgiveness from the important people in his life, in deference to Muslim custom. Moffett speaks more than passable Bahasa Indonesia, and for a tall, loose-talking Texan he has somehow managed to master Indonesia's cultural sensitivities. He made his obligatory appearance at the open house of the Department of Mines and was seen standing beside Sudjana. Two months had passed since Moffett had appealed directly to Suharto, not jockeying for position for Freeport, but rather to have his men clean up this Busang mess. Freeport insiders, even as late as the second week of February, assumed the "prize" would go to Placer. Moffett was clear on one other point: Bob Hasan was not going to do business with Peter Munk.

Everyone was running right to the wire. Some even found a moment of humour here and there. When Norm Keevil was in town,

John Willson ran into him by the house phones in the Shangri-La lobby. "I'm here to talk about a potential coal project with the Indonesian government," said Keevil with a straight face. Willson was under intense pressure, but did not allow himself to lose sight of the absurdity of moments such as these. A coal project? Sure enough, Gerry White then hove into view, on his way to a first meeting with Keevil. Willson good-naturedly introduced the two.

Placer's pride of place was slipping. The deal-churning, the wheel-spinning, had gone on interminably. During one spell, having spent weeks in Jakarta with no substantial progress, Willson asked Bob Hasan if it was worth his while staying on there. Bob Hasan said it was.

But John Willson should have been familiar by then with affirmative answers that, in truth, signalled nothing positive. He and his troop had taken sensitivity training, getting the lowdown on how to shake hands, to sit, to gesture. The company seemed to have done the right thing by Indonesia, carving off a substantial piece of Busang for local interests. And the architecture of the marriage with Bre-X—a stock swap, effectively—actually allowed Willson to describe the arrangement as a merger of equals, which must have seemed flattering to Bre-X. But Placer had two black marks against it on Bob Hasan's ledger. The first was the too-public, too-aggressive public relations battle with Barrick. The second was the Marcopper tailings spill.

John Willson's final meeting with Bob Hasan took place in the deluxe corporate environs of one of Hasan's myriad companies. This one happened to be an insurance firm. The two met in Hasan's office, which again registered with Willson as something so outsized that it could have swallowed five like his own.

Willson had brought along a golf ball, a gift from Philippine President Ferdinand Ramos, who had presented a signed set to Willson in September 1996. It was a goodwill gesture meant to convey that Placer, in spite of the Marcopper spill, was in no way blacklisted from future Philippine mine activity.

Willson knew that Hasan and Ramos were occasional golfing partners, so he took along this small token. It had been a draining five
months for John Willson: invited in by Bre-X and seemingly adopted
by Hasan initially, he had watched it drift away. Hasan told Willson
that Busang would not be his. As the two walked toward the front
entrance of the sumptuous corporate quarters, Hasan studied his new
toy. He bounced it on the tile floor. Ping. Ping. Ping. "You know, John,"
murmured Hasan, "it was nice to know you. I appreciated the relationship. Maybe it's next time. Maybe we do business another time."

Willson tried to play the courteous loser, chin held high. He did not
know who the winner was.

Friday, February 14. John Felderhof was at his desk in his sparse office
within the grim PT WAM premises on Rasuna Said. The imposed deadline was heart-stoppingly close. And there was no deal yet done. This
was bigger than money. This was about securing a place in history,
and Felderhof wanted to see this fairy tale through. Seeing it through
meant seeing Busang into production, perhaps even taking a place on
the management committee of whatever mining company ended up
running the thing—a prospect that might give any interested major
mining company the heebie-jeebies.

Felderhof's hair was just starting to grey at the temples. He was
tired and he looked old. The skin under his blue eyes avalanched into
his cheeks. His thin, near lipless mouth was drawn. There were many
cigarettes, lit in rapid succession. Felderhof was a walking, sweating
nerve end, simultaneously hounded by phone and fax.

Down the hall, Michael de Guzman was outwardly less anxious
than his friend. He was wearing a cheap polyester shirt in tones of
black and grey that effected a snakeskin look. The top two buttons
were undone, disco style, and a black thread poked from one. Underneath, barely peeking, was a white singlet and just a hint of the obviously long gold chain that he wore about his neck. De Guzman could
be any man. He did not look rich. He did not smell powerful.

De Guzman's unfashionable aviator glasses had a light-yellow tint, which was unbecoming, lending a jaundiced look, as someone suffering from hepatitis might appear; the glasses themselves emphasized a nose that was both bulbous and broad across the nostrils. His eyes were small, deep brown and bloodshot. Across his upper lip ran a sparse, untrimmed moustache. His eyebrows too were very spare and sat on an almost Neanderthal ledge. His head of black hair was thick and luxuriant, glossy as a beo bird. His face was full, fleshy. His jaw was slightly protuberant, what unkind children call "monkey mouth."

The duo seemed like a couple of luckless geos, who had stomped the jungle under the noonday sun a day or two too many. "We've been portrayed as a bunch of assholes," Felderhof groused. A couple of rubes and a former bankrupt.

John Felderhof had proposed a meeting time and I had arrived at the appointed hour. But he was jittery. I wanted to ask some questions about land title. I showed him a map I had been given. He gave at first a small smile. "Where'd you get this?' he asked.

De Guzman spoke briefly about the Merukh menace. "It's becoming a fashion," he said, meaning that every great discovery will have at least one claim laid against it.

Felderhof requested that no tape-recorder be used. He was very clear on that point. How curious. He suggested we meet again, the following day.

I had been presented with a chronology of the Busang title issues, prepared by someone in the Department of Mines. A ministerial representative met with me to outline the various Bre-X transgressions. With him was a director of PT Panca Minevatama. Panca's parent was a Hong Kong-registered holding company. Behind Panca was a cousin of Suharto's, and two of the president's sons. Later, over dinner, the men drew on their Kretek cigarettes, the clove-scented smoke twisting in the air. Bre-X had no title to the Southeast Zone, they insisted. The Canadian company must be ousted.

The deal was going down, and it was not the deal that most had expected. Jim Bob Moffett had attended the annual open house of the Department of Mines two days earlier, and had been seen standing alongside I.B. Sudjana. Journalists who were making second careers out of the Busang guessing-game were starting to study Mr. Moffett's movements much more closely. Moffett already had a formal Hasan connection. PT Nusantara Ampera Bakti, aka PT Nusamba, aka Bob Hasan, had bought into Freeport's Indonesian subsidiary, which in turn controlled the copper- and gold-rich Grasberg mine. Nusamba had bought a company that had a 9.4 percent stake in PT Freeport Indonesia. Helpfully, Freeport had agreed to guarantee up to US$256 million of the purchase price, which had been extended to Nusamba through a syndicate of Indonesian banks. Freeport had gone one step further, lending the monies to service the interest on the debt.

So Jim Bob Moffett and Bob Hasan were partners. Together in December they had appealed to President Suharto to settle Busang. Hasan had said no to Placer. To Teck. CRA had given it up months before. The list of suitable mates had grown rather short.

David Walsh had quit Jakarta on February 6 and retreated to Ocean Place, his Bahamian home. He would monitor the final hours of the stewardship of his stock market creation by phone. Francisco would lead the negotiations, with Felderhof and the investment bankers. Francisco, besieged by reporters and by this time utterly paranoid about the amount of underground surveillance he believed was going on, switched to the Four Seasons Regent, checking in under Greg MacDonald's name.

When the call came it came from Bob Hasan. He said he had a partner in mind, Freeport-McMoRan. What did David Walsh think of that?

What did David Walsh think? What did he think? After weeks of growing agitation, after potential partners had been shut down, after the notion of expropriation had become rooted in his brain? Thank suffering Christ.

On the evening of February 12, Bob Hasan notified Felderhof and

Rolly Francisco that they would be meeting with Jim Bob Moffett at Hasan's home in Menteng. Bre-X would have 45 percent of Busang; Freeport, the operator, would take a slim 15 percent. The Indonesian interest, as the government liked to bill it, would be a stunning 40 percent, or at least it would have seemed stunning had it not been for the Placer offer. Of the 40 percent, just 10 was going to the government or "the people." A full 30 percent was to be funnelled Askatindo's way. While there were vague assurances that much of that piece was going to be "redistributed," no specifics were forthcoming. For putting no money down, aside from his buy into Askatindo through Nusamba, Bob Hasan had got for himself 30 percent of the world's richest gold mine. After all that talk of being screwed by Barrick, the Bre-X shareholders now came face to face with the fears that had been mounting for four months: they were being screwed by the power base in Jakarta. There was no discussion on the split. Bre-X had no say in setting the terms. Walsh signed for Bre-X. Hasan for Nusamba. And Moffett for Freeport.

While agreeing to acquire 15 percent of Busang II and Busang III, Freeport committed to providing 25 percent of the project financing, up to US$400 million. Further, the company arranged, on behalf of its Indonesian partners, a $1.2-billion financing commitment from the Chase Manhattan Bank in New York for the remaining estimated costs. "We are excited about establishing proven and probable reserves at the Busang properties and swiftly bringing these reserves into production for the benefit of all shareholders and the country of Indonesia," said Moffett. The joint venture was predicated, however, on the ability of Freeport and its advisers to satisfy themselves on a number of due diligence issues. Financing was only half of it. Freeport would immediately put in motion an exploration group to draw up a plan for the due diligence at site: Freeport would drill its own holes, just as CRA, the first company to attempt to partner with Bre-X, had tried to do.

John McBeth, an Australian with a bum leg and a ruddy complexion who was bureau chief for the *Far Eastern Economic Review*, had superb contacts within the government and the corporate community in Indonesia. McBeth was well liked by his fellow journalists, and much respected as a chronicler of the Indonesian scene. McBeth was the first journalist to get the word. The deal was going down. Hasan had dictated his preferred solution: Jim Bob Moffett.

Walsh would say later that the closest contender had been Teck. But Teck wanted 25 percent. Given the Indonesian 40, that would have left Bre-X with only 35. So life could have been worse for David Walsh on this day. He must have known that no other mining company would have accepted 15 the way Freeport did.

Certainly Barrick would not have. The point, though, was moot. Barrick was slapped down on the twelfth. Bill Birchall had tabled the ultimate Barrick offer. Munk heard the negative news at his winter retreat at Klosters. "I didn't know Hasan was to be the kingmaker," he said. "I thought the [mines and energy] minister was going to do that."

By the time the sun set on Valentine's Day, the Blue Bird and Steady Safe taxis were disgorging road-weary foreigners onto the stoop of the Shangri-La. Wealthy locals tossed their Mercedes keys to eager car-jockeys. Inside, a chanteuse swathed in red silk fondled a grand piano as she purred her Johnny Mathis lines: "You make me smile with your heart . . ." Smartly outfitted bellhops smoothly pushed brass baggage carts. The scene was all a-glister, befitting the richness of the corporate dealmaking. A defeated Randall Oliphant checked out of Jakarta that morning. The multibillion-dollar gold discovery that had created $6 billion in shareholder value was now in Jim Bob Moffett's lap.

At 6:00 a.m. on February 18, Kuntoro was ordered to draft a ministerial statement on the ownership of Busang. By mid-morning, more than one hundred media representatives sat listlessly within the Department of Mines fortress, awaiting the official government declaration. Some munched on the warmed boxed breakfasts passed through the gathering. Others wandered and waited. At last, I.B. Sudjana, an hour and a half late, presented his heavily Brylcreemed self. He read Kuntoro's statement, outlining the percentage interests, then slid away, Umar Said following in his oily wake. Kuntoro took the questions from the media. Yes, he said, Bre-X's contracts of work would now be processed.

Jim Bob Moffett was born at his family's home in Golden Meadow, Louisiana, in 1938; his birthplace, though, is officially listed as Houma, the closest town registry. Moffett's parents divorced when he was small, and his mother moved Jim Bob and his sister, Marilyn, to Houston when he was five. It was a "housing project type life," he said. "But nobody considered it because we didn't know any better."

There were summers on his grandfather's peanut farm in Polk County, suppers of squirrel stew and a life of few amenities: no running water, no electricity, outhouses, and odd summer jobs in later years. He attended the University of Texas at Austin under a football scholarship and graduated with special honours, earning his B.Sc. in geology. He played tackle for coach Darrell Royal and was a two-year letterman in the sport. He is a captain in the U.S. Army Reserve, past chairman of the board of the Horatio Alger Association, member of the All-American Wildcatters and holds memberships at half a dozen golf-and-country clubs in Louisiana, Texas, Florida, New Jersey and North Carolina. His daughter is named Crystal. He sang "You Ain't Nothin' But a Hound Dog" at her debutante ball; she wore a strapless bobinette Scaasi gown. His son, James Jr., is known as Bubba. Jim Bob is the all-American boy. "The Texas Tornado," they call him. It would be a challenge to manufacture a character so completely opposite to Peter Munk as Jim Bob. An associate reflecting on the Jim Bob phenomenon for a southern magazine described Moffett, who works eighteen-hour days, as a man with two speeds: "He's either wide-ass open or he's fast asleep."

Unlike many corporate titans, who now rise to lead mining companies from beginnings in accountancy and corporate finance, Moffett was a geologist, who pursued graduate studies at Tulane University in New Orleans. They called him Tex-*ass*, and he knew what it was like to spend a summer high-booted in muck, salting leeches off limbs, working with a geophysical crew. Moffett did just about every job known to the geo: roustabout, jug-hustler, doodlebugger.

In the mid 1960s, Moffett started an oil company with his mentor, Ken McWilliams. They called it McMoCo, and when Mack Rankin joined them a few years later, they changed the corporate name to McMoRan Oil & Gas Co. McMoRan was an exploration company, trying to roust investor interest in hopeful drilling plays, tapping the deep pockets of the same acquaintances time and time again.

In the spring of 1981, the company merged with Freeport Minerals Co., and Freeport-McMoRan Inc. was born. Freeport's own beginnings went back more than fifty years, to development of its sulphur wells in the marshes off the Mississippi. Moffett, much younger than his two originating partners, became CEO of the new company in 1984. The next year he moved Freeport's headquarters to New Orleans, and the company eventually became the corporate sponsor of the pre-Masters professional golf tourney there. Jim Bob was Horatio Alger come to life. He referred to himself as a field and research geologist who got lucky.

Freeport certainly needed help. In the spring of 1960, Cuba's Fidel Castro introduced a new mining law, imposing a 25 percent tax on the export of shipments of nickel concentrate, as well as claims taxes. Freeport Sulphur had barely started to ship nickel concentrate from its spanking new nickel mine at Moa Bay. The company quickly announced the suspension of operations, which was followed by the Castro government's formal announcement that it would be taking over Moa.

Moa Bay would, at full production, have been one of the country's largest taxpayers. But the new mining law had not only introduced an economically unworkable tax base, it had shut down Freeport's attempts to obtain the financing it needed to complete the mine. The mine would reopen quickly, Freeport officials said, just as soon as new agreements were reached with the Castro government. That never happened.

Freeport followed with a hyperactive phase of spinning off subsidiaries into individual, publicly traded corporations. The company controlled the largest sulphur discovery in the world, in the Gulf of Mexico, and it had Grasberg. Jim Bob Moffett once said that "the real potential is limited by the imagination of the guy who's looking at it."

Freeport's Indonesian operations consisted of the single largest gold reserve on the planet. Freeport states publicly that there are 72 million ounces of the precious metal at Grasberg. Barrick's Goldstrike mine, considered huge by North American standards, has 30 million ounces. Freeport's weight in gold was often overlooked, as the company put its mining operations in Indonesia forward as a copper reserve, with the world's third-largest copper mine.

By 1997, the company had operated in Indonesia for more than three decades, and was often among the top five corporate income tax payers in the country, its income swinging with the price of copper. Its largest shareholder is Rio Tinto-Zinc Indonesia Ltd. (RTZ), which owns 28.4 percent of the stock. Its most notable director is Henry Kissinger. Kissinger Associates, Inc. in 1996 was paid $200,000 to provide to the company "advice and consultation on specified world political, economic, strategic and social developments" affecting the company's affairs.

Freeport had not been able to operate free of pressure from Indonesian corporate interests. Aburzial Bakrie, owner of one of the richest corporations in the country, had bought in years before. According to a magazine on Asian business tycoons: "In 1990 while on a cruise up the Mississippi River in the U.S., he reportedly told his hosts he wanted to buy into their Indonesian copper and gold mine, even though it was then not for sale. Six months later they agreed to sell him 10% of Freeport Indonesia. That same year, after Freeport discovered the world's largest gold reserve, he sold back half his stake for $212 million." It was the Bakrie piece that eventually ended up with Bob Hasan.

Busang presented Freeport with an opportunity beyond the merely monetary. A $1.5-billion construction project, a fifty-year mine life, the requirements to train local labour and introduce health and social programs: managing Busang gave Freeport a second chance to prove to the people of Indonesia that it could get it right.

The company's glossy brochures trumpet outpatient clinics, freshwater wells, training departments and venture capital programs to promote local business development. The company has said it is committed to doubling the number of Irianese employees over five years, a number they have pledged to double again five years after that. And, it says, PT Freeport Indonesia will double the number of Irianese managers and supervisors in the ten years ahead.

The Grasberg mine was in full operation, hauling 125,000 tonnes of ore to its mill daily, producing 1.67 million tonnes of concentrate a year, from which more than 500,000 tonnes of copper is ultimately derived, and 1.7 million ounces of gold. Gold mines have been built on fewer reserves than Freeport pulls from Grasberg each year.

Virtually all of Freeport's asset base is located in Irian, a risky proposition for any company. Moffett has likened the company's accumulated land mass to "something the size of the state of Vermont."

In 1995 the Overseas Private Investment Corp. terminated Freeport's $100-million political risk coverage, citing environmental concerns and the increased scope of Freeport's mining activities in Irian. The company continued to explore the region, and, the same year, formed a joint venture with RTZ PLC for this purpose. The potential of further ore discoveries led the company to dub its enormous land claim around Grasberg the "Golden Triangle."

Grasberg had irrevocably changed the contours of the region, shearing more than 120 metres off a mountain peak, bulldozing hauling roads that snake beneath the terraces of ore. Billions of tonnes of overburden, the valueless rock that overlays the minerals, would have to be moved off in order to get at the copper, gold and silver, altering forever the biodiversity of more than 14,000 hectares of land. As with any mining operation, the handling of the mine's "tailings" was a key concern. It was tailings that spilled from Marcopper in the Philippines. At Grasberg, 125,000 tonnes of tailings were being deposited daily into the adjacent watershed.

Freeport insisted that its tailings were not toxic and had no adverse effect on the fish in the Ajkwa watershed, or the wildlife. A landfill with a synthetic membrane liner had been constructed to take on the solid-waste tonnage from the mine site and the mill site. The reclamation and revegetation of Grasberg would be one of the largest ever undertaken in the history of mining.

The area was once populated by a few hundred Amungme, an aboriginal tribe. Now there is a 16,000-strong workforce, and a twenty-year plan to build New Town, to be formally called Kuala Kencana, "Golden Estuary," located north of Timika. A global village, promises Freeport. A "state-of-the-art designed community" featuring an Olympic-sized swimming pool and badminton courts. The focal point for the town would be the *alun-alun*, or town square, which would be circled by five pillars representing the five principles of *Pancasila*.

On February 19, Walsh, Francisco and Felderhof were linked for a conference call with a group of market analysts. Leslie Morrison and Doug McIntosh from J.P. Morgan were in on the call as well. The Bre-X executives now had to sell the new ownership structure to the markets, which were not at all pleased with this latest development. Bre-X was ending up with an awfully small piece of something they had claimed so vociferously to own.

Walsh weighed in first, and dropped a bomb within seconds. "Under the terms of the agreement Bre-X will own 45 percent of the new joint venture. Some have mistakenly thought that we somehow own 90 percent of this property. That was never the practical reality. Nor was it ever a basis for the valuation of Bre-X's stock."

This surely came as a surprise to investors who'd bought the stock with exactly that understanding, and surely, too, to the analysts who had evaluated the worth of a Bre-X share based on the company having 90 percent of Busang.

Greg Chorny was driving his truck along the icy roads of rural Ontario when he heard Walsh's comment on the ownership stake played over the radio. He nearly crashed when he heard Walsh say those words. What about the dozens of press releases, and certainly the private assurances to shareholders, as big as Walsh, that Bre-X had a clear 90? "There's a multimillion-dollar heist going on here," Chorny fumed. "I'm sick and fed up with my management . . . David has potentially bought himself a class-action suit for serious non-disclosure."

During that conference call, Walsh blathered about the political reality that the Busang deposit was of national importance to Indonesia. That was surely true, but it had taken Walsh a long time, years even, to come around to that understanding. "The program is exactly as we had envisioned it. Unfortunately, I do not think that the market understands the deal."

The questions from the analysts were restrained, polite. When might Bre-X get its COW? How many tonnes a day? Is this the best deal, better than any other offers tabled? Leslie Morrison took that question: "It is certainly the case in the real world that this is the only deal which is acceptable, which is available to Bre-X," he said. It was "in the ballpark." "This is the one which was available and it's the one which has been blessed by our local partners and I think it's true to say it's the one that the management of Bre-X and its advisors is particularly pleased about in its totality . . ." It is too painful to continue.

The zinger came from Felderhof. "We are dealing with a very unusual deposit here and it's one of a kind in the world. Once we finish the drilling program we are currently doing, I think that which will be completed and a new resource estimate will be provided by mid-April, my estimate is 95 million ounces. Mike de Guzman, my project manager, he estimates 100 million ounces. If you would ask me what is the total potential, I would feel very comfortable with 200 million ounces."

Shareholders needn't feel put out, in other words, for while Bre-X's stake had been cut in half, taking the proportional interest of common shareholders with it, there was twice as much gold. Egizio Bianchini sounded momentarily as though he was going to blow the air out of such nonsense. This contract of work, "we now know what type of paper it's printed on ... we all know what's going on here." Felderhof admitted he was a "bit disappointed." But Bre-X could still end up with 90 million ounces for its own account. "That's my feeling and that's a pretty good mine," said Felderhof. Bianchini veered suddenly off course. "From your lips to God's ears, John. Thank you."

Walsh later clarified that what he had meant to say was that his expectation of not retaining the 90 percent was based on the fact that a major mining company would of course be brought in to partner. The absurdity of this defence was not lost on investors with even the shortest attention spans. David Walsh was just a putz after all.

But there was so much gold. On February 17, the same day that the world was told of the "Busang Indonesian Gold JV," the company upped its resource calculation yet again. "An updated resource calculation has been completed by KILBORN SNC LAVALIN," crowed the company, putting that last bit in bold-faced, capitalized letters. The Busang resource was now 71 million ounces, give or take a few thousand ounces.

"I want to congratulate Mr. Mohamad 'Bob' Hasan for his diligence and guidance during these lengthy negotiations," said Walsh. "There is no doubt that he was instrumental in bringing this project to fruition."

On the surface, Freeport professed its pleasure at being given a chance to participate in Busang. But in truth the company had its hands full with Grasberg—not the technical aspects, but grassroots issues with the indigenous peoples of Irian Jaya.

Tom Beanal, an Amungme, had become the spokesperson for the Traditional Deliberation Institute of the Amungme Tribe. In February, he was readying himself to launch a suit against Freeport at home, in Louisiana, seeking US$6 billion for human rights and environmental violations. Water contamination and deforestation were issues pertaining to the latter. Arrest and detention of local peoples, and the destruction of their property, were part of the human rights allegations.

The Amungme charged Freeport with exploitation in the mountainous region that was, they said, the "cradle of their culture." A group called the FKGMIJ (Forum Komunikasi Generasi Muda Irian Jaya) charged that Freeport had not sent indigenous Irianese for training to the United States, as it had promised. There was not a single indigenous Irianese manager at site.

Deep in the Irianese interior, tribespeople had once thought that these planes bearing foreigners were their ancestors ferrying riches from the sky. But the riches had been beneath their feet all along, and now they were being exploited for the benefit of a foreign company. The wealth that would extend to Indonesia in the form of taxes and royalties might have seemed impressive when viewed on an accountant's ledger, but it did not mean much to the Amungme.

Like all major mining companies, Freeport was deep in the conundrum of how to pay for sustainable development. Would profits be soaked up refilling pits and growing grass? That was the ultra-right cynicism, insisting that the costs of reclamation be tightly contained. Otherwise, there was no prospect of pursuing mining as a growth industry. Freeport liked to see itself pulling the levers of economic growth in underdeveloped countries. There would be prosperity for all.

Hasan had a quiet message for Moffett. He did not want any flashy PR around the introduction of Freeport to this partnership. "We know you're excited. You're the operators. But you're the minority. Take a low profile." Freeport in turn had a message for David Walsh: any Bre-X press releases henceforth will not be disseminated until after consultation with Freeport. It was time to rein in the hapless Walsh, who fumed still about the press treatment he had got. He vowed henceforth to communicate with shareholders solely by post, e-mail and website. He bleated that it was only the requirements forced by the securities regulators in Canada that compelled him to release assay results as he had. Why, had it been a private company, Bre-X need not have released any results at all. And those nasty claim-jumpers would not have got so uncontrollably greedy.

This was rich, because Walsh owed his fortune to the public markets, the continuing ease with which he could push stock to the public, then bump up its price via ever more impressive resource calculations. Were it not for the adoration of Canadian stock exchanges for small mining companies, Busang would never have had the run that it did.

Bre-X did some quick tabulations. Let's see, at $350 an ounce, and 70 million ounces, and recovery costs of $96 an ounce, why, that was a gross economic value of $24.8 billion, in u.s. dollars, meaning a gross economic value of $11.2 billion for the piece that Bre-X got to keep. David Walsh's job now was to convince shareholders that they should be happy with that. "We were ultimately victimized by our own success," he said. "We could not lose sight of the fact that we are guests in Indonesia."

Of course, he had lost sight of precisely that. Walsh liked to complain that the trouble Bre-X found itself in was a result of the "black hats." Perhaps he was reflecting on John Craig's warnings all those months before, of the "black hand." Walsh did not quite get right the characterization that Craig had provided. Was he referring to Barrick and its inner workings in Jakarta? Very likely. But that overlooks the point that Bre-X had been warned, before Barrick started flexing its muscle, that without title it was out of control, that strange things happen in Indonesia.

Judging by the efforts Walsh put into market-making, and the efforts that were *not* put into learning Javanese protocol, investors had a right to damn Walsh and his henchmen for their bungling. And yet his hands were tied, Walsh moaned. Bre-X had been excluded from negotiations.

Michael de Guzman's posturing around Barrick, his very clear statements that he would move off once Barrick moved in, had left him in a bit of a spot now that Barrick had vaporized. He had said he was going to clear his Bre-X interests, specifically his options, in order to get as far away from Barrick and Busang as possible. He still wanted to exercise those options. He took a new tack. On February 20, de Guzman faxed Felderhof. "As a group consensus Jonathan, Cesar, Greg and myself intend to sell 50% of our respective share options, issued on 19 January 1996 at a share price of $85.25; to be sold on/before 28 February. Jerry and Bobby have intended to sell also the remaining 50% balance of their shares."

De Guzman had been granted options on 25,000 shares, which he could exercise any time over a four-year period, to January 19, 2001. One of the contractual provisions was that the option agreement would expire thirty days after de Guzman ceased to be an employee of the corporation. Should he choose to exercise the option, he was compelled to notify Bre-X in writing. He was prohibited from assigning the agreement to anyone else.

De Guzman wanted to cash out quickly. He knew he would not be part of the new show. But 25,000 shares, in the scheme of things, in this play in which someone, somewhere, must have made hundreds of millions of dollars, was pocket change. Where were de Guzman's big winnings? Did they exist?

And just what was the man's plan? He was carefully booking an itinerary that would take him to Toronto in March. And with the leadership of Busang now clearly set, he was agreeing to lead the Freeport geological crew on a site tour before his Toronto trip. Mike de Guzman would show off his great discovery to experts representing the greatest mine in the region. One of those representatives would be Dave Potter. Potter had found a truly great mine. Grasberg was in production. Busang was just a bunch of rock. What would Potter see there? And why would Michael de Guzman agree to go along for the ride?

THE CRACKUP

ON THE AFTERNOON OF MARCH 1, Dave Potter and his Freeport team made the march along the oxblood-tiled walkways of Jakarta's Sukarno Hatta International Airport. The glass-walled corridors showed off the lush greenery, reminding travellers to and fro of the tropical setting, hinting at the orchidaceous scent in the land beyond. The team piled aboard a Sempati Airlines flight headed for Balikpapan: Keith Parris and Colin Jones, Freeport geologists; Wayne Beaupre, a driller; Joe Macpherson, a geologist-cum-computer-geek; Bruce Marsh, Freeport Indonesia's expert on social and environmental issues.

Potter had had precious little time to familiarize himself with the Busang gold prospect. He had spent the last nights of February up late, reading through much of the Busang material, including a three-volume intermediate feasibility study prepared for Bre-X by Kilborn Pakar Rekayasa.

Kilborn had tabled its report, a follow-up to its pre-feasibility analysis, the previous December. The result was far from a swift read. From site geology to orebody modelling, from capital-cost estimates to operating-cost analysis, the report was a comprehensive pitch from a company that clearly saw itself as first in line to construct the mighty mine.

Kilborn had dotted many "i"s. Included was an environmental evaluation prepared by PT Beakindo Pacific, which documented an array of issues: from a checklist of the fish life in the Mahakam River Basin, to the most common ailments recorded in the Kutai Regency between 1991 and 1994 (upper respiratory tract infections, skin inflammation and generalized stomach distress), to an ongoing dispute over land ownership between three of the local villages and the Plantation Forest Timber Company. Residents of the region had been asked about their perceptions of the Busang project. Sixty percent indicated that they believed their economic situation would improve.

Kilborn's project proposal included a baseball diamond, swimming pool and badminton courts, and detached housing for senior management. The townsite plan could have been any expat community in any mining region anywhere in the world.

The mine and mill facilities called for rigorous security measures. Metallurgical results conducted for Kilborn by Hazen Research Inc. of Golden, Colorado, and Normet Proprietary Ltd. of Perth, Australia, had concluded that the gold grains at Busang were generally liberated, and thus a high recovery rate through a so-called gravity circuit seemed a certainty. Kilborn proposed a separate building, which it dubbed "the gold room," for the gravity shaking tables and the refinery. "No one will be allowed to enter the gold room alone.... The vault will be housed within a reinforced concrete structure within the refinery building. Doorways to the gold room will be locked at all times.... Closed circuit video camera surveillance will be provided."

As for the geological aspects, Kilborn reached back to many de Guzman reports to attempt to explain the Busang discovery. Terry Leach and Gregg Corbett, New Zealand-based experts in epithermal deposits, were cited. "However," the report cautioned, the abundance of the gold at Busang "may indicate a totally separate deposit category." Had Felderhof and de Guzman discovered something never before known to geologists?

The report opened with a broad disclaimer. "While all care has been taken with the compilation of this study and it is believed that information contained in the report is reliable, this study is based partially on work generated by others over which Kilborn has no control. However results presented in this study should not be treated as a final assessment of the Busang project. Therefore the use of this report or any part thereof shall be at user's risk."

There were some interesting tidbits. The yawning 250-metre drill spacing in the Southeast Zone was a problem. "Such distance is inadequate to build an ore body model that would accurately represent mineralization." Fire assay tests had produced enormous reproducibility problems. And that gold that was so "liberated" was recorded as rounded, with beaded outlines.

Normet had commenced its metallurgical work during a site visit to Busang between March 31 and April 2 of the previous year, at the request of Mike de Guzman. The firm's representative, Tony Showell, had visited the Indo Assay laboratory, where John Irvin's workers were bottle-rolling the 750-gram Busang samples. "The laboratory looked clean and professional," said Normet. "John [Irvin] stated that repeat bottle rolls do show considerable variance."

Normet lauded the site operations. "Excellent core logging and core preparation facilities have been provided at site. . . . The mineralised and non mineralised zones can be distinguished visually. . . . Excellent facilities for assay sample preparation have been installed at site. . . . The facility is not currently used for drill core."

Normet had retrieved so-called "splits," the leftovers from the Indo Assay sampling, which had been shipped to storage at Bre-X's open-air warehouse at Loa Duri, forty minutes outside Samarinda. Normet in turn had commissioned Roger Townend and Associates of Perth to conduct mineralogical examinations of the samples. It was from this mineralogical work that the gold was recorded as "particle shapes . . .

mostly rounded with beaded outlines," shaped, in other words, like placer gold that has been rounded by the washing of water. Some particles, said Townend, "show distinct gold rich rims with argentian core, other particles are of uniform colour of varying silver content." Such characteristics are typical of placer gold, though this went unremarked in the Normet report. The study included photographic blow-ups of the Busang gold particles. In one of these the gold grains look like popcorn.

Sometimes the Dayak form an amalgam with their gold findings, forged with mercury, like the Acupan workers. The mercury is then burned off, and the stuck-together gold takes on a bumpy, almost puffy appearance.

Potter nuzzled his six-foot, three-inch, 225-pound frame into the modest Sempati Airlines seating. His trim beard, forming a neat rectangle beneath his lower lip, had started to grey. He had been in Indonesia for thirteen years now. Both of his children, a boy and a girl, had been born here. For all his experience in the region, though, Potter did not know Kalimantan. So he had read everything he could get his hands on. He was up to his ears in Busang. He knew of course of Mt. Muro and Kelian. Same rocks, same trend. So now all of a sudden we're talking 200 million ounces? God those Bre-X guys sure are lucky.

Potter had been infatuated with the gold search ever since his days in Elko, Nevada. He had been a good student of geology at his hometown college, Bowling Green State University in Ohio, but it was Elko that set the gold lure deep down in his belly. At Jarrett Canyon he learned how fickle a mistress gold can be, infusing one rock, then bypassing another just 2 metres away.

It was after Potter had left Nevada that a theretofore unknown Canadian mining hopeful called American Barrick made its enormous discovery at the Carlin Trend nearby. Mine finds oftentimes come to unlikely souls. Often they are as much about intuition and luck as anything else. Someone once estimated that it takes the careers of fifty-four geologists to unearth a single mineral deposit. Depressing for realists, but not for explorationists.

Still, a rock is a rock, and Busang seemed awfully rich. Months earlier, at Grasberg, Potter had met Egizio Bianchini, the gold analyst from Nesbitt Burns in Toronto. Bianchini had requested a site tour of Grasberg, and Freeport, which tightly controls the region, agreed. Potter had raised with Bianchini the fabulous numbers pumping out of Busang. Might the resource be overstated? An exaggeration? Bianchini blew a gasket. "Look, I've seen the data," barked the believer. Bianchini really took a chunk out of Potter that day, implying that he was not up to the Busang standard. "There are probably ten great geologists in the world," the analyst said to the geologist who had discovered Grasberg. "I dunno. Maybe you're one."

Potter prided himself on his pattern recognition, his knack for walking across a piece of ground, then another, recalling similarities. At Grasberg, he was struck by the limestone, which was broken up in a way that suggested the kind of plumbing system that truly excites a geologist. In order for silica-rich ore fluids to move into the rock, they have to have a way in, and a break-up like the one Potter saw provides for that. From the surface, the rock, in the lexicon of geologists, appears "altered." At Grasberg, Potter had knocked off a few chunks with his pick and had them assayed. They came back two grams per tonne gold.

Potter's Grasberg discovery had taken Freeport's Indonesian operation from forty-five million tonnes of ore to half a billion and climbing. Grasberg was a career-maker. Now Potter was based instead in Jakarta as Freeport Indonesia's senior vice-president of exploration. Potter sat on the executive committee that managed Grasberg, but more significantly he stickhandled the company's $30-million exploration budget.

Potter mentally scanned the plan that lay ahead: a due diligence program that would include "twinning" four of Bre-X's sweetest holes, and running three scissor holes, as CRA had planned to do all those months before. Potter would get a better feel for Felderhof, "the Mouth," and de Guzman, "the Brain," outside of the stifling office setting. Potter had met the duo earlier at Freeport's offices. Felderhof had done all the yammering. But de Guzman seemed to have the answers. Funny how it seemed to take the two of them to make one. Ah, well. If one were to meet Bill Gates on the street, would one peg him as the richest working man in the world?

The bullshit feel of Busang had been rolling around Jakarta for months. Not bullshit in the it's-gotta-be-a-fraud sense, more like the I-don't-want-to-believe-that-some-jokers-from-nowhere-have-found-the-motherlode kind of bullshit. Bullshit in the broad sense. Funny how the mind works. The taller the Busang tale grew, the more the people at Freeport came around to believing that Busang was the real thing. It was too big not to be. Now, it probably was not as big as the Bre-X folks were claiming. Maybe it wasn't 70 million ounces. Maybe it was 30. What was the "mineable" resource? Why had the company not drilled along closer fence lines so that outside parties like Freeport could get a better understanding of the property?

Potter had not even landed in Balikpapan yet, and he could already see the difficulties ahead. The in-house Freeport engineers were practically wetting themselves as they scoped an airstrip and talked about sending bulldozers in, renting barges. Money was no object. The people who ran the soft issues—social policy, etc.—were thrilled with the work done with the local communities. Bre-X was seen in Kalimantan as a friendly force. The Freeport enthusiasm could not be quelled, or even tempered. Potter had not yet so much as touched a piece of Busang, yet the company's view was intensely eager. Oh Christ, you know it's gotta be a mine. Get out of our way. That's the pressure Dave Potter felt.

Mid-afternoon, the Freeport crew checked into the Dusit Hotel, by far the best spot in town, and one where travellers can actually get a night's sleep, often an impossibility at the smoky, overly noisy Benakutai. The

Dusit had a calming atmosphere, attentive staff, and, fronting on the Makassar Strait as it did, could make visitors forget, if briefly, that they were holed up in a stinky oil town and not some luxury resort. And if one were too tired to hit Bondy, the best fish and seafood place in town, with the Mahakam prawns that individually make a meal, one could be assured that the food at the Dusit would not disappoint.

Potter dumped his stuff: his luggage, his computer, his dictaphone, his $200 bifocalled Ray-Bans and that little leather case in which he likes to stick his aspirin and such. The Freeport people were set to have dinner with John Irvin, at Irvin's favourite dining retreat, Jack's Place.

Irvin and his lab were well known to Freeport. His reputation in Indonesia was rock solid, and he had done good work for Freeport before. A relaxed meal at Jack's Place was in keeping with Irvin's style. Irvin knew Jack himself, a former U.S. Navy man who had come to Kalimantan in the 1960s and never gone home. His open-air restaurant sits above the sandy shores of the Makassar, where one of the last major battles of World War II was fought. More than a thousand Allies had stormed the beach, from near the "town," such as it was then, to past Jack's. It was June 29, 1945. The town was being held by more than four thousand Japanese, half of whom died that summer. Two hundred and twenty-nine Australian men lost their lives. It was a dirty battle as the Japanese tried to secure the region's oil riches, more of the money-and-colonial-politics play. Fifty years on, Jack takes a metal-detector down to the beach from time to time, scanning for artillery shells. Irvin likes the place for Jack himself and for the history that comes with it. Jack's sidelines include selling sepia post-cards of Balikpapan in her early days and pottery beer mugs, on which "Jack's Place, Borneo" is roughly printed.

John Irvin led the group out of town and to this coastal spot. The men moved through the deep dark, their boots echoing along the wooden platform that runs alongside the restaurant. Irvin led them to a table at the railing. When the tide is high, the waters of the Makassar lap at the footings below. At night the oil platforms of the vast

Pertamina refinery twinkle in the distance, and by the glow of the table's candles Jack's creation seems hopelessly romantic.

Dave Potter sat across from Irvin, who looked perfectly at home, sporting his preferred tan safari wear, with a white singlet underneath. It could have been 1939 all over again, and Irvin could have been a character out of Somerset Maugham, recounting tales of his days in "The East."

Irvin's voice drifted softly through the night air, skipping out of range whenever he turned out to the horizon, which was difficult to discern as the water met the black sky. Irvin liked to host visitors from the West. It was very isolating here. The evening passed pleasantly, the talk turning of course to the exercise that lay ahead. The beer was wonderfully cold.

The drive back to the Dusit offered another view of Balikpapan. The city is the home of BRIMOB, Indonesia's special military force that has recently dealt with "The Troubles" in West Kalimantan. The army and the "*polisi*" here throw big parties for themselves, and their presence is felt in every corner. Big money is wagered in the Chinese gambling halls. To Dave Potter, Balikpapan seemed an evil place.

Late on the night of March 1, Dave Potter inserted his coded room card into the door handle of his hotel room. Perhaps he felt a traveller's momentary disorientation, as his brain quickly clicked through the architecture of the place, the placement of the furniture, recalling where he had left his various belongings. Something was amiss, a feeling first, then confirmation. The Ray-Bans were gone. And the dictaphone. Yet the million rupiahs had been left untouched. Whoever rifled the room had a key. None of the rooms of the other Freeport guys had been messed with. Such skulduggery. But who was playing? Large Indonesian interests? Barrick?

Barrick's attempts to muscle in on the property had not played well in Jakarta's mining circles. No matter what was thought of Walsh or de Guzman or Felderhof, the activities of Mr. Munk had been seen as worse than ungentlemanly. So for the other mining companies there had been some satisfaction in seeing Munk cut off at the knees by Bob Hasan. It was easy to imagine that Barrick had something to do with this latest episode.

The following morning, Potter et al. boarded a helicopter out of Balikpapan, stopping to refuel in Samarinda, then travelling on to site. Busang offered swish accommodation by camp standards. The fridge was well stocked with cold Bintang beer. The red-and-grey-tiled patio provided a pleasant after-hours gathering spot, where the top workers would shed their clay-clogged boots and slide into rubber thongs. From this vantage point, sitting beneath the ceiling fan, workers could watch the sun set over the well-trimmed garden and beyond to the low-lying jungle. At site, Freeport was met, if not exactly greeted, by John Felderhof, Mike de Guzman, Jerry Alo and the Puspos brothers, Cesar and Manny. PT Nusamba sent one of their guys over too, to keep an eye on things. And a photographer for *Gatra*, the Bob Hasan-owned magazine based in Jakarta, had been invited along too.

For Potter, there was much to hate about this operation, beginning with the people. De Guzman was terse and uncommunicative. Prising an answer to any question was like pulling teeth. Getting more than one word or two was nigh impossible. Cesar Puspos offered a gibbering jackrabbit, mouth-shaking performance when he was cornered, which was rare. Puspos was adept at staying away from the Freeport people. Colin Jones needed Puspos to help him size up the Southeast Zone, but the guy was incredibly nervous, indirect, casting his glance away from Jones, avoiding eye contact. John Felderhof would not shut up even when he did not know what he was talking about, which, given the number of times he would look to de Guzman for head-nodding confirmation on geological matters, seemed rather often. Sometimes de Guzman would shake his head from side to side instead. Shit, thought Potter. These guys must really be afraid of me.

Felderhof knew how to blow smoke up someone's ass, and he spent a lot of time blowing it Dave Potter's way. Exploration geologists make shitty development people, and that went for the lot of them, from

Felderhof on down. In the mining community, they like to joke that when you ask an exploration geologist what three plus two is, the answer will be, "Ah, somewhere between three and seven." So who was dotting the "i"s, crossing the "t"s at Busang? That the answer was Mike de Guzman was not reassuring. Bre-X had not moved management in to oversee the exploration geologists. That seemed damn strange. The Freeport crew made it clear to Felderhof and de Guzman that they were going to lose control of the project. De Guzman seemed not to mind. He said he had many irons in other fires. Felderhof, who had never worked in an operating mine in his life, was less ready to accept this fate. "Well I'm going to be on the management committee," he insisted. That was fine with Freeport. They would see John Felderhof every quarter, they figured. He would have no involvement in the day-to-day.

Felderhof seemed happiest knocking back a beer, a classic tropical bum, the kind who come to Indonesia for the women, the booze, the loose society, the political leverage. They often arrive on the backs of biggish mining companies, and when good fortune turns against them, they spiral down through a series of smaller and shadier outfits, desperate to hang on in Indonesia, drinking themselves into the ground. Even when they're old and shrivelled and balding, with broken capillaries spreading across the maps of their faces, they squire gorgeous young Indonesian women, for whom western men are trophies of a sort.

Busang had halted John Felderhof's spiral. To the salaried workers of Freeport, the multimillionaire who had over the years cashed in approximately $71 million worth of Bre-X stock showed off a photo he had on hand of the red Lamborghini El Diabolo, first in the 1997 series, that his wife Ingrid had purchased for him. One quarter of a million dollars for a car. He was a rogue, but he was an appealing rogue. People laughed at the story of how he had ordered a piano placed on the balcony of his Cayman Islands home, with a CD player buried beneath, so he could entertain his friends standing around the grounds below as if he really were Rachmaninoff. The Felderhof mansion was next door to Michael Hammer's, son of

Armand. Hammer had had a beach-load full of sand dumped on his own property, but a storm blew up and carried it over to Felderhof's.

Judging by its personnel, it was certainly clear that through Bre-X's 3 1/2-year bull run at Busang the operation had not transformed itself into a professional one. The number of geos on site were few, and the four young outsiders from Canada—Mike Leverman, Sasha Mihailovich, Trevor Cavicchi and Steve Hughes—were just about the most virginal geologists Freeport had ever had a chance to lay eyes on. Green as grass.

Potter, fitted out in hiking shorts and a bright-yellow field vest, grabbed his geo-pick and headed off with Puspos and de Guzman. De Guzman had his wellies on, and a black Nike hat, and as they traversed the Southeast Zone, de Guzman motioned this way and that, giving a sparse overview of his gargantuan discovery in his trilling girly voice. He later played a pick-up game of basketball with the Freeport men.

One of the Freeport guys took an immediate dislike to Jerry Alo, feeling that the guy was greasy and crooked as the day is long. "We'll have to get rid of Alo," was the comment he made to his peers. Alo presented himself as the logistics person, running the place, making sure that bulldozers and drills were where they were needed, that people were fed, that things moved when they were supposed to move. There was talk that Alo had taken kickbacks. Kickbacks—in Indonesia? So what else was new?

Felderhof intermittently railed on about Barrick. He had a real hate for Barrick. He had told just about anyone who would listen that Barrick had greased big palms in Jakarta. A $30-million payoff was what some people had heard him say. There had been helicopters circling overhead, Freeport was told. Spies. Geological spies.

When the Freeport boys were shown the remnants of the building that burned down in early January—the one that rather conveniently held all of the project's on-site records, field notes, drill records—they were told that someone had come in and set it. More skulduggery.

Freeport was assured that there was a duplicate set of records in Samarinda. More delay.

There was much to see. The prep lab seemed a good, clean, typical John Irvin job, though it was curious that it was used only for crushing waste rock and channel samples. Freeport had two on-site prep labs, one at Timika and another at Grasberg. That Bre-X had had a prep lab built at Busang made some sense, given the enormous quantity of the rock that was being shovelled out. The existence of an on-site Busang lab did not throw up a red flag for Freeport.

As for the drilling, well, PT Drillinto Tiko seemed to have done a good job out there. Freeport itself had used Tiko on and off, and the firm's attitude was that you were buying the men more than the company they worked for. Jim Rush and the boys had done a good job here.

The list of irregularities was longer. The core was sitting in logging boxes three and four deep, so the project was far behind on the logging of the core and the retrieval of the so-called mineralized sections for shipment to Samarinda. Yet that had not stopped the drills from turning. The spotting of the drilling—that is, the process of deciding where to drill next—seemed haphazard.

That the boys were not splitting the core was an issue. Freeport always split the core at Grasberg. But raising the fact that Bre-X was operating outside normal industry practice was a hot button with Felderhof. Everyone had heard the "nuggety gold" speech before, so it really was not worth exploring. When Potter plotted the holes Freeport would sink on the property, he made the decision to mimic the Bre-X process step by step. He would not have the core split. If anything went awry, no one would be able to claim that the problems lay in not understanding the geology, in doing anything in a way that was infinitesimally different than Bre-X's.

The ground was a horrendous mess of muck. The tractor tires were wrapped with chains, and Potter and de Guzman went about together, de Guzman pointing out the collars of previous holes, the really rich ones.

The Freeport drill plan was comprised of seven sites, four of which would twin Bre-X holes—that is, sink deep into the ground just 1.5 metres away from where Bre-X had drilled theirs. Freeport would also drill a number of scissor holes, which would cut across the drill lines. The objective was obvious enough: to prove that something was there with a minimum of drilling. No one would have expected to duplicate precisely the results Bre-X had achieved in its own holes. If a Bre-X assay showed three grams of gold per tonne, and the Freeport result showed half that, no one would bat an eyelash.

After three days on the property, with the program underway, Potter and Marsh returned to Jakarta via Samarinda and Balikpapan. They stopped at Bre-X's Samarinda offices, where sample bags were piled in the breezeway.

Potter and Marsh were optimistic, though for different reasons. To Potter, the prospect appeared clean overall; to Marsh, it appeared that this was a project that could be done the right way, right from day one. There would be none of the social and environmental missteps that had occurred at Grasberg. Bre-X, to its credit, had done a commendable job of community relations. The company had built a school, a church, and had sponsored sewing classes in one of the small yellow bungalows erected on site.

Potter left Colin Jones in charge, overseeing the program, getting the core shipped, as Bre-X had done, to John Irvin's lab. The first check hole, the first batch of rock, was a twin of one of Bre-X's best. The Bre-X methodology was followed. Two-metre pieces were broken up and bagged, the entire core. No splits. The rock was shipped to Indo Assay, the drill rigs still turning on later holes.

The results were faxed to Freeport. The rock was stone cold dead. What had gone wrong? Had Freeport inaccurately surveyed the hole? Was it possible that something was wrong with the lab? Was there gold at the bottom of the hole?

On March 7, Mike de Guzman, Jonathan Nassey, Cesar Puspos, Jerry Alo and John Salamat boarded the 8:45 Garuda Airlines flight out of

Jakarta, headed to Hong Kong, business class. There they would connect with the first-class Cathay Pacific flight at 3:30 in the afternoon, headed to Toronto direct. Cathay was always the airline of choice for the long haul. Its generous grey-blue leather recliner, the softness of the lighting, the attentiveness of the purser, made airline travel a hopeful approximation of an airborne resort.

The night before leaving, de Guzman phoned his mother in Manila. "Pray for me, mama," said Chel. "They want to kill me." Or so Leila would later recount to investigators hired by Bre-X.

The entire Bre-X cast was jetting to Toronto for the annual Prospectors and Developers Association convention. The year before, the headliner had been Robert Friedland, honoured for Voisey's Bay. This year, it would be John Felderhof's turn. The Bill Dennis Award would be presented at the annual black-tie dinner. This was to be John Felderhof's big day—and Bre-X's big day, for that matter.

The Busang team checked into the Royal York Hotel. March is a bitter month in Toronto, and this one was no exception, though at least there was no snow on the ground. The cold air cut through the spring coats of hopeful Torontonians. De Guzman and Puspos quickly sized up the mining gathering at the faded, dowager hotel and decided that their Toronto escapades would be focused on a strip joint a mile away called For Your Eyes Only.

De Guzman, Puspos, Nassey and Salamat took a booth at the rear of the main floor, settling into the black-leather banquettes that offer a view of the main stage, but also afford a degree of privacy. The city had imposed a no-contact code in the strip bars, and some bars were looser on this rule than others. For Your Eyes, more than most, tried to keep it clean, and when they did critics called it the place that gave visitors the worst bang for their buck. The booths improved patrons' petting chances.

Up on stage, behind the semicircular bar, barely post-teen women, their tight poly togs sitting as high as their crotch, sullenly spin around and around a silver pole stuck through centre stage. Above them, a plexiglass siren hangs suspended, backlit by frigid blue floodlights. The rest of the atmosphere is dark, red, smoky and hot. Non-performing strippers sit at the bar, yawning, playing on the Countertop Champion machines. They are indolent and overly lipsticked women, uninterested in their work, performing their numbers with all the eroticism of schoolyard kids playing "I'll show you mine . . ." Ten bucks a table dance; a hundred bucks for an hour of table dancing.

Like birds to breadcrumbs, the strippers flock to the booths, where the pay is twice what it is on the open floor—twenty dollars a dance, two hundred an hour. That night, four of them were successful in catching the attention of the exuberant visitors: Michelle, Nina, Goldie and Maria.

Maria and Michelle were roommates. They had come from Romania and adopted these stage names for their new careers. Maria was petite, about five foot four, with sandy-blonde shoulder-length hair. Her eyes were small and blue, and she did not carry much of a chest on that tight little body of hers. Without make-up she could pass for a teenager. Michelle was taller, five foot nine, voluptuous, with green eyes and black curly hair. She said she had been a police officer back home in Romania.

De Guzman liked Maria right away; Puspos favoured Michelle. For the next four days, when the Bre-X geologists did not have some formal function to attend, they spent their time in the girls' company.

The girls drank Cristal, the boys rum and coke. Mike de Guzman revelled in the atmosphere. When Maria took to the stage, as she did three times a night, wearing a long red body-hugging halter dress with a little hole at the chest, he would emerge from his booth, admiring his latest woman, dancing on the floor. Who is that little man dancing away? He had everyone's attention. He would dance back to the booth. He danced in the booth. He seemed inordinately happy.

Maria and Michelle favoured cheesy, early-1980s pop songs for their numbers. They rarely changed their music. They were not the club's most creative dancers, and when they spread their bum cheeks or opened wide the lips of their vaginas they had the bored look of long-suffering domestic help.

The bar tabs ran high, up to $2,500 a night. The waitress lucky enough to be assigned Mike's booth received a $500 tip each night. The strippers would be paid in $100 chips, which de Guzman would charge to his credit card. The girls would cash out their chips at the end of the night, the club taking its percentage.

Mike and Cesar took their new girlfriends shopping. Versace dresses. Gold and diamond jewellery. They said they were geologists, but that's about all the professional talk they offered. Mike showed up at the girls' door one day, bearing flowers and a ring. He wanted Maria to marry him. She declined. He gave her his phone number and address in the Philippines.

On the night of March 10, John Felderhof, in black tie and tux, made his way to the PDA podium to accept the biggest honour of his life. He had made it at last. He was introduced as the epitome of the prospector, credited with a long list of discoveries, including Amphalit, Mt. Muro and Mirah. Felderhof discovered the Busang diatreme, the audience was told, which de Guzman "enhanced," a comment that would later carry an ironic ring. He was insightful, persevering, diligent, the audience was told, a world traveller. Well, he was that, a world traveller.

Felderhof had recently fine-tuned his affidavit in the Merukh case. He had spent as much as 70 percent of his time in Indonesia since 1980, he stated. "Over that period of time I have learned that the pursuit of mineral interests in Indonesia is unique to that area and requires a detailed knowledge and understanding of the geology, the administrative, legal and political regime and the nature of the people. I believe I have developed unique expertise regarding all of these matters."

Felderhof took to the podium to the theme music from *Raiders of the Lost Ark*, draped himself over its top, and spat out his words in that staccato Dutch accent of his. Here was Indiana Jones come to life, telling the crowd that exploration is tough work, that winning this award was like winning the Stanley Cup. There were Oscar-winning moments. "I think we should expand the PDAC to include the tree-shakers, all right? Those are the companies that shake the trees to see if something will drop out, all right? The only exploration they do is explore the ways and means of how to get something from you." (Applause.) "The jungle they know is the concrete jungle. When they explore they explore not the real stuff, all right? The closest they get to rocks is scotch on the rocks. Now we work hard and I say to them go find your own."

Peter Munk was not in the audience, but Barrick chairman John Carrington was. No question, this spitfire message was directed at Barrick. And perhaps some of it was aimed at Freeport, too.

This David vs. Goliath shtick was tremendously appealing. Felderhof had lost twelve mates, he told the audience, in landslips, flash floods and helicopter crashes. And he certainly had the look of someone who had spent a miserable decade or three tromping through swamp in search of the elusive. He deserved this award, no question. Many had heard that Felderhof had had malaria more than a dozen times and was now immune. This river-walker routine was what had turned off so many fund managers three years earlier.

The background buzz was fed in part by the Bre-X people themselves. The field building had been burned down by Freeport—that's what some were now saying. There was no longer any point in pinning that on Barrick. Daniel McConvey asked de Guzman how confident he was of the 200-million-ounce figure. De Guzman paused. "Eighty percent," he said. De Guzman seemed upbeat, and joked about beating the Freeport team in that on-site game of basketball.

Felderhof introduced his team. "O.J. Simpson had his dream team and I got mine," he said, using a discomfiting analogy in his thanking of Puspos, de Guzman, Alo and Nassey. He tipped his hat to Francisco for his negotiating skills and Steve McAnulty for his "excellent" public relations.

He saved his most fulsome praise for David Walsh. "I used to call David Walsh. Send more money. And he did, amazingly enough," he said. "David, I made you a promise. I said to you I'd pick up three properties and find you two mines. I lied. I find you more."

Was John Felderhof one of the best actors in the world or was he dumber than dogshit? Freeport's assay results continued to come back half a hole at a time. When the next batch came up equally dry, the earth started to shake at Busang. Surveyors rechecked their work on site. Every inch of the due diligence plan was scrutinized. Freeport head office was reassured that the on-site crew were 100 percent convinced that there was nothing amiss on their end. The storm was brewing.

Freeport moved into top gear. An Airfast charter plane, a Boeing 737, was called up from Irian Jaya and flown to Balikpapan. The Freeport drill, which had been monitored every step of the way, twenty-four hours a day, was sealed and helicoptered to Balikpapan, loaded aboard the 737, then flown to Jakarta. At Sukarno Hatta Airport, Jim Bob Moffett's $51-million custom-fit 757 was commandeered to carry the entire core hole to New Orleans. Freeport had $4 billion invested in Indonesia. Virtually its entire asset base was housed in that one mighty mountain in Irian Jaya. Grasberg is a fifty-year deposit, and the future of the company rests on being able to hang on to her for those five decades. Potter's huge exploration program, the exploration potential of the country, was critically important, too, to Jim Bob Moffett. Freeport could not fuck up.

Freeport shipped the samples to Crescent Technology in New Orleans, along with stockpiled Bre-X samples from John Irvin's lab. Crescent had more than assay capabilities. It was outfitted with electron-microscopy equipment to analyse those Indo samples. Every link in the chain of custody was documented and videotaped. In New Orleans the core was kept under armed guard as it was scrutinized, fire assayed, cyanide leached, you name it. But just like the previous results out of Indo Assay, this stuff was dead as dirt. Moffett was advised daily, sample by sample, on what was coming out of Busang.

On the morning of March 12, de Guzman and Puspos had planned a car trip with Nassey, Alo and Salamat to Niagara Falls, a little more than an hour's drive outside Toronto. That same day, Jim Bob Moffett phoned David Walsh. He hated to interrupt their joy, Moffett would say later, but the Freeport crew was having serious difficulty at site. Walsh bleated that he was just the money guy, he did not know anything about the technical aspects of the project. He said he would get Felderhof to call him. Felderhof reassured Walsh by recalling the early grim results achieved by Barrick, and the much improved second run. Walsh and Moffett spoke again the following day. For David Walsh, backed by his crack team of geologists, there was a simple explanation for the discrepancy between a 200-million-ounce gold mine and a pile of Kalimantan dirt. Freeport had screwed up, he told Moffett, ignoring the fact that the team, headed by Potter, was likely one of the best in the universe. Walsh would later say that Moffett flew off the handle when Walsh made that remark.

John Felderhof took a call from Dave Potter. Potter was in Timika. Felderhof was still at the Royal York. He told Felderhof flat out that they had found nothing for their efforts.

"You're wrong," protested Felderhof.

"Then you'd better get somebody out here to show us what we did wrong," said Potter.

Potter made plans to go back to Busang, where he would be joined by Steve Van Nort, who heads Freeport's exploration office in New Orleans. Potter expected that John Felderhof and Mike de Guzman would be arriving at Busang too. The Filipinos, and Nassey, were already scheduled to leave Toronto on March 13.

The morning of the thirteenth, Felderhof called Puspos and de Guzman to his room. Someone had to be picked to face Freeport. De Guzman was it. Following the meeting, de Guzman and Puspos picked up their new best girlfriends and travelled in a different car to the Falls from the one ferrying Nassey, Alo and Salamat. When both cars stopped at a souvenir stand, the car carrying de Guzman and Puspos took off.

Late on the night of March 13, de Guzman, Salamat, Nassey and Alo boarded the Cathay Pacific night flight back to Hong Kong. There they would disperse. Nassey connected almost immediately back to Jakarta. Alo and Salamat headed to Manila together, where they would spend six days, before heading back to Jakarta on March 21.

De Guzman stuck to the schedule he had arranged before leaving for Toronto. His destination now was Singapore, where he would meet Genie, who would have retrieved his cash pay from the Bre-X office in Jakarta and who would be waiting for her husband at the Marriott Hotel on Orchard Road. De Guzman would attend to his banking, and his check-up at Mount Elizabeth Hospital. Before the group broke up, Nassey turned to de Guzman. He was having, he said, some difficulty with the drill plan and needed Mike's advice. "Go ahead," said de Guzman. "Drill whatever you want."

Puspos had already left Toronto, taking an afternoon flight to Los Angeles. He said he had a girlfriend there and she had given birth to twins. Puspos had booked the stopover before leaving Jakarta. He had planned, too, to spend five days in Manila before returning to Busang.

Before the group had broken up at the PDA, Felderhof had informed them that they would not be allowed to exercise their options just yet. The Busang scam was collapsing, yet only a tight circle knew this to be true. At the exploration site, PT Drillinto Tiko continued with the Bre-X drilling program. Dozens of Indonesian workers continued hammering up houses. Box after box of drill core was logged, the subsequent samples shipped on to Indo Assay. A batch of eighty-six was sent to the lab March 13. One hundred and thirty more were sent two days later. The veneer of normalcy remained set, everyone going about their business. A Potemkin village.

On March 19, in the Jakarta headquarters of Freeport Indonesia, a group gathered to discuss the plan for Busang. Greg MacDonald was supposed to represent Bre-X but could not make it and sent Bernhard Leode instead. Bob Hasan sent four representatives, including Gerry White. Paul Murphy and Bruce Marsh were there for Freeport, along with Dan Bowman, Freeport's in-house legal counsel in Jakarta.

There they were, discussing power plants, access to ports, various construction contractors. There was talk too about the establishment of the new joint venture company between Bre-X, Freeport and Nusamba. Hasan, outside of Nusamba, had now assumed the role that Tutut had taken on in the Barrick design. One of his companies, IKAPT, would take on the infrastructure projects. Freeport would provide accounting services. As for Bre-X, well, it would have no role in the future whatsoever.

Freeport knew they had drawn nothing but blanks. Legions of securities lawyers had been retained to advise them about their duty to shareholders. Freeport knew that if they were to announce publicly right then that Bre-X was a hoax, they would be sued right out of existence.

Dave Potter and Steve Van Nort, Freeport's senior vice-president of exploration, were back at Busang, staring at the village that had created $6 billion in shareholder "value." Potter knew, in his very bones, that Freeport had been taken for a ride—along with Barrick, Placer, Teck, Newmont, CRA. Busang was a scam—the most successful scam in mining history—and the whole world had fallen for it.

Potter pointed to a nice long piece of brand-new core sitting in a core box at site. Manny Puspos and Bobby Ramirez were there.

"I want that two-metre core right now," Potter said.

The lackeys protested. "It hasn't been assayed. We can't do that without Mike's permission."

"Get de Guzman on the phone," Potter ordered.

From the site office at Busang, Puspos and Ramirez conducted one of the last phone calls that Mike de Guzman would have on God's green earth. They spoke in Tagalog, and Potter, sitting very close in the radio room, could certainly hear de Guzman's voice. He just did not know what the hell he was saying.

"Get him to speak English," snapped Potter.

"Let him have it," said de Guzman, switching to English. "It doesn't matter anyway."

Bobby Ramirez was videotaped saying the two-metre piece was going to run three grams of gold a tonne. Right to the very end, to the last miserable minute, the putzes at Busang played this game of pointing at dross and spinning expectations of golden riches. Bobby Ramirez was a believer. He had spent years sitting on a small chair on the core pad, logging metre after metre, kilometre after kilometre of core.

De Guzman hung up the phone in the lounge of Temindung Airport and walked out to the tarmac. The Pertamina trucks were in for refuelling. Passengers were milling about. The orange hibiscus, the pretty children's kites. The tropical breeze ruffling the air. Mike de Guzman had passed through this scene hundreds of times before.

De Guzman climbed aboard the PK-TRY helicopter, sitting expectantly on its metal heli pad. He placed his yellow denim jacket on the seat in front of him. His seatbelt was snapped shut. He picked up the headset and placed the padded gear over his ears. The chopper powered up. Mike de Guzman listened to Edy Tursono make contact with the control tower.

In his bag de Guzman had placed the lined sheets of stationery that he had purchased the previous day. The 2,000-rupiah stamp, decorated with a grand garuda with his wings held high, was stuck on the lower left of the authorization letter he had written the night before. The one giving Bernhard Leode the authority to act on his behalf "in case of disability or my death." Disability. Could one fall from a helicopter mid-flight and end up merely disabled? From 250 metres? What had Michael de Guzman been thinking? He had made modest financial arrangements for Lilis, or so he thought, asking Grace Kapal to give her some cash. He had phoned Susani, murmuring of love. He had had a reunion with Genie, the one he loved, next to Teresa, most of all. Was everything tidy in his life now?

The PK-TRY helicopter lifted into the air. Was de Guzman's heart pounding? Did his mind race? He had sounded resigned on the phone to Manny Puspos at site. Calm. Already removed from this drama.

But the notes. Big, loopily scrawled notes. "Pls. accompany my body (death) to Manila.... Stay at funeral parlour.... Bring my black bag w/ all my very important notes.... Sorry I have to leave.... God bless you all.... Do not bury me. Burn—cremate me in Manila." So dramatically different from the fax he had sent to the Jakarta office the previous day, in which he had gone over a number of business matters, and which he had jauntily signed "Cheers, Mike de Guzman."

By early afternoon it was clear that something was amiss. Where the hell was de Guzman? Freeport called MacDonald at Bre-X's offices. MacDonald said he knew nothing. Then the phone rang. It was Jim Bob Moffett, who had had a call from Walsh. De Guzman was gone. Freeport phoned the Balikpapan airport, which confirmed that the helicopter had returned sans Mike.

Adrianto Machribie, president director of PT Freeport Indonesia, put in a call to Dave Potter at Busang. There is no privacy in a radio room, and when Machribie said he had personal information to relate, Potter said he would have to find a more secure listening post. He went to another company's drill site nearby, kicked everybody out and placed the call to Jakarta. The conversation was brief. "Something happened to de Guzman. The report is that he fell out of the chopper. Get the hell out of there. Don't talk to anybody." Potter returned to site. Clearly, the inside group knew what had happened. Potter stared at Manny Puspos, his mind racing, not wanting to deal with the prospect that something horrible had happened to Mike de Guzman as he prepared himself to meet again with Dave Potter. "Manny?" said Potter. "Is there something you want to tell me?" Puspos shook his head. Within half an hour, forty-five minutes tops, the Freeport people were hell and gone from Busang.

At 2:00 p.m., John Irvin's phone rang in his office in Balikpapan. It was John Felderhof, calling from the Caymans, where he had flown after the PDA. It seemed so curious that the man credited as co-discoverer of Busang, who had only just accepted an award in honour of this great geological find, would have flown, not to Busang to defend her honour in front of Freeport, but rather home to his offshore, tax-haven palace.

"Mike's missing," Felderhof told Irvin. Fallen from a helicopter? Irvin turned to his colleagues, Shane and Jimmy, who knew the Bre-X group as well as he did. What in God's name was going on? They later headed out for a beer, and as they were sitting in the gathering dark, the mystery of Busang just being born in their minds, Freeport's Colin Jones came by. "We're out of here, man," he said.

Greg MacDonald phoned Rolly Francisco at his home. It was very late on the night of March 18, Toronto time. Francisco and Bryan Coates, who had come in from Calgary and was staying at a hotel, had been working that day with the Freeport legal delegation, up from New Orleans, on the joint venture agreement. MacDonald informed Francisco that de Guzman was dead. Rolly Francisco did not believe what he was hearing.

David Walsh was at his Ocean Place plantation house, West Bay Street, in the Western District of the Island of New Providence in the Commonwealth of the Bahamas. Was he fretting? He must have been. Freeport had said they could find no gold.

The renovation of Ocean Place was a long way from completion, but David and Jeannette Walsh were in top shape financially. In Jeannette's name, an international business company incorporated in the Bahamas had been established on March 7, 1995, under the name Balogh Investment Ltd. Balogh had a u.s.-dollar account and a Canadian-dollar account as well as shares in Bre-X and Bresea. Two years later, on March 27, 1997, Jeannette Walsh's cash accounts totalled us$12.1 million, with 2.5 million shares of Bresea, 1.5 million shares of Bre-X and 160,000 shares in Bro-X Minerals.

Jeannette Walsh was the beneficial owner of Balogh through yet another company, Ark Ltd., also a Bahamian company, which held the Balogh shares in trust. Ansbacher (Bahamas) Ltd. had been appointed Balogh's bank early in 1996. Ansbacher then opened a brokerage account at Nesbitt Burns in Calgary in order to deal in securities—that is, Bre-X and Bresea—on behalf of Jeannette Walsh.

David Walsh beneficially owned a separate company, Hearn Ltd., also incorporated in the Bahamas as an international business company. In August 1996, three months after Bre-X had split ten-for-one, Walsh had sold 300,000 shares for net proceeds of $6.7 million, which he deposited in the Hearn account. The stock split had taken David Walsh's Bre-X share holdings to 8 million shares, and 9 million unexercised stock options. Walsh too established a securities trading and custodian agreement with Ansbacher.

In their Ocean Place hideaway, David and Jeannette Walsh were sitting on their pot of gold. And in their Cayman Islands hideaway, John and Ingrid Felderhof were sitting on their own treasure.

In a stinky, infested swamp south of the greatest gold discovery in human history, Michael de Guzman lay in the 100-degree heat, the 100 percent humidity. Wild pigs waddled through the muck, nudging his carcass, neatly, almost with a surgeon's precision, tearing him across the midsection. Something nibbled away at his nose, his ear, and chomped on his backside. The brackish mire was a warm pool about his body. The maggots came, and he was crawling with their white, opalescent shapes. The sun at noon, high overhead, baked everything in its path. One day. Then two. Then four. Michael de Guzman lay in wait. Somerset Maugham once wrote, "Death ends all things and so is the comprehensive conclusion of a story."

Not this time.

CONSPIRACY THEORIES

"BIGDUDE" WAS STARING AT HIS computer screen at the offices of the brokerage firm where he worked in downtown Toronto. The analysts were cheek-by-jowl in these unprepossessing quarters—desks overrun with papers, baffles tacked with family photos. If the outside world could only see the corporate innards of such brokerage houses, where the low-ranking serfs like Bigdude toiled, they would see that Bay Street is not exclusively about big money and shiny cars. The trading desk set-up had the feel of a cluttered newsroom, which was fitting, for there was some investigative work to be done.

Bigdude, aka Warren Irwin, had been following the Busang saga intensely. He had talked his way onto the site, as part of the mining analysts' visit the previous summer. Bigdude was not a geologist, nor was he a mining analyst, nor was he formally following the company. Bigdude's job was to make investments for the firm's own account. The company had not taken a position in Bre-X, but Bigdude had, for his personal account, and he was a high-volume trader. Bre-X had become a full-time pastime.

Bigdude had retrieved a rock sample from Busang, which he had had assayed upon his return to Toronto. When it came up barren, his curiosity had been heightened. But the sample was small, and he had carefully monitored Bre-X drill results to compare his piece to the results of the hole itself. Bre-X stopped releasing hole-by-hole assays after that summer trip, and Bigdude had nothing to compare against his little piece of a hole punched 1.5 kilometres off into Never Land, far beyond the presumed sweet spot of the Busang discovery. The site fire in January had bothered him some. But accidents happen, and he was still long on the stock. He was still betting that the stock had a distance to run yet. He still believed.

Bigdude had been subsumed by Bre-X. He wanted the company to succeed in the worst way. After the ownership resolution in February, Dude had written up a list of questions for David Walsh at the suggestion of Don Carter, a broker at Nesbitt in Ottawa who handled some of Walsh's personal accounts. Bigdude wanted to prime Walsh for that analyst's call, the one Walsh ended up bungling so badly. Bigdude had faxed the questions to Walsh in the Bahamas, and when fat boy blew the call, Dude was pissed.

Now de Guzman had "fallen" out of a helicopter. Having been snapped into a helicopter seat on a PK TRY chopper just eight months previously, Bigdude knew that the pre-flight safety measures at Samarinda would not have allowed for such a bizarre occurrence. So now the Busang saga featured a dead man, and not just any dead man, but one of the script's main characters. The Busang plot had shifted dramatically. Bigdude had 60,000 shares left in what had been a 200,000-share position. At one point he had had $1 million borrowed against his position. Had Bre-X collapsed when Bigdude was long, he would have been pushed toward bankruptcy. He had been far enough inside the Bre-X loop to know that those investors deemed very special, whom David Walsh held very close, were hearing reassuring noises from Bre-X all the time. To get off any stock would have felt like an act of betrayal, infidelity. Bigdude was having a pool sunk in the backyard of the big new house he had financed with his Bre-X investment. The guy putting the pool in was a Bre-X investor too. By 1997, anyone who was not a Bre-X investor was a schmuck, a putz.

There was not much that was dude-ish about Bigdude. He had the earnest, satchel-carrying look of a schoolkid. Still, he liked the sound of the moniker he had chosen for writing his missives on the Internet, joining in on one of the many Bre-X threads that had become a favourite pastime for stock players.

De Guzman's vertical descent into Borneo, despite Bre-X's immediate chatter about "the fall," had to be bogus. Bigdude pecked at his keyboard, stating the obvious. "People don't just fall out of Alouette helicopters." He got that right. On March 19, Bre-X shares closed down 40 cents to $17.25. Nesbitt's Egizio Bianchini offered this assessment to *Globe and Mail* mining reporter Allan Robinson: "Geologically, [de Guzman's] expertise was unparalleled."

In the small hours, Bigdude would stare at the screen, studying the messages posted by people calling themselves "Drumbeat" or "Ole 49er." The glow of the monitor was sucking Bigdude into the mind-bending crevasse that had become Bre-X. The shadow players, the agendas: that all looked like child's play now.

Bre-X quickly amended the story. De Guzman had jumped, having chosen suicide over a future as a carrier of hepatitis B. But chronic carriers of the hepatitis B virus must test positive for the hepatitis B surface antigen for six months, and de Guzman did not fit that characterization. There were 200 million hepatitis B carriers worldwide. Dr. Cheriyan had not painted a dire picture for Mike de Guzman at the time of his medical assessment in Singapore.

Bigdude was not convinced of anything yet. If he had been, he would have shorted the shit out of Bre-X. Instead, he hung in.

Graham Farquharson has the austere, modest bearing of a parson. Brushcut, short-sleeved shirt in the dead of winter, a pocket-pal for his pens. His nose has an aquiline cut and is squeezed thin; his hairline is high; his smile is small but warm. When he played recreational hockey, which he was passionate about, he would take his teeth out before a game, but never, ever wear a helmet.

For years a bachelor, Farquharson seemed to be married to his work. He married late in life, battled his own cancer, then watched his new wife struggle with kidney failure. Farquharson's stoicism prevented him from sharing his burdens.

In the mining community he was known as "Dr. Death," an epithet, and not an unaffectionate one, that he had drawn for offering the straight goods on a mine's potential. Everyone in this tight fraternity agreed that Graham Farquharson was above reproach, straight as a die, would never bend the prospect of a discovery's potential to make it appear more rich.

In the entranceway of the office quarters of Strathcona Mineral Services Ltd., the Toronto company he steers, Farquharson has hung a cartoon of an elderly woman getting shilled by a penny mining con man. The promoter has a cigar wedged in his face and he's promising that this discovery of his will be a great gold mine. The company is named Great Canadian Gold Mines Inc. It's the ever-repeating tale of the easily duped investor, his pockets turned inside out by some fat boy promising a great gold discovery in who-cares-where.

Late in the afternoon of March 19, Graham Farquharson took a call in his downtown office. Hours earlier, in the offices of Bennett Jones Verchere, Bre-X's legal advisers, Bryan Coates and Rolly Francisco had convinced the Bre-X board that the company should quickly retain Strathcona to perform an independent audit of Busang. Farquharson was asked to make an appearance at the Bennett Jones offices, which he did do, posthaste. There had been a problem with some of the work done at Busang, he was told. Freeport could not duplicate their astronomical results. But Bre-X had no Freeport numbers yet to pass along to the Strathcona experts. And the project's chief geologist had fallen from a helicopter.

There was certainly no time for pleasantries. Farquharson made immediate plans to head straight to Indonesia. He would not bother meeting first with David Walsh, whom he did not know. His only connection to the story was through previous meetings on unrelated projects with Francisco and Coates. He called a follow-up meeting with these two and legal counsel on March 20.

By the time of the meeting, the story had already changed somewhat. Freeport had faxed a letter to Michael Melanson, one of Bre-X's lawyers at Bennett Jones Verchere in Toronto, that day. The assay results from the four holes were negative, Freeport said. Farquharson was informed of another twist in the tale: de Guzman had jumped. Graham Farquharson headed for Toronto International Airport. He wanted to see Freeport's information first-hand. That was the first step.

As Graham Farquharson settled into the twenty-four-hour flight to Jakarta, *Harian Ekonomi Neraca*, a Jakarta-based paper owned by Bob Hasan, quoted an unnamed Askatindo insider questioning the economic viability of Busang. There was far less than 70 million ounces, he said. Busang might not even be mineable. The leak was not that great a surprise in Indonesia. The buzz there had been growing for days. Bernhard Leode heard the talk at Ahmad Yani's wedding. This was not a brotherhood that kept a secret well. The *Harian Ekonomi* story was picked up by a North American wire service. Bigdude picked it up from there and posted it on the Net. Furious trading in Bre-X shares caused the Toronto Stock Exchange to halt trading for more than three hours. The stock closed at $15.20. David Walsh said Freeport was still carrying out its due diligence and had not commented "to the press" on its progress.

Walsh offered up an interview on a Canadian radio program. "He was forty-one years old," he said of de Guzman. "A remarkably bright fellow, extremely well thought of, and indeed an unbelievable geologist. And he had his own theories. He liked working with Bre-X. We do give our geologists the freedom of developing their theories." The interviewer commented that it seemed de Guzman had chosen a rather dramatic ending to his life. Was he dramatic? "No," said Walsh. "He was a very warm, friendly [guy who] had a good sense of humour, but took his work very, very seriously. He was a perfectionist."

The following day, March 22, at 8:45 p.m., Bigdude posted a Bigdude alert on the Tech Stocks thread. "Felderhof in Jakarta" he typed in boldface letters. "Spotted at the Shangri-La. . . . He would never be there if he believed it was a scam. I would hate to be the sorry assed Freeport dude that gets caught leaking info on Freeport's due dilly." Bigdude was thick in the mystery now. "Man I hate this crap. I can't sleep, I can't concentrate on anything else, I am in denial that my friend Mike de Guzman is gone, I am a mess."

The Internet speculation was wildly fantastic. De Guzman was spotted in Alabama, of all places. "Drawing a line on an atlas, Alabama is almost a straight line between Kalimantan and the Cayman Islands," wrote one participant, attempting to explain how the hell de Guzman had ended up in the Deep South.

Still, there was therapeutic value to the Internet talk. In the absence of clear information from Bre-X since, well, since the beginning, and without any ability to understand what was actually going on in Jakarta, daily hits on the Internet became a cleansing ritual.

Jerry Alo had come off site to attend a memorial service for Mike in Jakarta. Everyone at the Bre-X office had been expecting the return of Cesar Puspos. Cesar never came. His brother Manny was left sweating at the site, with Bobby Ramirez.

The same day, Daniel McConvey at Lehman Brothers wrote up his assessment under the headline: "Tragedy Strikes. Raises Questions on FCX Due Diligence." FCX is Freeport's trading symbol, trading on the New York and Australian stock exchanges.

The death of Senior Bre-X geologist Michael de Guzman who fell from a helicopter yesterday over Kalimantan may raise questions as to the integrity of the geological data relating to the Busang gold resource. We are not overly concerned. While we are not geologists, everything we have seen and heard makes us believe that the work done in determination of the resource was done in a respectable way. De Guzman was one of our heroes in the discover [*sic*] of the Busang Deposit. He lived for geology. We saw him in Toronto last week and he was as confident as ever, over the prospectivity of Busang. His bizarre death, is a huge and sad tragedy.

On March 24, Egizio Bianchini—such a booster, such a supporter of Bre-X—checked in with the Nesbitt sales force by conference call. Bianchini's zeal for Bre-X had not lessened in the least, or if it had, he was not about to let on to his broker support network. By now Bianchini was driving about Toronto in his late-model car with a licence plate that said "AU GUY," "au" being the symbol for gold. Others had grabbed the Bre-X-related vanity plates. Michel Mendenhall, the Nesbitt broker in Ottawa, had been given a BXM licence plate by his boss, for his 911 Turbo Porsche; BXM represented the Bre-X trading symbol. Now shares in Bre-X had started to sink. And Mendenhall, for one, was fully invested in Busang.

"If you didn't know any better out there, you'd think there might be a conspiracy going on," Bianchini told his team. Bianchini cited the *Harian Ekonomi* story, not by name, just as a third-rate newspaper. Bianchini did not discount its alarmist predictions for Busang. To the contrary. "Given the work that I've done since then, and over the weekend . . . Freeport's initial results were probably quite low." Bianchini calmed the Nervous Nellies. "Do not be alarmed," he said. "I'm going to explain this."

Bianchini said that three separate entities had "sampled" the deposit, that the results had been similar to, in some cases higher than, those reported by Bre-X. He was, presumably, referring to Barrick, Placer and CRA. But the samples had all been provided by Bre-X, so Bianchini's protestations should have done nothing to dispel the growing suspicion that someone had tampered with the samples. Bianchini had an answer for that, too. Kilborn, he said, would "audit the process from the time that the core comes out of the casing all the way to the audit—sorry, to the assay number. They are . . . They are . . . They have audited the process. Obviously they have not sat on every drill hole, but they've audited the process."

So what, then, could account for Freeport's troubles? Bianchini put that down to assaying methodology. Remember, he told his flock, that Bre-X's first drilling on the Central Zone had not turned up any gold. "Fire assay does not give a representative sample of the gold in this deposit," he said. "That's been tested." Only cyanide leach, he claimed, could capture the true value of the gold.

Picture the broker. Twenty-five. Green. A high school education, perhaps. Took the securities course in the evening, after his shift at Tip Top Tailors. Manages to get through the page on sinking fund debentures without ever truly understanding what the hell they are. Gets his registered representative credentials. Leaves Tip Top. Enters brokerage. Hopes to make gobs of money.

There he sits, with no qualifications whatsoever to check Bianchini, to tell the star analyst what the star analyst, with a geologist's credentials after all, surely should have known: if you can't get the gold out with fire assay, the gold ain't there. "If it comes out that they [Freeport] have used fire assay we'll know that the whole—that the . . . you know, that the report was—was bogus," offered Bianchini, helpfully. Further, said Bianchini, in some parts of the deposit, up to 96 percent of the gold was "coarse free gold so there are some special things that you have to do in sample prep and I won't get into the details. But if those have not been done, there's a very strong likelihood that you are not going to get a representative . . . a proper representation of grade in the deposit."

He said he had spent the weekend trying to run down what had happened. "First of all, I'd like to start with the conclusion first so that everybody is clear as to what . . . what's going on. The gold is there. There's no question about it." But of course there was a question about it. And it was precisely due to the questions raised that other analysts had retreated to, at minimum, a neutral stance. Bianchini still rated the stock a buy. Why, it was cheap. Bianchini's "target price" was $29. At $15, Bre-X was a steal.

Bianchini was now slightly more forthcoming about what he knew. Freeport's results were "less than overwhelming. In fact, they've probably been duds." He had his explanations, as we now know, the "three outside entities checking the numbers" argument, the "Kilborn 'auditing' the process" argument. He said he had to be vague for "confidentiality reasons." Well what did *that* mean? It sounded as though Bianchini was talking as a Bre-X insider. But he was supposed to be an objective outsider. Thousands of investors, directly and indirectly, were relying on him for that. The gold was plentiful, free and coarse, he insisted, and Freeport simply did not know how to find it.

"Now I understand," Bianchini continued, "many of you out there have speculated or have heard speculation that, you know, the lower than expected results for grade from this deposit are somehow linked to Mr. de Guzman's death. Many of you now know—it was reported in the *Globe and Mail* that they found Mike's body unfortunately— or fortunately that they found Mike's body. Unfortunately, he is dead. And, you know, any of you that know the man—that knew the man, I'm going to say publicly here, know that the possibility of any funny business on the part of Mike de Guzman or his knowledge of any funny business . . . . It's just impossible for me to believe that. . . . So to those of you that . . . are speculating that . . . the core was salted . . . it is so preposterous . . . I'm not even going to address the possibility of that happening because I just . . . it's infinitesimal. So our conclusions remain that, you know, the deposit is as it's represented."

In a conference call of this kind, the analyst makes his introductory comments to whoever has phoned in, then opens it up for questions. The first question that morning came from Jim Steel from Toronto Dominion Securities. "Hi Egizio. Could you tell me what the average grade is throughout the deposit?" No, he couldn't. "I can get that to you, Jim," he said. He took a question from Kim Stephens with Schneider Capital. What if Freeport *had* used a cyanide test, and had used an independent lab to carry it out? "My conclusion would not be different." Bianchini jumped around the coarse grain issue again, the part about losing gold in the crushing. "We're getting into a little bit out of my league here," he said. In the previous conference call Bianchini had relied heavily on the cyanide leach defence. Now he was explaining that even the presence of the technology would not have guaranteed success for Freeport. The problem could have been in the sample preparation.

Another question. How closely does Kilborn shepherd the core? "They're there at the drill rig," answered Bianchini. "They watch, you know, how the core is put into the, into the core boxes, how it's brought back, how it's logged, how it's then prepared for sample ... they did not, of course, supervise every single drill hole. I don't think they even supervised ten drill holes. They may have only supervised one through the whole process, but they have spent time and at different key spots during the process and I think that ... that Kilborn will substantiate those comments that I have just made."

Bianchini noted that there was loads of crushed Busang core untested by Indo Assay if anyone wanted to carry out some due diligence, a check assay. Just 750 grams went into the test, he said. That presumed, of course, that there had been no funny business with the bags of core themselves. And how could Bianchini know that?

Could politics be to blame? "What's the prospect that Freeport may be trying to improve their stake in a deal right now through all of this?" Bianchini hemmed, hawed, sensitivities you know, but then, "The reasonable man would come up with a yes to that," he said. "This deposit, and when it is shown once again that it is as represented in the market right now, is going to be bigger than—well, the deposit itself will be bigger probably than the whole North American gold mining industry when measured on proven and probable reserves." There was evil at work in the marketplace, Bianchini suggested. Unnamed interests who were driving the stock into the ground. But the story would turn right again, he suggested. "As far as Bre-X is concerned, I mean, you know, they, they fully expect Freeport to come up with the same conclusions that they've come up with."

Bianchini may have been Bre-X's biggest booster, outside of its own corporate officers. But there were legions of followers who believed still in Busang, that Freeport must have screwed up somehow. "While shaken by recent events," said Lehman's Daniel McConvey, "we believe that the Busang discovery exists as Bre-X has disclosed it . . . Kilborn has reviewed the procedures. J.P. Morgan, Bre-X's investment bankers have, we understand, reviewed the procedures and Barrick Gold . . . . has done its own checks. No one has, to our knowledge, questioned the premise of the deposit to date."

On March 26, Graham Farquharson and his team taxied to the corporate head offices of PT Freeport Indonesia on Rasuna Said. Dave Potter and Steve Van Nort were waiting, itching to offload, eager to make it damn clear that all this shit talk about the games Freeport was playing was entirely unfounded. Potter and Van Nort did not welcome the prospect of having to convince a new group that they knew what they were doing. Paul Kavanagh joined the gathering. The Mouth was not there. The Brain, of course, was dead.

Freeport had done a first-class job. Farquharson could see that right away. Ninety percent of what Freeport had drilled was not, however, split, in keeping with the Bre-X practice. So Farquharson had nothing to take away clean from the Freeport drill. Paul Kavanagh attended the same meeting, in which Freeport's Van Nort and Potter went through its processes. He kept circling back to the same point. Barrick had found gold in their samples. How could this be?

Potter lost no time taking the men from Strathcona through Freeport's attempts to verify the Busang results. He told them of the 1,000 metres of core drilled, of where the holes were spotted, and of the shocking assay results: there was no gold within a country mile of an economic ore deposit.

All reports were made available to Farquharson and his team: the Kilborn intermediate feasibility study; the results of the Barrick assays. The Strathcona men headed back to their hotel rooms at the Shangri-La. The gossamer hope that the fairy tale was still true had dissolved. At 6:00 p.m., Jakarta time, Farquharson picked up the phone to call Rolly Francisco, still asleep beside his wife, Dorrie, in the early hours of a miserable March morning. Farquharson's hand was shaking slightly as he pushed all those buttons. This, he knew, was a $6-billion phone call.

Dorrie answered, and passed the phone across to her husband. "Sorry for getting you out of bed," said Farquharson, "but we don't like what we've seen so far. There's a strong possibility that the samples have been tampered with. In fact, there may not be any gold there at all."

Francisco tried to stammer a response. "I can't believe it. Are you sure?"

"No," said Farquharson, "I'm not sure. But we're going to find out. There are some real warning signs there."

"I can't believe it," said Francisco again. "Incredible."

"Rolly, we're going to have a letter on your desk this morning. There's no choice but to advise the Toronto Stock Exchange to shut down the stock." Farquharson did not want the widows out there buying all those Bre-X shares.

Farquharson asked for, and was granted, permission to move on to Busang and drill 1,500 metres. Strathcona would need, he said, nearly four weeks to complete its work, at a cost to the company of about $900,000.

For Rolly Francisco, the Busang affair had been nothing but trouble since the day he arrived. Some fucking gold mine.

The letter Farquharson's wife had typed up was delivered to Bre-X. "Based on the work done by Freeport and our own review and observations to date, there appears to be a strong possibility that the potential gold resources on the Busang property have been overstated because of invalid samples and assaying thereof."

Freeport made its own announcement. "During the past three weeks, FCX has drilled seven core holes within the Busang II project area to confirm the results of core holes previously drilled by Bre-X," said Freeport. "To date, analyses of these cores, which remain incomplete, indicate insignificant amounts of gold."

After a prolonged halt, Bre-X shares resumed trading at 3:00 p.m., March 28. With just ninety minutes to go until the closing bell, the share price was massacred in a sell-off that wiped out $3 billion worth of shareholder "value."

The rumours piled as high as Freeport's own mountain of gold. That Jim Bob Moffett was acting deliberately in an effort to suppress Bre-X's share price. That this was the evil hand of Bob Hasan at work. That the Indonesian government was at work in this, setting the stage for Freeport's ouster. Maybe, surmised McConvey, the Freeport results, whatever they were, were due to improper assaying. The holes Freeport drilled were too small in diameter, some proclaimed hopefully. They must be in the wrong spot. Perhaps, most simply and most broadly, Freeport did not know what it was doing. In its release of March 26, Freeport politely ran over the terms of the joint venture one more time, the percentage share splits, and the financing that would be required to take the deposit into production. "FCX will elect to participate in the development of the Busang project only if development is, in FCX's opinion, economically feasible." It knew Busang was not.

Farquharson flew to Balikpapan on March 27, where he ran into senior Bre-X staff coming out of Busang for the memorial for de Guzman. They were hostile, questioned the firm's integrity, insisted that they were all honest people and had carried out a diligent exploration program. They had some funny theories about why Freeport was not getting the gold. It was the first time he met John Felderhof, who was

more hostile than all the rest put together. The gold was erratic, the
Bre-X workers said, for they had certainly heard this line many times
before. Perhaps Freeport had not drilled in the right place. That day,
the *Global Gold Stock Report* issued a "Hot Stock Fax Alert." "A
couple of weeks ago I was told that Freeport and certain Indonesians
were going to initiate a campaign to totally discredit Bre-X and the
Busang gold deposit. I was told that Freeport would downgrade the
Busang deposit in an effort to decimate the price of Bre-X shares and
then take over the company at a $3 to $4 share price."

John Felderhof made preparations to prove Freeport wrong. He
contacted geologists Terry Leach and Gregg Corbett, at Leach's home
base in New Zealand. Felderhof had not met either man, but he had
cited their important work on epithermal gold deposits in his own
papers on the geology that he said applied to Busang. Felderhof
retained both men as his personal Busang experts. They were to fly
to Kalimantan to provide their own assessment of what this ground
was made of. Felderhof also retained Phillip Hellman, a geochemistry
expert in New South Wales. Leach and Corbett met Felderhof at the
Sheraton in Perth. They gave their working file a code name: The Sheraton Project.

When Felderhof arrived on site he had not only Ingrid in tow, but
Brian Cooper, a private bodyguard from the U.K. Two inspectors from
the Indonesian Department of Mines moved in, along with representatives from the Indonesian police, and two from the government's
geology department. Nusamba sent a young geologist. And, in a nice
scene-setting touch, the Indonesian paramilitary police arrived to
oversee the proceedings.

As the Felderhofs waited for Leach and Corbett, they hovered over
the shoulders of the Strathcona team like buzzards eyeballing tomorrow's feed. That they did not trust Farquharson and his men was
clear. Ingrid kept screeching about the legal avenues that she and her
husband were bound to pursue to put the lot of them out of business.
The Strathcona men noticed some very interesting things right away:

there appeared to be no Dayak working anywhere on the fabulous Southeast Zone. There was no geochem anomaly over the Southeast Zone. There was no gold in the outcrop samples, a point made to Bre-X workers, who variously suggested that the gold had been leached, evaporated, or had just "gone someplace." The spotting of the drill holes seemed not to be influenced by the previous drilling. In more than 60,000 metres of core-logging there had been no visible gold reported. The prep lab was well equipped, but under-utilized. Why?

The drilling program went smoothly, despite the histrionics. Long, smooth pieces of core came from the Southeast Zone. Like butter. Just as it had for the PT Drillinto Tiko drillers who had moved onto the site early in 1994.

When Leach arrived, he examined the skeleton core from hole 198 in the Southeast Zone. The mineralized core from 198 had assayed spectacularly high values, with the gold running unbroken through 400 metres at an average twelve grams per tonne. If it were true, Terry Leach would not have seen anything like it. Like any zealous geologist, Leach jumped at the chance to get on the ground at Busang, and hole 198 was one of the first pieces of evidence he chose to explore.

And therein lay the problem. Leach and Corbett examined the skeleton core from the hole, and were wholly unimpressed. The rock did not have the characteristics, the fracturing, to even hint that it would be host to such fantastic results. They raised their concerns with Felderhof, who could not "fucking" believe it. "Somebody is out to get us."

Leach gathered seventy-four samples from the site, fifty-one of which were taken from the Southeast Zone. "Gold was not observed in any of the polished sections from the 51 samples," said Leach in a memo to Bre-X. "This absence of microscopic gold is in agreement with the petrological work carried out by Anne Thompson." Leach was referring to a study by a Vancouver-based expert who, curiously, had been commissioned by de Guzman. There were, however, gold grains in the other samples, which had been taken from the Central

Zone. One he described as very large. "This is the only grain in the section that illustrates the nuggety distribution of the gold." Farquharson held out a piece of rock, showing it to Leach. "This assays 30 grams a tonne. What do you think?"

Before leaving the site, Felderhof instructed Cooper to take some whole core samples back to England for assaying there, Felderhof's personal check assay. When he came off site, Felderhof rang up John Irvin and asked to meet him at the Dusit. Felderhof brought Ingrid, and the three sat at the bar, the glass-walled view looking out to the strait.

"Can you believe he jumped?" Ingrid asked of Irvin. "He was so happy, so positive." John Felderhof asked another question, one that was growing as large as the curious demise of de Guzman. He turned to Irvin. "You don't think we salted it, do you?" he asked.

"No," said Irvin softly. "It's too hard to believe."

Felderhof's blue eyes drooped wet in their sockets, his tumbledown face dragging at the corners of his mouth, his large hands that had seen so much good work forming a mitt around his drink. "All ya gotta do," he said, as the others studied him very closely, "is drill one hole and find gold." He looked at Irvin and smiled, quizzically. The best result on Felderhof's own check assay was 0.47 grams per tonne. Nothing.

Farquharson oversaw a six-hole drill program, spreading the breadth of the property, holes that would audit Freeport holes, which in themselves mirrored Bre-X's, and others to be drilled alongside hot Bre-X holes that were not part of the Freeport program. Strathcona strapped 13 tonnes of drill core, assisted by the U.K. security hires and the Indonesian military, aboard a 737 jet headed for Perth.

Finally, even the supporters turned to sellers. Calls came in to Balikpapan from all over the world. Daniel McConvey sounded distraught when he phoned Irvin, seeking reassurances. McConvey had left Lehman and moved to Goldman Sachs, a star gold analyst. Suddenly his reputation did not look so hot.

Far away in Kalimantan, PT Drillinto Tiko driller Jim Rush was marching through the muck with Bobby Ramirez, who had logged miles of core at lightning speed and was well liked by the workers here. Ramirez had not flown the coop as Puspos had, and as de Guzman had, in his way. Rush turned to Ramirez. "Where have the Canadian geologists gone?" referring to Steve Hughes, Sasha Mihailovich and Trevor Cavicchi. Said Ramirez: "Their balls went up into their guts." Ramirez was sure to be implicated. Why had he stuck around?

On March 23, Police Lieutenant-Colonel Boedhi Santoso, from the subdirectorate of general investigation, police headquarters, Jakarta, commenced his investigation into the mystery of Busang. He studied the trail of the samples, from the early days. What was this rental facility in the village of Loa Duri, outside Samarinda, used for? He was told that Loa Duri was rented in 1996, long after the scam commenced, and was used to store the Indo Assay leftovers, course rejects, sent after assaying. When the sample bags came downriver, they went to Bre-X's Samarinda offices: first to the modest premises on Jalan Gaja Madha, then to the more middle-class set-up across town. Cesar Puspos was the primary steward of the samples. Only if Cesar was in residence would the samples flow to Indo Assay, and then they would arrive tonne upon tonne, making life difficult at the lab. It was physically impossible to keep up with the load.

The lab itself was held under suspicion at first, and the police demanded an average gold showing of all the data run on all those samples. Whatever for? To see if there are 71 million ounces of gold at Busang. The Indonesian police attempted an intimidating interrogation of John Irvin, taking his statements down on an aged typewriter, clacketing in the heat, and when the return carriage was hit a little too vigorously, it flew off. It seemed amusing, but in Indonesia, it is best not to laugh.

Strathcona had retained Colin Parker, a security specialist based in London. Parker's job was to oversee the security of the sampling. But he couldn't help but notice the way Bobby Ramirez and Manny Puspos were burning documents. "It's my brother," said Puspos to Parker by way of explanation.

Fidelity, which had held 7.62 percent of Bre-X at year's end, started aggressively selling off the stock. By the end of March, Fidelity had less than 2 percent of Bre-X. For those investors suddenly wondering why this great big mutual fund outfit had put such a heavy investment in such a speculative play, 2 percent was roughly 2 percent too much.

Toward the end of the month, Inco's Scott Hand met with Kuntoro Mangusubroto in Jakarta. Kuntoro knew then that he would be "released" from the department. Someone had to fall. Kuntoro was curious. What might happen in North America as a result of this? The osc, the sec, what will they do? Talk turned to the nickel market.

Munk did not believe that the Bre-X guys had salted the mine, had forged their samples. At least, not then. Too many analysts had been to site. How could you fool so many people for so long? It was impossible.

Wednesday, April 2, the bell at the Toronto Stock Exchange rang the opening as it does every work day at 10:00 a.m. In the next hour and forty minutes, nearly 12 million shares traded, till the exchange shut down the stock.

In early April, David Walsh paid a visit to Alan Lenczner's law office in downtown Toronto. Walsh's woes were far greater now than when he had retained Lenczner in the first place, over the Merukh suit. He was due at a meeting elsewhere in the city but needed a place to hide out in the interim. Could he stay here? He could not be seen on the street. The hounds were on David Walsh's tail.

A verbatim interview ran on April 6 in the *Calgary Herald*. Walsh was asked if he thought Mike jumped. "I knew him well," said Walsh. He found a fresh audience in mid-April with *USA Today*. "There's really been a well-oiled disinformation campaign against us," he said. "I stand by our test results. . . . We wanted to build this company on a business-like basis, not with promotion or a fly-by-night operation," he groused. *Angin*, blowing air. The Bresea Bre-X affair had been a

classic promote, and it was hardly appropriate to argue professionalism when, as a defence, Walsh would later embrace the notion that
he did not have a clue what was going on in Indonesia and did not
have a clue what this mining business was all about.

Greg Chorny headed into the uptown studios of TVOntario.
Chorny had become a regular media gadfly through all the excitement.
He and his wife, Kathy, had made millions on Bre-X, and for a long
time had sat on the list of the company's largest shareholders. In fact,
Chorny had calculated that he and his wife had made a fatter profit
on their Bre-X shares than David Walsh had.

Chorny had long been on the outs with Bre-X management, but
he could not entertain the notion that there was no gold there. The
results were in from Freeport, I told him that evening. "Yeah, but
where are they drilling? The back 40?" "Well, no, actually, the holes
were twinned." "Oh." A look of worry passed across Chorny's face.
It was one thing to vigorously fight so many battles on so many
fronts, championing the shareholder cause. It was quite another to
face the growing fact that there was no gold at Busang: the proverbial pot of gold wasn't.

Indonesian authorities announced that they would await the
Strathcona results before saying anything further. "Maybe the loss
will be the name of Indonesia," said Mines Minister Sudjana. "A little
embarrassing."

On April 11, Farquharson sent a letter to John Irvin and Keith Sarbutt at Lakefield Research in Peterborough. "Personnel from Bre-X
and Freeport are specifically prohibited from having any access to the
samples, or to be present when the samples are being treated."

On April 16, David Walsh and the companies he had promotion-
ally created were hit with seven lawsuits by shareholders from New
York to California. Walsh had already cut off most of the media, long
before the troubles hit, claiming reporters were assholes, or stupid, or
in the pocket of Barrick.

The posse of Bre-X intimates hung on to their belief that something other than the gold was amiss. "What's really going on here is that Hasan and Jim Bob Moffett have cooked up a way to grab the whole fucking thing," Hill and Knowlton's Richard Wool told *Fortune* magazine senior writer Richard Behar. "I came to that conclusion myself."

Investors phoned their brokers. What to do? "Absolutely do not sell," said one Nesbitt broker to her client. "This thing is blue chip. The gold is there. Believe it."

Bob Lindquist is what is known today as a forensic investigative accountant, a specialist in tracking white-collar fraud. Lindquist practically invented the practice of forensic accounting in Canada, and had formed a partnership in Toronto with an aim to selling such services, at a high price, to corporations. Lindquist later had a falling out at the firm he helped found, Lindquist Avey Holmes, and went over to Price Waterhouse in the same capacity.

Price Waterhouse had been retained by Bre-X, in the third week of March, as part of its mounting internal investigation into Busang. On April 22, Bob Lindquist widened the investigative net by bringing in Doug Hunt. Hunt was a Toronto lawyer. He knew two of Bre-X's outside legal counsel, Michael Melanson and John Sabine, from his earlier days in practice in a firm where the three had all once worked. Hunt had left the practice of law to help form a new firm, Forensic Investigative Associates (FIA), based in Toronto, with a hopeful worldwide mandate of tracking white-collar fraud for corporations and governments. FIA's most prominent founding partner was Rod Stamler, a former member of the Royal Canadian Mounted Police.

In approaching FIA, Price Waterhouse had a specific line of inquiry in mind: what was the connection between the fall of de Guzman and the assay discrepancies? Was de Guzman pushed? Was it suicide? Was it murder? Was the maggot-infested body truly de Guzman's? More specifically, FIA was to inquire into the discrepancy between the assay results recorded by Freeport and those claimed by Bre-X.

After a meeting in Calgary, Stamler struck an investigative team of four, and on April 28, Doug Hunt was on his way to Jakarta. Perhaps Freeport had done something wrong. That was one possibility as FIA saw it, though that would run counter to what Graham Farquharson was saying about Freeport's methods. Perhaps there was some sort of conspiracy. What was the real reason for the fire on site in January? There did not, at least for the moment, seem to be much concern about the gold itself. At the end of the day, the gold would be there, or at least that was the message from Bre-X. This was a fact-finding exercise, an audit of what had transpired. Strathcona's results were due soon. But Strathcona had not gone to site to interview people.

Hunt very quickly met with Price Waterhouse representatives in Jakarta. They set the scope of interviews to be conducted. Manny Puspos, Sonny Imperial and Bobby Ramirez—the three Filipinos still on site after Michael's fall—were the key targets. Hunt wanted to get to them fast. By noon, May 1, he was being squired around Busang.

Hunt has no geological background, and the other investigators had none to speak of. And so while Hunt recorded the beehive of activity at site, the making of drill core boxes, the erection of a fence around the core pad, he had no expertise to aid him in his assessment as to whether any of the site activity seemed untoward. Did the drilling program seem to be running too far in advance of the logging and the sampling? Hunt would not be able to say. On his way back to Balikpapan, Hunt stopped at Samarinda to view the office there. It was, in his assessment, a quite secure facility. He was prevented from entering two locked rooms off the office's casual area, which featured a pool table. He was told they were empty. He could see through the window that was not the case. Yet the new, high-priced investigators were unsuccessful in convincing Bre-X staffers to allow them access.

Back in Jakarta, Hunt and his team spent Saturday reviewing videotapes that they had taken at site. Strathcona's results were due to be tabled the following day.

The gun-metal sky seemed to seal the city of New Orleans on the morning of April 29. The board of Freeport had gathered for the company's annual meeting in the company's headquarters on Poydras Street, a green, granite-clad highrise across from the Superdome. "MDC XV" was cut grandly in bas-relief near the top of Freeport's headquarters, a pretentious way to advertise the company address. The place seems out of sync with New Orleans, with its antebellum mansions, its gumbo soil.

The outside world wants to hear from Jim Bob Moffett on two matters. The first and more obvious is Busang, about which Moffett has pledged to say very little. The second is the company's operations in Irian Jaya, over which Moffett et al. are facing a lawsuit from Tom Beanal and the Amungme.

For the ceremonials, the media had to drop their tape-recorders outside a dingy beige meeting room. No sensible explanation was given as to why the journalists were being prevented from recording the proceedings, or why they had to observe Jim Bob and his allies on closed-circuit television. Corporate representatives announced that the lawsuit was "an attempt to shakedown shareholders of Freeport-McMoRan." Having thus dispensed with it, the company would not entertain any discussion about the suit itself. Frequently moving off camera, his presence recorded only by the laser pointing at overhead acetates, Moffett danced across the company's cash flow, expansion plans, production costs. But Jim Bob Moffett, the all-American boy, the epitome of the American dream, could not bring himself to go face-to-face with the media.

A slide showed the audience Grasberg, at 4,000 metres, what Moffett called an old volcanic cone. "What you're looking at is the throat of this volcano," he said, marvelling at Mother Nature. The company, he said, brings $40 million worth of goods into the mine site's commissary annually. "You literally cannot buy salt or sugar or a hammer or a nail," said Moffett, signalling that Freeport had to import everything. The largest discovery of the century, he called it. The largest existing gold reserve in the world.

David Walsh had claimed for months that Busang was the largest. "We were invited in by Bre-X and Nusamba to look at the project," Moffett said nonchalantly. "We have a right to participate." He knew, of course, that the property was a fraud, but Moffett had given no interviews on what the company knew. If the property proved to be uneconomical, Moffett said coolly, "the company will basically withdraw and we will not be involved in Busang." Should that happen, "Bre-X can then go forward and find a partner of its own."

A representative of the Seattle Mennonite Church called for a resolution to postpone the expansion of Grasberg until the concerns of indigenous people had been addressed. The resolution was roundly defeated. Questions about Moffett's compensation were shut down. The big question, the appropriateness of this investment benefiting a murderous, oppressive military regime, never got an airing.

The following day, in the courtyard of a law office in New Orleans, Tom Beanal takes me through the trajectory of his life, from his birth fifty years earlier in Pelora, in the Stjuggal Valley, through his studies in theology and philosophy and his six years as a member of Golkar, the ruling party of Indonesia, in the 1970s. He has been battling Freeport for years. He says he wants fairness for his people, not charity. He complains that Freeport is so close to Suharto that the company "can do anything it wants without difficulty from our government."

Beanal's thumbnails are long and curved. He moves his Abita! beer, using the bottle to represent gold. "They say to me I will get gold from this place," he says quietly. "This is for you—this is for your government." But for Beanal, this is no good. "They must sit down with me and talk about my mountains, my rivers, my forests. All the trees," he says, then his words drift across the courtyard. "Everything is dying. Everything."

By the tinkling of a fountain, a scrum of energetic environmentalists plan their public relations assault on Freeport. A Project Underground worker was recently expelled from Irian Jaya attempting to take stream samples downriver from the mine. There is talk of Suharto, and the trouble brewing in the streets there. The power struggle is looming. Everyone can feel it. "When he goes," says one, speaking of Suharto, "Indonesia will make the Falklands conflict look like kindergarten."

Sunday, May 3, Graham Farquharson arrived at the low-rise corporate premises of Bre-X Minerals at 11:30 in the morning. Walsh, Kavanagh and Francisco were there to greet him. John Sabine. Brett Walsh. Karen Seymour, representing Bre-X's u.s. counsel, Sullivan Cromwell.

They were certain that Farquharson's news would relieve them of this wretched burden of the past days, that his report would validate their gold find. John Felderhof remained rooted in the Caymans. Curious? Not really. Even if John Felderhof were so stupid as to have not known over the previous three years what had transpired at Busang, he sure knew now.

The Bre-X people had spent the entire previous day strategizing, mentally preparing for news from Strathcona that there were not seventy million ounces of gold, but rather thirty, or perhaps even less than that. No one was prepared for the worst possible news.

Farquharson laid his neatly prepared report before the executive group. In ten minutes he presented the news in his ascetic style, his barrel-deep voice not searching for any grace notes. There was no gold. The group stared at him, stunned for a second of silence, before caving into an emotional meltdown. Now the tables were turned. Farquharson was not prepared for this reaction. He was quite surprised that the Bre-X people were so surprised.

Farquharson's report did not waste a verb, nor offer a superfluous adjective. "The magnitude of the tampering with core samples that we believe has occurred and resulting falsification of assay values at Busang, is of a scale and over a period of time and with a precision that, to our knowledge, is without precedent in the history of mining anywhere in the world."

Rod Stamler was in Calgary, meeting with Bob Lindquist and the

Bre-X group. He phoned Doug Hunt in Jakarta. "No gold at all?" asked Hunt, who then spent his time between the hours of midnight and 4:00 a.m. on the phone with Stamler and Bob Lindquist. FIA's mandate had quickly changed. The company now needed to determine where the salting had occurred, how and by whom. The next day, Doug Hunt headed back to Samarinda with Bernhard Leode. The same day, the Royal Canadian Mounted Police started a new investigation file called Bre-X.

Felderhof issued a press release from his comfortable Cayman Islands retreat. Shocked and dismayed, he said he was, to read the Strathcona conclusions. "I personally still believe that there are significant amounts of gold at Busang." He said he would co-operate fully with authorities.

So now Felderhof and Walsh were sharing the shock and dismay of shareholders. They were not, however, sharing the penury of those who had held on through all the accusations of their unprofessional management. Felderhof phoned Walsh on May 6, and spoke briefly to Walsh's son Brett. "My fuckin' heart has been ripped out of me," said the younger Walsh.

Felderhof was not interested in commiserating. He wanted to find David. He had sent faxes. Left messages. Perhaps he sensed the gathering mood that he, John Felderhof, river-walker, star geologist just a few scant weeks ago, was about to be left twisting in the wind.

"They fooled me completely," said Walsh of the Filipino crew. "When do you think this all started?"

"Right from the beginning," said Felderhof. "Right from day one I would think. I really have no fuckin' idea, Brett. No idea, no idea. Because I never stopped in Samarinda, you know, very seldom, right?"

Walsh: "I feel empty. I feel, I mean I just cannot—this is the scam of the century."

Felderhof: "But they fooled every goddamn guy. You know—Larry Kornze from the Barrick, the Barrick people. Ingrid is absolutely shattered too you know."

Walsh: "For Christ's sake."

Felderhof: "It is like seeing a whole lifetime gone before your eyes."

Walsh: "This thing has been going on for three and a half years. I mean, every single day was a lie."

On May 7, John Felderhof faxed David Walsh. "Dear Mr. Walsh," it began. "I received your letter of May 7, 1997 with regret. I understand the Company's need to conserve its financial resources at this time. . . . I have greatly appreciated the opportunity to work with you and your fellow Bre-X employees over the last few years, many of whom I understand will be leaving the company shortly. Please consider this letter also to constitute my resignation. . . . Again, let me state without reservation that I was not aware of any fraud at Busang, Loa Duri, or Bre-X."

Bigdude spent much time on the Net. "Dudes," he posted, "a buddy of mine overseas said he heard a rumour that there is a newspaper in Southeast Asia/Australia that has a story on de Guzman. It features an interview with one of the pilots that said they dropped de Guzman at a river's edge. (Remember my post saying I believe 66% chance that de Guz is still alive.) Could you guys help me confirm this rumour. BD."

ALL TO DUST

JOHN IRVIN, HIS HEAD TILTED BACK, holds a small, clear plastic pouch up to his office lighting. "Beautiful, isn't it," he says softly, as a man admiring, perhaps, a naked form, a piece of art. He tilts the envelope, a slight movement that sends the small gold grains within it tumbling to its corner. A lovely, lambent image, rounded beads of gold, *kencana*, dancing in the light, brought to John from Busang, ferried by a good friend, who had bought the gold from Salin, the Dayak panner. The friend had tried to make such purchases before, in the heady days of Bre-X, but Salin would say, "So sorry, pap. Pa Cesar, Pa Mike want this gold."

Hunters for gold or pursuers of fame, they had all gone out on that stream.... The dreams of men.

And when they find none they get desperate. Thirty-five milligrams of gold pannings would have given a five-gram assay in a single Busang sample. One-sixtieth of Irvin's souvenir. And from there grew the richest gold mine in the universe.

In his khaki safari shirt, his white singlet showing in a small v, his skin rising in a reddish sun-tint above, Irvin has the appearance of an expat but the gentle demeanour of a Javanese. Irvin has been years in this place, and he now ponders leaving Indonesia.

Strolling the simple Indo Assay office complex, Irvin pauses at the cupelling furnace, rows of cruells lined like soldiers, the red-hot heat from the fire assay reaching across the laboratory floor. In the room beyond, bottles are rolling cyanide-leached samples, hour after hour. The flow of work has slowed. Dozens of bags heavy with Busang samples have been humped on pallets, then covered with tarpaulins. In the storage yard, core boxes from Freeport's work sit piled high, leaning against a chain-link fence. Irvin surveys the detritus of a $6-billion fraud. "I'm going to throw it all in the river pretty soon," he says quietly.

Mario Possamai, one of the investigators with Forensic Investigative Associates, came through yesterday, asking the obvious questions. He was on his way to Busang, where he would purchase a sample of Salin's pannings and thence pass a portion of that on to Strathcona.

Strathcona would not chemically "fingerprint" the gold, a method developed by Anglo American to control gold theft in their mines. No one would compare the gold in the salted Busang samples to other placer operations in Kalimantan, or outside Indonesia for that matter. And so, the examination will rest on the conclusion that this one man with his pan—as simple an image as mining can possibly offer—provided the raw materials for a massive scam. One of the geologists in the drama found this very puzzling. "I never would have bought gold from the Dayak," he said. "They can't keep their mouths shut."

The Royal Canadian Mounted Police have notified Irvin that they are on their way. It seems very late. Strathcona's Reinhard von Guttenberg will soon be back, this time to retrieve samples from the Bre-X warehouse at Loa Duri. The memo from Cesar Puspos, the one that refers to the megascopic gold, sent back in the dying days of 1993, has provided a tantalizing clue. Von Guttenberg will retrieve the stored sample from hole number three, from which will come the proof that the gold-salting fraud started very early, as Michael de Guzman prayed to any God to show him some gold, as fine curlicues of pink gold were shoved into the rock.

One day, unannounced, a man named Phillip Hellman showed up, his business card identifying him as an ore reserve consultant from Beecroft, New South Wales, Australia. Hellman was bearing a small bag of rock, which he asked Irvin to put through Indo Assay's crushers. Irvin wondered if Hellman might be representing Hasan, or the Suharto family. Even in the aftermath, there were numerous agendas at work.

Hellman was clearly on a mission to investigate. Hellman had done an analysis of hard-rock gold that nevertheless displayed some of the characteristics of its alluvial cousin. He did not say he was representing John Felderhof. Nor did he say, though this was implicit, that he was here to investigate the lab. Felderhof himself had asked a question of Irvin: if it was salted, why was there so much silver in the assay results? The alluvial deposits of Kalimantan are known for their purity: 90 percent gold, even higher. Irvin's tests showed 70 percent gold, jibing with a hard-rock deposit. Whoever salted Busang was so clever. Brilliant.

Irvin has survived the ignominy of having his work questioned, the suspicions about the reliability of his testing procedures, about whether he knew anything of what went on at Busang. For months since that fateful day in March, Irvin's mind has tripped through the Busang fantasy. Were there any clues? What was the strategy? What was the plan? If Mike orchestrated this, why did he return to Busang that day? He recalls the time when Felderhof advised him to buy into Bre-X at $60 a share. After all, said Felderhof, even Cesar was a millionaire now. Instead, Indo Assay had $65,000 in unpaid Bre-X bills.

Sitting at Jack's Place, the sweat beading down the curves of the cold beer bottles, the breeze rising high across the Makassar, Irvin recounts the dying days of Busang. It is fitting that the sky on the far horizon, beyond the Pertamina platforms, flashes with lightning. A queer obsession takes hold as one stares too closely at the small, twisted details of this tale. "Mind-bending," whispers Irvin. After Freeport's first damning press release, he recalls, Bre-X samples kept arriving in Balikpapan. Batch after batch. Each of them dry, goldless, stone cold dead.

The two-lane blacktop from Balikpapan to Samarinda is a two-hour journey past skinny roadside tree growth, girdled in white to serve as markers on the unlit road. *Bukit Suharto*—Suharto's Forest—speeds by on the twists and turns.

The Bre-X offices are a short walk from the roadway to what could be a middle-class suburban home. A truncated concrete basketball court fronts the modest building. To its left, a carport, and beyond that a breezeway separates the office from the rooms of workers who live here.

Yani is still here in July. Yani is Genie's sister and Cesar Puspos's girlfriend. A couple of other workers lounge, listening to the radio, splayed on incongruous teal leather furniture. The obligatory photograph of Suharto hangs framed in the reception area.

Outside Cesar's office, plastic binders—blue, green, red, pink—fill bookshelves. Boedhi Santoso, lieutenant-colonel with the Indonesian National Police, has claimed them as evidence. A string runs across the binders, four times each set, stuck then with white paper strips and clear cellophane tape. Wax sienna seals affix the investigator's labels to the shelving.

In Cesar's office, a white lace curtain flutters in the breeze of an open window. As the curtain ruffles, it offers glimpses of pink bougainvillea blossoms. Cesar's chair is high-backed, brown. A drafting table nearby offers mapping space. A drill hole location map pinned to a bulletin board is dotted with pink and blue spots: the blue signifies the presence of gold; the pink its absence. On the map's right is the Luun Beren River. The drill lines charted run to its east. sEz-69. The Southeast Zone. Holes 215, 216. A list of holes drilled, sampled and dispatched to Indo Assay is recorded with Manny Puspos's name on it.

A fax is posted, addressed to Mike de Guzman, dated January 10, 1997. The faxes fade so quickly in this humidity, and this one is yellowed. "Mike: For your information and record, the samples [*sic*] numbers of the 'whole' untreated drill core sent to Lakefield Research on behalf of Barrick Gold were as follows..."

A preliminary schedule of mine development, drawn up by Kilborn, is affixed to the wall too. A sequence of phases: intermediate feasibility study; detailed feasibility study; engineering, procurement and construction; then, lastly, start-up and commissioning.

Half an hour away by car is the Bre-X warehouse in the village of Loa Duri. Between the street and the Mahakam, three long bunkers sit parallel to the road. Inside they are stacked high with the fibreglass Busang bags.

An adjacent alley offers an arresting contrast to this stark warehouse scene. Here, mothers sit on benches outside wretched housing, tending to lovely, round-faced babies, skin as soft as rose petals. The mud road is paved with garbage. Bits of laundry hang from metal rods that jut through windows. Grains of rice dust the bottom of a rattan bowl. *What then must we do?*

Down the alley and around the corner, two blue-and-yellow boats are docked behind the warehouse. Their "Busang Bre-X" signs have been knocked flat, but they are still legible.

At #87 Jalan Gajah Mada, Achmed Maulana is sitting in his living room, his front door open, as he tutors his students. He wears a gold and brown *pitji*, and his sarong shimmers in reds and burgundies. Five minutes away, Dzia Uddin offers watermelon and Coke and chats about his days at the Busang site. People are very nervous here, he says. Many believe that there was a fourth person in the helicopter March 19, and that Michael de Guzman was murdered.

In Jakarta, many believe he made his escape. In a highrise in the capital's core, Canada's ambassador to Indonesia, Gary Smith, has conducted many interviews on the Busang affair. "Have you been to his tomb?" he asks. "Have you asked yourself why no family members are there?" The city is chock-full of theorists who do not believe de Guzman died that March day.

The companies that rushed into Kalimantan on the heels of Bre-X are shutting up shop. It's tougher raising capital now. The mine-seekers and fortune-hunters will merely go elsewhere. A news item in a Manila daily was date-lined Kinshasa: "Every day Western businessmen in suits and ties risk riding in creaky elevators at the Ministry of Mines. . . . A Western mining executive, standing before a geological map hanging outside the minister's office, explained why. 'This is all money,' he said, his hand sweeping an arc over the eastern rim of this vast country, passing over symbols for cobalt, zinc, magnesium, iron, copper, diamonds and gold."

Those hanging on in Indonesia are battling El Nino. The fires have come to Kalimantan. Umar Olii has gone to work for a company called Kalimantan Gold, and when the smoke is on, it takes six days to get to site, the last three on foot. When there's water in the rivers, the trip takes half as long.

Mansur Geiger, who runs Kalimantan Gold, has been exploring for the precious metal for seventeen years, so he has lived through two booms now. Kalimantan Gold got its listing on the Vancouver Stock Exchange during the Bre-X boom. Geiger went to Vancouver to help sell the stock. He need not have bothered. The brokers there were not interested in his geological speeches. His property was on Kalimantan, and therefore was part of the Busang play. It was a gold rush, and the rush begat a fever, and that's all any company needed to prosper. Geiger has spent enough time on the island, studying her rocks, to know that Busang "was the perfect geological beast to fraudulate."

Not everyone is having a hard time. Genie de Guzman has remarried, and she and her new husband, Irvan, whom she married on Valentine's Day, Mike's birthday, have gone back to Palangkaraya, Central Kalimantan, to raise the two children she had with de Guzman.

The ground is quaking in Indonesia. It is the summer of 1997, and the local papers report the country's financial rot. On June 26 the *Jakarta Post* reports that the country's Supreme Audit Agency has unearthed multibillion-rupiah losses "caused by government over-spending, overpriced projects, unpaid taxes, bad loans at state-owned banks and other irregularities in state finance management."

It is just the beginning. The Asian currency crisis, born in Bangkok, has brought its infection here. The rupiah is headed for massive deval-uation. The price of gasoline, and of basic foodstuffs, has begun to skyrocket. The country's total foreign debt approached us$105 bil-lion. The banking sector is choking on nonperforming loans, many of them affixed to Suharto-related enterprises.

Yet when the Asian flu hit Indonesia, the severity with which it hit caught the world by surprise. Paul Krugman, an economist at the Massachusetts Institute of Technology, said that even Asian skeptics, himself included, "who regarded the claims of the Asian economic miracle as overstated, and argued that Asia was bound to run into diminishing returns eventually," did not expect those returns to wholly collapse. "What we have actually seen is something both more complex and more drastic: collapses in domestic asset markets, wide-spread bank failures, bankruptcies on the part of many firms, and what looks to be a much more severe real downturn than even the most negative-minded anticipated."

"Don't blame us," said Muhammad Sadli, chairman of a Jakarta-based think tank. "Those willing banks from the West and North just push money down our throats. Look at all those tall buildings we have built since 1986. All that was built with borrowed money."

The International Monetary Fund came calling. But it was not dis-posed to focusing first on the currency crisis. Instead, the IMF zeroed in on the Suharto empire, its greed and cronyism. International observers had warned for almost a decade that Suharto's talents for lining the pockets of family and friends could take the country to cri-sis. Some even warned as early as 1990 that when the backlash came, it would likely come in the form of a movement against the ethnic Chinese as well as against Suharto. By the dawn of 1998, the country was caught on a knife-edge. Fed up with Bambang, Tutut, Tommy and the lot, and the likes of Bob Hasan, too, they wanted to see an end to the carnivorous feeding frenzy.

In February, facing rampant food riots, Suharto ordered advanced military aggression in Jakarta against anti-government activists. They were plotting Indonesia's disintegration, he charged, with these "unconstitutional" behaviours. He shuffled his commanders. Tutut's husband, Major General Prabowo Subrianto, was named to the post of the army's strategic command chief. Bob Hasan, laughably, became minister of industry. Tutut became social welfare minister, an ironic touch. And B.J. (Rudi) Habibie, a man renowned as much for his megalomaniacal industrial projects as Sukarno was in his day, was named vice-president.

Suharto stood at the precipice, and it was electrifying. Students took to the streets by the thousands, demanding at last the democracy that had never come in his more than thirty years at the helm. Suharto held his placid visage, the benign father, *bapak*, of his country. As he smiled, the great man's great army gunned down student protesters. In the chaos that followed, more than one thousand people died, many in fires set in the rampage.

On May 19, 1998, Suharto at last stepped down, handing the presidency to Rudi Habibie. Suharto's man, literally the deposed autocrat's adopted son. Hasan and Tutut were dropped from the cabinet, and anti-Suharto forces started hunting down the estimated US$40 billion that the ex-president and his family had pilfered from the Indonesian people. Echoes of the downfall of the Marcos regime.

Indonesia was approaching the boiling point as David Walsh was signing off on the bankruptcy of Bre-X Minerals Ltd. "I, David Walsh, president of Bre-X Minerals Ltd., make oath and say . . ." He had been here before, back in Calgary, in his basement days, when he dreamed of what might lie buried at the end of the rainbow, if only he could find the rainbow. The assets of Bre-X on November 4, 1997 consisted of just under $5 million. Included in the corporate debts was $2,760,000 claimed by Suharto's son Sigit, via Panutan.

Six months previously, Bre-X had been removed from the Toronto Stock Exchange at the last traded board price of 90 cents.

Perhaps David Walsh still saw every day as a fresh start. It certainly seemed that way as he proposed that he convert Bresea into an oil and gas play and that he, David Gordon Walsh, should be free to run it. Instead, the trustee ordered the Walshes' assets frozen and limited, for an unspecified period of time, holding the Walshes to a weekly allowance of $3,000.

Perhaps it was the stress, though experts say stress is not a key factor in such medical circumstances. The weight, the drinking, the smoking: none of that could have helped. Two weeks after the fall of Suharto, David Walsh suffered a massive stroke. On the afternoon of June 4, 1998, he was pronounced dead of a brain aneurysm. The promoter would not have his day in court. Investors would not get the satisfaction of pressing the stock pusher on how he could have so utterly failed in his corporate responsibilities. Even if he did not know.

From his Cayman Islands estate, John Felderhof, whose assets had been frozen before Walsh's and who remained in what surely must have begun to feel like purgatory, offered his heartfelt regret at the passing of the man who had always sent him the money.

Dr. Jerome Bailen remembers that the meeting took place the day before All Soul's Day, and that the de Guzman family was making preparations to offer their prayers to the dead. They were seeking, first, their own peace. Who was this man buried in the Estate of Peace Three, Holy Cross Memorial Park, Quezon City?

Addressing his audience—Laurence de Guzman, brother of the deceased, and Teresa de Guzman, wife of the deceased—Dr. Bailen carefully detailed his investigation of cadaver No. N-97-591. Dr. Bailen had top credentials for this work. An anthropologist, he had achieved some fame in the Philippines seeking the proved identities of "the Disappeared" from the Marcos years. Bailen sees himself as a holistic thinker. "I'm a little impatient with mere cadaver-cutters, you know, who think the body is devoid of poetry, poignancy and pathos."

Dr. Bailen had studied the photographic evidence over at the National Bureau of Investigation, and the NBI's X-rays, too. He confirmed, first, the obvious: that the body was that of a male southern-Asian Mongoloid with distinctly developed brow ridges. He studied pictures of the hands and feet: that these feet appeared to be those of Michael was all that Laurence could offer. Certainly, thought Bailen, they were very similar feet. He studied the dental evidence, and the carious portions of Michael's teeth. Most significantly, a photo of the body taken as it lay in the swamp in Kalimantan showed clearly the lump on the left shoulder, Michael de Guzman's identifying characteristic. In the post-mortem X-rays taken by the NBI, the upper inner angle of the cadaver's left shoulder blade was far more developed than the right, extending above the collarbone. There was no question, Dr. Bailen told the family, that this was a match.

Mike de Guzman had made a phone call to his friend Mike MacDermott in March 1997, when he was attending the prospectors' convention in Toronto. MacDermott had played his own role in the Bre-X saga, having been hired by John Felderhof back in 1996 with the objective of countering the intelligence moves being made against Bre-X in Jakarta, when so many different players were fighting over ownership of Busang. De Guzman said he was looking forward to a holiday that the de Guzmans and the MacDermotts would take together two weeks hence. MacDermott had helped de Guzman get his family residency stamp for Australia. De Guzman seemed very happy about that.

Within a week of their last conversation, Mike de Guzman had jumped out of a helicopter. For six months, Mike MacDermott was convinced that his friend was still alive.

By the time Dr. Bailen presented his finding to the de Guzman family, Mike MacDermott, too, had concluded that the geologist was, in fact, deceased. He also believed that de Guzman had been murdered.

Through the early months of 1998, Dr. Jerome Bailen assiduously pursued this possibility. He grew four batches of maggots, comparing them with photographs of the cadaver as it lay in Samarinda. The maggots in the body, he says, appear to be younger than they should have been, "as claimed by the narrative." But the evidence is soft. "The Indonesian guys didn't even collect the maggots," he says. "So terribly inept. They should have collected the god-damned maggots."

He studied the fracturing of the bones. There was none at the base of the skull. There was no misalignment of the angle of the heel bone with the lower leg bone. When Michael de Guzman was found in the swamp, his left leg was entangled in an overhanging vine. He was belly down, the left side of his face resting in the crook of his right arm. Yet, the most fractured side of the face was the right. The fracturing, Bailen believes, is inconsistent with the fall Michael presumably made. He noted the lack of blood pooling around the fractures which should have occurred had the tissue been live at the time of the break.

He wondered why the body was so cleanly empty. Jerry Alo told Bailen that the body reminded him of an animal butchered as it would be in the Philippines, with a hole cut around the anal opening and the connection cut at the neck and the organs simply pulled out. "The people who might have processed Mike's body might have really cleaned it up," says Bailen. "They know the kinds of information that internal organs might have that would help us figure out the cause of his death."

On Michael de Guzman's back, Bailen observed a pair of horizontal imprints, on either side, a little bit below the armpit level. He surmised that these indentations might have been made by the top end of a wooden chair. He believes there is another imprint below the level of the chin.

By the summer of 1998, Dr. Bailen had been wholly sucked into the mind-bending vortex of the Bre-X saga. He now envisions a man, heavier than he was in this Acupan days and far less handsome, sitting on a wooden chair, somewhere in the interior of Kalimantan. He is being interrogated to wrest information that will go into the suicide notes that he will be forced to write. When this is done, this man will be pulled back hard against this wooden chair. Standing behind him is a military man, who pulls the ligature, tightening it across his neck, until death. Bailen sees this body then dumped into the jungle, the left leg catching on that overhanging vine.

The sun sits directly overhead. In the dizzying, delirious atmosphere of Indonesia, the truth is a slippery thing to grasp. Not far away, by a spit of a creek called Busang, the remnants of a fabulous fraud start to fade in the blistering heat.

ACKNOWLEDGMENTS

Fever was not my idea. Literary agent Daphne Hart called me up one wintry day in 1996, having been referred by my great friend Kimberley Noble. Hart thought the Busang tale had the makings of a wonderful book. At the time, Peter Munk and many Barrick Gold lieutenants and investment advisers were dancing about Jakarta, attempting to ensure that Busang would become part of the growing Barrick gold mining empire. Busang then was a great, great gold mine. The biggest ever.

I found the prospect of shaping the Busang odyssey into book form compelling for a number of reasons: the size of the touted deposit; the cast of characters who discovered and promoted it; the intriguing battle over ownership; and, above all, the exotic awayness of the assignment. I had not been to Indonesia in a decade. Suharto's power was on the wane and it seemed inevitable that when he fell, he would do so in dramatic fashion, and the world would hear the earth shake.

In February 1997, I travelled to Jakarta. I was then a writer at *Maclean's* magazine, Canada's newsweekly, and desperately eager to claim the first on-the-ground story from Indonesia on the fight over Busang. Of course, doing so meant travelling without a journalist's visa, but there was no time for protocol. Once in Jakarta I was hooked.

I had lunch with Meg Masters and Kevin Hanson from Penguin Books after my return. I recall that Meg at one point asked what at the time seemed a wild question: What if there's no gold? A month later we all knew the truth. Busang was a dry teat, and somebody somewhere pulled off one of the most brilliantly contrived frauds of all time.

My first thank-yous go to *Maclean's*. To Bob Lewis and Geoff Stevens for encouraging me always. To Ann Dowsett Johnston for helping me get to Indonesia. To Phill Snel for the chocolates and the Moet.

At *Maclean's*, my editor, mentor, and unflagging supporter was Ross Laver. Ross held my hand across the phone wires, getting a story out of me as I lay ill and mewling. I would not have covered Busang, nor written this book, had it not been for Ross. Thank you from the bottom of my heart.

At *Report on Business Magazine*, Patricia Best offered me a job knowing that I had not yet come through book-writing slaughter. Everyone at the magazine patiently watched the process unfold, praying, I think, for my survival. A special thank-you to Charles Rowland for his ever-sharp researcher's eye and Shelley Cathers for her biblical knowledge.

This is a work of primary research. Hundreds of interviews were conducted; many of those contacted agreed to be interviewed at length numerous times. Not surprisingly, some of those interviewed requested anonymity. Among the crew who requested no such shelter I would particularly like to thank: Glenn Greisbach, John Irvin, Bernhard Leode, Umar Olii, John Willson, Kevin Waddell, Barry Tannock, Laurence de Guzman, Diane de Guzman, Mary Jane Lapaña, Bruce Kennedy, Tom Malihan, Dr. Ed Kalalo, Dr. Noel Minay, Bayani Palad, Paul Damasco, David Harries, Jim Macgregor-Dawson, Dick Walters, Dale Hendrick, Warren Irwin, Dr. Robert Ginn, Chong Fong Fatt, Beni Wahju, Arif Arryman, Hartojo Wignjowijoto, Dzia Uddin, Tom

Ajamie, Don Jack, Harvey Strosberg, Graeme Chuck, Jim Rush, Rachman Wiriosudarmo, Graham Farquharson, Reinhard von Guttenberg, Scott Hand, the late David Allen, Birl Worley, Malcolm Bailey, Giselle de Mege, Ineke Felderhof, Rudy Vega and Mansur Geiger.

I would like to single out Richard Behar, senior writer at *Fortune* magazine in New York, who provided critical insights and resource material. Richard was a tremendous supporter of this project. I hope it lives up to his expectations.

The book was ultimately birthed by Meg Masters and Catherine Marjoribanks, to whom I am very grateful, and would not have happened at all were it not for my dear friend, Erma Canaleta.

Finally, my biggest love to my husband, Peter, and our three boys. Mexico. I promise.

Toronto, June 4, 1998

BIBLIOGRAPHY

Abdulgani, Roeslan. *Nationalism, Revolution and Guided Democracy in Indonesia*. Clayton, Victoria, Australia: Monash University, 1973.

Amnesty International. *Indonesia/East Timor: The Suppression of Dissent*. July, 1992.

Anderson, Benedict and Ruth McVey. *A Preliminary Analysis of the October 1, 1965 Coup in Indonesia*. Ithaca, New York: Cornell University, 1971.

Blair, Lorne and Rio Helmi. *River of Gems: A Borneo Journal*. Jakarta: Image Network Indonesia, 1991.

Budiardjo, Carmel. *Surviving Indonesia's Gulag*. London: Cassell, 1996.

Chomsky, Noam. *Perspectives on Power: Reflections on Human Nature and the Social Order*. Montreal: Black Rose Books, 1997.

Cleary, Mark and Peter Eaton. *Borneo, Change and Development*. Oxford: Oxford University Press, 1992.

Cribb, Robert, Ed. *The Indonesian Killings: Studies from Java and Bali*. Clayton, Victoria, Australia: Monash University, Centre for Southeast Asian Studies, 1990.

Crouch, Harold. *The Army and Politics in Indonesia*. Ithaca, New York: Cornell University Press, 1978.

de Jesus, C. *Benguet Consolidated: 75 Years, 1903-1978*. Manila: 1978.

Forensic Investigative Associates Inc. FIA *Interim Report of Investigation into Tampering with Bre-X Minerals Ltd. Busang Core Samples*. Toronto: October 3, 1997.

Goshal, Baladas. *Role of the Military in Indonesia*. Madras: University of Madras, 1980.

Hill, Napoleon. *Think & Grow Rich*. New York: Fawcett Books, 1960.

Hillen, Ernest. *The Way of a Boy: A Memoir of Java*. Toronto: Penguin Books, 1994.

Hillen, Ernest. *Small Mercies: A Boy After War*. Toronto: Viking, 1997.

Keynes, John Maynard. *The World's Economic Outlook*. New York: The Atlantic, 1932.

Koch, Christopher J. *The Year of Living Dangerously*. London: Penguin Books, 1978.

Krugman, Paul. "What Happened to Asia?" Web posting: January, 1998.

Laber, Jeri. "Smoldering Indonesia." *The New York Review*, January 9, 1997.

Lefolii, Ken. *Claims: Adventures in the Gold Trade*. Toronto: Seal Books, 1987.

McBeth, John and Michael Vatikiotis. "The Endgame." *Far Eastern Economic Review*, May 28, 1998.

McDonald, Hamish. *Suharto's Indonesia*. Blackburn, Victoria, Australia: The Dominion Press, 1980.

Mealey, George A. *Grasberg*. New Orleans: Freeport-McMoRan Copper & Gold Inc., 1996.

Mody, Nawaz. *Indonesia Under Suharto*. New Delhi: Sterling Publishers Private Ltd., 1987.

O'Hanlon, Redmond. *Into the Heart of Borneo*. London: Penguin Books, 1984.

Orwell, George. *The Road to Wigan Pier*. London: Victor Gollancz, 1937.

Pintz, William S. *Ok Tedi: Evolution of a Third World Mining Project.* London: Mining Journal Books, 1984.

PT. Kilborn Paka Rekayasa, PT. Westralian Atan Minerals. *Busang Gold Project, East Kalimantan; Intermediate Feasibility Study.* Jakarta: December, 1996.

Schwarz, Adam. *A Nation in Waiting: Indonesia in the 1990s.* St. Leonards, New South Wales, Australia: Allen & Unwin, 1994.

Shulman, Morton. *The Billion Dollar Windfall.* Toronto: McGraw-Hill, 1969.

Simatupang, Marangin, Soetaryo Sigit and Beni Wahju, Eds. *Mining Indonesia: Fifty Years Development 1945-1995.* Jakarta: Indonesia Mining Association, 1996.

Strathcona Mineral Services Ltd. *Busang Project—Technical Audit for Bre-X Minerals Ltd., Interim Report.* Toronto: May 3, 1997.

"Suharto & the Reins of Power." *The Economist,* November 17, 1990.

"Suharto's End-Game." *The Economist,* June 26, 1997.

Sykes, Trevor. *The Money Miners: Australia's Mining Boom 1969–1970.* Wildcat Press, 1978.

Toronto Stock Exchange/Ontario Securities Commission. *Setting New Standards: Mining Standards Task Force, Interim Report.* Toronto: TSE Publications, 1998.

van Leeuwen, Theo M. "25 Years of Mineral Exploration and Discovery in Indonesia." *Journal of Geochemical Exploration,* 1994.

Vittachi, Tarzie. *The Fall of Sukarno.* London: Andre Deutsch Ltd., 1967.

"What Price Stability?" *The Economist,* August 3, 1996.

INDEX

A. Wahab Syachrani Hospital, 28
Abacan Resources, 166
Aber, 108
A.C.A. Howe, 70–71, 87, 102
A.C.A. Howe Australia Pty., 72
Aceh, 234
Acupan, 30, 39, 47–52, 54–5, 85,
   116, 130, 145, 157, 323, 382
Adamson University, 35–8
Adyningsih, Siti Hutami, 221
Aidit, D.N., 209–11
Airlangga (*see* Hartarto, Airlangga)
Ajamie, Tom, 297
AKM, PT, 17
Alberta Securities Commission,
   108, 124
Alberta Stock Exchange (ASE), 99,
   107, 120, 140, 163–4, 166, 189
Alberta Treasury, 169
Alice Springs, 8
Allen, Herbert Sr., 44–6
Allen, Peter, 197

Allen & Co., 44, 46
Alo, Jerry, 95, 142, 159–60, 166,
   194–6, 242, 289, 319, 328, 330,
   332, 336, 338–9, 350, 381
Altamira, 108
American Barrick, 78, 246, 323
Amnesty International, 223
Amphalit, 72, 90–91, 93, 335
Amphalit Mas Perdana, PT, 54, 71
Amsya Lyna, 288
Amungme people, 314, 316–7, 366
Aneka Tambang, PT, 231
Anglo American of South Africa
   Ltd., 172, 299, 372
Ansbacher (Bahamas) Ltd., 343–4
Apkindo, 280
Applegath, Bert, 197
Ara Tutut, PT, 95, 143
Aracus, 93
Arequipa Resources, 196, 265
Argus Resources, 107–8
Ark Ltd., 343

Armado, 31
Arryman, Arif, 295–6
Asian World Stock Report, 152,
    272
Asiaweek, 221
Askatindo, PT, 165, 240, 257,
    288–9, 308, 349
Aspac Center, 14
Aspecindo Kreasi, PT, 225
Atkinson, Dorothy, 107
Attunga, 82
Austin, Ian, 286–7, 293
Australian Financial Review, 93
Ayrex, 120

Badan Pelaksana Pasar Modal
    (BAPEPAM), 90
Baguio, 40–41; mining history,
    41–4; nightlife, 48–9
Bailen, Dr. Jerome, 32–3, 379–82
Baker, David, 172
Baker, Howard, 239, 259
Bakrie, Aburzial, 312
Bakrie Nusantara Corp., 95
Balatoc Mining Co., 43
Balikpapan, 61–2
Balogh Investment Ltd., 343–4
Banco do Oro, 56
Bank Central Asia, 272
Bank of Montreal, 45
Barrick Gold Corp., 161, 163, 168,
    177, 181, 185, 256, 259–60,
    263–6, 269, 271, 274–6, 281,
    284–5, 289–90, 295–6, 298,
    304, 308, 312, 318, 327–8, 330,
    336, 340, 351, 355–6, 363, 370,
    375; Bre-X partnership discus-
    sions, 131–5, 137, 141, 148–50 ;
    Bre-X takeover bid, 187–8,
    232–5, 237–42, 246, 248–50,
    254–6, 273–4, 276–84, 286–8,
    293, 297, 299, 301, 309
Barrick Investments Ltd., 262

Barrick Petroleum Co., 262
Barrick Resources, 262
Bataatsche Petroleum Maatschappij
    (BPM), 62
Batt, Warren, 93
Batu Hijau, 270, 293
Beakindo Pacific, PT, 321
Beanal, Tom, 316, 366
Beaudoin, Armand, 95, 191
Beaupre, Wayne, 320
Beck, Howard, 262
Beckwith, Warren Talbot, 111, 114,
    188, 269
Behar, Richard, 99, 364
Belfranlt Hotel, 55
Bell, David, 107
Bell Canada, 179
Benakutai Hotel, 16–7, 19–20, 325
Benguet Consolidated Inc., 38
Benguet Consolidated Mining Co.,
    42
Benguet Corp., 30, 38–9, 41–6,
    49–56, 93, 117, 130, 159
Bennett Jones Verchere 282, 348–9
Bettles, Keith, 286
Betze deposit, 135, 260
Beverly Hilton, 296
Bianchini, Egizio, 170, 172, 193–6,
    201, 316, 324, 347, 351–5
"Bigdude", 345–7, 349–50, 370
Biggar, Bill, 255
Bimantara Citra, 221
Birchall, Bill, 238, 262, 293, 309
Bird, Mike, 10, 15, 17, 23, 53, 85,
    87–8, 90–91, 110, 242, 299
Bock, Carl, 59–65
Bond, Alan, 85
Bond group, 85
Borneo: history, 59–63; forest
    industry, 60, 62; missionaries in,
    62–3
Bowling Green State University, 323
Bowman, Dan, 340

breccias, 50–51, 88, 112, 117, 128

Bresea Resources Ltd. (*see also* Bre-X Minerals), 15, 97–8, 101–3, 107, 179–80, 343–4, 363, 379; Indonesian prospects, 110–11; share trading with Bre-X, 103, 123, 151

Bre-X Minerals Ltd. (BXM) (*see also* Bresea Resources; Bro-X Minerals; Busang; de Guzman, Michael; Felderhof, John; Walsh, David), 4, 94, 97–8, 116; bankruptcy, 378–9; Barrick partnership proposal, 131–3, 137, 142, 148–50; Barrick takeover bid, 188, 234–8, 241–2, 248–50, 255–7, 273–4, 276–84, 286, 288; Busang II acquisition, 165, 184, 252; CRA interest, 173–5, 267–8; Freeport deal, 307–8, 340, 367; growth, 14–5, 103, 251; Kennecott Canada deal, 106, 108; Kroll investigation, 246–8; lawsuits, 288; offices, 10, 14, 19, 21, 121, 125, 155–6, 186; partnerships, potential, 172–3, 267–8, 272–3, 292–307; Placer Dome interest in, 234–5, 268–72, 277–9, 281, 284–8; promotion methods, 121–5, 130, 135, 139–41; prospects, 103–4, 106–8, 110–11, 128–30, 139; security concerns, 246, 289, 302, 330; share issue, 103–4; share prices, 103, 106, 108, 121, 123, 141, 151, 153, 166, 168–70, 172, 177, 179–80, 201, 232–3, 252, 267, 270, 274, 299, 301, 347, 349, 353, 357, 379; share split, 232–3; share trading with Bresea, 103, 123, 151; shareholders, 179–80, 345–7; shareholders meeting, 177, 179–81;

trade/media coverage, 130, 135–7, 150, 152–3, 162–4, 179, 274–5; TSE 300 listing, 189

Broken Hill Proprietary Co. (BHP), 69, 106, 113

Brooke, James, 62

Bro-X Minerals (*see also* Bre-X Minerals), 180, 343

Bull & Bear, 121, 135–6, 150, 161, 163

Bupati, 18–9

Burnham, Daniel Hudson, 40

Busang, 14, 18, 30–32, 66, 110, 139–40, 148–50, 154, 163, 335; Central Zone ownership, 137–9, 236–7, 240, 250; contract of work, 117, 137, 170, 245, 258, 275; de Guzman's assessment, 115–8; drilling practices, 142–7, 150–51, 153, 158, 169, 174; expansion to Southeast Zone, 167–70, 175, 178, 183, 256; Freeport due diligence, 320–32, 337, 339–41; history, 111–5, 185; living conditions, 159–60; mine plan, 164, 244; police investigation, 361, 363; resource estimates, 154, 171, 177, 232, 244, 280, 315–6, 336; rumours, 185–7, 193, 270, 349; sample handling (*see also* Loa Duri warehouse), 156, 195–6, 243–4, 352, 354; sample logging, 158–9; sample procedures, 127–8, 131, 143–4, 150, 162, 174, 188, 243; sample prep lab, 166–7, 243, 331, 359; sample results, 33, 131, 145–9, 196, 258, 281–3, 288, 322, 331, 346, 360, 364; sample tampering, 148, 152, 351, 353, 356, 362, 368–9; site plans, 125, 140; site visits, 134, 171, 193–6, 242–4,

279; Strathcona audit, 348–9,
355–63, 368–9; trade/media
coverage, 130; working
conditions, 158–9
Busang I (Central Zone), title claim,
182, 184, 190, 236, 240, 250,
288
Busang II (Southeast Zone), 150,
164–5, 357; drilling plans, 300;
Freeport acquisition, 308; SIPP,
252, 255, 257, 266, 283; title
claim, 184, 240, 306
Busang III, 273; Freeport
acquisition, 308
Bush, George, 239, 259, 265–7

Calgary Herald, 123, 151, 362
Calgary Sun, 107
Camat, 18–9, 156
Canada Permanent Trust Co.,
100–101
Carlin Trend, 134, 259–60, 323
Carrington, John, 279, 336
Carter, Donald, 180, 346
Carter, Ted, 140
Carter's Choice Newsletter, 140
Casa Berardi, 120
Castro, Fidel, 206, 312
Cavicchi, Trevor, 244, 330, 361
Charles, Prince of Wales, 265
Chase Manhattan Bank, 308
Cheriyan, Dr. Achamma, 13, 347
Chevron, 231
Chong, Fong Fatt, 93–4
Chorny, Greg, 179–81, 295, 297,
315, 363
Chorny, Kathy, 363
Chua, William, 31–2
Chuck, Graeme, 111–3, 116, 185
Citra Lamtoro Gung Persada, PT,
40, 221, 242
Clairtone Sound Corp., 260–61,
263–4

Coates, Bryan, 257, 282, 343,
348–9
Cominco, 103
Commonwealth, 108
Consolidated Gold Fields, 247, 263
Consolidated Golden Arrow Mines,
189
conspiracy theories, 57–8, 370
contract of work (COW) (*see also*
KP, SIPP), 73–9, 119, 135,
230–31, 289
Cooper, Brian, 358, 360
Corbett, Greg, 259, 321, 358–9
Cortés, Hernán, 41
COW (*see* contract of work)
CRA Ltd., 86, 113, 173–5, 183–5,
188, 237, 240–41, 249, 267,
269, 301, 307–8, 324, 340, 351
Craig, John, 173–5, 183–5, 237,
245, 267, 318
Crescent Technology, 337
Cribb, Robert, 212–3
Crouch, Harold, 216–9
Crowne Plaza Hotel, 255

Dalhousie University, 67
Damasco, Paul, 30, 51, 53, 55–6
Dar Tadine Tanzania Ltd., 95
Dattels, Stephen, 190
Davidson, Alex, 148–9
Davies Ward & Beck, 234, 248,
262
Dayak people, 60, 243;
architecture, 159–60; belief in
supernatural, 12, 158–9;
cannibalism, 63; conversion by
missionaries, 62–3; gold
panning, 112, 147–8, 278, 323,
359, 372; traditions, 160
de Albuquerque, Jorge, 61
De Beers, 107
de Guzman, Genie (*see* de Guzman,
Michael, under wives)

de Guzman, Michael Antonio
Tuason (Chel), 130–31, 133,
136, 144, 156, 278; autopsy –
Indonesia, 6, 27–9; autopsy –
Philippines, 4–8; Bre-X stock
options, 168, 172, 318–9; children, 11, 20, 25, 30, 48; death,
346–7, 349–51, 353, 364, 376;
early years, 37–9; employment
by Benguet Corp. (Acupan), 30,
38–9, 46–54; employment by
Bre-X Minerals Ltd. (Busang)
115–8, 122, 128, 133–4, 141–6,
148–9, 151–2, 159, 160–65,
167–9, 171, 174, 176–182, 186,
194–6, 234, 237, 242–3, 245,
255, 257, 279, 286, 288, 315,
321–2, 325, 327–44, 371, 373,
375; employment in Indonesia,
various, 94–5; employment by
Pelsart, 54, 84–5, 87–8, 91–2,
94; employment by research
interests, 49–52; Felderhof,
initial dealings, 54; final days,
8–23, 339–44; health problems,
12–3, 18, 290, 303; identification of body, 1–4, 32–3,
379–82; last wishes, 23–5;
memorial services, 29–30, 350,
357; parents, 4–5, 9–10, 37–8,
66, 333; pastimes 10–11, 19,
48; personality, 15–6, 24–5,
157, 258, 305–6; remains, 31;
siblings, 9–11, 50; Laurence
(Owie), 4–5, 379–81; wife
Sugini Karnasih (Genie), 8–9,
11–4, 16, 20, 24, 91, 95, 115,
177, 303, 339, 341, 374, 376;
wife Lilis, 20, 341; wife Susani
Mawengkang, 19–20, 24, 341;
wife Teresa (Tess), 9–11, 14,
24–5, 30–31, 48, 95, 115, 252,
341, 379, 381

de Guzman, Teresa (Tess) (see de
Guzman, Michael, under wives)
de l'Mari, Grover Whitney, 49–50,
117
Department of Mines and Energy,
Indonesia, 18, 72, 75, 78–9,
90–91, 111, 117, 119, 137, 140,
165, 182–3, 191–3, 225–6,
229–30, 240–41, 252, 255–7,
273, 276, 288, 290, 297, 299,
303, 306, 309, 358
Dermawan, 248
Dewan Perwalikan Rakyat (DPR),
222
Dewar, Elaine, 247
Dia Met Minerals, 106–8, 121, 172
Diadem Resources Ltd., 242
Diamond Fields Resources, 172,
180, 198–9
diatremes, 49–50, 116–8, 168, 170,
178, 335
Directorate of Geology, 228
Dizon, 45, 55, 145
Dow, John, 293
Dow Jones, 162
Doyon Lands, 114
Drillinto Tiko, PT, 66, 142, 161,
168, 290, 331, 339, 359, 361
due diligence, 152, 175, 184
Dulla, 16
Dusit Hotel, 16–7, 286, 325–7, 360
Duvalier, Jean-Claude, 247
dwifungsi, 207, 216

East Tara Malawi Minerals, 86
Easterday, Clark, 92
Eastern Trust, 100
Echo Bay, 103–4
Econit Advisory Group, 295
Edge, Bill, 276, 282
Edison, Thomas, 101
El Paso Chem–Tec Laboratories,
197

Elk International Corp., 263
Ertsberg, 74–6, 137, 139
Export Development Corp., 45

Fagan, Brian, 152, 168, 272
Falconbridge Ltd., 199
Far Eastern Economic Review, 308
Far Eastern University, 5
Farquharson, Graham, 347–9,
   355–8, 360, 363, 365, 368
Felderhof, Ingrid, 29, 90, 109, 236,
   245, 300, 329, 344, 358, 360,
   370
Felderhof, John, 17–9, 23–4, 30,
   66, 94, 96, 111, 157, 162;
   Bre-X stock options, 252, 300;
   childhood & education, 66–7;
   employment at A.C.A. Howe,
   70–73, 84–90, 92; employment
   at Bre-X Minerals Ltd., 121,
   123–5, 127–9, 131–3, 135–6,
   139–40, 144–5, 148–9, 152–4,
   164–5, 167–71, 173–5, 177,
   180–85, 186–8, 232, 234,
   236–8, 240, 242–6, 248–9,
   251–2, 255–9, 270, 272, 276–7,
   279, 282–4, 286, 288–9, 294,
   300–302, 305–7, 314–6, 319,
   322, 325, 327–31, 333, 335–9,
   342–4, 350, 358–60, 368–70,
   373, 379–80; employment of de
   Guzman, initial dealings, 54,
   115; employment by Kennecott,
   68; employment by Minindo
   Perkasasemesta, 95; employment and Ok Tedi discovery,
   69–70; employment by PT WAM,
   115; employment by Walsh,
   initial dealings, 102, 108–11,
   118–9; family, 66–7, 160, 186,
   300
Fidelity, 200, 300, 362
Financial Post, 188, 196, 243

Financial Times, 263
Fipke, Chuck, 106
Fishburn, Doug, 69
Flood, Ed, 200–201
Fly River, 68–9
Ford, Gerald, 220
Foreign Capital Investment Law,
   73–5, 89
Forensic Investigative Associates
   (FIA), 364–5, 369, 372
Fortune, 99, 364
Four Seasons Regent, 255, 297,
   307
Fowler, Michael, 193, 270
Fox, Steve, 179
Francisco, Dorrie, 282, 356
Francisco, Rolando (Rolly), 180,
   183–5, 236–8, 245–6, 248–52,
   255, 257–8, 266, 271, 273,
   276–7, 279, 281–3, 286, 297,
   302, 307, 314, 336, 343, 348–9,
   356, 368
Franco Nevada, 172
Freeport Indonesia, PT, 74–7, 307,
   313, 324, 339, 342, 355
Freeport Kaolin Co., 74
Freeport–McMoRan Copper and
   Gold Inc., 14, 17–8, 135, 137,
   139, 166, 202, 229, 268–9,
   281, 285, 293, 303, 307–308,
   311–4, 316–7, 319, 324, 336,
   342–3, 348–9, 351–5, 363–6,
   368, 372, 374; due diligence,
   Busang 320, 332, 337, 339–41,
   355, 357–8, 360
Freeport Minerals Co., 311
Freeport Sulphur, 311
Friedland, Robert, 198–202, 333
Fung, Bob, 238

Galbraith, Richard, 142–4, 146,
   150
Ganaja, 226

Ganto, Adnan, 232, 238, 252, 266, 280
Garama Dhananjaya, PT, 241
Garver, Pat, 248–50, 256, 262, 280, 282
Gates, Bill, 325
Gatra, 328
Geiger, Mansur, 376
Gilmour, David, 260–62
Global Gold Stock Report, 150–51, 163–4, 358
Globe and Mail, 101, 270, 347, 353
Glover, Danny, 204
Gold Fields, 299
Gold Standard Inc., 262
Goldman Sachs, 360
Goldstrike Mine, 78, 134–5, 177, 248, 259–60, 264–5, 296, 312
Gordon Capital, 238, 278
Goshal, Baladas, 207, 216
Grand Hyatt Hotel, 204, 245, 250, 275, 277, 279, 293
Grasberg, 76, 137, 139, 202, 268–9, 307, 312–4, 316, 319, 324, 331–2, 337, 366–7
Green, Jeff, 278
Griffith, Melanie, 204
Gunung Bijih, 113–4

Habibie, B.J. (Rudi), 378
Hamilton, John, 214
Hammer, Armand, 329
Hammer, Michael, 329
Hand, Scott, 228–31, 233, 238, 362
Hang Lung Developments Co., 90
Harian Ekonomi Neraca, 349, 351
Harjojudanto, Sigit, 221, 239, 272–4, 289, 379
Harsono, Mr., 17, 238, 272
Hartarto, 221, 273

Hartarto, Airlangga, 241–2, 245, 248, 256, 266, 272–3, 276, 280
Hartarto, Gunadharma, 239, 241
Hartina, Siti (*see also* Tien, Madam), 222
Harvard University, 225
Hasan, Haji Mohamad (Bob), 14, 211–2, 220–21, 224, 241, 278, 280–81, 284–5, 287, 289–90, 293–9, 303–305, 307–309, 312, 316–7, 328, 340, 349, 357, 364, 373, 378
Hausserman, John, 43
Hawkins, Stan, 120, 242
Hazen Research Inc., 321
heap leaching, 198
Hearn Ltd., 344
Hedderwick, David, 116, 118–9
Heffernan, Virginia, 107–108
Heldi (Eddy), 64–5
Hellman, Phillip, 358, 373
Hemlo, 78, 88, 107, 179, 247, 250, 288
Hendrick, Dale, 185–8, 196
Hernanto, Johnnie, 238, 272
high-grading, 47–8
Hill, Allan, 133–4, 137, 141, 148–9, 232, 234, 279
Hill, Napoleon, 101, 104–106, 167
Hill & Knowlton, 296, 364
Hillen, Ernest, 65
Hodgson, Jay, 286
Holmes, Oliver Wendell, 31
Holy Cross Memorial Park, 31, 379
Holy Trinity Academy, 38
Horsham Corp., 263
Horsham Securities Ltd., 263
Hotel Senyiur, 156
Howe, Peter, 70, 72, 102, 237
Howlett, Karen, 101
Hughes, Steve, 244, 330, 361
Humpuss Group, 272

Hunamas Putra Interbuana, 15, 94–5, 115, 278
Hunt, Doug, 364–5, 369
Hutasoit, Takala, 15, 278
Hutchinson, Bob, 67–8, 70

Ibu Yoke, 276, 280
ICI Chemicals, 15
Igorot people, 41–2
IKAPT, 340
Imperial, Sonny, 56, 365
Inchcape, 195
Inco Ltd., 199, 228–30, 362
Indo Assay (Indo Analisa Laboratorium), 116, 128, 131, 141, 144–5, 147, 151, 156, 160, 162–3, 166, 171, 195–6, 243, 286, 288, 322, 337, 339, 354, 361, 372–3, 375
Indochina Goldfields, 201
Indonesia: corruption, 204–5, 219–26; culture, 204–5, 210, 214, 216; human rights violations, 212–3, 223–4; military influence, 206–7, 210–13; political & economic history, 89–90, 203–26, 377–8; political parties: Golkar, 222–3, NASAKOM, 209, PKI, 209–13, 215; poverty, 203, 208; Suharto presidency, 203–6, 210–26; Sukarno presidency, 206–11; U.S. relationship, 208–9, 213, 216–7, 219–20
Indonesia Air Transport, PT, 20, 23
Indonesian Foreign Investment Review Board, 187
Industrial Estates Ltd. (IEL), 261
Ingold, PT, 96, 113
International Monetary Fund (IMF), 216–8, 377
International Nickel Indonesia, PT (PT INCO), 229

International Pursuit, 190
Ireland, Dean, 92
Ireland, Len, 92
Irvan, 376
Irvin, John, 116, 141, 146–7, 149–50, 156, 160, 166, 196, 243–4, 286, 322, 326–7, 331–2, 337, 342–3, 360–61, 363, 371–4
Irwin, Warren, 196, 345
Iwan, 16, 19

Jackson, Karl, 224
Jakarta Post, 377
Jakarta Stock Exchange (JSE), 80, 89–90, 95, 192, 220, 229
Jambi, 87
Jason Mining Ltd., 54, 71–2, 78, 84–7, 164
Jerritt Canyon, 76
John the Baptist, 214
Jones, Colin, 320, 328, 332, 343
J.P. Morgan & Co., 184, 237, 242, 257, 268, 276, 282–3, 294, 314, 355

Kadri, Tariq, 263
Kalalo, Dr. Eduardo Antonio (Ed), 2–8
Kalimantan: forests, 21–2; history, 22, 61–3; resources, 62; swamps, 7, 25
Kalimantan Gold, 376
Kapal, Grace, 19–20, 341
Karnasih, Sugini (see de Guzman, Michael, under wives)
Karpa Springs, 92–3
Kasongan Bumi Kencana, PT, 54, 92
Katili, Dr., 87, 89
Kavanagh, Paul, 131–4, 137, 141, 147, 150–53, 161–2, 168, 181, 258, 274, 279, 282, 355, 368
Keevil, Norm, 293, 303–4

Kelian, 86, 89, 173–4, 177, 323
Kennecott, 67–70, 174
Kennecott Canada Inc., 106, 108, 139
Kennedy, Bruce, 90–92
Kennedy, John Fitzgerald, 31
Kennedy, Peter, 188, 243
Kertanegara, 61
Khashoggi, Adnan, 262–3
Khashoggi, Essam, 263
Khoo, Tan Sri, 262
Kilborn Engineering, 178–9, 189, 233, 316
Kilborn Pakar Rekasaya, PT, 10, 244, 320–22, 352–6, 375
Kindwall, Nils, 74
King, Joel, 103, 168
King Edward Hotel, 255
Kingking deposit, 129–30
Kissinger, Henry, 219, 312
Kissinger Associates, 312
Koch, Christopher, 214
Kok, Jan, 67
Kornze, Larry, 134–7, 141, 161, 168, 260, 279, 370
KP (see also contract of work, SIPP), 230, 257
Kroll, Jules, 246–8
Kroll Associates, 246–8, 256
Krueng Gasui, PT (PT KG), 137–9, 182, 236, 240, 288
Krueng, Taungah, PT, 137
Krugman, Paul, 377
Kuntoro (see Mangusubroto, Kuntoro)

La Jolla Securities Corp., 136–7
Lac Minerals Ltd., 180, 188, 197, 234, 257, 265, 288
Lakefield Research, 279, 282, 286, 363, 375
Lam, Dr. Leslie, 13
Lassonde, Pierre, 172

Lavoie, Luc, 296
Leach, Terry, 259, 321, 358–9
Leduc, 101
Lee, Dr. Kevin, 8
Lehman Brothers Inc., 242, 274, 303, 350, 355, 360
Leishman, Doug, 124
Lenczner, Alan, 288, 362
Leode, Bernhard, 15, 17, 20, 23–4, 30, 85, 340–41, 349, 369
Leverman, Mike, 330
Lévesque Beaubien Geoffrion, 193
Levings, John, 112–3, 116, 185–7
Lindquist, Bob, 364, 369
Lindquist Avey Holmes, 364
Liong, Liem Sioe, 220
Livermore, John, 260
Loa Duri warehouse, 58, 322, 361, 370, 372, 375
Loewen, Ondaatje, McCutcheon Ltd., 152–4, 163, 168
Loney, John, 269, 271
Longos, 94
Lupin Mine, 103–4
Lyons, Hugh, 282

maar diatremes, 89, 116, 118, 170, 178, 243
MacDermott, Mike, 380–81
MacDonald, Greg, 10, 17–8, 23–4, 186, 257, 307, 319, 339, 342–3
Machribie, Adrianto, 342
MacLachlan, Neil, 248, 256
Maclean's, 197
MacMillan, Viola, 189
Macpherson, Joe, 320
Magnum Minerals, 128, 164–5
Mahabarata, 205
Mahakam River, 60, 62–5
Mahmud, Ridwan, 74, 240, 256
Majelis Permusyawaratan Rakyat (MPR), 222–3
Malihan, Tom, 30, 54–6

Malik, Adam, 87, 216
Mandarin Hotel, 279
Mandor, 71, 102
Mangusubroto, Kuntoro, 182,
    230–33, 238–40, 245–6, 252–2,
    266, 272–3, 309, 362
Manila Mining Corporation, 143
Manila Stock Exchange, 44–5
Marcopper, 235, 297, 304, 314
Marcos, Ferdinand, 36, 205, 378,
    380
Marcos, Imelda, 36, 205
Mario the Blind, 31
Marion, Rene, 286
Marriott Hotel, 11, 339
Marsh, Bruce, 320, 332, 340
Martin, Dean, 261
Martinus, 25
Marunda Group, 114
mas, 64
Massachusetts Institute of
    Technology, 377
Maugham, Somerset, 344
Maulana, Achmed, 156, 375
Mawengkang, Susani (*see* de
    Guzman, Michael, under wives)
McAnulty, Steve, 140, 171, 282,
    336
McBeth, John, 308
McConvey, Daniel, 242, 274–5,
    303, 336, 350, 355, 357, 360
McDonald, Hamish, 207–8, 211–2
McIntosh, Doug, 276, 282–3, 294,
    314
McLucas, Willy, 114–5, 118,
    236–8, 245–6, 250, 283
McNamara, Robert, 217
McMoRan Oil & Gas Co., 311
McWilliams, Ken, 311
Mealey, George, 74–5
Meilan, Andrian, 20
Melanson, Michael, 282, 349, 364
Mendenhall, Michel, 180, 351

Mercur, 248, 262, 264
Mercurindo, 284
Mercury Asset Management, 172
Mersch, Frank, 108
Merukh, Jusuf, 17–8, 111, 138,
    165, 182, 185, 188, 190, 236,
    240, 245, 249–50, 252, 256,
    269–70, 275, 283–4, 288, 293,
    306, 335, 362
MGM Grand, 287
Midland Doherty Ltd., 101, 140
Mihailovich, Sasha, 244, 330, 361
Min, 160
Min people, 68–9
Minay, Dr. Noel, 4–8
Mincon Abadi, PT, 86
Mindoro, 190
Mineralindo Rejeki Alam, PT
    (MRA), 185
Minindo Perkasasemesta, PT, 96,
    115, 138, 143, 229
mining: diamond, Canada, 106–7;
    gold: Indonesia, 78–80; North
    America (*see also* Hemlo), 78,
    107–8; Philippines, 41–6;
    Indonesia, 71, 77–80, 84, 191–2,
    230–31; laws; Indonesia, 73–9;
    Philippines, 44
Minorca Resources, 187
Mintech, 113
Mirah, 54, 87–8, 90, 92–4, 142,
    168, 242, 335
Moa Bay, 311
Mobang, Sibau, 63
Moffett, Jim Bob, 76, 202, 229,
    281, 303, 307–12, 337–8, 342,
    357, 364, 366–7
Monopros, 107
Montague Gold NL, 113, 137–8
Montague Pacific, 113–4, 116–9,
    128, 131, 141, 152, 159, 164,
    182, 188, 236, 288
Montreal Exchange, 187

Moore, Demi, 203
Morrison, Leslie, 276, 282–3,
    314–5
Mount Elizabeth Medical Centre,
    12–3, 303, 339
Muara Atan, 111, 114–6, 118–9,
    137
Muir, Andrew, 124
Mulroney, Brian, 239, 259, 265–6
Munk, Melanie, 265
Munk, Peter, 78, 131–2, 134–5,
    148, 187–8, 233–4, 238–9,
    241–2, 249, 254–6, 260–67,
    269, 275–7, 280–2, 285–7, 290,
    295–6, 298–9, 303, 309–10,
    327–8, 336, 362
Muro, Mt., 85, 89, 93, 169, 323,
    335
Murphy, Paul, 340
Mutiara, 168
Muyup, 86–7, 89, 111, 169

Nainggolen, John, 15, 95, 278
Nassey, Jonathan, 87, 111, 122,
    136, 148, 168, 242, 288, 319,
    332–3, 336, 338–9
Nasution, General, 212
National Bureau of Investigation
    (NBI), 1–8, 32–3, 380
Nazareth School, 38
Nesbitt Burns Inc., 152, 168, 170,
    180, 193–4, 201, 255, 324,
    346–7, 351, 364
Nesbitt Thomson & Co., 260
Neuhaus, David, 242
Nevada Mining Association, 259
New Cinch Uranium Ltd., 197, 246
New York Stock Exchange, 14, 44,
    234, 350
New York Times, 213
Newmont Gold Co., 172, 242, 249,
    260, 269–70, 340
Newmont Mining Corp., 293

Noranda Inc., 93, 103
Noranda Mining and Exploration,
    233
Normet Proprietary Ltd., 258,
    321–3
Northern Miner, 78, 106–8,
    130–31, 179, 294
Nova Corp., 233
Novotny, Mike, 71, 85, 90–92
Nusantara Ampera Bhakti, PT
    (Nusamba), 220–21, 289,
    307–8, 328, 340, 358, 367

Ok Tedi, 69–70, 89, 96, 115, 122,
    132, 145
Olii, Tommy, 96, 134
Olii, Umar, 71, 86–7, 89, 96, 102,
    110, 122–3, 126–8, 130–31,
    133–4, 136, 376
Oliphant, Randall, 248, 255, 276–7,
    279, 281, 283, 293, 298, 309
Olympia & York, 132, 248
Ongpin, Jaime (Jimmy), 45–6
Ontario Securities Commission
    (OSC), 362
OPEC, 231
Opp, Michael, 197
Ordona, Jamie, 243
Orogrande, 197
Orwell, George, 47
Outer Space Health Institute, 208
Overseas Private Investment Group,
    313
Oyam, Pedro, 30, 94

Pacific Amber Resources Ltd., 185
Pacific International, 124
Palad, Bayani, 32
Panca Minevatama, PT, 306
Pancasila, 206, 215, 314
Pangalinan, Rod, 94
Panutan Duta, PT, 238, 272, 283,
    379

Panutan Group, 238–9, 241, 272
Parker, Colin, 361–2
Parris, Keith, 320
Parry, Kevin, 71, 85
Parry Corp., 90
Parsons Behle & Latimer, 248
Pebit, 159
Pelsart International Ltd., 71
Pelsart Resources N.L., 54–6, 78, 84–5, 90–91, 93–4, 115, 142, 164
Pemberton Securities, 102
penny stocks, 43–4; Australia, 82–4; Canada, 80; promoters: (*see also* stock promoters), 80–82, 99–100; Canada, 80–82; U.S., 135–6
Pennzoil group, 93
Perilya Mines, 93
Petrominer, 191–2
Peusahaan Pertambangan Minyak dan Gas Bumi Negara (Pertamina), 218–9, 327, 341, 374
Pezim, Murray, 78, 88
Philippines, the; history, 41–2, 45; mining industry, 41–6
Phillips, Kevin, 206
Pines Hotel, 51, 117
Pintz, William, 70
Placer Dome Inc., 172, 179, 188, 234–5, 237, 239, 242, 245, 249, 268–72, 277, 279, 281, 284–91, 293, 295, 297, 303–4, 307–8, 340, 351
Placer Exploration Pty., 67
Placer Pacific, 137
Planet Hollywood, 203–4
Plantation Forest Timber Company, 321
Pohl, Karl Otto, 239, 259
Pooley, Roger, 164
Porgera, 234, 268

Poseidon, 82–4
Possamai, Mario, 372
Potter, Dave, 17, 76, 319–20, 323–32, 337–8, 340–42, 355
Prabowo, Sitit Hediati, 221
Price Waterhouse, 364–5
Princeton University, 151
Project Underground, 368
Prospectors and Developers Association (PDA), 176, 186–7, 300, 333, 335–6, 339, 342
Puregold, 108
Puspos, Augustine (Augus), 257
Puspos, Cesar, 15, 30, 52, 55, 56, 58, 87, 95, 131, 134, 142–6, 149, 151–2, 155–6, 159–60, 163, 167–8, 171, 196, 242–4, 246, 257, 319, 328, 330, 332–6, 338–9, 350, 361, 371–4
Puspos, Emmanuel (Manny), 53, 55–7, 328, 340, 342, 350, 362, 365, 375
Puspos, Mrs., 57
Puspos, Rene, 57
Putra, Hutomo Mandala (Tommy), 204, 221, 224, 272

Quezon City Science High School, 38

Rais, Amien, 295
Ramayana, 205
Ramirez, Bobby, 56, 159, 319, 340–41, 350, 361–2, 365
Ramly, Rizal, 289
Ramos, Ferdinand, 304
Rankin, Mack, 311
RBC Dominion Securities Inc., 99, 102, 104, 277
Reichmann, Paul, 132, 247
Reid, Les, 136
Republic National Bank, 237, 257, 268, 276, 282

Reston, James, 213
Reuters, 171, 280
Revis, Tex, 41
Reyes, Dr. Alberto, 2–3
Ridwan (see Mahmud, Ridwan)
Rijanto, Captain Dr. T.B., 28
Rim of Fire, 67–8, 121, 129, 140, 200
Rio Tinto, 71, 86, 102, 113, 173, 184
Rio Tinto-Zinc Indonesia Ltd. (RTZ), 173, 312–3
Riquel, Fernando, 41
RJR Nabisco, 254
Robertson, John, 10
Robertson Stephens & Co., 199, 201
Robinson, Allan, 347
Roger Townend and Associates, 322–3
Rogers, Loretta, 260
Rogers, Ted, 260
Royal, Darrell, 310
Royal Bank of Canada, 132
Royal Canadian Mounted Police, 364, 372
Royal Darwin Hospital, 5, 8
Royal Dutch, 62
Royal York Hotel, 176, 179, 333, 338
Rucker, Steven, 248
Rukmana, Siti Hardyanti (Tutut), 40, 204, 221, 223–4, 242, 249, 267, 272, 276, 289, 340, 378
Rush, Jim, 160, 290, 331, 361
Russell, Bertrand, 213

Sabine, John, 282, 364, 368
Sable prospect, 129, 148–9, 156–7, 165–6, 180, 234, 242
Sadli, Muhammad, 377
Said, General Umar, 252, 256, 272, 277, 280, 282, 289, 294, 309

Salamat, John, 30, 56, 332–3, 338–9
Salim Group, 220
Salin, 147–8, 160–61, 257, 371–2
salting, 82–3, 244; Attunga, 82; Busang, 148, 152, 369, 373; Karpa Springs, 93; New Cinch, 197, 247
Samarinda, 59–62
San Jose, Jeffrey, 31
Santoso, Lieutenant–Colonel Boedhi, 361, 374
Sapulidi, 156
Sarbutt, Keith, 363
Sari Pan Pacific Hotel, 110
Schaefer, Michael, 163
Schneider Capital, 354
Schwarz, Adam, 206–7, 219–20, 222
Scotia McLeod, 170
Scribben, Rod, 233
Securities and Exchange Commission (SEC), 190, 362
Semar, 216
Seng, The Kian (see also Hasan, Bob), 211, 280
Sepinggan Airport, 20
Seymour, Karen, 368
Shangri-La Hotel, 10, 245, 276–7, 284, 291–3, 298, 300, 303, 309, 350, 356
Shell, 62
Shell Canada, 119
Sheraton, 358
Showell, Tony, 322
Sigit (see Harjojudanto, Sigit)
Sigit, Ari Haryo, 272–3
Sigit, Sutaryo, 74, 229
Sinatra, Frank, 261
Singhe prospect, 110, 165, 180, 242
SIPP (see also contract of work, KP), 77–8, 119, 183

Sirait, Umar, 192
Sivarena, 31
Smith, Bob, 134, 232, 239, 264, 276–7
Smith, Gary, 375
Smith, Ian, 264
Smith, Scott, 262
SNC Lavalin, 233, 316
Soetarto, Bas, 227, 231
Soetjipto, Rozik, 240, 252
Soroako, 228–30
South Pacific, 190
South Pacific Hotel Corp., 262
South Pacific Properties Ltd., 261–2
Spooner, Ed, 33–4
Sriwijaya, 275
Stallone, Sylvester, 204
Stamler, Rod, 364–5, 368
Steel, Jim, 353–4
Stephens, Kim, 354
Stephens, Paul, 199–202
Stikine, 179
stock promoters (see also penny stock promoters), 199–200
Strathcona Mineral Services Ltd., 348, 355–63, 365, 368–9, 372
Subrianto, Major General Prabowo, 378
Subroto, Colonel Gatot, 211–2
Sudirman, General, 206
Sudjana, Ida Bagus, 225, 228, 231–3, 239, 251, 266, 272–3, 276, 288–9, 293–4, 297, 303, 307, 309, 363
Sugeng, Lieutenant Dr., 28
Suharto, 32, 73–4, 84, 87, 190, 193, 203–6, 210–26, 228–30, 239–40, 266–7, 273, 280–81, 284–5, 295, 297, 300, 303, 306–7, 367–8, 377–8; childhood, 215; children, 40, 204–5, 219, 221–4, 239, 241–2, 249, 267, 272–3, 281, 289, 294, 373,

378–9; mother (Sukirah), 215; regime, 203–6, 210–26; Sukarno, overthrow of, 210, 214–5; wife (Siti Hartina, also known as Madam Tien), 204–5, 222, 224, 241
Sukarno (Bung Karno), 3, 73–4, 206–11, 214–4, 217, 219, 240, 378; Pancasila principle, 206, 215; Suharto, overthrow by, 210, 214–5
Sukarno Hatta International Airport, 16, 204, 320, 337
Sukirah, 215
Sullivan Cromwell, 368
Sumalindo Lestari Jaya, PT, 28
Sumber Hema Raya, PT (SHR), 242, 267
Summitville, 198
Sungai Atan Perdana, PT (PT SAP), 138–9, 165, 182, 236, 288
Surya Veneutasakti, PT, 115
Sutrisno, General Try, 223
Sutton Place Hotel, 238
Sy, Henry, 56
Syakerani, Haji, 111, 138, 150, 165, 182, 187–8, 234, 236, 240, 246, 256–7, 288–9
Sydney Park Hyatt Hotel, 172
Sykes, Trevor, 82–4

Tambang Timah, PT
Tandem Resources, 242
Tannock, Barry, 119–25, 129–30, 139–41, 146, 149, 151, 171, 201; family, 119–20
Tanqueray Resources, 107, 190
Tara Group, 87
Target Mas Perdana, PT, 87
Target Petroleum, 87
Taware, 129, 132, 139–42, 148, 153–4
Tech Stocks, 350

Teck Corp., 293, 307, 308, 340
Temindung Airport, 20–21, 23, 341
Tempo, 224
Tenggarong, 61–2; King, 60
Texaco Inc., 262
Texas Gulf Sulphur Co., 189–90
Thahir, 25
Thompson, Anne, 359
Tien, Madam, 204–5, 222, 224, 241
Time, 217
Times (London), 211
Timika, 331
Timmins, William, 103
TNK Resources, 278
Tobing, Adam, 18–9, 87, 96, 110, 123, 125
Toledo, Santiago, 3
Toronto Dominion Securities, 353
Toronto International Airport, 349
Toronto Stock Exchange (TSE), 14, 80, 154, 189, 234, 255, 264, 301, 349, 356, 379; TSE 300, 14, 189–90
Toukmanian, Jeannette (*see also* Walsh, Jeannette), 100
TransCanada PipeLines, 233
Triad International Corp., 262–3
Trihatmodjo, Bambang, 204–5, 221, 249, 272
TrizecHahn, 275
Tropic Endeavor, 85
Tulane University, 310
Tursono, Edy, 20–23, 341
Tutut (*see* Rukmana, Siti Hardyanti)
TVOntario, 363
Tyler, 108

Uddin, Dzia, 66, 155–8, 160–61, 375
Umar, Dr. Daniel, 28–9
United Overseas Bank, 13

United Paragon Mining Corp., 94
United Siscoe Mines Ltd., 263
University of the Philippines (UP), 36, 38
University of Texas at Austin, 310
University of Toronto, 33
University of Utah, 248
Untung, Lieutenant-Colonel, 210
USA Today, 362

Van der Schurren, Father, 30
van Doorn, Rob, 153–4
van Langenberg, Michael, 213
van Leeuwen, Theo, 71, 78, 96, 173–4, 184
Van Nort, Steve, 338, 340, 355
Vancouver Stock Exchange (VSE), 197, 376
Vega, Rudy, 16, 19–21, 94, 194
Villarba, Waynefred, 1–4
Vincent de Paul, St., 36–7
Vittachi, Tarzie, 208–10, 213–4, 218
Voisey's Bay, 198–200, 333
von Guttenberg, Reinhard, 372

Waddell, Kevin, 109–10, 121, 123, 129
Wahju, Beni, 228
Walsh, Brett, 98, 102–3, 151, 270–71, 368–70
Walsh, David, 66, 119–25, 129–30, 136, 139, 141, 146, 151–4, 161, 163–4, 167–8, 170, 174–5, 180–1, 183, 185, 187, 233, 235, 239, 251–2, 257, 267–75, 288, 292–307, 327, 337, 349–50, 362–3, 367–70, 378–9; bankruptcy, 97–9; Barrick dealings, 132–3, 137, 148–50, 234, 237–8, 241, 255–6, 274, 276–7, 280, 282, 284, 290; Bre-X stock options, 252, 300,

343–4; childhood & education, 100; credibility, lack of, 174, 182–4, 201, 297, 301; death, 379; employment history, 100–101; Felderhof, initial dealings, 102, 108–9, 118–9; Freeport dealings, 307–8, 314–8, 338, 342; Indonesia, travels to, 102, 109–11, 161–2, 292–307; inspiration, 101, 104–6; Nassau residence, 172, 246; Placer Dome dealings, 235, 268–72, 277–9, 285, 287, 291; questionable dealings pre-Bre-X, 101–2

Walsh, Jeannette, 100, 103, 124, 172, 180, 201, 246, 252, 269, 302, 343–4

Walsh, Sean, 98, 102, 109–10, 121, 151, 160

Walsh, Vaughan, 100

Watson, Sir Malcolm, 22

Waverley Management, 114

wayang, 204–5, 210, 214, 216

Weld, Tuesday, 261

Weston, Galen, 260

Weston, Hilary, 260

Westralian Atan Minerals, PT (PT Westralian, PT WAM, WAM), 14, 111–5, 119, 128, 137–9, 143, 149, 155, 182, 236–7, 283, 288, 305

Westralian Resource Projects Ltd.

(WRPL), 111, 137–9, 190, 236, 283, 288

White, Bill, 67

White, Gerry, 281, 284, 295, 304, 340

Whitehouse, Laurie, 85

Whittingham, Tony, 197

Wignjowijoto, Hartojo, 225–6

Wilkins, Gregory, 149

Willis, Bruce, 204

Willow-Q Explorations Ltd., 121

Willson, John, 235, 249, 268–72, 277–81, 284–7, 290–91, 293, 297–8, 303–5

Wilson, Forbes, 74–5

Windfall Oil & Mines, 190; scandal, 189–90

Wiriosudarmo, Rachman, 90–91

Wolff, Ian, 114

Wool, Richard, 364

World Gold Council, 225

Worley, Birl, 46

Yamana Resources, 298

Yani, 374

Yani, Ahmad, 187–8, 288, 349

Yoga, Dharma, 232

Yorkton Securities, 100, 103, 124

Young, Kenneth, 213

Yunawati, PT, 71

Zufrein, 126, 134